ULTIMATE ART : ESSAYS AROUND A
ML1700 .L59 1992

DATE DUE

~~DE~~ ~~'94~~		
~~MR 2 4 '95~~		
~~JE~~ ~~1 '95~~		
MY 2 4 '96		
~~NO 9 '02~~		
~~DE~~ ~~'02~~		

DEMCO 38-296

THE ULTIMATE ART

David Littlejohn

THE ULTIMATE ART

Essays Around and About Opera

UNIVERSITY OF CALIFORNIA PRESS   BERKELEY   LOS ANGELES   LONDON

FRONTISPIECE Photo montage of the first
performance (Puccini's *Tosca*) in the War
Memorial Opera House, October 15, 1932.
Morton Studios photograph. Courtesy of
the San Francisco Opera.

University of California Press
Berkeley and Los Angeles, California
University of California Press, Ltd.
London, England
© 1992 by The Regents of
the University of California

First Paperback Printing 1994

Library of Congress
Cataloging-in-Publication Data
Littlejohn, David, 1937–
The ultimate art : essays around and
about opera / David Littlejohn.

      p.   cm.

Includes bibliographical references
and index.

ISBN 0-520-07609-5

1. Opera.   I. Title.

ML1700.L59   1992
782.1—dc20   91-39025
                              CIP
                              MN

Printed in the United States of America

9 8 7 6 5 4 3 2 1

The paper used in this publication meets
the minimum requirements of American
National Standard for Information
Sciences—Permanence of Paper for Printed
Library Materials, ANSI Z39.48–1984. ⊚

CONTENTS

For Kori Lockhart

*As many musicologists have come to realize (and verbalize),
musicology cries out, at this stage of its development, for enrichment
from other disciplines; in this it is far behind art history, literary studies, and
the rest of the humanities and social sciences, perhaps because of the peculiar
self-contained nature of musical syntax and structure, so seemingly recalcitrant to general
humanistic understanding. Music, however, is of this world, not of the musician's world
alone. It must be talked about from the outside as well as from within, if it is to
maintain itself as a humanistic study, and not collapse into itself entirely
to become a self-contained "windowless monad."*

PETER KIVY
Osmin's Rage: Philosophical Reflections on Opera, Drama, and Text

All but one of the essays that follow the Introduction were written for the *San Francisco Opera Magazine*, the program book of the San Francisco Opera, during the last sixteen years. They add up to no statement about or position on the phenomenon we call "opera," except insofar as the fact that one person wrote them may lead you to detect some sort of "unified sensibility" behind them. I have added a couple of updating footnotes or postscripts, and have tried to correct a few earlier errors; I'm sure others remain. I like to think (but am not convinced) that the more recent pieces are better. They are frequently longer, in any event.

The one exception is a piece written after, rather than before, a particular event— my description of and response to Peter Sellars's productions of *Così fan tutte*, *The Marriage of Figaro*, and *Don Giovanni* at Purchase, New York, in the summer of 1989, originally written for *The Opera Quarterly*. Although I have written critical reviews of many individual opera productions, none of the others seemed to me sufficiently reflective or substantial to warrant collecting and preserving. It is only the very exceptional critic who can turn rapidly written reviews of the passing scene into literature worth reading long after the event.

Partly because of their original occasion—as background essays intended for people who had already made the decision to attend a particular opera—and partly because of my own interest in opera as a cultural phenomenon, a product and inhabitant of other-than-musical worlds, many of these essays deal with things other than music.

But then so does opera. Considerations of the history of culture, of literary, historical, and topographical sources, of librettos in their own right, of the lives of artists, of theatre history, of set design, of great singers, and of changing public taste—all of which I write about here—are as pertinent to the understanding and the enjoyment of opera as are music history, analysis, and criticism.

The standard opera repertory is madly heterogeneous, drawn from a broad array of historical and cultural sources. Our experience of opera is enhanced, I believe, by knowing something more about the different worlds from which it sprang. Different pressures, different impulses throughout cultural and musical history have led to many different sorts of opera, all jumbled together today in a repertory that spins us from Vivaldi to Offenbach by way of Wagner. To know what led to the conventions of opera seria, why the Paris Opera demanded ballets, or how a librettist may have hobbled a composer (or challenged him to new inspiration) enlarges the nature of the operas we see.

There is relatively little here of what is usually called "musical analysis." The more of it I read, the less faith I have in its cogency or effectiveness: very few people perform it persuasively or well, and I am not likely to be one of them. As a musical amateur, in both senses of the word, I have no desire to betray any more of my inexpertness than I absolutely must. I make frequent use of the work of musicologists, but I don't pretend to compete. This collection is intended for people interested in opera who are neither professional musicians nor "opera fanatics"— i.e., obsessional voice-connoisseurs who dote on particular singers or particular styles of singing. It is intended for men and women who enjoy opera (I have no dream of converting the unconverted); who attend performances when they can; who listen to broadcasts and recordings; and who are curious to know more about the works they are seeing and hearing.

Since most of these people cannot readily read musical scores, or understand the specialized language (what Shaw called the "Mesopotamian words") of musical analysis, I have tried, like most music critics who address themselves to general audiences, to keep such things out of my writing.

In the essays that follow, I have turned to the scores in an attempt to explain my emotional reactions to certain moments in certain operas: *Alceste, Don Giovanni, Norma, Die Meistersinger, Otello, Oedipus Rex*. In the process, I have reduced complex verbal and musical effects to a series of adjectives and metaphors which I only hope will suggest to others both the music I heard and the feelings it aroused.

But the feelings are (or were) only in *me*. There is no way I can "demonstrate" any cause-and-effect relationship between a particular musical form, and a particular feeling-in-me; let alone demonstrate that the feeling I claim to have experienced is (or ought to be) shared by anyone else. All I (or for that matter, any more sophisticated musical analyst) can do is try to describe a personal experience honestly; point to the piece of music drama that preceded or accompanied it; and suggest that there is a connection between them.

For all the uncertainty and solipsism of this enterprise—the common practice of almost all music criticism—I see no reason to stop indulging in it. When I read other analysts and critics, making their own assertions of musical cause and emotional effect, I feel no obligation to accept their assertions as the truth, and you should feel none to accept mine. I am free to test their assertions, as you are free to test mine, for their cogency, their persuasiveness, their coincidence with our own experience.

Much analysis of and commentary on operatic music depend on artificial parallels drawn between qualities of music and qualities of character, linked by no more than common adjectives ("unstable," "impulsive," "nervous"); or by assertions that an emotion felt by a particular listener (boredom, pain, sadness, erotic arousal) is in fact a quality inherent in the music, and therefore one that should be felt by all listeners.

But analysis that depends on adjectives and metaphors is no more than impressionism. It may be verbally deft, even poetic. But it comes no closer to demonstrating the power or meaning of music than did the once-popular "narrative readings" (birdsong and brooks, moral struggle and triumph) of nineteenth-century orchestral works.

There is no question that many of the devices of music—the decision to achieve or avoid resolution, certain tonal modulations or changes of rhythm, the use of instruments of a particularly affective timbre (solo violins, cellos, oboes, trombones, tympani), the rich possibilities of repetition and recall—may be turned to effective and efficient dramatic use. But the most a critic or commentator can do is to point them out; and suggest their possible appropriateness to the dramatic situation. Since there can be no assurance they will affect others as they affect you, the analysis of musical expressiveness can, in the end, be no more than autobiographical. To call a particular phrase "menacing," "ethereal," "grotesque," "mellow," "urgent," "bleak," "crying," "dull-rooted," "radiant," or "beautiful" (all these attributions come from twelve lines of Joseph Kerman's analysis of the murder scene in *Otello*) is only to apply verbal tags to one's own emotional responses; it is not to define the music, or the necessary response of anyone else.

If a writer about music is sufficiently engaging, appears to know what he is writing about, and appears to share some of my basic tastes and values, then his assertions are likely to lead me, at the very least, to listen more carefully to the music, perhaps even to study the text and score; two not unworthy results. I may be led by his claims to keep a closer watch on my own responses the next time I hear the work. This, in turn, is likely to keep me more open-eyed a spectator, more open-eared an auditor; to lead me to pay closer attention; to stay wider awake: surely no bad thing in an opera house. My emotions will not be the same as those of the critic whose comments I have read, any more than yours will be the same as mine—I am I, he is he, you are who you are; our inner and outer worlds are too different. We may end up disagreeing absolutely about the musical source of our experiences in any case, let alone their value. (I actually enjoy being moved to tears by the plights of fictional characters, in opera and elsewhere; why, I don't know. I certainly expect no one else to.)

But in the process of reading one another's responses, we may have been seduced into getting more out of an opera. We may either enjoy ourselves more or understand better why we did not.

Our emotional (and intellectual) responses to music depend on many more things than the words and notes of the score; our responses to live opera productions depend on other things still. Much of what we experience has to be at least potentially present in us already: an ability to be penetrated by particular vocal timbres; a fascination with the European past; a familiarity with Shakespeare; an ability to yield to the pulses and swoops, the endlessly unresolved ideas of Wagnerian chromaticism; a taste for theatrical excess and unreason; a patience with da capo repeats; a tolerance for melodrama, or secco recitative, or the musical equivalents of madness.

I like to think of myself as perpetually educable, open to interesting, possibly valuable new experiences and ideas. But every so often I come near to concluding that there are certain singers and types of singers, certain forms of music or musical effects, even certain operas and composers that other intelligent and sensitive people can admire, and I cannot. And then I hear a countertenor who can act with his voice, see a resolved and ingenious production of Meyerbeer or Menotti, and my catalogue of prejudices alters.

The same thing, I believe, applies to the varying interpretations of conductors, producers, and performers. Because music is essentially nonreferential, because the meanings we assign to it are in the end so arbitrary and so personal, the most cogent, convincing, step-by-step written analysis of the "meaning" of a scene or a work, the most assured theoretical explication of the way a role should be played or a passage performed, can be shattered by the next performance we experience that makes it "work" a different way.

Each opera we see has its own context: when and where (and how) it was written and first performed; the other works of art, musical and nonmusical, that preceded and surrounded it; the events or ideas that fed into its creation; where it fit in, how it grew out of, the life of its creator.

All of this matters considerably, I believe, in our experience of opera. So I investigate and write about such things. I beg music lovers to be tolerant of my excursions into history and biography, art and architecture, stage design and production, the evolution of taste, and other fields that may seem only tangentially related to opera. For me, the Ultimate Art adjoins many other domains. In writing about them, I hope I may still be saying something useful about opera.

I wish to thank Phillip Brett, Daniel Heartz, Roger Parker, and Paul Robinson for their helpful comments on all or parts of this text; and Kori Lockhart, editor of the *San Francisco Opera Magazine*, a woman of great tact, charm, patience, and understanding, who commissioned and edited most of these essays in their original form. An earlier draft of this book, which grew to be unconscionably long, included four additional essays (on the devil as character in opera, the historic original of Verdi's Don Carlos, the Cairo première of *Aida*, and the actual Roman settings for Puccini's *Tosca*), cutting which occasioned no great loss; and a far more extensive, chapter-by-chapter bibliography, whose absence some readers may regret. As I note at the end of my Suggestions for Further Reading, readers interested in the missing pieces are welcome to write to me for copies.

Berkeley, California, 1991

CHAPTER ONE

Introduction: The Difference Is They Sing

I

It is easier to explain the attractions of ballet, bullfighting, pro football, religious revivals, stadium rock concerts, TV talk shows, or Woody Allen films than the persisting, in fact the growing, appeal of opera. Tens of millions of intelligent adults in Europe, the Americas, Australia, and a few other countries, year after year, spend considerable sums of money, or wait in line for hours, in order to attend reenactments of nineteenth-, eighteenth-, occasionally twentieth-, and once in a great while seventeenth-century dramatic spectacles, frequently performed in languages they don't understand, in which most of the words are sung by specially trained performers accompanied by (indeed, often in aural competition with) an orchestra of musicians.

In 1989, as part of its celebration of the bicentennial of the French Revolution, the city of Paris opened a new opera house on the site of the Bastille, at a cost of more than $400 million. During the incendiary 1960s, the French composer and conductor Pierre Boulez had proposed blowing up the world's opera houses, as French revolutionaries had once destroyed earlier symbols of superannuated power and prestige, like the Bastille.

Since he made that remark, Boulez has conducted performances of eight well-known operas at well-known opera houses. Perhaps he has changed his opinion. What he was apparently implying in 1967 was that this particular art form had become shamefully passé, absurdly costly to maintain, and socially indefensible. No longer, its detractors continue to insist, does opera as it is most often performed bear any relation to what matters or is worthy of public support in the last decade of the twentieth century.

But opponents of opera were making such charges in the seventeenth, eighteenth, and nineteenth centuries, even more forcefully than they make them today. Early detractors were impatient with what they saw as the unnatural conventions of the form and the unnatural behavior of its practitioners, compared with those of the spoken drama. "The whole piece is sung from beginning to end," complained the French critic and freethinker Charles de Saint-Évremond in 1677,

> as if the characters on stage had conspired to present musically the most trivial as well as the most important aspects of their lives. . . . There is nothing more ridiculous than to make someone sing while he is acting, whether he is arguing in a council meeting, or giving orders in a battle. . . . Who can endure the boredom of a recitative, which possesses neither the charm of the song nor the forcefulness of the spoken word? . . . [Opera] is a bizarre mixture of poetry and music where the writer and the composer, equally embarrassed by each other, go to a lot of trouble to create an execrable work. . . . Nonsense filled with music, dancing, stage machines, and decorations may be magnificent nonsense; but it is nonsense all the same.

Jean-Jacques Rousseau (who wrote a successful comic opera of his own in 1752, and who was in part arguing a case against the excesses of French opera, and in favor of the Italian) put words in the mouth of one of his fictional characters, in order to describe with disgust the unhealthy strain and artifice of the court-sponsored tragic operas he had witnessed in Paris.

> What you could not possibly imagine are the frightful cries, the long-drawn-out groans which fill the theatre throughout the performance. . . . One sees the actresses, almost in convulsions, violently extracting this screeching from their lungs, their fists clenched against their breasts, their heads held back, their faces inflamed, their blood vessels swollen, their stomachs quivering. . . . The most difficult thing to understand is that these screeches are almost the only things the spectators applaud.

Soon after Italian opera arrived in London in 1705, Joseph Addison, in *The Spectator* papers, mocked what he regarded as the absurdity of foreign-language productions, improbable scenic allusions, recitative, and bel canto vocalise. "I have known the word 'And' pursued through the whole Gamut, have been entertained with many a melodious 'The,' and have heard the most beautiful Graces, Quavers, and Divisions bestowed upon 'Then,' 'For,' and 'From,' to the eternal Honour of our English Particles." In 1779, Samuel Johnson characterized the Italian opera (quite correctly) as "an exotick and irrational entertainment, which has always been combated and always has prevailed." Lord Chesterfield, Johnson's legendary adversary, dismissed operas in a letter to his son as "essentially too absurd and extravagant to mention. I look upon them as a magic scene, contrived to please the eyes and ears at the expense of the understanding. . . . Whenever I go to an opera, I leave my sense and reason at the door with my half-guinea, and deliver myself up to my eyes and my ears."

The most notorious antiopera statements by a writer of note are those of Leo Tolstoy, who attacked the genre first in his novel *War and Peace*, and later, even more resolutely and radically, in a tract called *What Is Art?* For the novel, Tolstoy invented a ludicrous Bellini-like opera attended by Natasha Rostova and her family in Moscow, in which the fatuousness of what takes place onstage is underlined by Natasha's girlish confusion and naïveté.

The floor of the stage consisted of smooth boards, at the sides was some painted cardboard representing trees, and at the back was a cloth stretched over boards. In the centre of the stage sat some girls in red bodices and white skirts. One very fat girl in a white silk dress sat apart on a low bench, to the back of which a piece of green cardboard was glued. They all sang something. When they had finished their song the girl in white went up to the prompter's box and a man with tight silk trousers over his stout legs, and holding a plume and a dagger, went up to her and began singing, waving his arms about.

First the man with tight trousers sang alone, then she sang, then they both paused while the orchestra played and the man fingered the hand of the girl in white, obviously awaiting the beat to start singing with her. They sang together and everyone in the theatre began clapping and shouting, while the man and woman on the stage—who represented lovers—began smiling, spreading out their arms and bowing.

After her life in the country, and in her present serious mood, all this seemed grotesque and amazing to Natasha. She could not follow the opera nor even listen to the music, she saw only the painted cardboard and the queerly dressed men and women who moved, spoke, and sang so strangely in that brilliant light. She knew what it was all meant to represent, but it was so pretentiously false and unnatural that she first felt ashamed for the actors and then amused at them. She looked at the faces of the audience, seeking in them the same sense of ridicule and perplexity she herself seemed to experience, but they all seemed attentive to what happened on the stage, and expressed delight which to Natasha seemed feigned. . . .

In the second act there was scenery representing tombstones, and there was a round hole in the canvas to represent the moon, shades were raised over the footlights, and from trumpets and contrabass came deep notes while many people arrived from right and left wearing black cloaks and holding something like daggers in their hands. They began waving their arms. Then some other people ran in and began dragging away the maiden who had been in white and was now in light blue. They did not drag her away all at once, but sang with her for a long time and only then did they drag her off, and behind the scenes something metallic was struck three times and everyone knelt down and began to sing a prayer. All these things were repeatedly interrupted by the enthusiastic shouts of the audience.

The imaginary third-act ballet and storm scene are described so as to appear even more foolish, from the disingenuous point of view of Tolstoy's ingenue. In the fourth act, "there was some sort of a devil who sang waving his hand, till the boards were withdrawn from under him and he disappeared down below."

When thirty years later he came to write *What Is Art?* Tolstoy had no need to invent an imaginary opera to deride. Instead he described, in much the same disdainful, amazed-rationalist, antitheatricalist tone, an actual performance he had attended of the Moscow première of Wagner's *Siegfried* in 1889 (or at least two acts of it): "I could stand no more of it and escaped from the theatre with a feeling of revulsion which even now I cannot forget."

He begins his case against *Siegfried* with a device the American comedian Anna Russell made famous, which is simply to relate the plot of an opera in a wide-eyed, Man-from-Mars way that makes everything about it seem absurd. (This was one of his standard literary tricks, called in Russian *ostranenie*, or "making it strange.") Tolstoy repeatedly describes the actors' physical and histrionic shortcomings and the odd way they open their mouths. He makes no reference to their voices or to what they are singing, except to call it "incomprehensible" and to complain of the excessive length of their "strange sounds," their nonmelodic chanting. He describes Wagner's leitmotivs in a mocking and elementary way, condemns the orchestral score for its expressive simplemindedness, and complains of the composer's frustrating practice of forever starting up musical ideas he doesn't finish. Tolstoy is severe on Wagner's practice of having one character recount to another (for the benefit of the audience) previous events both of them must already know. He dismisses the dragon scene as something out of a booth at a village fair. "It is surprising that people over seven years of age can witness it seriously; yet thousands of quasi-cultured people sit and attentively hear and see it, and are delighted." He adds:

> Of music, that is, of art serving as a means to transmit a state of mind experienced by the author, there is not even a trace. . . . What is happening onstage meanwhile is so abominably false, that it is difficult even to perceive these musical snatches, let alone to be infected by them. . . . The author's purpose is so visible that one sees and hears neither Siegfried nor the birds, but only a narrow-minded, self-assured German of bad taste and bad style, who has a most false conception of poetry and in the crudest and most primitive manner wishes to transmit to one these false and mistaken conceptions.

What disgusted Tolstoy more than anything else was the witless complacency of the upper-crust Moscow audience—"a crowd of three thousand people who not only patiently witnessed all this absurd nonsense but even considered it their duty to be delighted with it. . . . The cream of the cultured upper classes sits out six hours of this insane performance, and goes away imagining that by paying tribute to this nonsense it has acquired a fresh right to esteem itself advanced and enlightened."

Tolstoy can explain the effect Wagner's operas have on other people only by comparing it to the experience of a medium's séance or to the effects of getting drunk or smoking opium.

> Sit in the dark for four days with people who are not quite sane, and through the auditory nerves subject your brain to the strongest action of the sounds best adapted to excite it, and you will no doubt be reduced to an abnormal condition and be enchanted by absurdities. . . . And this meaningless, coarse, spurious production finds acceptance all over the world, costs millions of rubles to produce, and assists more and more to pervert the taste of people of the upper classes and their conception of art.

One could simply class this notable harangue as one of the many nineteenth-century attacks against Wagner (and more specifically against Wagner's *Ring*) rather than as an attack against opera in general.[1] But elsewhere in this notorious booklet, and elsewhere in his writings, Tolstoy extends his condemnation to opera of every kind. Of an opera rehearsal he once attended, he writes, "It would be difficult to find a more repulsive sight. . . . The opera . . . was one of the most gigantic absurdities that could possibly be devised. . . . People do not converse in such a way as recitative, and do not place themselves at fixed distances, in a quartet, waving their arms to express their emotions."

> Instinctively the question presents itself: for whom is this being done? If there are occasionally good melodies in opera, to which it is pleasant to listen, they could have been sung simply without these stupid costumes and all the processions and recitatives and hand wavings.
> The ballet, in which half-naked women make voluptuous movements, twisting themselves into various sensual wreathings, is simply a lewd performance.
> So one is quite at a loss as to whom these things are done for. The man of culture is heartily sick of them, while to a real working man they are utterly incomprehensible.

To be fair, I should point out that Tolstoy *had* enjoyed operas—in particular Rossini's—as a young man; but by the time he wrote *What Is Art?* at the age of

---

1. The first edition of Nicolas Slonimsky's *Lexicon of Musical Invective* (1953) cites twenty-seven pages of outraged attacks on Wagner, probably the most-hated serious composer in musical history.

sixty-nine he had converted to a kind of radical-puritan hatred of *all* art that did not directly appeal to the suffering masses, inspire elevated religious sentiments, or "unite people in a community of feeling." If Wagner's neurotic depravity felt the sting of Tolstoy's lash, so did virtually all of the music, art, and literature of his century, including most of his own earlier work. "I saw plainly that all this music and fiction and poetry is not art," he wrote in his diary at the time, "that men do not have the slightest need for it, that it is nothing but a distraction for profiteers and idlers, that it has nothing to do with life." In "The Kreutzer Sonata," he turns a Beethoven violin and piano sonata into something lewd and diabolical.

But if he censures Beethoven and Berlioz, Ibsen and Zola, Rodin and Monet as decadent, godless, and inaccessible to good common folk—if in the end he feels obliged to dismiss as well Shakespeare and Dante, Michelangelo and Raphael, even the "rude, savage, meaningless" Greek tragedians—it is for opera, this exclusive, insincere, dramatically absurd, outrageously extravagant, and socially useless (indeed, socially harmful) form, that Tolstoy reserved his harshest scorn.

The attacks on opera—opera as an art form, opera as it is currently produced, opera as a social institution, opera as a drain on the public purse—continue today, and will no doubt go on until the institution dies. In 1962, the German sociologist and philosopher Theodor Adorno declared that conscientious people (like him) had been expecting the death of opera for at least thirty years. As early as the late 1920s and early 1930s, according to Adorno,

> People began to realize that opera, by reason of its style, its substance, and its attitude, no longer had anything in common with the people on whom it depended; its pretentious forms could not possibly justify the extravagant resources they required. Already, at that time, it was impossible to believe that any public was capable of making the antirationalist, antirealist efforts that the stylization of opera demanded. . . . The reduction of the entire current repertoire in America to at most fifteen titles—including Donizetti's *Lucia di Lammermoor!*—only confirmed the petrifaction of the institution.

In September 1987, a typically rabble-rousing piece entitled "Do We Need Opera?" appeared in a London paper:

> There are some fine tunes in them, decent orchestral stuff, some good choruses, and some tolerable dancing. There can be dreadful dross between the arias—recitative is surely the most tiresome form of communication devised by man—but the pleasure of hearing a tenor or soprano busting a gut belting out "Celeste Aida" or "Casta diva" at Covent Garden can be most affecting, and is not to be sniffed at. As popular entertainment, grand opera is no more to be faulted than melodrama or music hall—Victorian art forms to which it is closely related.

But the writer, George Gale, asks, Is it art?[2] "Watching and hearing *Aida* [on TV] from La Scala, I thought no one could possibly claim that the characterization was other than perfunctory and the action other than merely melodramatic; we are involved in no tragedy, but were simply spectators at a spectacle. It was noisy and moving and empty, like a beaten drum."

Why, then, he asks, does it continue to demand and attract millions of pounds in public subsidies, in cities all over the world? "The answer," he answers,

> can only be that grand opera, meaning and saying nothing much, does not and cannot threaten any regime, however obnoxious; that little or no understanding of what is going on is necessary to enjoy it; that it provides an undemanding but flashy way of showing off; that grandiose spectacle is especially attractive to the vainglorious; that opera-goers are so unsure of their own taste, discrimination, and position in society that they support these 19th-century continental equivalents of Cecil B. De Mille's epics, fondly hoping thereby to establish their own true cultural ancestry and social worth; and that we would be culturally better off not bothering to subsidize so vain, inferior, and foreign an expression of art. . . . It is its failure to attract the mass audience, for which it was originally devised and remains intellectually suited, that finally characterizes grand opera as minor and meretricious art, rather than rubbish.

Two and a half years later, Geoffrey Wheatcroft, a columnist for the London *Sunday Telegraph*, "sated and exhausted" by a year of operagoing, raised much the same question: "Why so much expenditure of time and money and effort on what, when looked at from one angle, is surely a marginal artistic activity?"

II

These people are not all objecting to the same things. As a hybrid form of drama combined with music, or as an institution—and (in either sense) as something that has changed greatly over nearly four hundred years—opera has offered its detractors a great many things to dislike. Simplest-minded of the antiopera crowd are the imagination-deficient literalists, who object to anything less on stage than absolute naturalism; those tiresome people who protest that characters in opera (or theatre or ballet or, I presume, puppet shows) do not behave the way people do in real life. Tolstoy appears to disdain the very use of costumes, sets, and stage lighting.

Others, slightly more tolerant, object that opera is *more* unnatural than other forms of theatre, further from "real life," because in real life people do not

---

2. A curmudgeonly and populist columnist—briefly editor of *The Spectator*—Gale regularly attacked all forms of subsidized art, among other sacred British cows.

regularly express themselves by singing or "converse in such a way as recitative." The fact that operas are sung, moreover, and frequently sung in a language other than that of the audience renders a large portion of them incomprehensible as drama. Beyond these basic stumbling blocks, such critics object that opera performances are full of dramatic absurdities no audience would tolerate in a spoken play. Although operas may *look* like drama, they argue, in fact they have none of the thought-filled, intellectual substance of serious plays.

In some ways more interesting than such critiques of opera's "unnaturalness," or its deficiencies when contrasted to the spoken stage, are objections based on its perversity, even its wickedness as a social and economic institution. One may discount the claims, made by patriots of one nation or another, that imported operas are dangerously "foreign" and thus unwelcome. The argument that opera is extravagantly costly is more complicated, involving as it does fundamental social and political values. A good deal of criticism is directed at opera audiences as much as at opera itself. The institution of opera, it is claimed (the claim was made in past centuries, as it is made today), plays a meretricious, antiartistic, exclusionist role in serving primarily as a self-certifying symbol of "cultural chic" for those who can afford to patronize it: hence the palatial houses, the private boxes retained by old families (or auctioned off to social climbers), the high price of tickets, the ritual of formal dress. Part of the attack on public subsidies for opera, which have replaced court and aristocratic support, is based on the argument that it does *not*— as it may have done at other times and places—enjoy sufficiently broadly based appeal, accessibility, or popularity. (Statistically, this argument is open to question. In some cities, more people attend opera than attend professional sport.)

Some antiopera attacks are openly moralistic in a more personal sense: opera is bad for you. This attitude is apparent in attacks on Wagner by people like Tolstoy and the Viennese critic Eduard Hanslick, who attacked the *Ring* (and the phenomenon known as Tristanism) as a vaporous, antirational, thought-dissolving drug especially dangerous to women; and in claims that the vain and vulgar showiness of opera (which includes exhibitionist vocalism as well as lewdly costumed dancers), the flashy tricks, and the opulent spectacle appeal to people at their most mindless, undiscriminating, and base.[3]

A large part of this criticism—and of opera criticism generally throughout the centuries—has been directed not so much at the genre itself as at inadequate realizations; not so much against all opera as against bad opera, or (most often)

3. Not only *Lulu*, *Salome*, and *Lady Macbeth of Mtsensk* (which are all explicitly erotic) but also *Carmen*, *La traviata*, *Louise*, and *Tosca* were roundly attacked on their first appearance as obscene and immoral entertainments. In a *New York Journal* editorial of January 21, 1907, William Randolph Hearst himself expressed his disgust at Strauss's *Salome*: "In a public performance, a woman is made to declare a desire to bite the lips of a severed head, 'as one would bite a ripe fruit'!"

against opera badly produced and performed. Tolstoy declaiming in 1889 against thick legs, cheesy costumes, or singers "waving their arms about," eighteenth-century observers protesting against extravagant stage spectacles and show-off vocalizing can be regarded more as judicious critics than as Jeremiahs, as sympathetic observers suggesting ways in which opera could be better.

In fact, a good deal of what might appear to be radically antiopera criticism is written by people who actually *like* opera, who take it seriously, and who wish that those who produce and perform it took it seriously as well. What they are objecting to, often fiercely, are the weaknesses or excesses of opera production practice—and, to some degree, the overly tolerant embrace of the established repertory—at the time or place they are writing.

In 1720, the Venetian composer and civic leader Benedetto Marcello depicted the grosser excesses of contemporary Italian performance practice in a satirical essay, at once revealing and clever, entitled "Il teatro alla moda" ("or A sure and easy method to compose well and produce Italian operas in the modern fashion"), addressed in part to his colleague and fellow Venetian Antonio Vivaldi. Marcello's fundamental point, in this richly detailed essay, is that spectacle-conscious impresarios and egocentric singers were calling all of the shots. All that the poor composer and librettist could do was to follow their orders, whatever the cost to dramatic or musical integrity. By means of his numerous "recommendations" (to writers, composers, singers, impresarios, musicians, stage designers, the soprano's parents and protectors et al.), Marcello compiled a catalogue of abuses, only very slightly exaggerating the grotesque, artistically indefensible circus that opera had become in many Italian theatres by 1720.

> Real life is imparted to the opera by the use of prisons, daggers, poison, the writing of letters on stage, bear and wild bull hunts, earthquakes, storms, sacrifices, the settling of accounts, and mad scenes. . . .
>
> The librettist should pay frequent social calls to the prima donna since the success of the opera generally depends on her. He should change his drama as her artistic genius may order him to do so, making additions or cuts in her part or that of the bear or other persons. . . . [The composer] should speed up or slow down the tempo of the arias according to every whim of the singer and he should swallow all their impertinences, remembering that his own honor, esteem, and future are at their mercy. . . .
>
> In an ensemble scene, when addressed by another character or while the latter might have to sing an arietta, he [the male lead] should wave greetings to some masked lady-friend in one of the boxes, or smile sweetly to someone in the orchestra or to one of the supers. In that way it will be made quite clear to the audience that he is Alipio Forconi, the famous singer, and not the Prince Zoroastro whose part he is playing . . . When he reaches the repeat in the *da capo* aria he should change it completely in any way he pleases, regardless of whether or not these changes will go with the accompaniment of bass or violins, and whether they will distort the tempo entirely. . . .

As soon as she [the seconda donna] receives her part she will carefully count both notes and words. If there should be fewer of either than in the prima donna's part she will insist that librettist and composer change this by making both roles equally long. She will be particularly insistent about the length of her train, the ballet, the beauty spots, trills, embellishments, cadenzas, protectors, little owls, and other equally important paraphernalia.

Between 1883 and 1894, George Bernard Shaw wrote reviews of London musical productions for a number of papers, under a number of names. Collected in three volumes, they comprise, for all of Shaw's idiosyncrasies, one of the wittiest, soundest, and most salient commentaries on "music as performed" ever written. During that time, he wrote reviews of hundreds of opera performances, (the greater part of which he disliked) including the British premières of *Otello, Cavalleria rusticana* and *I pagliacci,* and *Manon Lescaut.*

Sometimes it was the work that displeased him. He "saw through" Meyerbeer and his imitators earlier than most operagoers and critics. *Le Prophète*, he wrote, "meant to be luridly historical, is in fact the oddest medley of drinking songs, tinder-box trios, sleigh rides, and skating quadrilles imaginable." "Who wants to hear *Samson et Dalila?*" he once asked, rhetorically. "I respectfully submit, Nobody." Of a mediocre new Italian opera that had been paired with Mascagni's *Cavalleria rusticana* in 1891, he wrote, "Any grasshopper with a moderately good ear could write reams of such stuff after spending three months in Italy. Offenbach's lightest operetta looms in intellectual majesty above this brainless lilting, with its colorless orchestration and its exasperatingly light-hearted and empty-headed recitatives, accompanied by sickly chords on the violoncello with the third always in the bass."

There can be no question that Shaw was a devoted and serious lover of opera. He was, in fact, an uncommonly prescient and perceptive admirer of the operas of Mozart, Verdi, and Wagner. What he hated was what Victorian London was doing to them. The wonder is that he was able to maintain his fervent admiration for their great works through the mutilated, unmusical, and antidramatic performances in which he inevitably saw them on stage.

Ever since I was a boy I have been in search of a satisfactory performance of *Don Giovanni;*[4] and at last I have come to see that Mozart's turn will hardly be in my time. . . . The vigorous passages were handled in the usual timid, conventional way; and the statue music, still as impressive as it was before Wagner and Beethoven were born, was muddled through like a vote of thanks at the

4. So have I.

end of a very belated public meeting. . . . The great sextet, "Mille torbidi pensieri," . . . deprived of its stage significance, became a rather senseless piece of "absolute music." . . . I am sorry to say that alterations of Mozart's text were the order of the evening, every one of the singers lacking Mozart's exquisite sense of form and artistic dignity. . . . [Zélie de Lussan] is one of those Zerlinas who end "Batti, batti" on the upper octave of the note written, as a sort of apology for having been unable to do anything else with the song. The effect of this suburban grace can be realized by anyone who will take the trouble to whistle "Pop goes the Weasel" with the last note displaced an octave.

Verdi's opera [*La traviata*] is one thing: the wilful folly of the Covent Garden parody of it is quite another. Take any drama ever written, and put it on a stage six times too large for its scenes, introducing the maddest incongruities of furniture, costume, and manners at every turn of it; and it will seem as nonsensical as *La Traviata*, even without the crowning burlesque of a robust, joyous, round-cheeked lady figuring as a moribund patient in decline. . . . The truth is that *La Traviata*, in spite of its conventionalities, is before its time at Covent Garden instead of behind it.

The popular notion of [Verdi's operas] is   founded on performances in which the superb distinction and heroic force of the male characters, and the tragic beauty of the women, have been burlesqued by performers with every sort of disqualification for such parts, from age and obesity to the most excruciating phases of physical insignificance and modern cockney vulgarity. . . . At the thought of that dynasty of execrable imposters in tights and tunics, interpolating their loathsome B flats into the beautiful melodies they could not sing, and swelling with conceit when they were able to finish "Di quella pira" with a high C capable of making a stranded man-of-war recoil off a reef in mid-ocean, I demand the suspension of all rules as to decorum of language until I have heaped upon them some little instalment of the infinite abuse they deserve. Others, alas! have blamed Verdi, much as if Dickens had blamed Shakespeare for the absurdities of Mr. Wopsle.

"I hate performers who debase great works of art: I long for their annihilation," Shaw wrote in 1894. Among the debasers he heard and hated were singers now regarded as part of one of opera's "golden ages"—Jean de Reszke, Nellie Melba, Emma Calvé, Victor Maurel. Of Calvé's performance as Carmen, he wrote: "She carried her abandonment to the point of being incapable of paying the smallest attention to the score." Of de Reszke: "His acting as Otello was about equally remarkable for its amateurish ineptitude and for its manifestations of the natural histrionic powers which he has so studiously neglected for the last fifteen years." Of Katerina Rolla's Amelia in Verdi's *Un ballo in maschera*: "Her acting consisted of the singular plunge, gasp, and stagger peculiar to the Verdi heroine, whose reason is permanently unsettled by grief."

Shaw cared profoundly for the *music* of good opera, as witness his outrage at the casual mistreatment and butchery of scores. But he was fundamentally a man of the theatre, and (as his appalled descriptions of Victorian opera acting suggest) he was most distressed by the blind, blank inability of contemporary productions to realize the vivid drama (even melodrama) implicit in the better opera scores and texts.

In 1962, another magisterial "man of the theatre"—Eric Bentley, at the time America's most insightful and authoritative drama critic, a great admirer of Mozart's operas and of the opera productions of Walter Felsenstein in East Berlin—undertook to describe a season at the Met for *Theatre Arts* magazine. (In 1955, Bentley had edited a paperback collection of Bernard Shaw's best music reviews.) At the Metropolitan, Bentley was appalled by the empty-headed foolishness of the audiences, which seemed to wake up only to cry out "Bravo" (or, to demonstrate their knowingness, "Brav*a*") at the end of arias. "The provocation for these little interruptions," he wrote, "is commonly an extremely high note sung very loudly, preferably (this season) by a soprano. . . . The spontaneity of the Italian outcries is suspect." To many people present, he thought the opera was no more than "an interruption of the intermissions."

While acknowledging that some great music was played (although often too loudly), that some great voices were on display (Richard Tucker's, Birgit Nilsson's), and that a few haute couture designers had been hired, "the issue for me," he wrote, "is the art of opera. Singers would sing had opera never been invented. The question of opera is the question of musical drama"—and drama was precisely what he found missing at the Met. Although every great opera composer, according to Bentley, is at heart a great dramatist, "the Met ignores dramatic values," whether comic, romantic, melodramatic, or tragic. "The Met employs singers, not actors; it provides a dog show for soprano-fanciers."

He preferred what theatre director Cyril Ritchard did to Offenbach's *La Périchole* (for all its lack of essential French values) to the Met's dead, waxworks stagings of Verdi: "At least it was *something*, something produced, something directed." Better second-rate music (like Offenbach's), or second-rate singers (like Felsenstein's), if the result is living theatre. "I have been speaking," Bentley concluded,

of two things: the public and the performance. Together they make up a perfect specimen of the effete. The public: overprivileged, overfed, overconfident, exclusive, uncommitted, uninvolved. The performance: overdecorative, overinflated, overcharged, chi-chi, lush, a mere exhibition, whether of coloratura or chiaroscuro. It's the familiar phenomenon of the jaded palate and the overspiced condiments that are used to please it. It is possible that nothing can be done except exactly what Mr. Bing is doing [Rudolf Bing was general manager of the Met from 1952 to 1974], in which case one can either admire him for his sense of reality, or pity him for his helplessness. But if it is inevitable that the Met be what it is, it is not inevitable that one continue to go there.

Andrew Porter is probably the most knowledgeable and influential music critic writing in English today. After writing in London for the *Musical Times*, the *Financial Times*, and *Opera*, he began serving as regular music critic for *The New Yorker* in 1972. In 1974, the composer and critic Virgil Thomson wrote, "Nobody reviewing in America has anything like Porter's command of [opera]."

He has also translated into English the librettos of several important operas, produced operas by Handel and Verdi, and performed scholarly investigations of *Macbeth* and *Don Carlos*. Most of his reviews, in fact, incorporate a fair amount of (sometimes irrelevant) state-of-the-art scholarship, to the point that reading them en bloc (they currently fill five volumes) provides one with a serendipitous education in musical history. Porter is open to new music and new production ideas, and frequently finds things to admire in the work of smaller (even amateur) opera companies, lesser-known festivals, and works dismissed as unimportant by other critics and scholars. But his published response to the "grand" opera of his day—which has generally meant, since 1972, the Metropolitan Opera in New York—is depressingly similar to that of Bentley and Shaw.

Between 1972 and 1990, Andrew Porter made more than passing mention of some 140 productions at the Metropolitan Opera in his *New Yorker* reviews. Writing a century after Shaw, he is disgusted at the sloppy, tasteless things that producers and singers are still doing to Verdi. "The Metropolitan Opera's current production of Verdi's *Macbeth*," he wrote in 1973, "is a limp, bloated relic." Eleven years later, he found a revival of the same opera equally depressing: "The Met chorus is surely one of the dullest and least dramatic opera choruses in the country. The choristers stood or sat about like dummies—features blank, postures inexpressive, eyes on the conductor—and produced much the same sort of timbre and attack whether they were playing warriors, courtiers, exiles, bards, or witches."

Of a 1973 production of *Il trovatore*, he remarked, "All in all, it was the sort of evening that brings grand opera into disrepute and keeps musical people away from the Met. . . . The time has come to treat Verdi's music as seriously in opera houses as it is treated by serious musicians." Of the Met's *Aida* and *Trovatore* in 1976, he wrote, "From a dramatic point of view both productions must be deemed failures." Eleven years later, things were no better: "At the Met, it was grand opera as usual—no, worse than usual—on the first night of *Il trovatore*." Taking note of the noises of displeasure that greeted the designer and director, Porter wrote, "Booing is an ugly sound, but here it reflected recognition that this staging is ill-conceived—inimical to the drama and unhelpful to the singers. The cast needed help. Luciano Pavarotti, who took the title role, is no sort of actor, physically, visually, or, any longer, vocally." Joan Sutherland's Leonora was distressing to hear; the Azucena and the Count de Luna both sang off pitch. "The performance made a poor case for [*Il trovatore*], and for grand opera in general."

A 1983 presentation of Verdi's *La forza del destino* "was put on with a lineup of big names . . . but it was an unworthy, an almost meaningless representation of Verdi's drama. . . . If there was any line or purpose in John Dexter's direction, I missed it." A new production of *Ernani* that year "was a tame and vapid affair," its stars (Leona Mitchell, Luciano Pavarotti, Ruggiero Raimondi) "dramatic ciphers. In the remarkable trio that constitutes the last act, they stood in a row, as if lined up before microphones in a recording studio. One forgives singers who can't act if by their singing they bring the drama to life. These singers didn't."

What appears to dismay Porter most, on the basis of the increasing number of "failing" reviews he gives to Metropolitan Opera productions, are poor singing by famous singers (colorless, weak, forced, off-key), many of whom cannot or will not act; bloated, extravagant, vulgar visual productions that contribute nothing to—in fact often war with—the drama; radical choppings and changings of the original scores, in works such as Handel's *Rinaldo* and *Giulio Cesare;* and a boring, depressing, overall absence of any sort of spirit or dramatic content: operas that are little more than what he calls "concerts in costume," and often not very good concerts at that. "The whole was undramatic, untheatrical, unworthy," he wrote of the Met's new *Der Ring des Nibelungen* in 1989. "This was a shallow, unpoetic, mindless account of the great drama." He was scarcely happier with the Met's previous *Ring* in 1975.

Again and again, Porter grows angry and bitter at the company's penchant for costly and overblown productions—the Zeffirelli *Bohème* and *Traviata*, a gross and joyless *Die Fledermaus*, an elephantine *Manon*. "While other big opera companies seek to rediscover dramatic values in familiar works of the past—sometimes stylishly, sometimes with reckless abandon—the Metropolitan Opera prefers elaborate, extravagant spectacle. . . . The company cultivates an audience that doesn't really listen to a score, that is eager to drown the music with its applause for scenic effects and for the entries of well-publicized artists."

Much of the weakness Porter traces to "the company's repertory system, essentially unchanged in a hundred years, [which] precludes the single-minded attention to one opera at a time which many European houses can now afford." He himself is often more enthusiastic about opera productions at less richly endowed companies and festivals in the United States and abroad.

The vociferous objections in all four of these last cases come from people not radically opposed to opera; not even from people who like operas only when the works performed are very, very good (Shaw defended Mascagni, and Porter has admitted to enjoying Meyerbeer); but from people who take opera seriously and who acknowledge, as I do, its potential as the "ultimate art." They are dismayed and disgusted by the ways in which producers and performers have betrayed this potential, either by the injustice they have done to the music, or by the fact that they have ignored the importance of opera as drama.

III

The basic production elements of live opera as most people think of it today—what the French, and later the Americans, took to calling "grand" opera—were set into place between 1870 and 1920. This kind of opera, opera as produced at the Metropolitan Opera, Covent Garden, La Scala, the Vienna Staatsoper, and the Paris Opera, could easily be starved to death by the public agencies and private philanthropies that maintain it—precisely because it is so expensive to produce, and hence so dependent on external support.

New productions of "grand" operas at the world's best-known houses now cost hundreds of thousands of dollars to mount, often (compared to successful productions in the commercial theatre) for relatively few performances. These productions frequently involve several elaborate sets, a great many custom-made costumes, intricately programmed lighting, and a corps of professional dancers. They may require the work of a hundred or more highly skilled musicians, as well as more hundreds of technical personnel, administrators, and office staff. They are presented in purpose-built, often palatial auditoriums seating from one thousand to three thousand or more. To perform the leading roles in such productions, audiences in many cities have come to expect (and occasionally the scores demand) singing actors possessed of rare and fragile gifts, a situation that allowed the best-known of these singers to command fees of $10,000 or more per performance in 1990.

It is impossible to write sensibly and analytically about "opera" as it exists today, to make coherent and universally applicable remarks about it as a written and a performing art. There are simply too many kinds of opera, performed in too many different ways, from *Help, Help, the Globolinks!* to Wagner's *Der Ring des Nibelungen*, from a church hall performance with piano accompaniment to a von Karajan première during Easter Week at Salzburg.

Student, amateur, semistaged, piano-accompanied, or otherwise inexpensive versions of opera can be heard in hundreds of places. These often provide excellent entertainment and respectable hearings of popular operas for audiences that would not otherwise be able to experience them live. Occasionally, student and amateur opera groups offer new or rarely performed works, or revealing insights into repertory standards.

With all appropriate respect for the college and church hall players, Gian Carlo

Menotti's *Globolinks* (an amusing children's opera), and the more than two hundred other-than-grand opera companies in America, what interest me are the kinds of opera and opera production that dominate the Western imagination, for better or worse: those that fill the big houses, attract the largest audiences (and the greatest amount of publicity), and end up recorded on disk, videotape, or film, broadcast by radio and television, thus to be seen and heard by millions of people.

The operas regularly performed by the so-called "international," or by the leading national/regional repertory companies are by definition the most enduring of the thousands that have been written since 1600. Occasionally, of course, such companies venture novelties and rarities, very few of which win places in the standard repertory. But it is by means of such ventures that the standard repertory *does*, in fact, alter over time.

In at least fifty-five cities—forty-seven of them in Europe, six in North America, and two in Australia—one could attend in any given recent year at least ten different operas, and a total of at least forty opera performances, in fully staged professional productions. (I lack figures for the Soviet Union and some cities in Eastern Europe.) At least eighteen of these cities are in Germany or Austria—thanks to exceptionally generous government subsidies, which generally cover 85 percent or more of a company's expenses; eight are in Italy; seven are in France; three each are in Switzerland and Britain; and two each are in Belgium and Spain. (The two British companies on the list based outside of London—Opera North in Leeds and the Scottish Opera in Glasgow—also tour extensively. In fact, with the three other professional touring companies of the United Kingdom—the Welsh National Opera, the Glyndebourne Touring Company, and the Kent Opera—they offer each year a total of almost five hundred performances of some fifty different productions in British cities outside London.) In nineteen of these cities (thirteen of them German-speaking), one could have a choice of one hundred or more opera performances a year staged by permanent and professional companies. And in five of them—Berlin, London, Munich, New York, and Vienna, each of which houses at least two full-time major opera companies—at least three hundred professional opera performances are mounted every year.[5]

Three of the best-known and most elegant European opera houses—the Teatro alla Scala in Milan (which opened in 1778), the Paris Opera (1875), and the Teatro

5. The 1991 *Musical America International Directory of the Performing Arts* lists 310 (self-reporting) opera companies outside the United States, 98 of which are in Germany, 35 in the former USSR, 25 in France, 13 each in Great Britain and Italy, and 12 in Austria. Sixty-eight are in what used to be called communist countries. These listings take no account of the size or offerings of these organizations. For the United States and Canada, the *Directory* ranks companies according to the level of their annual budgets. Eighty opera companies in these two countries fall in the $1,000,000 and greater categories. One hundred eighty U.S. opera groups claim an annual budget of more than $100,000. "Music festivals" are listed indiscriminately—there are fourteen in Finland alone—but about thirty of them worldwide appear to be devoted primarily to opera.

dell'Opera in Rome (1888)—offer relatively limited seasons, closer in numbers to those of Chicago or San Francisco than to those of, say, Hamburg or Zurich. With the opening of the Opéra-Bastille, in fact, the "old" Paris Opera is now used primarily for dance and baroque music concerts. The historic eighteenth-century houses in Naples and Venice offer too few performances today to make the list.

Qualitative distinctions among these companies are difficult to make, unless one is able to attend several productions in each of them over a number of seasons. Over thirty-eight years, I've attended more than six hundred productions of 160 different operas in thirty of these cities, as well as in several other places. But this is nowhere near enough to venture meaningful comparisons.

Many serious devotees and regular music critics have seen a great deal more opera than I have. Such assiduous operagoers may learn a great deal about the repertory, about individual performers, and about productions, but they are still likely to know the offerings of only one region. Only a few music critics and opera fans have enjoyed the freedom to travel extensively year after year and compare performances around the world.

The important second companies in the cities that have more than one—the Komische Oper in (East) Berlin, the Volksoper in Vienna, the English National Opera in London, the New York City Opera, the several "second companies" in Paris, and the Theater am Gärtnerplatz in Munich—tend to offer more light opera and operetta, as do many of the smaller German companies. In the latter, as at the Volksoper and the Gärtnerplatz, an "opera" season will often include performances of *My Fair Lady* or *Fiddler on the Roof* as well as *The Gypsy Baron* and *The Merry Widow*—and Mozart, Puccini, and Weber.

Most European companies, some with an annual repertory of thirty, forty, or even more different operas performed in what seems like random order night after night over a nine- or ten-month season, depend almost entirely on a resident company of performers whose names and voices are likely to be unknown beyond the immediate region. (This applies to Eastern Europe and the former Soviet Union as well as the West.)

But this need not mean that a serious and well-managed "regional rep" opera house achieves a lower level of overall quality than the house that tends to import its lead singers from the international pool. Summer festivals (there are perhaps twenty summer opera festivals worldwide deserving more than regional attention) such as Glyndebourne and Santa Fe have earned much of their high reputation from putting on distinguished, carefully rehearsed productions cast with good but lesser-known singing actors.

The opera companies that make most use of well-known, nonresident, international singers (and frequently of visiting producers and conductors as well) are New York's Metropolitan, the Royal Opera at Covent Garden in London, and the Vienna Staatsoper—the Big Three; the San Francisco Opera, the Lyric Opera of

Chicago, La Scala in Milan, the Teatro dell'Opera in Rome, the Teatro Liceu in Barcelona, the Teatri Comunali in Genoa and Florence; and to a slightly lesser degree the companies in Bologna, Houston, Madrid, Paris, and Toronto. (The Los Angeles Music Center Opera, which had its first season in 1986, hasn't yet reached my arbitrary ten-opera/forty-performance minimum, despite a formidable annual budget. When it does, it will join this list, because it also makes use of star singers and producers drawn from the international/recording pool.)

Residents of or visitors to many other cities—(West) Berlin, Geneva, Hamburg, Lyons, Marseilles, Munich, Nice, Turin, Washington, Zurich—are likely to be able to see several international class singers each season, along with a company of local or lesser-known performers. Other important opera companies, some with very extensive seasons and repertories—Cologne, Dresden, Duisberg/Düsseldorf (the two cities share one company, which puts on more than three hundred opera performances each year), East Berlin, Hannover, Liège, Mannheim, Strasbourg (the companies based in Liège and Strasbourg also perform at neighboring cities), and Sydney, plus the four Scandinavian capitals (where most operas are performed in the local language) depend almost entirely, and in some cases entirely, on resident troupes. On occasion, these troupes have included performers who are also, or who go on to be, international stars: Theo Adam in (East) Berlin, Joan Sutherland in Sydney, Martti Talvela in Helsinki, Elisabeth Söderström in Stockholm. But the same is true of most of the world's serious resident companies, small as well as large.

There are opera houses in Cairo, Istanbul, and Tel Aviv that offer annual seasons from the traditional Western repertory. Elsewhere in the non-Western world—particularly in wealthy, West-oriented cities like Tokyo and Hong Kong—citizens can receive frequent doses of opera by means of visits from important American or European companies. Between 1988 and 1990, the Japanese subsidized extensive and expensive visits by the Teatro alla Scala of Milan, the Bavarian State Opera of Munich, the Bayreuth Festival Opera, and the Opera Theatre of St. Louis. A lavish new music center in Hong Kong opened in November 1989 with a two-week visit from the Cologne City Opera, performing *Fidelio* and *The Barber of Seville*.

Except for the pure voice fancier or star follower (a not insignificant category of opera fan), the presence of "name" singers does not of itself guarantee a memorable, even necessarily a tolerable, evening of opera. Singers like Caballé, Carreras, Domingo, Freni, Pavarotti, or Te Kanawa (the names at the top change every ten or twenty years) may sing from forty to eighty opera performances a year, in perhaps a dozen or twenty different cities, in productions that range from brilliant to deadly dull. Although it is the "starriest" company in the world, performance for performance, the Metropolitan in New York is not everyone's idea of opera heaven. Some of the most interesting opera producers and conductors—who often have more to do with the overall quality of a performance than individual singers do—tend to concentrate their activities in their home cities, which helps to guarantee certain places a consistently high level of production. In the eighteenth century, the quality of the resident *orchestras* in Dresden, Prague, Mannheim, and Munich led composers like Mozart to prefer them for premières. The same may be true today of cities like Vienna, Berlin, Munich, Milan, and London, where the opera orchestras tend to be led by conductors of greater-than-usual distinction.

The range, depth, and adventurousness of a given company's repertory may also give some clue to its quality. If an overabundance of *Mikado*s or *Merry Widow*s may hint at a certain shallowness in the repertoire, the ability and willingness to mount Wagner's *Der Ring des Nibelungen* may be taken as a sign of serious resources and intentions. In the past twenty-five years, new and complete *Ring* cycles have been mounted by at least thirty different cities, including those at the Wagner festivals in Bayreuth and Seattle. One should expect to see more Italian operas in Italy, more German operas in Germany, more French operas in France; all three countries, moreover, retain a popular fondness for their own lighter operas (*Le comte Ory, Zar und Zimmermann, Mireille*), many of them little known outside their borders. The Finns do more Finnish operas, the Russians more Russian, the Czechs more Czech; but all of them depend on the standard Western European repertory as well. The Metropolitan Opera and Covent Garden, like other U.S. and British companies, are more evenly international in their repertory, because so few English or American operas have made their way to the list of accepted standards.

Among them, the fifty-five most operatically active cities might produce six "world premières" of totally new operas—out of some three hundred or four hundred works altogether—in a typical year. At best, two or three of these will go on to be produced again somewhere else. The most recent operas to have had several sequential productions at major houses were Aribert Reimann's *Lear* (Munich, 1978), Philip Glass's *Satyagraha* (Amsterdam, 1980), and John Adams's *Nixon in China* (Houston, 1987). The more adventurous companies, those that take their "educational" or creative responsibilities most seriously, try to offer several recent or rarely performed works every season, in order to expand the acquaintance and taste of their audiences beyond the standard repertory.

IV

Which leads to the next question: what *is* the standard repertory? *Aida, Barber, Carmen,* and so on down the alphabet, as it was in the beginning, is now, and ever shall be, world without end, Amen?

Yes and no. The standard repertory—the list of operas most often, most regularly, and most universally performed—changes more over time than many people think. In any decade, the Top 40—or 50 or 100—operas in the world repertory may appear to be cemented in place with incredible fixity, which is one of the many things about opera its detractors pretend to dislike. Of course, the world's leading symphony orchestras and chamber music groups draw heavily from a common stock of old music as well. Repertory theatres the world over continue to perform the same "classic" plays. But the conservative tastes of the world of opera, it is presumed, far outrun either of these. The caricature of the complacent operagoer is that of someone who never grows beyond *Aida-Barber-Carmen,* who goes on tapping his toes and hurling his bravos at *Faust*s and *Lohengrin*s and *Lucia*s and *Tosca*s long after he should have moved on to better things.

In the calendar years 1988 and 1989, professional companies in the fifty-five cities to which I referred offered eleven operas at least 200 times each: *The Barber of Seville, Tosca, The Marriage of Figaro, La Bohème, Madame Butterfly, Don Giovanni, Rigoletto, Così fan tutte, The Magic Flute, Die Fledermaus,* and *La traviata.* With the exception of *Così* and *The Magic Flute,* one would probably have found these same titles in the standard repertory fifty years ago. So the charge of dug-in conservatism in the opera world might appear to be justified.

But if you cast your net wider and deeper, to include all 252 professional opera companies and festivals whose schedules are reported in *Opera* magazine, a list of the 100 works they perform most often takes on considerable interest. The special tastes of all those German companies become more evident, including their taste for mixing operettas and American musicals in with "proper" operas. The world-wide penchant for lighter, more singable, and more salable works interspersed with the heavier classics gives to the present-day operatic Hit Parade considerable heterogeneity—one more thing that makes it difficult to discuss the phenomenon called "opera" in any logical, univocal way. Admired works that are difficult to cast, such as *Tristan* and *Norma,* end up far below the frothy light operas and tired Victorian war-horses (*Faust, Adriana Lecouvreur*) that many critics would be happy to see retired from the lists for all time.

What follows is a list of the 100 works most often performed by professional opera companies and festivals around the world in the calendar years 1988 and 1989, compiled by means of an arbitrary (and inherently flawed) tallying process. The titles I give first—which are the titles I'll be using throughout this book—are those colloquially used in the United States and Britain. Sometimes we tend to translate (*The Flying Dutchman, The Marriage of Figaro*); other times (*Die Fledermaus, Così fan tutte*) we don't.[6]

6. Works generally thought of as "light operas," "operettas," or "musicals" I have identified by asterisks. Although I am writing in this book primarily about the nonasterisked sort of work, this list is intended to suggest the actual nature of the current repertory of opera companies around the world—which includes works one may not normally think of as "operas." It may soon, for economic reasons, come to include more.

1. *The Marriage of Figaro* (*Le nozze di Figaro*) (Mozart, 1786)

2. *Tosca* (Puccini, 1900)

3. *Don Giovanni* (Mozart, 1787)

4. *The Barber of Seville* (*Il barbiere di Siviglia*) (Rossini, 1816)

5. *La Bohème* (Puccini, 1896)

6. *La traviata* (Verdi, 1853)

7. *The Magic Flute* (*Die Zauberflöte*) (Mozart, 1791)

8. *Così fan tutte* (Mozart, 1790)

9. *Madame Butterfly* (Puccini, 1904)

10. *Rigoletto* (Verdi, 1851)

11. *Carmen* (Bizet, 1875)

12.* *Die Fledermaus* (J. Strauss, Jr., 1874)

13. *The Abduction from the Seraglio* (*Die Entführung aus dem Serail*) (Mozart, 1782)

14. *Fidelio* (Beethoven, 1805/1814)

15. *Aida* (Verdi, 1871)

16. *The Flying Dutchman* (*Der fliegende Holländer*) (Wagner, 1843)

17. *Salome* (R. Strauss, 1905)

18. *Un ballo in maschera* (Verdi, 1859)

19. *The Tales of Hoffmann* (*Les Contes d'Hoffmann*) (Offenbach, 1881)

20. *Turandot* (Puccini, 1926)

21.* *The Merry Widow* (*Die lustige Witwe*) (Lehár, 1905)

22. *Falstaff* (Verdi, 1893)

23. *Der Rosenkavalier* (R. Strauss, 1911)

24. *Hansel and Gretel* (*Hänsel und Gretel*) (Humperdinck, 1893)

25. *L'elisir d'amore* (Donizetti, 1832)

26. *Ariadne auf Naxos* (R. Strauss, 1912)

27. *Lucia di Lammermoor* (Donizetti, 1833)

28. *Eugene Onegin* (Tchaikovsky, 1879)

29. *Faust* (Gounod, 1859)

30. *Otello* (Verdi, 1887)

31. *Il trovatore* (Verdi, 1853)

32. *Die Walküre* (Wagner, 1870)

33. *Parsifal* (Wagner, 1882)

67.   *Mefistofele* (Boito, 1868/1875)

68.*   *The Mikado* (Sullivan, 1885)

69.*   *The Gypsy Princess* (*Csárdásfürstin*) (Kálmán, 1915)

70.   *The Pearl Fishers* (*Les Pêcheurs des perles*) (Bizet, 1863)

71.   *L'incoronazione di Poppea* (Monteverdi, 1642)

72.   *Manon Lescaut* (Puccini, 1893)

73.   *Idomeneo* (Mozart, 1781)

74.   *L'italiana in Algeria* (Rossini, 1813)

75.   *Tristan und Isolde* (Wagner, 1865)

76.   *Die Frau ohne Schatten* (R. Strauss, 1919)

77.   *Giulio Cesare* (Handel, 1724)

78.*   *West Side Story* (Bernstein, 1957)

79.   *Arabella* (R. Strauss, 1933)

80.*   *La belle Hélène* (Offenbach, 1864)

81.*   *My Fair Lady* (Lerner, 1956)

82.   *Gianni Schicchi* (Puccini, 1918)

83.   *Norma* (Bellini, 1831)

84.   *Peter Grimes* (Britten, 1945)

85.   *Bluebeard's Castle* (Bartók, 1911)

86.   *The Merry Wives of Windsor* (*Die lustigen Weiber von Windsor*) (Nicolai, 1849)

87.   *La finta giardiniera* (Mozart, 1775)

88.   *The Turn of the Screw* (Britten, 1954)

89.*   *La Grande Duchesse de Gérolstein* (Offenbach, 1867)

90.*   *A Night in Venice* (*Eine Nacht in Venedig*) (J. Strauss, Jr., 1883)

91.   *Albert Herring* (Britten, 1947)

92.   *Pelléas et Mélisande* (Debussy, 1902)

93.   *Thaïs* (Massenet, 1894)

94.*   *The Land of Smiles* (*Das Land des Lächelns*) (Lehár, 1929)

95.   *Les Dialogues des Carmélites* (Poulenc, 1957)

96.   *La Gioconda* (Ponchielli, 1876)

97.   *Il signor Bruschino* (Rossini, 1813)

98.   *Samson et Dalila* (Saint-Saëns, 1877)

99.   *Le comte Ory* (Rossini, 1828)

100.   *La sonnambula* (Bellini, 1831)

All sorts of games can be played with statistics, especially statistics you have contrived and collected yourself. But despite its obvious weaknesses and omissions, I believe this list reflects fairly accurately the state of contemporary taste. It also leads me to a few reflections.

1.   The operas that head the list seem relatively secure in their positions. The bottom third or quarter, however, will vary considerably from year to year, depending on producers' search for variety, how long a work has been off the schedule, and the changing preferences of singers and audiences. In trying to fix an image of the current "standard repertory," therefore, one should also take note of the next twenty or so, any one of which may appear on a Top 100 ranking in a different set of seasons.

As of 1990, the runners-up would include Verdi's *Luisa Miller*, Auber's *Fra Diavolo*, Prokofiev's *The Love for Three Oranges* and *The Fiery Angel*, Shostakovitch's *Lady Macbeth of Mtsensk*, Jerry Bock's *Fiddler on the Roof* (called *Anatevka* in Germany, where it remains a repertory staple), Britten's *A Midsummer Night's Dream*, Stravinsky's *The Rake's Progress*, Carl Millöcker's *Der Bettelstudent* (but only in Germany), Puccini's *Il tabarro* and *La rondine*, Janáček's *The Makropolous Case* and *The Cunning Little Vixen*, Richard Strauss's *Die schweigsame Frau*, Cimarosa's *Il matrimonio segreto*, Weber's *Oberon*, Borodin's *Prince Igor*, Mussorgsky's *Khovanshchina*, Donizetti's *Viva la mamma* (as his farce *Le convenienze ed inconvenienze teatrali* is popularly retitled), Cherubini's *Médée* (or *Medea*), Gershwin's *Porgy and Bess*, Purcell's *Dido and Aeneas*, Dvořák's *Rusalka*, Lehár's *Der Zarewitsch*, Gounod's *Romeo et Juliette*, and two or three other Gilbert and Sullivan operettas.

2.   An obvious conservatism is evidenced by the staying power of a great many old favorites, from *Tosca* to *La sonnambula*, which should be no more surprising than the durability of Ravel's *Boléro* and Tchaikovsky's *Pathétique* on orchestral rosters. The estimate, made by Meirion and Susie Harries in their useful book *Opera Today*, that two thirds of the "international standard repertory" is made up of nineteenth-century works, is borne out exactly: sixty-six out of these one hundred date from the nineteenth century, as against twenty-four from this century (not all of them "modern," of course), nine from the eighteenth (seven

Mozart, one Gluck, and one Handel), and one from the seventeenth, Monteverdi's *L'incoronazione di Poppea*.

3. More interesting to me than the "conservatism" of this list are its variety (opera today clearly means a great many things) and the vitality displayed by its changes over time. Despite the durability of many "war-horse" works, such a list of favorite operas would have been remarkably different fifty, thirty, even twenty years ago—as I think I can demonstrate.

My old copy of *The Victor Book of the Opera* (published sometime in the late 1930s) describes and illustrates 106 operas in greater or less detail, greater in the case of anything by Wagner (the *Ring* gets 47 pages; *Die Meistersinger* and *Parsifal*, 14 each) and other Golden Horseshoe hits—*Aida, Barber, Bohème, Boris, Butterfly, Carmen, Cav* and *Pag, Faust, Figaro, Gioconda, Giovanni, Lucia, Martha, Mignon, Otello, Rigoletto, Tosca, Traviata;* lesser for everything else. The selections are skewed somewhat by the Victor Company's desire to sell records (selections available are noted throughout the text) and by the author's tendency to take the Metropolitan Opera of New York as the international norm. But it's still, I think, a fair index of "the opera world" of just over half a century ago.

The 106 works described in the book include four American operas written between 1927 and 1937, all of which have effectively disappeared. Operetta is in general excluded, although the author, Charles O'Connell, describes eleven Victor-recorded Gilbert and Sullivan standards, perhaps at the request of his sponsor. The remaining ninety-one operas include nine once-popular French works by Meyerbeer, Massenet, and Halévy rarely revived even in France anymore (*L'Africaine, Dinorah, Hérodiade, Les Huguenots, Le Prophète, Robert le diable, Le Cid, Le Jongleur de Notre Dame, La Juive*); and operas such as Balfe's *The Bohemian Girl*, Rimsky-Korsakov's *Coq d'or* and *Sadko*, Weber's *Euryanthe*, Thomas's *Hamlet*, Wolf-Ferrari's *The Jewels of the Madonna*, Delibes's *Lakme*, Montemezzi's *The Love for Three Kings*, and Glinka's *Ruslan and Ludmila* that most of us cannot expect to see produced. (I've caught four of them so far.) None of these is among the Top 100 of 1988–1989.

4. An even more telling proof of the vitality and mutability of the standard opera repertory is the fact that in the 106 operas described in the *Victor Book*, one will *not* find thirty operas—all first produced before 1935—that *are* among the Top 100 today. Operas returned or risen to favor since the 1930s include five by Mozart (*Così* was first performed professionally in the United States in 1922, *Idomeneo* in 1951, *Tito* in

1952), four by Strauss, two by Janáček (see "The Janáček Boom," in the essays that follow), and long-ignored early Verdi operas like *Macbeth* and *Nabucco*.

A comparable measure of changing tastes is provided by a recently published list of the works most often broadcast or telecast by the Met in the years between 1940 (when its broadcasts began) and 1990. All but one of their Top 50 (the missing title is Gounod's *Romeo et Juliette*) are among my current Top 100; but the difference in rankings is marked. Works such as *Figaro*, *Così*, *The Magic Flute*, *Falstaff*, *Fidelio*, and *Turandot* rank much higher today than they did over the Metropolitan's half-century of broadcasts. A great many others show up in the 1988–1989 list at far lower places worldwide than on the Met's list, which may indicate changing tastes over fifty years, the basic conservatism of the Metropolitan Opera, and the entry or reentry of many works into the worldwide lists in recent years. As "standards" such as *Aida*, *Norma*, *Samson*, *Cav* and *Pag*, *Faust*, *Tristan*, *Manon Lescaut*, *La gioconda*, *Tannhäuser*, and *Lucia* have fallen in the ranks, new favorites such as *Ariadne*, *Cenerentola*, *Elektra*, *Der Freischütz*, *Manon*, *Nabucco*, *Eugene Onegin*, Gluck's *Orfeo*, and Mozart's *Seraglio* (none of which figured in the Met's half-century favorites) have risen to take their places.

Most noteworthy among these changes is the rise to clear current dominion by Mozart, a phenomenon that has taken place largely in our own lifetime. Between the bicentennial celebrations of his birth and death (1956–1991), Mozart has moved to the number one rank among opera composers in terms of productions and performances; his works now hold four of the top eight positions. The astonishing climb to favor of *Così* only began at Glyndebourne in the 1930s. But I would guess that the most fervent Mozartean at Glyndebourne fifty, even twenty years ago could never have predicted that *La Clemenza di Tito* would have ended up more internationally popular among producers and operagoers than *Die Meistersinger* or *Forza*, *Idomeneo* more popular than *Tristan;* or the eighteen-year-old Mozart's *La finta giardiniera*, of all things, ahead of *La Gioconda* and *Samson et Dalila*.

5.   Other messages of interest one might draw from the current standard repertory listings include the general acceptance of Handel, Monteverdi, Gluck, and, of course, Richard Strauss; and the entry of Britten, Berg, Janáček, and Bartók into so many regular seasons, year after year. And yet chroniclers of opera as an institution, like Herbert Lindenberger, continue to insist that "the commercially viable operatic repertory today [1984] has not grown within living memory."

6. In some ways, almost as interesting to me as the rise and fall of the leaders are the two hundred or more *other* operas that are now professionally performed every year. As Andrew Porter points out in the fortieth anniversary issue of *Opera* magazine (February 1990), the repertoire at almost all serious opera companies, large and small, has expanded astonishingly since World War II. Whether you live in or visit one of the great opera cities, have near to hand a company that offers no more than a handful of works, or vacation in any one of a dozen or more festival venues, you can be fairly certain of hearing works, new and old, that your parents and grandparents could never have heard—and this does not take into account the immensely extended repertory available now on record and tape.

In the article just mentioned, Porter laments the lack of public interest in new operas (actually this seems to vary considerably from place to place). But he is positively rapturous about the rise to visibility, even to fame, of so many forgotten operas of the past: operas by Monteverdi, Handel, Rameau ("I have seen six Rameau operas staged," Porter announces with obvious pleasure), Gluck, Mozart, Verdi, Janáček—all operas "that my grandfather had no chance of seeing." But Porter is also pleased to have been able to see and hear little-known Mascagnis and Donizettis, long-retired bel canto showcases of Rossini and Bellini, even an occasional glimpse of the long-maligned, all-but-forgotten grand operas of Massenet and Meyerbeer.

Peter Conrad wrote in 1987 that "the operatic canon is closed, our attitude to the art necessarily retrospective." But in the summer of 1990, I was able to see the American premières of both Nicolò Jommelli's *La schiava liberata* of 1768 and Aribert Reimann's *The Ghost Sonata* of 1984, virtually without leaving home. In the two years before that, traveling no farther than my home state and a nearby summer festival, I saw for the first time Prokofiev's *The Fiery Angel*, Vivaldi's *Orlando furioso*, Cavalli's *Ormindo*, Massenet's *Cherubin*, Philip Glass's *Satyagraha*, Handel's *Giustino*, and Penderecki's *The Black Mask*—along with my now standard fare of operas such as *Lulu*, *Idomeneo*, *L'Africaine*, *Tancredi*, *Mefistofele*, and *Lady Macbeth of Mtsensk*.

Summer opera festivals in cities like St. Louis, Santa Fe, and Wexford (Ireland) regularly offer new or little-known older works. In 1990–1991, the English National Opera offered, apart from three bicentennial Mozarts, *nothing* but twentieth-century works—a total of nineteen, including nine new productions, one a world première. (The list, admittedly, included three Puccinis.) For better and worse, the "standard repertoire" of opera has never been larger or more diverse.

V

For all its evident vitality, its widespread (and growing) popularity, this peculiarly hybrid form of drama is still often identified by its adversaries as a "cultural dinosaur"—a creature doomed to extinction because its body has grown too big for its brain. But if opera is doomed, it is not because it is intrinsically outdated as an art form, but because it has become so costly to produce. At the busiest and best-known houses and festivals, the production of opera has become so extraordinarily expensive, so archaically labor intensive that—unlike the most extravagant Broadway or West End musical—opera simply cannot pay its own way.

Even after setting top ticket prices at $100 to $250 (in 1990)—and tickets at or near these prices account for a large fraction of the seats in many houses—all of the world's major opera companies are obliged to search elsewhere for a substantial portion of their expenses. "Elsewhere" means either local, state, or national government grants, private philanthropy, commercial broadcasts and recreations, or a combination of all three.

There is no guarantee that audiences of the future will continue to pay the ever-rising prices of opera tickets, or that future governments and philanthropists will share the priorities of their counterparts today. Should such individuals and institutions begin to balk at the cost of contemporary-scale productions, the end of "opera as we know it," the twilight of the gods and goddesses, could well be in view.

In 1968, and on several occasions afterward, the opera houses in Milan, Rome, and Paris became symbolic targets of antiestablishment protest demonstrations. A series of violent demonstrations in four Swiss cities was set off in 1980 when thousands of students took to the street in protest against the government's 61-million-franc ($36 million) subsidy of the Zurich Opera. A Paris Opera première I attended in 1986 was delayed for an hour by a cordon of demonstrators blocking the front steps.

Personally, I expect that "grand" (i.e., Covent Garden– or Vienna Staatsoper–style) productions of opera will continue for at least one more generation, unless fundamental changes beyond my imagining occur in the Western world at large. The prestige value of opera, and more particularly the symbolic value of opera houses and companies, have become such established articles of political faith that local, state, and national governments (or groups of wealthy individuals) insist on maintaining them at almost any cost. Grand opera throve during the Great Depression. New opera houses were built or destroyed old ones rebuilt throughout Europe—throughout the former Axis countries in particular—after World War II. The reopening of the bombed-out Vienna State Opera (with Beethoven's *Fidelio*, Karl Böhm conducting) in 1955 was regarded as the single most important symbol of Austrian recovery.

On the other side of the now-melted Iron Curtain, every communist government in Europe has subsidized at least one opera company, often lavishly. (One of

FOYER OF THE PARIS OPERA (Palais Garnier), 1875. Drawing by
A. Deroy. Courtesy of the Bibliothèque Nationale, Paris.

the collateral losses of a reunified Germany and of a decommunized Eastern Europe is likely to be the loss or reduction of many of these subsidies.) The Sydney Opera House, the Opéra-Bastille, the recent visits of opera companies to Japan and Hong Kong (which are very costly to the host country), and the more than 200 new opera companies started in the United States in recent decades are all evidence of the symbolic importance, the political prestige, and the public relations value of opera, and hence of its probable survival. Apart from anything else, the investment in operatic real estate around the world, and the predictable resistance of existing groups with a stake in the survival of opera as an institution (companies, orchestras, conservatories, trade unions, suppliers) would make the dismantling of the existing order very difficult indeed—as Parisian authorities learned at the old Palais Garnier.

On the other hand, it seems certain that established gestures toward economy will continue and increase: the sharing or underwriting of new productions by several companies (of the new Los Angeles Music Center Opera's first thirty-three productions, a majority were either rented or shared, or made use of designs originated elsewhere); the sharing of a single company between two or more cities, which is the case in the two Rhine River companies in Germany and France; the recording of productions for sale to television or on videocassette; and an increased fostering of and dependence on less expensive local talent. A few impressive productions in the big houses have made skillful use of inexpensive staging.

But to be properly done, many operas from the standard repertory—Wagner's *Der Ring des Nibelungen*, for example, or Verdi's *Aida*—demand extensive theatrical resources. In the 1870s, when these works were first performed, the low wages of musicians and theatre staff (and generous subsidies from local kings and khedives) helped make their first performances possible. Today, lighting technicians, stagehands, and costume makers must be paid at the equivalent of union scale. Musicians skilled enough to play such works adequately must have had many years of special training, must devote hundreds of hours to rehearsal, and must possess one-in-a-thousand gifts. They, too, now demand adequate compensation. Singers, conductors, producers, and designers equal to the task of an adequate *Aida* or *Die Walküre* may be among a hundred or fewer people available in the world. (Some observers put the number of "great" sopranos or tenors performing at any time at no more than twenty, as if some sort of global gene pool limited the available talent.) In a market economy, such people, like star athletes and other popular entertainers, can ask for, and expect, very high wages indeed.

Opera can, of course, be done inexpensively. One can do a Rossini extravaganza without costumes or decors, a condensed-concert *Ring*, a little theatre *Don Giovanni* sung in English, with a single set and an amateur chamber orchestra. In several countries, touring versions of small-cast operas are sent by bus and truck into the hinterland, with advanced student performers and a single pianist. All of these I have seen and enjoyed. Without good, economical productions of this sort, in fact, which may cultivate new audiences for the art form more effectively than televised or recorded "star" performances, future audiences for opera in *any* form may begin to dry up. But if such performances were to become the norm, we would still be talking about the end of opera "as we know it."

I once thought it unlikely that any city would ever again spend the $130 million (which was ten times the first estimates) that Sydney, Australia, devoted to its opera house between 1957 and 1973—until the city of Paris found itself, between 1982 and 1989, spending $400 million on the politically embattled new Opéra-Bastille. In the last few years, Cairo, Essen, Hong Kong, Houston, and Ludwigsburg have all opened impressive new houses; those in Frankfurt (after a fire), Genoa, and Munich closed down for costly rebuilding. Sometime after 1995—the date keeps moving forward—Covent Garden is to be shut down for at least three years, at a cost of who knows how many hundreds of millions, so that it can be refit to the technical standards of these newer houses. The Metropolitan Opera (which moved into its lavish new quarters in 1966) now has expenses in excess of $100 million a year, less than 40 percent of which is recouped at the box office. Covent Garden operates in about the same range. At the main houses in (West) Berlin, Hamburg, Milan, Munich, Paris, Rome, and Vienna, ticket sales account for less than one fifth of the bill, even when every performance is sold out.

If opera producers and audiences in the leading opera cities continue to insist on elaborate new stagings of each work in the repertory at least every ten years, and if the famous singers these audiences and producers expect to hear continue to command million-dollar-a-year incomes, then "grand" opera, "international level" opera, "world class" opera—call it what you will—may well be spending itself into extinction, except by means of electronic transmission.

If someone were to pull out the feeding tube of public funding that has prolonged the life of opera in all of the countries where it has apparently prospered, it would in fact die a "natural" death. All that public subsidies are doing, argues the antiopera faction, is to subsidize the exorbitant fees of singers who jet from one country to another, along with the archaic and irrelevant tastes and status aspirations of upper- and middle-class patrons.

Whatever the cost of opera, many people opposed to it dislike the very idea, the fundamental concept of the thing. Almost from its inception, they argue, this "exotic and irrational entertainment" was sustained by a decadent love for spectacle and a sensationalist love for unnatural voices. Consider only the 200-year-long vogue of the castrato, the male singer who was kept a soprano for life by having his testicles deformed, even surgically removed, while he was still a young boy.

This odd form of musical drama, invented by Italians around 1600, was patronized early in its history by aristocrats and princes. For many of them, it served as an ostentatious, court-controlling demonstration of their wealth and good taste. As princes lost their thrones and aristocrats their power, the financial support of opera was maintained by upper-class burghers, first in Europe, then in its former colonies, as a ritual form of socializing, status assertion, and self-display. There were (and still are) large popular audiences for opera who occupied the less expensive upper balcony seats. But most theatres and companies were kept alive by box holders, subscribers, and other wealthy patrons. And in neither court theatres nor civic opera houses, it must be admitted, did many of these patrons know or care much about music.

Critical observers have been making fun of wealthy people who go to operas largely to socialize and be seen in elegant surroundings (and I concede there are such people) since the seventeenth century. But such sneering seems more impertinent today than it may have been 100 or 200 years ago. What matters to most of us is what happens on the stage and in the pit, not who sits in the boxes. Both the quality of the product, and the fact that many of us can be there at all, depend considerably on the largess of these fashionably dressed philistines in the more expensive seats.

What members of the radical opposition really dislike about opera, however, has less to do with politics, society, or economics than with opera itself: with what happens on the stage. (They tend to be more tolerant of what happens in the pit. In fact, they are often willing to hear excerpts from the orchestral scores of operas—Rossini's overtures, Wagner's preludes, Britten's interludes—inserted into symphony programs.)

The people I have encountered who are ill-disposed toward opera fall into several categories. First, there are a great many music lovers who find all of the stage business a distraction, and all but a very few operas second-rate or worse when analyzed on strictly *musical* terms. They wonder, frankly, how I can tolerate all of the melodramatic nonsense and turgid musical infill, when I could be listening to something so much more consummately wrought, so much less compromised and crude, at the symphony hall or on record. (Actually, I do both.)

Very few works in the standard operatic repertory are judged worthy of close attention by analysts, historians, or theorists of music in general.[7] It seems to be taken for granted that the extramusical compromises the composer of an opera has

---

7. According to Joseph Kerman, "The Verdi cult has never recruited heavily from among musicians who are devoted principally to analysis. . . . How could it? There is not much work for the analysts in 'Di quella pira.' . . . Even when they try to map out key schemes for the operas they run into inconsistencies and frustrations, as well as arguments. What analysts care about is the way a piece of music is put together, and the more dogmatically they care about this, the more antipathy they must feel for composers who subordinate purely structural concerns to, say, an overriding theatrical vision. . . . Music such as Verdi's . . . depends on relationships among words, stage movements, and human motivations as well as pitches and rhythms."

to make virtually guarantee that his score will be less "interesting," as music, than that of a good symphony, concerto, or sonata. Among composers who primarily wrote operas, Herbert Lindenberger points out, only Wagner—and more recently, and to a lesser degree, Verdi—is ever granted a place in the "canon" of great composers. "Anyone who included Bellini, Bizet, or Puccini would risk intellectual embarrassment." As Geoffrey Wheatcroft more provocatively, even pugnaciously, puts it, "Surely any *music*-lover would give all of Puccini for a single Haydn quartet, or even a single Schubert song." (Joseph Kerman typifies such absolute-music purists as people who believe that "*Otello* is somehow vulgar as compared to a good fugue by César Franck.")

There is no way or reason to answer such people. "It seems the world is divided into two classes of people," writes Gary Schmidgall in *Literature into Opera*, "those 'poor, passionless, bluntminded creatures' (Stendhal's words) who dislike opera, and those to whom it comes naturally and who subject themselves as willingly to its absurdities as to its compelling expressive powers."

Second, there are the drama lovers who find the singing and the orchestra a distraction—or, worse, a virtual guarantee that the intellectual and dramatic values *they* love in the theatre will be diluted or lost. To cite Gary Schmidgall again: "In the sheer triumph of vocal beauty, unfortunately, we are often willing silently to sacrifice other more subtle artistic values, among them dramatic momentum, integrity of plot, intelligibility, and balance. For many who like opera, beauty is sufficient. This is partly because, as Shaw pointed out, many people 'have little or no sense of drama, but a very keen sense of beauty of sound and prettiness of pattern in music.'"

Like operagoers in other categories who pick and choose their works, pure-drama lovers may find a place for *The Marriage of Figaro*, *Tristan und Isolde*, and *Otello* (although they will inevitably prefer Shakespeare's original), and perhaps a few other operas that "work," in their opinion, the same way good plays do. But they would still rather have, hear, and be able to think about all of the words.

Third, there are sensible people—or, if you like, "poor, passionless, bluntminded" people—who find the conventions of opera absurd, the acting unconvincing, the use of foreign languages alienating, the dramatized "history" perverse, the librettos inane. All theatre is built on performing conventions, some more distant than others from a direct simulacrum of life-as-we-live-it. People who are troubled by these distances, these conventions (soliloquies, verse drama, painted sets, the use of dancers or puppets, actors who burst into song), people who are affected, consciously or unconsciously, by what Jonas Barish calls "the antitheatrical prejudice" are likely to be especially annoyed by opera. Whatever ineffable truths about life an opera production may convey, in its onstage action it is considerably farther from life-as-we-live-it, considerably less "realistic" and more "theatrical" in its conventions than most other forms of drama.

Fourth, there are "up-to-date" people who cannot understand why anyone in 1990 (or 1950 or 1970) should still feel the need to see and support such out-of-date displays. To them, even the secondary trappings symbolize a dead and alien world: the swaggering solo bows, the bravos and thrown bouquets, the yards of velvet and satin, the private boxes and dress-up galas; bewigged pages, for heaven's sake, pulling back Great Golden Curtains! They complain, as did Tolstoy and Shaw, of the stand-and-deliver poses, of young and heroic roles performed by overaged and ungainly singers. They scorn the melodramatic contrivances, the "sexist" plots, the conventional formats (long-retired elsewhere) of kings and heroes pretending to be torn between love and duty.[8] They mock the inauthentic presentation of the past, the ancien régime parades of dutiful peasants, all of the dramatic conceits that other forms of theatre abandoned more than a century ago. These formulaic, old-fashioned dramas, which devotees sit through dutifully season after season, are to them of the most tiresome predictability. In no other form of theatre, they insist, musical or otherwise, could producers get by with such antiquated stunts.

Fifth, there are those who tolerate, even admit to liking, *some* operas, but agree in denouncing all of the others. The seasons of most major companies nowadays are made up of an eclectic and carefully distributed mix: one Monteverdi or Cavalli every few years, lots of Mozart-Verdi-Puccini-Wagner-Strauss, perhaps a few operettas and musicals, at most one work (already performed elsewhere) by a living—or, better, recently dead—composer. This means that such people—should they be subscribers or regular patrons—are bound to be discontented a good part of the time.

The "I like *some* opera" people can be divided into four separate camps:

1. The Italian-traditionalist crowd prefers, above all else, middle and late Verdi (except *Falstaff*) and Puccini—that is, opera as memorable tunes, as hummable pop music. A good deal of Donizetti will pass, as will Rossini's comic operas; Bellini's *Norma;* maybe *Faust, Carmen, Manon;* but nothing *too* French. Of the German repertoire, at most a jolly *Rosenkavalier* or *Meistersinger*, though even those are a bit tedious and, well, you know . . . German. My suspicion is that this group still includes the operagoing majority in North America, Britain, Australia, and Italy, most of whom would prefer a nice *Rigoletto* or *Butterfly* any day.

---

8. Sexist plots are the subject of two recent French feminist studies: Catherine Clément, *Opéra et la défaite des femmes* (translated as *Opera, or the Undoing of Women*); and Hélène Seydoux, *Laisse couler mes larmes: l'opéra, les compositeurs, et la féminité.* I have more to say about both of these studies in my chapter on Bellini's *Norma.*

2. There are still many doctrinaire Wagnerites; there were once a great many more. One meets them whenever a major *Ring* cycle is offered. They fly in from all over the country and all over the world, and compare notes in the foyer on all of the Brünnhildes they have stood for and cheered. To them, no other composer's operas can compare; few of them are even worth listening to. (To the first Wagnerite—Richard Wagner—this was virtually an article of faith.) They will tolerate Strauss, Mahler, or Bruckner. But your perfect Wagnerite believes, in good late-nineteenth-century fashion, that all earlier music was secretly aspiring to the condition of *Tristan* (or *Parsifal*) and will settle for nothing less than the antirational, hyper-romantic, quasi-religious experience that only the Master can provide.

    This faction was very big indeed between 1880 and 1920, as much in "advanced" social London and New York as in Germany. But two world wars and a more levelheaded approach to music history have helped to thin it out.

3. Then there are what the British call "canary fanciers" and Americans "voice freaks": people who go to opera only for the singing. Depending on what kind of singing they prefer, such people may seek out Verdi and Puccini, Wagner, bel canto works in general, or any opera that features their own favorite tenor or soprano—as many operagoers did in previous centuries. (Voice freaks rarely get hooked on the lower vocal ranges.) This group, like the larger group of opera lovers in general, appears to include an unrepresentatively large number of gay men, for reasons I don't understand.

    A subgroup of (3) is made up of the paid or unpaid claques, the devoted fans of individual singers—Zinka Milanov, Renata Tebaldi, Mario Del Monaco, Luciano Pavarotti—and, of course, Maria Callas. They have been with us for many years.

4. Another category of the more selective or specialized operagoers is made up of demanding and impatient intellectuals. A first group of these will ask, Is the *music* serious enough? This generally rules out Puccini, Bellini-Donizetti-Rossini, Gounod, and Meyerbeer (though scholarly revisionism is always at work); and favors composers like Mozart, Wagner, the harsher Strauss and the later Verdi, and twentieth-century opera except when it's too easy. In *Opera and Ideas*, Paul Robinson writes an eloquent appreciation and analysis of Berlioz's *Les Troyens*—a superchallenging grand opera he admits to be all but unperformable. But still he questions the values of a world that "has appar-

ently unlimited time and money for the workmanlike stuff of Berlioz's fellow-countryman Massenet" (one of the composers all serious critics love to hate), while denying us adequate versions of Berlioz's five-hour doubleheader.

A second group of intellectually critical operagoers will ask, Is the *drama* serious enough? Or will we be made to suffer through foolish Verdian melodrama, Puccinian sentimentality, Straussian "decadence," or (what is "serious" depends on one's own susceptibilities) the symbolic-idealistic nonsense of Wagner's *Ring* or *Parsifal?* Such judgments tend to be based at least as much on the libretto, the plot, and the stage action as on music, voices, or production—as if one were choosing whether to attend a straight play with a bit of musical accompaniment. The three Mozart–Da Ponte operas may survive this kind of screening, along with the two Verdi-Boitos, and modern works with respectable literary pedigrees, like *Wozzeck* or *Death in Venice.*

A third group will ask, Is the work sufficiently new and different (or old and forgotten)? This subgroup appears to be populated mainly by music critics and German impresarios (who have already seen the standard repertory operas more often than they wish) and by insistent novomaniacs. For such people, a tissue-thin new work by Philip Glass, a piece of Peter Sellars's cheeky revisionism, a *L'Olimpiade* or a *Dinorah* is preferable to anything they've seen more than twice before. The one thing opera must not be allowed to become, they insist, is a "museum," a haven for great works of the past—as if museums had suddenly become reprehensible institutions.

Then there are people like me. We (and I like to think we still represent a sizable fraction of opera audiences) remain willing to take a gamble on almost any halfway-promising opera production because we prefer good opera (when it works) to any other form of music *or* theatre; and because we've been happily surprised in the past by impressive productions of works we had dismissed, or had been advised to dismiss, as second rate. I am almost ready to concede that a good production team—which includes conductor, orchestra, and singers, as well as director and designer—can work magic on *any* text and score.

Most extended, nonjournalistic critical writing about opera has dealt entirely with texts and scores, just as most serious critical writing about Shakespeare has dealt with the words we read from the printed page. One can go a long way toward the evaluation of a work destined for the theatre by a careful, critical

GERD ALBRECHT (producer, left) and THOMAS STEWART (who played
the title role) discussing Aribert Reimann's opera *Lear* backstage
during rehearsals at the San Francisco Opera, 1985. Photograph
by Ira Nowinski. Courtesy of the San Francisco Opera.

reading of its text. Producers, performers, impresarios, and dramaturgs must do
this all the time to decide which works they want to produce or perform.

But coming to opera from the perspective of the theatre (rather than that of the
study or the music room), I still regard such texts as nothing *more* than scripts, to a
degree revealing, perhaps delectable when examined in one's armchair (or at the
piano): but incomplete until produced and performed, until realized on stage.
Read privately, by oneself, they are not yet in my judgment operas.[9]

Three things, I believe, must come together for a satisfactory operatic experience
to take place: the right opera, the right production, and the right spectator. And
each of the three must be "right" in terms of the other two. I would like, as my
contribution toward an "aesthetics of opera," to consider each of these three for the
space of a few pages.

9. Peter Kivy, who works both as a philosopher and as a theorist of music, has come close to admitting
as much in *Osmin's Rage*. After referring to "the text" of an Mozart opera, he backtracks to add, "to the
extent that we can speak of 'the text' as something apart from its interpretation."

VI

Independent of productions and spectators, is it possible to classify works of the lyric stage absolutely on a scale from best to worst?

In 1956, the London-born, Princeton-trained, Berkeley-based critic and musicologist Joseph Kerman (then thirty-two) published a short, original, extremely readable, and notoriously provocative book entitled *Opera as Drama*, in which he proposed to establish standards for distinguishing good operas from bad.

He began (as I have begun) by referring to the antiopera critics. As far as he was concerned, the only respectable way for serious defenders of opera to counter their attacks was to become more selective, to separate the few grains of wheat in the repertory from the mountains of chaff. Writing in 1956—but retreating very little in a second edition prepared thirty years later[10]—Kerman has nothing good to say for the "hardening repertory," "the slag-heaps that have kept opera thriving."

> Flabby relativism is certainly the danger, as anyone knows who buys an opera season ticket. Under the tacit assumption that everything is all right in its own terms, extremes of beauty and triviality are regularly placed together. In our opera houses, art and *Kitsch* alternate night after night, with the same performers and the same audience, to the same applause, and with the same critical sanction. Confusion about the worth of opera is bound to exist when no distinction is drawn publicly between works like *Orfeo* and *The Magic Flute* on the one hand, and like *Salome* and *Turandot* on the other.

If a case is to be made for opera as a viable form, he insists, it can be only in terms of the *best* operas, operas that work "dramatically," in the same way that good plays do. The radical difference is that in good operas (on the evidence of this book, Kerman appears to think there are about twenty; Hans Keller, writing in a wholly different context, puts the number at "about 25"), the basic elements of drama—characterization, action, psychology, and so on—are defined and conveyed *by the music*, not by the words. These few operas, he sometimes appears to be saying, are the only ones that really ought to be produced. He takes music critics to task for wasting their time judging new productions of standard repertory works, when they should be trying to *reduce* that repertory by judging operas—old operas as well as new ones—according to more rigorous standards.

---

10. The main distinction between the two editions—beyond a new "contextual" prologue and an epilogue on critical theory—is Kerman's lopping off of a dated conclusion, which rather mercilessly attacks the 1950s American vogue for Menotti and predicts "that works like *Turandot* and *Salome* will fade from the operatic scene." A few pages of the attacks on Puccini and Strauss have quietly disappeared, and Mozart's *Idomeneo* is treated with new respect. Some judgments of other critics have been modified, a few no longer timely remarks have been excised, and a couple of absolutes are now qualified. But the thrust, the tone, and the substance of the book remain the same.

Kerman begins his own sifting of the repertory with a quotation from the musicologist Edward Cone: "In any opera, we may find that the musical and the verbal messages seem to reinforce or to contradict each other; but whether the one or the other, we must always rely on the music as our guide toward an understanding of the composer's conception of the text. It is this conception, not the bare text itself, that is authoritative in defining the ultimate meaning of the work."

Whenever there is an apparent conflict between the drama implicit in the libretto and the drama implicit in the score, Kerman insists, it is the composer who wins.

We trust first what is most emphatic in the music. (*Orfeo*)

In opera we trust whatever is musically forceful. (*The Marriage of Figaro*)

In opera, we trust what is most convincing in the music. (*Così fan tutte*)

In opera we trust what is done most firmly by the music. (*Don Giovanni*)

As always, the dramatist is the composer, and the Rake's progress is articulated by a progress in the music.

Most of *Opera as Drama* is devoted to close, selective investigations of about a dozen operas Kerman frankly admires. ("The significant operatic canon is not large. Monteverdi, Purcell, Gluck, Mozart, Verdi, Wagner, Debussy, Berg, Stravinsky, and a few others have left a body of musical drama which is rich and various, but not large.") In these chapters, he describes and analyzes differing ways in which drama can be created and conveyed by the score. His explications of the "musical dramaturgy" of certain individual scenes—the Act II trio of *Don Giovanni*, the Act II finale of *The Marriage of Figaro*, Otello's murder of Desdemona, Tristan's long Act III "Delirium"—are about as good as purely verbal musical-dramatic analysis can get. In them, he demonstrates how music works simultaneously to create, compel, and contain action, to define and express subtle and evolving changes in and among characters. Especially impressive is his relation of the simple "progress forward" of music—the alterations of structure, rhythm, and tonality in time—to the parallel forward progress of the drama, the evolution of feeling in the characters.

The standard Kerman applies to opera, in his attempt to distinguish better from worse, is closely related to literary criticism of the post–World War II years (his early essays on music, which evolved into this book, were published alongside the work of leading literary New Critics in *The Hudson Review*), and more specifically to theoretical works on drama by critics like Francis Fergusson, Eric Bentley, T. S. Eliot, and Una Ellis-Fermor, all of whom he cites. If he is to demonstrate the viability or ultimate worth of an opera, he must prove that it contains rich characterizations, a coherent progress or plot, and a unified world, like those of the best spoken drama. "The spoken theatre serves as a court of appeal," he writes, "or at least of analogy, when the dramatic efficacy of opera or any other non-verbal medium is likely to be tested." Unfortunately, as Herbert Lindenberger once pointed out, "as long as opera is seen from the point of view of spoken drama, it is always likely to seem wanting. . . . As soon as opera is compared to drama, the former comes to look deficient in 'intellectual' content."

Beyond that, Kerman depends considerably on the ideals of formal coherence, integration, and unity, the kind of "organic economy" proposed and promoted by leading British and American literary critics of the 1940s and 1950s (whom today he labels "classics"). By the standards of many literary critics of the time, one could ask for nothing more than maximum complexity under maximum control; and it was presumed that one could demonstrate this kind of perfection by the close analysis of a text.

But when Kerman applies similar standards to opera, the works of Baroque and bel canto composers are inevitably seen as wanting. "The fault, almost always," he writes, "was in the abysmal lack of integration of lyricism into a sensible dramatic plan." Purcell, by contrast—one of Kerman's two seventeenth-century exceptions—understood "how to organize arias into a total, coherent dramatic form." The action in the operas of Mozart—Kerman's model of ultimate success—is "infinitely more complex . . . included within a single musical continuity, and unified by it."[11]

This particular set of ideals leads to what appears to be an aesthetic of historical progress—at least up to Wagner and Debussy—whereby operas became better as they moved away from separable "numbers," away from the expressively limited alternation of arias and recitatives; and *toward* greater musical/dramatic continuity: which, of course, is what the Wagnerians have been telling us all along. "Conflict, passage, excitement, and flux could [with the development of the Classical sonata form] be handled within a single musical continuity," Kerman writes; and at the same time be "made to cohere, to present unified impressions," permitting a much richer presentation of the human psyche. While acknowledging that in certain circumstances traditional arias may still "work" dramatically, he appears to give his most wholehearted approval to operas that manage to do without arias, or to depend more on ensembles.

But it is neither his theory of what makes for good opera nor his short list of works that succeed that has made *Opera as Drama* the most often-quoted book on

---

11. In an early (1949) review-essay on *Peter Grimes*, however, Kerman concedes that "in opera the overall coherence, subtlety, and even credibility of the dramatic conception are less urgent than a practical series of individual scenes with which the composer may establish his own dramatic point, his own subtlety and credibility, if only for the moment."

the subject of the last forty years. It is his near-absolute dismissal of the works of Giacomo Puccini and Richard Strauss, which still account (as we have seen) for a huge part of the standard repertory—eleven of the 100 leading works, including three of the Top 10. He is arguing, in effect, that critics and impresarios should stop granting these two composers serious attention.

> I do not propose to analyze the musical texture of *Tosca* [he writes, after savagely disposing of its ultimate scene]; it is consistently, throughout, of café-music banality. If Joyce Kilmer or Alfred Noyes had taken it into his head to do a grand poetic drama on Tosca, that would have been something analogous in the medium of language. . . .
>
> But if *Turandot* is more suave than *Tosca* musically, dramatically it is a good deal more depraved. . . . [The score] is consistently, throughout, of café-music banality. . . . Rarely has myth been so emptily employed as in this absurd extravaganza. Drama is entirely out of the question. . . . Puccini clings to his limited ideas and repeats them protectively. . . . There is almost a sense of despair in the meaninglessness of *Turandot*.

Strauss, Kerman concedes, was a more advanced and innovative composer than Puccini, masterly in power and technique. But as a musical dramatist of human situations, Kerman finds Strauss cynical, shallow, false, and sentimental. The conclusion of *Salome* he regards as "the most banal sound in the whole opera," the final coming together of the young lovers in *Der Rosenkavalier* "the poorest thing in the opera."

> Was it for this minimal level of consciousness that we have had to suffer the Marschallin's self-pity and to sacrifice Ochs? for this, the silver rose and the white suit, the Three Noble Orphans and four finicky hours of leitmotivs, modulations, and program-musical wit? . . .
>
> No one who understood *The Marriage of Figaro* could ever have taken *Der Rosenkavalier* seriously. . . . *Salome* and *Der Rosenkavalier* . . . are insincere in every gesture, meretricious and doubly meretricious on account of their show of outer formal integrity.

"From the start," he concludes, "Puccini and Strauss revealed a coarseness of sensitivity and a deep cynicism towards true dramatic values. . . . The operas of Strauss and Puccini are false through and through; the trouble runs much deeper than mere faults in conception or technique. . . . The response, the quality of the action, is insensitive or simply sham all the way. . . . In the deepest sense the operas of Strauss and Puccini are undramatic, for their imaginative realm is a realm of emotional cant. They are unable to match any action, however promising, with anything but the empty form of drama."

Kerman also dismisses all opera between Monteverdi and Gluck (except Purcell's short *Dido and Aeneas*) as of "unparalleled dramatic fatuity." He makes no mention of Handel beyond a line of very faint praise in the epilogue of the second edition. He is generous to *La traviata* and *Rigoletto;* rejects Bellini (but for the end of *Norma*), Rossini, and Donizetti; tosses out *Aida;* and appears (in *Opera as Drama*, although not in a later essay in *The Hudson Review*) unfavorably disposed to Wagner's *Ring*.[12]

If I am to begin working toward a definition of "the right opera," Kerman's standards and strictures are as good a place as any to begin. I am obliged, in any case, to live with the existing repertory. Like other critics and opera lovers, I must therefore come to some sort of terms with his responses to Puccini and Strauss.

Although creditable and well argued, Kerman's aesthetic of opera seems too restrictive for me, too limited, too purist. It is only partially able to account for my (and I presume other people's) actual experience in the opera house. He has (in *Opera as Drama*) almost nothing to say of the specific power of the singing voice alone, in ensemble or chorus, or with an orchestra—which I would have thought was the fundamental distinction of an operatic experience. Outside of his reviews, he makes no reference to production or performance, to the impact of live actors on stage, to the legitimate power of melodrama in opera, to the legitimate place of

---

12. Kerman has reviewed opera performances himself, notably for *Opera News* (from San Francisco) and for the *San Francisco Chronicle* (from New York) between 1954 and 1960, and occasionally elsewhere and since. As a periodical critic, he has been more tolerant of the "slag heaps" of the repertory than he is as a theorist of opera in general. But his high standards remain generally intact.

Enraptured by the expressivity, dramatic commitment, and sheer musicianship of Maria Callas in the title role (at the Met in 1958), he still pauses to remind us that "*Lucia* is a vile piece." Reviewing a concert version of another Donizetti tragedy (which he went to expecting "violent low entertainment") he admits, "Of course, *Anna Bolena* is a pretty dreadful work," despite "a sort of subartistic spontaneous vigor." Bellini's *La sonnambula* he calls "amiable fluff." Even so, in a thoughtful 1981 review-essay on Callas's career, he praises her for single-handedly reviving the whole bel canto repertory.

In general, as a journalist-critic, Kerman avoids any mention of Puccini, except to refer to the adoration that certain singers receive when performing his works. ("*Tosca* proved once again a wild success for Renata Tebaldi.") He praises the San Francisco Opera, in 1954, for its daring in offering only a single *Bohème*, only a single *Butterfly*. In New York, he pointedly refuses to go hear Inge Borgkh in *Salome*, Patrice Munsel in *La Bohème*, any "grimly reviewed" Wagner, or "*Andrea Chenier* in any shape, size, or condition." *Louise*, he declares in a passing mention, "must be the most inept piece in the repertory."

After praising everyone concerned for the American première of *Die Frau ohne Schatten* at San Francisco in 1959 (because "anything by an important composer is of interest"), he concludes, "As for the opera itself, I regard it, as I regard everything else by Strauss, as second rate, especially so in this instance because of the libretto, which is pretentious and obscure to the point of distraction, and because of the music, which is overblown and impoverished."

And yet just a year before, he was so bowled over by Elizabeth Schwarzkopf's American debut in *Der Rosenkavalier* in San Francisco—in fact, by everything concerned with that production ("the best production of any opera that it has been my pleasure to witness in this country, on either coast")—that his review left one with the impression that it is now okay to like Strauss; that, in fact, a great production of an opera may have forced him to change his mind about its value.

spectacle. In fact, he often simply labels such concerns as "vulgar" and "coarse," compared to musical-dramatic integrity.

Musical effects in opera intended primarily to be exhibitionistic, shocking, or bathetic, to move an audience to tears or gasps or bravos, are no more (and no less) admirable than the high-wire turns of a circus acrobat, the scream scenes in a movie thriller, a tear-jerking soap. But I tend to think that certain extradramatic, even vulgar, aspects of opera production—melodrama, vocalise, the stage presence of real actors, spectacle and setting, a conductor's or a director's particular reading or concept—are at least as essential to potential success as whatever drama may be crafted into the score.

Kerman's focus on overall coherence and dramatic integrity leads him to ignore or belittle our ability, perhaps even our innate tendency, to separate out and enjoy individual scenes, voices, and moments in opera. The sum of such pleasures may or may not be less intellectually worthy than the pleasure we take in an overarching musical-dramatic unity. But by the very creative conditions of opera, such unity is likely to be rare. "Opera by its very nature is a gigantic series of compromises," writes Winton Dean in *Handel and the Opera Seria*. To this, Herbert Lindenberger adds, "The whole institutional setting within which opera has traditionally flourished requires so many compromises that only a few operas demonstrate the intensity and evenness of craftsmanship that nontheatrical music can more easily attain."

For some critics, historians, and theorists of opera, the list of fully realized musical-dramatic unities appears to come down to one: *The Marriage of Figaro*. Rather than apply such reductive standards, I prefer to make a case for a broader base of appreciation: for trying to enjoy opera other than generically—in bits and pieces, if necessary, rather than as a coherent musical-dramatic whole. This is what Kerman might call "hedonistic," rather than "aesthetic," appreciation—a distinction he made in an early analysis of Virgil Thomson's critical standards.

In drawing his ideals of music drama largely from mid-twentieth-century theorists of spoken drama canonically certified as "literature," Kerman slights the fundamental importance of *melodrama* to opera. He does have favorable things to say about scenes in *Rigoletto*, *La traviata*, and *Norma* that might strike one at first glance as melodramatic. But a commitment to high-dramatic standards may lead a critic to prefer works drawn from more "respectable" sources, or works that make use of more subtle and less hysterical plots. Despite its contemporary position of disfavor as a "low" and pop-obvious genre, melodrama—as I argue in chapter 8, on Victor Hugo's opera plots (borrowing my case in part from Eric Bentley)—is closely related to human needs, is sometimes ideally adapted to operatic rendering, and, as the word *melodramme* originally implied, can be unusually viable when sung.

There is also a place for, and considerable pleasure to be taken in, the cultivation of a historical or cross-cultural imagination at the opera house, by which we make an effort to place ourselves into the situation of audiences not our contemporaries, and try to enjoy the conventions of other times and places. ("With a strong exercise of historical imagination," Kerman writes of Donizetti's *Anna Bolena*, "one can perhaps see why the piece made its mark in 1830." I recommend such exercise.) In the attempt to apply mid-twentieth-century standards of unity, continuity, controlled richness, and overall coherence to pre-twentieth-century works—admirable as such standards may appear to us today—we run the risk of condemning unheard, or hearing unsympathetically, a great deal of opera created at a time when such standards counted for less.

Beyond a single reference to "the emotional power of the human voice" (and a passing jibe at "the vulgar taste for vocal virtuosity"), there is virtually no mention in *Opera as Drama* of the affective force of singing, which is surely—even more than the orchestral score—what most clearly distinguishes opera from any other form of drama, both as an art form and as an experience. At times, in fact—sounding rather like Verdi or Wagner on a bad day—Kerman makes it seem as if live singers and physical productions are a hindrance, an obstacle to the composer of operas, when in fact they are the means by which his works are brought to life.[13]

Kerman admits, in the preface to the second edition, that there is a "total absence of any discussion of performance values in *Opera as Drama*." In this, he is simply behaving like most musicologists, who tend to see printed notes on a page (and, in the case of opera, the accompanying printed words) as composing something finished and complete, ready to be analyzed and judged and, perhaps, somewhere along the way, enjoyed. In trying to snatch Alban Berg's *Wozzeck* back from more microscopically analytic musicologists, Kerman reminds them that "the ultimate judge is the ear, not the eye, and that the work is destined for the opera house, not the analyst's study." But there is little reference to that destination elsewhere in the book.

It is here that Kerman's search for a code of values, an aesthetic for opera, most widely diverges from mine. By nature or training I am disposed to regard operatic scores, as I regard the texts of plays, primarily as scripts for production, incomplete until performed. Kerman (quite justifiably) regards both *Così fan tutte* and *Don Giovanni* as imperfect works, because the librettist provided texts that were either cynical and empty-hearted (*Così*) or clumsy and improbable (*Giovanni*), to a composer who was unable to take emotions other than seriously.

But what Kerman sees as flaws I see as opportunities; as, in fact, two of the greatest challenges the producer of an opera can face. (I use the term "producer" as

---

13. This is counterbalanced, of course, by the comments on individual singers in Kerman's journalistic reviews, and by essays such as his fine appreciation of Callas's theatrical skills. But it is *Opera as Drama* that goes on being read and quoted.

a kind of shorthand, rather as one speaks of a film's "director." I am fully aware that a whole team of creative individuals may be responsible for an opera production—often beginning with a conductor, rather than with what the French call a *metteur en scène*.)

Can Mozart's and Da Ponte's two magnificent, problematic works be produced in such a way as to realize simultaneously, even to reconcile, their warring worlds of discourse; in such a way as to make these operas "work," somehow, despite their troublesome *décalage?* Kerman complains that he has yet to see an explanation (or, I presume, a production) of *Così* that makes sense of both the action and the music—as George Bernard Shaw lamented that he would probably never in his lifetime see an adequate production of *Don Giovanni*. I put my faith in the ingenuity of producers, and wait in hope.

I regard works such as *Carmen, Boris Godunov,* and any so-called opera by Handel in a similar, tentative way: can they be made to work, made to matter, made to hurt? Can a producer fight the sentimental, lockstep stage directions Strauss and Hofmannsthal inscribed into *Der Rosenkavalier?* Can he or she make Puccini's Butterfly *really* suffer? Jean-Pierre Ponnelle's jaunty, knife-edged, totally rethought production of *I pagliacci* (1976) resurrected for me an old war-horse I had given up for dead. Other producers, conductors, and singers have performed similar miracle cures on similar works.

Even so, I do have standards of my own by which I distinguish better operas from worse, apart from their productions. Other things in the theatre being equal (which they never are), I too prefer coherence, a felt sense of continuity and unity, the overall arch of a single musical-dramatic conception, to a sequence of ill-matched musical scenes (like that of Boito's *Mefistofele*) that seems to defy one's dramatic expectations. (There are, of course, disunified works, like those of Alban Berg, that make good emotional sense.) I also agree that this drama should be achieved through an artful fusion of sung music, orchestral commentary, and onstage action, rather than simply through the libretto itself.

A good opera, I believe, is one written by a composer who is fresh, ingenious, and inventive; who can come up with interesting musical ideas that illuminate, illustrate, and help to tell his story.

Ergo, there should be a story. I find I am emotionally and intellectually compelled by stories that deal with characters whose situations represent or reflect those of human beings, rather than ideas or abstractions. I respond with greatest fervor and commitment to a dramatic action I can be made to care about (in the way one "cares about" actions in a theatre), to works with a high potential for characterization (which need not mean "realism" or "naturalism"); to works in which I feel myself potentially implicated in the persons and plights of the characters on stage. They can be animals—as in Janáček's *The Cunning Little Vixen*—or the nonhuman creatures of Wagner's *Ring*, as long as they allow me some means of emotional entry into the characters they represent. In any good production of the *Ring*, I find myself caring quite a lot about Alberich and Fasolt. There is also something quite wonderful about music dramas that offer a rich and still unified combination of tragedy and comedy—if only because "life is like that," as we say, and the challenge to the composer is greater. This may partly explain the enduring appeal of the Mozart–Da Ponte operas.

I realize that singing one's feelings aloud, along with or over an orchestra, to a theatre full of one or two or three thousand people invites a degree of exaggeration in both characterization and plot. That's all right with me. This in part explains why "melodrama" often seems more appropriate than realism, than so-called verismo. The onstage worlds of Operaland virtually demand people considerably larger and certainly more passionate than are we, their poor wizened counterparts in real life, who don't have to sing our emotions or pretend to sustain them for hours on end.

Dedicated producers, musicians, and singers, I have discovered, all of them working very hard, can maximize the faint, relatively uncomplicated human potential of opera seria. But most of the pleasure I take in it is musical, rather than dramatic, so I tend to regard it as a lesser form of opera.

I seem unable to respond with the same kind of fictive "belief" or intellectual approval that others can muster to operas like *Pélleas et Mélisande*, *Parsifal*, *Die Frau ohne Schatten*, or Michael Tippett's symbolist works (the best I can do, dramatically, is to regard them as some kind of dream); to the ideological elements of *The Magic Flute* or Wagner's *Ring*, or even to the "inspiring message" of *Fidelio*. However much I may enjoy their music (or the more "human" parts of their progress), I have a hard time warming to onstage abstractions, or crediting musical works for the supposed depth or righteousness of the ideas they express.

I prize operas that provide good occasions for singing (solo, ensemble, and choral), but preferably singing that makes dramatic sense. I grow impatient at mere circus-turn inserts, even when sung by large and famous canaries with priceless golden throats. I dislike irrelevant choruses and interpolated dance numbers, unless the producer has found a way to fit them into the plot. I have learned to live with, even enjoy, all manner of operatic conventions. But I most admire composers, like Mozart and Verdi, who can turn the conventions they are saddled with to genuine dramatic point.

The best opera composers are those who love, as I do, the human voice singing. They learn how to write for it, how to take advantage of it, and how to use it to captivate and compel, to win our attention and assent by exploiting either its sheer beauty or its potential for resonant dramatic expression.

The best operas are those in which the music—vocal and orchestral—is remarkable and captivating all by itself, but is also heart seizing and transcendentally

CLARAMAE TURNER (center) AND CHORUS MEMBERS backstage
during a rehearsal of Wagner's *Die Meistersinger*, San Francisco
Opera, 1959. Courtesy of the San Francisco Opera

affecting when experienced as the vehicle for a human drama about which one can
care. The orchestra should be intelligently and dramatically used; it should contribute to, and sometimes create, the action. It can (as many writers before me
have pointed out) describe inner thoughts, comment on events, foreshadow and
recall, and create fear or suspense far more potently than words alone can do. It can
motivate characters, define precise social relationships, bring new worlds into
being, and (as in Mozart) even undercut the apparent meaning of the text. I am
happiest when an opera orchestra does these things in interesting and original
ways, with something less than movie-music obviousness.

Potential for good theatre is nice to have as well. It is no accident that the three
greatest opera composers—Mozart, Verdi, and Wagner—were all theatrical geniuses, regardless of whether (as Shaw pointed out) the people who undertake to

stage their works always realize that. I find many operas, in and out of the standard repertory, to be fundamentally uninteresting both dramatically and musically, to the point where I doubt that *any* new production, however ingenious, could shake me out of my lethargic inability to respond. I once attended such works, when reviewing a whole season of which they were a part, as a professional critical chore. I no longer do. "I have difficulty with stupid works where bombastic music exceeds dramatic necessity," producer/impresario Michael Hampe has said. (The example he cited was *Andrea Chenier*.) I couldn't agree more.

There are other popular, and in few cases critically acclaimed, works that I actively dislike, usually because of a combination of what strikes me as either insipid (*Louise*) or aggressively "ugly" (*Elektra*) music, together with an over-wrought, artificial human story that simply cannot compel my attention, however pertinent or meaning-laden it once might have seemed; or because they embody (inescapably, in the music) attitudes and values that repel me. (See chapter 9, "Sex and Religion in French Opera.") But most of my nays are still tempered and tentative, decisions not altogether closed. I try to leave room in almost every case for the possibility that a great conductor working with good singing actors and an insightful director may yet open my ears and my mind.

A few operas—my list is probably no longer than Kerman's or Keller's—do seem to me beyond critical question. That is to say, I *know* they are great, and need no production to prove it. They may, of course (and often will), be abysmally produced and performed. But I can always try to imagine the angels singing them, the composer directing them, through all of the squawking, scraping, and stumbling on stage; then go home and read the score, or listen to a good recording, and imagine the perfect production staged in the Opera House Under My Hat.

The greater part of the standard repertory—and a good many operas not in it—I like *potentially*. I tend, far more than harsher critics, to accept the repertory as it has evolved, and to worry less about the perfect opera, or the twenty tolerable operas, or some Olympian standard of acceptability. The bent of mind that seeks to form "canons" seems to me, in the 1990s, archaic and uncomfortably authoritarian.[14] My job, both as critic and as simple hedonist, is not to narrow the possible inlets of

14. Joseph Kerman himself, despite his remark on the "significant operatic canon" in *Opera as Drama*, appears to acknowledge this point in a later essay. "Repertories," he wrote in 1983, "are determined by performers, canons by critics—who are by preference musicians, but by definition literary men or at least effective writers about music." He cites the authoritarian tendencies of would-be canon-formers of the early twentieth century such as Heinrich Schenker and Donald F. Tovey (and their successors), and the hostility of later music lovers to many of their judgments—even though most contemporary critics tend to think in terms of "canons" of their own. "Scholars who see the reality of a musical tradition in its social function within a supporting culture can only regard the activity of poring over revered scores 'in a kind of Meistersinger environment' as not only elitist and compulsive but myopic (and possibly chauvinistic), a deflection of scrutiny from where it belongs."

joy, but to remain as open as possible to what a good production team can make of a tolerable text and score. I am at least as fascinated by the challenge of making a problematic opera "work" as I am by the imputed dramatic perfection or imperfection of its score.

George Bernard Shaw once wrote, "Nobody has ever greeted a performance of *Tristan und Isolde* by such a remark as, 'We shall never be able to go back to *L'elisir d'amore* after this'; or declared that [Donizetti's] Lucrezia was impossible after Brünnhilde." Actually, I think people may very well have said something like that; I know I have *thought* things like that, after an especially moving evening of Wagner. But Shaw's intelligent point is that work of the first class does not displace work of the second class, any more (the analogies are his) than Ibsen displaces melodrama or Shakespeare displaces the circus. We need and enjoy good Shakespeare; we need and enjoy a good circus. We cannot breathe permanently the air of Olympus. After one good seventeen-hour *Ring* cycle, I find I don't require another for quite a while. After the Rhine has finally overflowed and Valhalla has gone up in flames, I find myself turning to diversions of a considerably lighter sort (which, of course, is simply a form of self-definition. There are good people who can happily sit—or even stand—through three *Ring* cycles in a row).

There is nothing arbitrary about the size of the standard operatic repertory. It takes about 150 operas, plus new additions and discoveries, to keep the existing houses and companies running, the audiences contented, the singers and orchestras paid. Although I have about had my fill of *Toscas* and *Bohèmes* (but only after a great many enjoyable evenings), there are new opera lovers starting out every season who should have their chance to see, and perhaps one day reject, these works. Revisionist productions in recent years of *Butterfly* and *Turandot*, cross-grained productions that stressed the cruelty against the lyricism, have affected me strongly. I never want to experience another *Faust*, which is one of the few top repertory standards I really would like to see dumped. But I will keep on going to *Rigoletto* and *Carmen* until I see and hear a production as powerful as the version in my head. Well-performed Offenbach (which is hard to find) I love, the five satiric operettas more than *Hoffmann*. Experience in the theatre has taught me that any of a dozen Verdi operas, the more durable bel canto tragedies, Monteverdi and Gluck, much of Janáček and Britten, *Der Rosenkavalier*, *Ariadne*, and *Arabella*, and almost any well-wrought opera buffa can be turned into silver (if not gold) by the right team of singers, musicians, and producers.

But that is my point: almost *any* tolerable script and score, I believe, can be made to work, can be rendered into a memorable theatrical experience, given the right production. And within "tolerable" I include Rossini and Vivaldi serias, Massenet and Meyerbeer, Henze and Shostakovitch, Penderecki and Poulenc: a list, in the end, so long that to speak of canons is to make no sense at all.

THE WAGNERITES. Drawing by Aubrey Beardsley from *The Yellow Book* (1894). Courtesy of the Bancroft Library, University of California, Berkeley.

VII

The early years of opera, from Rinuccini through Metastasio, could reasonably be considered the Age of the Poet. For many years the written words were regarded as more permanent, and were treated more like art, than the scores. Next came the Age of the Singer (these "ages," of course, overlap), described and satirized in Benedetto Marcello's "Il teatro alla moda" and chronicled by many other observers. Lasting through much of the eighteenth and early nineteenth centuries, this was the age of Baroque and bel canto opera, when the services of uniquely gifted singers (including castrati) were regarded as indispensable.

Around 1860, by sheer force of will and popularity, Verdi and Wagner were able to impose, or superimpose, what one might call the Age of the Composer. At long last, the person most responsible for what mattered in an opera was able to give orders regarding the libretto, the singers, the staging, and the conductors he wanted. Composers regularly conducted their own works as well, at least for important premières and gala events, which extended that authority even further.

As opera composers with this kind of power and popularity began to die out (the last two were Puccini and Strauss), dominion shifted again, and the Age of the Conductor was born. For a few decades in the first half of this century, important productions of opera—almost all of old operas now, because the repertory had begun to cease growing—were identified with, and in a major way created by, their conductors: Krauss's *Salome*, Furtwängler's *Tristan*, Toscanini's *Traviata*, Busch's *Così*.

Now a fifth age in the history of opera appears to be upon us: the Age of the Producer. During the past forty years, the nature and variety of opera productions around the world have altered to an astonishing degree. Traditional productions more or less like those our parents and grandparents saw still account for most of the thousands of performances given each year. But audiences in several major centers, some festivals, and a few smaller cities are now regularly confronted with assertively, even defiantly novel reinterpretations and reconceptions of standard repertory works. All of these are the creations of a type of opera/theatre professional virtually unknown less than a century ago.

Most older operagoers grew up on visual and musical incarnations of popular operas little changed since the days of the later Wagner and Verdi, the days of Shaw and Ernest Newman—little changed, that is, since the days when electric lighting and three-dimensional sets first seriously altered staging techniques. If the libretto declared that an opera was set in seventeenth-century Spain, efforts were made to dress the performers and design the sets according to someone's idea, at least, of the costumes and buildings of seventeenth-century Spain. Depending on the resources available, village plazas, mountain crags, Egyptian temples, or Paris cafés identified in the text would be recreated either sketchily, with painted back-

OPERA LOVERS. Anonymous illustration from Scrici (John H.
Swaby), *Physiology of the Opera* (1852). Courtesy of the Institute
for Studies in American Music, Brooklyn College.

drops and a few movable thrones, tables, altars, or rocks, or in painstakingly
naturalistic detail. In the larger houses, where extravagance for its own sake was
sometimes the rule, garrets and boudoirs grew to be sixty or eighty feet wide—a
convention audiences rapidly learned to accept.

A few librettists and composers (notably Wagner and Verdi) left explicit instructions on how they wanted their stages to be set and their actors costumed, moved,
and motivated. If a libretto called for, or the music indicated, a sword fight, a
dragon, a ghost, a little table, or a chaste kiss, that's what audiences saw. Almost
from the start, a few operas (*The Magic Flute*, Wagner's *Ring*, *Pélleas et Mélisande*)
seemed to invite stylization, even abstraction, in design, and occasionally they
got it.

The beginnings of the current revolution in the worldwide staging of opera, in the
years after World War II, are usually traced to the work of Wieland and Wolfgang

Wagner (the composer's grandsons) at Bayreuth, to the work of Walter Felsenstein in East Berlin, and to parallel innovations on the nonmusical stage by people like Peter Hall in England. For many operagoers this "revolution" will be something they have read about rather than experienced. A few companies in the United States have dipped a toe into the New Wave, but the "majors" have experimented only diffidently or rarely: one could cite producer Goeran Järvefelt's *Bluebeard's Castle/Erwartung* double bill at the Met, Peter Sellars's *Tannhäuser* in Chicago, Nicholas Joel's *Parsifal*, Nikolaus Lehnhoff's *Salome*, and a number of productions by Jean-Pierre Ponnelle in San Francisco. Opera productions in Spain and Latin America are still for the most part solidly nineteenth century. There are innovators at work in Britain and France, but the most radical of them have tended to work outside the largest houses. La Scala in Milan and the Comunale in Florence have taken a few eccentric stabs at postmodern production, but most of Italy remains determinedly traditionalist. The home of avant-garde production ideas remains essentially where it began, in the German-speaking countries—although ideas travel far and fast in today's opera world, partly because German producers travel also.

I describe a number of the new style, postmodern productions in the essays ahead, so I won't rehearse them here. Catalogues of revisionist outrages are included in books such as A. M. Nagler's *Misdirection: Opera Production in the Twentieth Century* (originally titled *Malaise in der Oper*) of 1981 and Henry Pleasants's *Opera in Crisis* of 1989. Nagler (who seems to be dissatisfied with *any* alteration from opera as it was produced sixty years ago) briefly labels and denounces more than 200 "misdirections" of 10 selected operas since 1950 (and sometimes earlier), most of them in Germany. Pleasants instances 29 British productions from 1977 to 1988—17 of them from the more "innovative" English National Opera—and (by way of secondhand accounts) 18 from other countries, including the 1976 and 1988 Bayreuth *Ring*s and Peter Sellars's versions of the Mozart–Da Ponte operas, on which I comment in the pages ahead. Although Nagler casts his net much more widely, many of the same "producer-kings" come under attack from both men: David Alden, Ruth Berghaus, Peter Brook, Patrice Chéreau, Walter Felsenstein, David Freeman, Götz Friedrich, Joachim Herz, Goeran Järvefelt, Harry Kupfer, Yuri Lyubimov, Jonathan Miller, Jean-Pierre Ponnelle, David Pountney, Luca Ronconi, Ken Russell, Peter Sellars, Andrei Serban, Peter Stein, and Graham Vick. Pleasants writes:

> The root of all this presumptuous, arrogant, and often licentious mischief is the crisis of opera in this century, i.e., the stagnation of the repertoire and the scarcity of great singers. . . .[15]

15. Opera producer John Cox, a highly respected *non*revolutionary, agrees with Pleasants's identification of the ultimate cause of "produceritis": "Many composers have deserted the popular language of

> Unable to update the music, . . . [opera managers] have looked to a new breed of producer, mostly from theater and film, to sustain the illusion of vitality and continuity by updating and altering the staging in cynical violation of tradition and oblivious of, or indifferent to, the consequent stylistic anachronisms, aberrations, abominations, and—not to mince words about it—vandalism.

Although all of the productions denounced in these books (as well as new postwar directions in opera production generally) have had their ardent defenders, many, perhaps most, local and international music critics, along with many apoplectic writers of letters to editors, have echoed the outrage of Nagler and Pleasants. Blame is sometimes spread to conductors and singers as co-conspirators; but more often they are regarded with sympathy as hapless puppets, imprisoned by tyrant-producers in their unspeakable new productions.

The new stagings most often criticized are of several sorts:

1. Those in which an opera originally set by its authors in one time and place is moved by the producer to another time and place (e.g., shifting *Rigoletto* to New York or Wagner's *Ring* to the nineteenth century), even if this forces the libretto into occasional anachronisms or nonsense;

2. Those in which specifically sited operas are moved "out of the world" altogether into a science-fiction or apocalyptic future, or a surrealistic fantasyland of the producer's and designer's own creating;

3. Those in which a producer flatly ignores or defies the original authors' own directions, the apparent and traditionally accepted meaning of the libretto, and the traditionally accepted "meaning" of the music;

4. Those in which an opera composed at an earlier time is used to argue or express contemporary, often controversial ideas, to make modern social or political "statements" the original work was obviously not intended to make. (This, in fact, often serves as a producer's justification for alterations that fall under categories 1, 2, and 3.)

---

the theater to write esoterically for one another. This leaves the field completely open to the director in search of originality. At the moment, we directors and designers have the field open to ourselves, and we must not forget that the situation is not going to change until composers come back into the theater with the works for our time, which are original, but also accessible. Until then we shall continue to recycle the same thirty standard operas, which circle the globe over and over, and we shall doubtless continue to indulge in these outré interpretations that are making the whole question of operatic staging such a critical matter today. If we were to desert, the whole species 'opera' would fossilize."

The French critic Guy Verriest traces the birth of the independent opera producer and set designer to postwar Germany, and in particular to Walter Felsenstein's influential concept of *Musiktheater*. Felsenstein (in Verriest's formulation), infusing Wagner's *Gesamtkunstwerk* with Brecht's antibourgeois "epic theatre," granted absolute priority to the overall *dramatic* effect of an opera by means of a minutely conceived and (usually) very original staging. What bothers this critic is that Felsenstein and his successors typically drew their "dramatic truth" exclusively from the libretto—even from its literary or historical source—and betrayed the original by creating a new work in conformity with their own taste and temperament.

> They [the producers] often ignore the music—which they generally don't understand; and nothing is more destructive to the comprehension of an opera. In each opera, we can judge whether the musical and verbal messages reinforce or contradict one another. In every case, we must take the music as our guide and try to understand the *composer*'s conception of the text. It is this conception, and not the naked text, that defines the ultimate significance of the work.[16]

16. To quote from Verriest's important (but little-known) essay at somewhat greater length: "The most serious and most current vice is the excessive interposition of the director between the work and the public. In his published conversations with Felsenstein, Siegfried Melchinger wrote, 'The major deficiency of the so-called modern theatre is that producers, instead of communicating an action to the public, stage their opinion of this action, and make use of actors as no more than marionettes.' In effect, the director denatures the work he is presenting either (1) to impose thereby his personal interpretation of a myth (e.g., Wieland Wagner's phallic scenery, or the interpolation of 'explanations' between the scenes of *The Magic Flute*); (2) to underline the dramatic element by downplaying the lyrical, as Felsenstein does; (3) to endow the work with political significance (which is even more common in Western Europe than it is in the East); (4) to disorient and astonish the spectator—*Carmen* in a nightclub, *Aida* or *Wozzeck* in an operating room; (5) to lose himself in the historical context and circumstances of the work's creation (e.g., staging *Manon*, *Faust*, or Wagner in nineteenth-century costumes); (6) to create a new work parallel to the old one (as Maurice Béjart does); or (7) deliberately to mock the original work, as Herlischka did with *Faust* at Frankfurt.

"In (1), the director sins by over-rationalizing, by making univocal what ought to remain nonrational, or at least ambiguous. As Alain has said, art is a way of *making*, not a way of thinking. In (2), he strips the work of one of its essential elements, thereby destroying its ambiguity. For (3), let me cite Henri Gouthier: 'The director betrays the duties of his commission when he considers himself more than a servant, and places the work at the service of his own political, religious, or even aesthetic opinions. His professional freedom does not confer on him the right to take liberties—it is closer to the "freedom" of an historian.'

"In the next two cases, the director destroys the image, perhaps even the substance of the work. It is as if he had never seen the original work—for, as Dufrenne says, the truth of an aesthetic object is its form. Is one truly seeing *Salome*, if the heroine is not crushed beneath the shields? Or *The Rape of Lucretia*, if Tarquinius does not put out the candle with his sword? 'You wipe out a myth when you cut it off from the unique and flexible gesture of mind that engendered it,' Maldiney has written.

"In the last two cases, the producer, by utterly destroying the context, turns himself into something insupportably pretentious. The naked dancer that Béjart introduced into *La traviata* can no more be reconciled with the world of Dumas than with the world of Verdi.

"Moreover, all of these unique and aberrant *mises en scène* destroy the intersubjectivity, that

Although original scores (or some modern scholar's reconstruction of them) tend to be more respected than in centuries past, producers, conductors, and singers are still criticized as well for cuts, interpolations, and transpositions. In general, however—except for Baroque opera—the music and words in these novel productions tend to be presented as written, or as rewritten, or as carefully reconstructed, or as "traditionally" edited and cut. (Many popular operas exist in several versions, each defensible on different terms.) What is being ignored or defied in postmodern productions, its critics argue, is not so much the score as the tradition of onstage performance practice—which is to say, the traditions of the bigger opera houses between 1880 and 1940—and the traditional "readings" or interpretations of text and score.

The range of works attacked by Nagler, Pleasants, Verriest, and like-minded operatic conservatives includes everything from productions that deviate only slightly from topographical realism, or the legacy of a librettist's minutest stage directions, to the most radical deconstructions of the original text. Because of this range, I find it impossible to declare the new breed of producers "right" or "wrong"; one would have to argue the case production by production. In any event, I would feel ill at ease debating the merits of any production I hadn't seen and heard myself. In my own experiences of the lyric (as of the spoken) theatre, I have found some extremely novel readings and interpretations of classics to work very well, to enlarge considerably my sense of the original. Others have struck me as reductionist and perverse.

Whatever one may think about such deformations of traditional operas—Bellini's Norma in a tank, Monteverdi's Ulysses in Vietnam—in one important respect the conservative critics and polemicists are right. Since 1950, the director or producer of an opera has become a far more significant figure generally than he was in the years before World War II.[17] Despite the occasional and isolated emergence of a dominating, "heroic" opera producer, like Alfred Roller or Max Reinhardt in the early years of this century, the very idea of the nonmusical *producer* of

---

communication with another cultural world that is made up of communal myths and supra-individual life stories—or at least destroy the circumstances that permit this encounter to take place."

17. The choice of terms is puzzling. This is partly because of the difference between British and American usage, and partly because of the modern theatre and film worlds' habit of labeling as "producer" the person responsible for raising or doling out the money, hiring a director, and so forth; and as "director" the person who conceives and manages the action, then rehearses and instructs the actors. Opera is further confused by the all-important presence of the conductor, or *musical* director, who in some rehearsals I have attended or productions I have studied seems to have been at least as responsible for the dramatic conception as the stage director. For the Bayreuth *Ring*s introduced in 1976, 1983, and 1988, Wolfgang Wagner first engaged a conductor, who then chose "his" director, who chose his own designer. If I tend to think of the more distinctive *metteurs en scène* of contemporary opera as "producers," it is because they have so much more control over every aspect of a production than operatic stage directors had in the past.

an opera becoming a creative force as important as, or even more important than, the singers or conductor of an opera is a phenomenon very much of our time.

A few conductors, like Herbert von Karajan, have served as their own producers. Some producers, like Franco Zeffirelli and Jean-Pierre Ponnelle, have taken on the role of designer as well. In extreme cases—which are themselves exemplary of the Age of the Producer—the producer assumes precedence over composer and librettist. Peter Brook's popular Paris entertainment of 1981 called *The Tragedy of Carmen* was a rewriting and condensation created by Brook out of Bizet's opera. In the case of John Adams's *Nixon in China* and *The Death of Klinghoffer*, it was the producer, Peter Sellars, who first conceived the idea of the opera, then assembled a sympathetic team of composer, librettist, and designer.

Two centuries ago, such a czarlike role would have been assumed not by an independent stage producer or by the composer but by the librettist. "It is therefore the poet's duty," wrote Francesco Algarotti in 1755, "as chief engineer of the undertaking, to give directions to the dancers, the machinists, the painters; nay even to those who are entrusted with the care of the wardrobe and dressing the performers. The poet is to carry in his mind a comprehensive view of the *whole* of the drama; because those parts which are not the productions of his pen ought to flow from the dictates of his actuating judgment, which is to give being and movement to the whole." Daniel Heartz has demonstrated that distinguished eighteenth-century poet-librettists like Metastasio, Goldoni, and Da Ponte all gave specific instructions for stage positions and movement, oversaw rehearsals, and "instruct[ed] the actors in the truth of the action and of the expression."

Critics unhappy about the new Age of the Producer will insist that these non-musical interpreters, these mere painters of scenery and shifters-about of singers, have assumed supremacy over composers and librettists in hundreds of cases less notoriously imperial than those of Peter Sellars and Peter Brook. Like old-line Catholic theologians, such critics refer to what they regard as the joint and equal authority of Scripture and Tradition: Scripture being what composers and librettists have in fact written down (which includes not only explicit or implicit stage directions in the libretto but also letters, transcripts of rehearsal notes, and production books); Tradition being the way in which their operas have "always" been done. ("Always," as I say, tends to mean the way operas were done at the Teatro alla Scala, the Royal Opera at Covent Garden, the Vienna Staatsoper, the Paris Opera, the Bayreuth Festspielhaus, and the Metropolitan Opera, between the introduction of electric lights and three-dimensional sets and the beginning of World War II.)

In earlier days, the poet told singers where to stand and how to move. The composer prepared and usually conducted (from the keyboard) at least the première performances. The theatre's resident musical director assigned roles and supervised the singing. Later on, chorus-masters came in to deal with crowds and stage movement in general, although (according to Wolfgang Hildesheimer), "there was no theory of stage direction in our sense of the term; action, gesture, mime were hardly synchronized; everyone did what he could; improvisation was substituted for rehearsal. . . . Actors were allowed to follow their interpretive inspiration of the moment."

Old singers' memoirs, from the days when most singers maintained a single home base all their lives, suggest that young members in a company learned expression from voice teachers and stage deportment from senior colleagues—out of which grew a tradition and a minimal need for stage directors as such. In many cities (particularly Paris and Milan) the design of opera sets developed into an elaborate and independent craft of its own, basically unrelated to concepts of acting or musical interpretation.

Today, the music critic typically addresses first the (new) *production* of an opera— which is presumed, for better or worse, to aspire to some sort of conceptual unity: Peter Hall's *Così*, not Bernard Haitink's; Jean-Pierre Ponnelle's *Così*, not John Pritchard's; Peter Sellars's *Così*, not Craig Smith's. What does the production look like, what do the actors do (and wear), what appears to be their character and motivation? How does this differ from other productions of the same opera? What, on the whole, does it (the production, not the opera) seem to "mean" or "say"? Does it roll along with or fight against, enlarge or reduce our previous conception of the work? All of this has become a fascinating, sometimes a maddening game for music critics (and for audiences) to play. It is one that they rarely had the opportunity or obligation to play in the past.

If the visible/theatrical production is in fact "traditional" (or tired, or very dull), or if the opera features a famous singer—especially one undertaking a new role—a critic may start at once with the voices. If Karl Böhm or Carlos Kleiber is making a rare and impressive appearance on the podium, the conductor's interpretation may still be addressed first. But the new 1976–1988 *Ring* productions at Bayreuth— conducted originally by Pierre Boulez, Georg Solti, and Daniel Barenboim respectively, each making use of some of the best-known Wagnerian singers in the world—are inevitably referred to today as Patrice Chéreau's *Ring*, Peter Hall's *Ring*, and Harry Kupfer's *Ring*.

Rarely, unless it is new to the audience, is an opera itself evaluated. For most critics today, the standard repertory is simply a "given." Joseph Kerman protests what he regards as this overturned set of priorities. Discourse in operatic criticism, he complains, is seldom about meaning but rather about peripheral topics, like "modern production methods."

In an ideal world, the order would perhaps be reversed. A critic would deal first with the value of the opera, then with the singing and conducting (focusing, of course, on dramatic values), and only finally, if at all, with the physical production. But when I once ventured to include my own opinion of Strauss's *Die Frau ohne*

Schatten—not one of my all-time favorite operas—in a London *Times* review, my editor asked me to keep my private judgments of repertory standards to myself. "Please confine your remarks to the new production," he instructed me. "We presume our readers have already formed their own opinions about the opera and aren't interested in knowing yours."

George Bernard Shaw was never backward in coming forward with his opinions of the *operas* he reviewed, however "established" in the repertory they may have seemed. Like Kerman, he obviously hoped he might help to disestablish one or two. But though he almost never referred to "producers" as such—except insofar as conductors like Thomas Beecham also took responsibility for productions—he did, as a conscientious man of the theatre himself, care a great deal about proper interpretation, realization, mise-en-scène. Before he mentioned singers at all (however famous) in his reviews, he tended to deal with the egregious weaknesses and errors that prevented most operas produced in London in the 1880s and 1890s from being fully realized on stage: the wretched acting (or nonacting), the total misreading of a composer's deeper meanings, the casual and foolish cuts and alterations made in the scores. Kerman, too, when working as a journalist-critic—though always ready to condemn any opera he dislikes—inevitably attends first to *dramatic* values, both in individual singers' performances and in productions as a whole.

I have said that "the right production" is the second essential ingredient for a successful operatic experience, that opera-as-written demands a proper production if it is to be completed and brought to life. What, by my lights, makes for a proper production? Given the repertory—and that is a very large given—what is it that I look for in a production?

I find myself applying many of the same standards to a production that Kerman applies to written scores. Where he looks for optimal dramatic coherence, I look for optimal *theatrical* coherence. This usually involves some sort of intellectual concept, ideally one drawn from the text, a concept that is tangible (or felt as evolving) throughout the opera, as we are experiencing it. This concept cannot be something arcane and imported, undiscernible except by way of a director's explanatory notes. In fact, many of the best directorial visions (in all forms of theatre) are impossible to express in words. Like a conductor's "interpretation" of a score—for scores do not play themselves—this involves a "reading," the discovery of an emotional and intellectual structure that permeates, vivifies, clarifies, and unifies everything we see and hear happening on stage. Ideally, the conductor's and producer's interpretations—of words *and* music, in both cases—would be worked out together. One would then sense in the opera house the excitement of a close and sympathetic collaboration.

Opera is, or at least can be, "total theatre" in the Artaudian sense: theatre to the max. Anything less than a total recreation, therefore, a controlled and integrated production in which every element contributes to a single coherent vision, seems to me inadequate. An indispensable subset of total theatre is *dramatic conviction;* it is far more indispensable, I believe, than "perfect" singing or "flawless" instrumental playing. I expect opera singers to be able to act, with their voices first, but ultimately with their whole bodies, no less than I do speaking actors.

With all respect for their extraordinary vocal abilities, I therefore find myself out of sympathy with singers like Joan Sutherland when she declares (Luciano Pavarotti has said essentially the same thing), "I think it is the sound of singing that people want when they come to the opera. If they want a good dramatic performance, they should go to a straight play." There are those of us who think we have a right to expect both—even at an opera. If singers can't or don't want to learn to act, perhaps they should stick to the concert stage.

That much said, I prefer to back off from more specific prescriptions about the ingredients of "the right production." Although there are important clues for production written into the words and music of every opera, these clues are not orders, nor do they yield a single "right" production. The detailed instructions left by some composers (Wagner's for *Parsifal* and the *Ring*, Verdi's production books for seven of his operas, Berg's for *Lulu*, Bartók's for *Bluebeard's Castle*) are certainly important for a producer to know; but they are not the *last* words, despite the "orders" of the original publishers.[18] Productions today that try to follow the originals precisely, such as the 1982 Parma *Forza*, are likely to be of primarily academic and historicist interest, like exact imitations of old buildings.

Within the score and its libretto is encoded a key for production—or rather several keys, since music is such an equivocal means of communication.[19] Studied carefully by a producer who either knows music well, or undertakes the task together with someone who does, the established text can provide not only the essential unifying concept; but also innumerable ideas for individual characterizations, movements, and gestures, as well as for settings, costumes, and lighting. The spectator should feel that the visual enactment blooms organically out of the text, even when (as in many contemporary productions of Shakespeare's *The*

---

18. In the original production book for Verdi's *Otello*, the publisher insisted, "It is *absolutely* essential that all artists familiarize themselves precisely with this *mise en scène* and conform to it strictly; and that directors and impresarios refuse to permit the least deviation regarding costume designs—these have been accurately researched and copied from paintings of the period. There is no reason for them to be altered according to the caprices of a particular singer."

This impressive book, based on the 1887 La Scala production, includes 270 diagrams of staging, lighting, set design, and crowd movement. As David Rosen has acknowledged, in "The Staging of Verdi's Operas," "This notion of a single, 'official' production would not be congenial to today's stage directors."

19. Producers, of course, differ even on this. Jacques Copeau has written, "I think that for any work well conceived for the stage, there exists one and only one necessary *mise en scène*, inscribed in the text

Merchant of Venice and *The Taming of the Shrew*) the production is actively commenting on or criticizing the text.

One can legitimately search for and make use of *external* clues for a production concept, beyond the more or less obvious ideas conveyed by the text, when dealing with any opera written before our time. The "modern" operas of Alban Berg, for example, no longer strike me as contemporary, any more than T. S. Eliot's *The Wasteland*, or a classic 1920s film. They seem to me to call out for a production concept that takes into account the distance we have traveled since they were written.

If this is true for operas of the 1920s, it is even more true for older works—which is to say, virtually all of the repertory standards. Unless one is aspiring toward a historicist revival, a study in the taste and ideas of another time (or nothing more creative than a harmless "concert in costume"), it seems appropriate, even desirable, to interpret and illuminate works of the past in the light of a number of external facts:

- what we know surely of the composer's own life and times (I find something both logical and revealing in performances of eighteenth-century opera seria—even when the operas are supposedly "set" in ancient Babylon or Greece—in eighteenth-century European court dress);

- what we know of the composer's own historical and literary sources (there are good clues for producing Bizet's *Carmen*, I believe, to be found in Prosper Merimée's short story);

- the traditional (1880–1940) image or performance style of the work, even if one elects to discard or work against it;

- the historical substance of the years that have passed between an opera's composition and today;

- the technical means at one's disposal, as well as the musical and vocal resources. Although I realize that this is not always possible at the international houses, where leading artists fly in and out, I greatly respect producers who build their conceptions around (while working with) the available performers, as composers themselves often did.

---

by the author." Au contraire, writes Jonathan Miller. "There is the idea that there exists a level of meaning that is fixed when a work leaves the composer's hand, and that as long as one can identify that determinant level of meaning in the production it must be preserved It follows, then, that there is a canonical performance towards which the cast must grope, and which, when attained, must remain fixed for all time.

"I find this view of the performing arts nonsensical. The arts are emergent, not static, containing properties that cannot be foreseen."

The very fact of the "archaism," the cultural distance from us of most repertory operas—and yet of their undeniably persisting musical/expressive power—invites the producer to *acknowledge* that archaism, to incarnate, not some image from 1787 or 1876 preserved, as it were, under a glass bell jar, but an onstage world that takes that distance (and the intervening history) into account. As Jonathan Miller has said:

> The author or composer is not necessarily the best authority on his own meanings. This is not to say that he is slipshod, or does not understand his meaning, but simply that no writer, no author, no composer has total access to all his own meanings. . . . The producer can provide this insight. He is the bystander, the intelligent critic who is in a position, sometimes, to identify meanings that were not directly accessible to the composer, and to extract new meanings with the passing of time. . . . One constantly has to make allowances for modern sensibilities, for unforeseeable changes in the perceptions of the modern audience. . . .
>
> Composers and writers working before about 1850 had little reason to suspect that the future would be any different from the past, or that their work would pass into a cultural environment very different from their own. History was relatively stable then. Now it is not so, and therefore the future of any particular work cannot be foreseen.

There are a number of ways in which a producer can discover "new meanings" in an opera, meanings of which the original authors may have been unaware. One can play melodrama so tightly that it hurts; one can make stock suffering heroines *really* suffer. One can openly dramatize what is problematic in a text—for example, the rigid and sometimes frustrating class distinctions in *Figaro* and *Don Giovanni*, the limited roles and images permitted to women in earlier times, Superman Siegfried's disgust for lower orders of beings, the Freudian undercurrents of *Elektra* and *Salome*. A producer who attempts to do such things—by dream or nightmare contexts, by modern dress and stage settings, by the dramatization of actualized neuroses and psychoses, by vivid symbolism and external reference, by taking a plunge into new emotional depths—will be inviting attack from critics like those cited previously. But all of these approaches strike me as legitimate and defensible, as long as the written work itself is not belied or betrayed in some essential way.[20]

This, I believe, is what happens (as I argue in chapter 6, on Peter Sellars's versions

---

20. Jean-Jacques Nattiez, in his brilliant study of the 1976 Bayreuth *Ring*, makes a good case for treason—but against the composer's "intentions," not against the work he has left behind. "On many occasions," he concludes, "I am convinced that Boulez and Chéreau have betrayed Wagner. But they have done right to do so. I am resolutely on the side of the traitors."

of the Mozart–Da Ponte operas) when a producer imposes from without a directorial conceit alien to the score. The producer's goal in such cases may be to shock—to defy the expectations of audiences he regards as half-asleep; or to editorialize—to force the opera to serve as a vehicle for some urgent personal message of his own. Some of the new productions that have been most vigorously denounced appear as well to defy, to play against the apparent message or meaning of the text and score.

This troubles me primarily, I suppose, because of the sublime arrogance involved. The words and music of a long-established work are turned into a plastic, pliable vehicle for a producer-king's late-twentieth-century ideas; the ideas of a producer-king who appears to regard himself as a creator, a maker of symbolic statements equal or superior to those of the original creators.

A case can be made for such apparently arrogant and perverse directorial "statements." I know, because I have heard versions of this case made time and again. One may decide (1) that composers of operas are not necessarily more important artists than the producers of their works; (2) that because the composer and librettist are dead—no more than names attached to a text, their intentions indecipherable or irrelevant—their words and score are now ours to play with as we will; (3) that modern producers of other people's texts need no longer play the self-effacing, secondary role of mere *réalisateurs;* (4) that in any case there are a thousand ways to "read" whatever "directions" may be encoded into the music; or (5) that because all values today are disputable, there can be no canons or "right ways."

All of these ideas may be found in contemporary literary critical theory as well. But a new, "deconstructionist" reading of a classic literary text differs considerably in its audience, its cultural effect, and its reality status from a similar reading of an classic opera, made by a person in a position to produce it. Having to live with a producer's strange new interpretation of Wagner's *Ring* at Bayreuth for five or more years (and the many other productions it is likely to affect) is quite a different thing from being able to read (or ignore) a critic's strange new interpretation of a Baudelaire poem. The case is even more serious with willfully outré productions of little-known works, because this particular interpretation is likely to be the only one the audience has ever seen or will ever see.

The producer of a standard repertory opera who based his interpretation on premises like those just cited—for example, Peter Sellars, in his productions of *The Magic Flute* or *Tannhäuser*—could insist that the only legitimate way to object to such a production would be to do battle, not with the producer's "misconception" or "perversion" of what we regard as Mozart's or Wagner's ideas, but with his own apparent statement. All productions, even the most traditional, the most dutiful, are interpretations of a sort, and hence implicitly critiques. A postmodern producer opposed to what he sees as the values of a composer or his time may take this idea one step further and mount an *anti*-Puccini *Madame Butterfly*, let us say (I have seen such productions), in which he attacks the composer and his values in the course of producing his work. (Of course, musical analysts, critics, and producers can debate endlessly over the nature of the original "meaning or message," in addition to the propriety or impropriety of defying it. There are almost as many musicologists' interpretations of the Mozart–Da Ponte operas as there are producers'.)

The chief weakness of such revisionist efforts is that the spectator cannot help but, in Kerman's words, "trust the music" first, because music carries so much more emotional impact than anything else: more impact than the words; more than buffoonish costuming, psychotic staging, cynical acting "against the text"; more than even the most vivid, the most hostile production. The producer, as I suggested, may even be presuming in the audience a shared *dis*trust, even disgust, for the score he has chosen to direct (Andrew Porter once suspected this of what he regarded as Jean-Pierre Ponnelle's trashing of Massenet's *Manon*); in which case, we are all implicated in the cynical, destructive enterprise.

Many operagoers are far more easily satisfied than I am with predictable, routine productions—Carmen with the spit curl and the rose between her teeth, flashing her knees flamenco-style beneath ruffled fuchsia petticoats as she clacks her castanets and dances atop an inn table *près des remparts d'*an apparently authentic *Seville*. Beyond that, they ask only for good music, well played and (if possible) spectacularly sung.

My preferences for fresh, alert, conceptually unified, and dramatically credible total theatre are based as much on autobiography as on any reasoned aesthetic theory. A literary and architectural education in the 1950s, several years spent as a critic and teacher of drama, a heady exposure at a very susceptible stage to the work of such people as Wieland Wagner, Walter Felsenstein, Peter Hall, Giorgio Strehler, and Maria Callas all disposed me to think of opera as theatre first; as drama, only better. In a frequently quoted remark, Michael Billington of the *Guardian* has claimed that "the lyric theatre has absorbed much of the dramatic theatre's energy and talent. . . . To put it crudely, opera now possesses [he was writing in 1988] the controversial dynamism theatre had 15 or 20 years ago." David Pountney (one of the postmodern directors conservative critics love to hate) says, "On good nights in the opera house, the acting you see is as good [as], if not better than, the acting that you see at the National Theatre."

I can't quite buy that. I remain an ardent follower and a fan of *non*lyric drama at its best, as well as opera. I know that one continues to see better acting—taken all in all—at the National Theatre than at Covent Garden, and at the better American regional repertory theatres than at the Met, and that it is foolish to claim otherwise. But I early learned of the far greater expressive potential of sung over spoken drama, however rarely that potential is achieved. Much of my indoctrination came at the hands of Kurt Herbert Adler, the Viennese-born general director (1953–

1982) of the San Francisco Opera, an impresario considerably more adventurous in his choice of operas, singers, and producers than either Rudolf Bing in New York or Carol Fox in Chicago. If I had been educated to opera in New York or Chicago, my responsiveness to "total theatre" values might conceivably have been less, and the likelihood of my thinking of opera primarily in terms of fabulous voices all the greater. (Contemporaries I met from those two cities who cared about opera were inevitably violently partisan fans of this or that particular singer.) On the other hand, if I had grown up learning about opera in any one of several German cities, I might not care about fabulous voices at all.

An ideal, total production of a major opera, by my standards, is very nearly unattainable, although I have seen many that came close. Exceptional resources and rehearsal time, rarely available outside of a few prime summer festival situations (Glyndebourne, Salzburg, Bayreuth), are probably indispensable. A first-rate conductor sensitive to voices is required. Many of the world's best conductors are unwilling to invest the time and energy required for a top-quality opera production (outside their home ports) when they can earn the same fees and acclaim for less demanding orchestral concerts and recordings.

This ideal conductor should have the time and will to work out a line-by-line interpretation together with a congenial and musically sensitive director. Ideally, the director would be his own designer, or would be working with one in sympathy with his ideas. The two of them would want, of course, the best orchestra, soloists, chorus, and dancers available, which implies a resident ensemble accustomed to working together, all of its members pliant and theatrically skilled, able and willing to undergo a great many rehearsals.

One is rarely likely to get all that, which is why a "perfect opera" is so hard to pull off. Most of the time I'm more than willing to compromise—as composers, conductors, producers, and singers have always had to do. If nothing essential is seriously harmed, I will settle for an imperfect realization of a great opera—a *Don Giovanni*, let us say (the text and score offer so much that even a partial achievement can be a feast); but I hope for something closer to a fully realized, 100 percent incarnation of a *Thaïs* or an *Arabella*. The pleasure of a well-produced minor work can be considerable, since a near-complete realization of almost any work of theatre yields (to someone possessed of a "theatrical sensibility") a sense of fulfillment; an ultimate, if a lesser kind of satisfaction. (My presumption is that 100 percent realizations of theatrical works, like perfect grades of "20" on French examination papers, never occur. The nearest I've come to what felt like a perfect realization of a great work of the spoken theatre was a production of Chekhov's *The Three Sisters* given by the new National Theatre at Chichester in 1963; of an opera, a *Der Rosenkavalier*—which featured Elizabeth Schwarzkopf's American debut—at San Francisco in 1955, reprised with great style in subsequent seasons.)

AUDIENCE AT THE GLYNDEBOURNE OPERA FESTIVAL THEATRE, 1969.
Drawing by Sir Osbert Lancaster. Courtesy of Lady Ann
Lancaster and the Glyndebourne Opera Festival.

Lesser achievements can still teach us many things, give us many pleasures.
Good music well played can offer, at the very least, the joys of the concert hall; fine
voices well deployed can yield a deep and intimate satisfaction, even if the vehicle
is weak, the production inadequate. In such cases, however, the frustration of
what has *not* been achieved may well undercut the satisfaction of what has.

VIII

The formula of right opera plus right production, the ideal work ideally realized, is
still an incomplete recipe for success. It lacks an essential ingredient—the ideal
spectator, the right person listening and watching. The ideal spectator would
not, obviously, be a Tolstoy or a Nietzsche, or any of the fundamentalist antiopera types conjured up some pages ago. The ideal spectator cannot, obviously,
be a woodenheaded literalist, one of Stendhal's "poor, passionless, bluntminded
creatures" who can tolerate art only at its most photorealistic, who accepts
what happens on a stage only when it resembles very closely what happens in
daily life.

Conversely, people who go to the opera primarily for the social cachet of being seen there—the operagoers Tolstoy and Nietzsche most despised—are probably doomed to boredom, frustration, and (insofar as they have one) an uneasy conscience. Let us permit these two types of non-opera lovers to cancel each other out.

What sort of person can spark a potentially fine operatic experience into life, within his or her own sensibility? What sort of person is likely to derive the greatest amount of pleasure (enlightenment, new understanding, moral and emotional enrichment) from a good opera well performed?

In the face of the heterogeneous list of 100 current standard repertory operas cited earlier in this chapter, it is clear that no two people—not even two people equally educated, open, alert, and responsive—are going to respond in the same way to the same works. Multiply the likelihood of variation in response by the different conductors and orchestras, the different actors and voices, and the different theatrical ideas and visual effects that may be involved in production, and it would seem impossible (except as a gesture of sheer solipsistic arrogance) to identify anyone's response as "ideal." Alan Rich defines this dilemma when he writes:

> Suppose I am going to *La Traviata*—a not out-of-the-way supposition, since there are times when I seem to be going to *La Traviata* four nights out of five. I've lived with this opera a long time, studied it in school, followed it with the score on records or at the piano. I have had plenty of time, in other words, to form my own set of ideas about the opera, the kind of voices I would ideally like to hear in the roles, the tempos at which it ought to move, how it should look onstage. This is the equipment I take with me to the opera house that night, but it is *my* equipment, which has taken shape inside *my* mind, conditioned by *my* personality, which happens to be that of an incurable romantic. My colleague across the aisle arrives with a similar set of equipment—similar in scope, that is, but conditioned by *his* personality. We sit there, a few feet apart, listening to a Violetta with a perfectly awesome technique; she sticks an E-flat into the end of "Sempre libera" which goes off like a rocket. She may not know beans about what the opera is about; her exchanges with Germont in the second scene may seem so many vocalises. But boy! she can get the tone out, and the crowd goes wild. In the next morning's papers my colleague erupts in ecstasy, I in fury. There's something I want from *La Traviata* that has to do with drama and sentiment and reaction to the text; my colleague is mad for vocal prowess. I am not immune to great singing, nor is he to dramatic values, but each has made his own decision as to which is the element more highly to be prized. Our reviews are opposed, and the strange and wonderful thing is that neither of us is "right" or "wrong."

On the whole, I expect that my response would be closer to that of Alan Rich than to that of his imaginary colleague. There are obviously people "mad for vocal prowess." There are people who relish opera primarily at its most voluptuous and irrational. Anyone who has spent much time in an opera house has probably encountered both sorts.

The Puccini scholar Mosco Carner once wrote, "As for *Tosca*, there is certainly an aspect of it [an 'undeniable streak of vulgarity,' as he called it] that may offend the purist. But it was not written for him, or the aesthete or the man of perilously refined taste. It is a bold man who will assert that to relish fullbloodedness in art is incompatible with aesthetic enjoyment—on the contrary it may be a sign of a healthy, unwarped aesthetic instinct." The French essayist Guy Verriest, unhappy with the overly demanding standards of rationalist opera critics (who "accept no more than about twenty works"), proposed *Mignon* as his test of the true opera lover. This opera (still popular in France), he writes, "signifies nothing for the analytic critics who are only trying to set up a relative scale of values, a normative judgment; while the sensitive, instinctive spectator will immediately be carried away by the 'unique and indefensible' poetry that characterizes Ambroise Thomas's work." The playwright Albert Innaurato, a self-confessed "opera fanatic," sets up Ponchielli's *La Gioconda* as his standard. "The question finally may be not whether the *opera* is defensible but whether *we* are who love it. *La Gioconda* is an extreme example, one where the expressive potential of music is used rather crudely, and not harnessed to insights of an intellectual sort. But I think there is something fundamental about its dramaturgy that may make it a litmus test to differentiate those who more or less like opera from those who adore it."

I fear I would pass neither Carner's test as a person of healthy, unwarped aesthetic instincts; nor Verriest's test as a sensitive, instinctive spectator; nor Innaurato's test as a defensible adorer of opera.

No one, except certain employees of an opera company (ushers, stagehands, orchestra members), professional music critics, and a few people who buy season tickets for other-than-aesthetic reasons, is *obliged* to attend every opera of the ten-, or twenty-, or thirty-production season of his or her particular resident troupe. In fact, only the most dogged and devoted fans are likely to do so, given the cost, the likelihood of imperfect performances, and the unlikelihood that every work will be of equal appeal.

And yet I believe that the happiest and most highly rewarded operagoer may be one who *can* take pleasure in almost any good production of a respectable opera. I am not convinced that the doctrinaire Wagnerite, who scorns Italian and French opera as trivial and thin, gets as much out of Wagner as the listener more catholic in attitudes and less difficult to please. The operagoer who can enjoy nothing later or more jarring to the ear than Puccini is obviously cut off from a universe of musical-dramatic satisfaction. I do not believe that the voice fanatic, and more especially the unique-voice fanatic, the Tebaldi or Domingo cultist, the devoted collector of Golden Age records, the exclusive connoisseur of bel canto sopranos—whatever ecstasies he or she may experience at particular moments with particular singers in particular operas—is ever going to get as much out of opera in general as someone whose cultivated inlets of pleasure are broader and more numerous.

From a consideration of the peculiar nature of the 100-plus operas in the standard repertory, and especially the fifty or so most commonly performed, one can begin to compile a list of "desirable characteristics" for our fictional (and probably unattainable) ideal spectator: the third element in my formula for an aesthetics of opera.

1. He (by which, of course, I also mean she) should probably be, if not Eurocentric, at least Europe oriented and more than usually interested in the European past. It would help if he were at least an amateur student of the history, literature, and art of Western Europe. A great deal of the standard repertory depends on Western literary classics and myths (the Greek myths and tragedies, Homer, the Bible, the Norse sagas, Ariosto, Shakespeare, Goethe and Schiller, Victor Hugo, etc.).

   In addition to such written works, the standard repertory depends on European history as it used to be written—the story of kings, popes, wars, royal marriages, conspiracies, revolutions. Typically, the settings and stage designs of standard repertory operas evoke, or were originally intended to evoke, European castles and cathedrals, European cities and towns, European mountain and valley landscapes. The places, the people and events, and the literary sources were usually falsified and distorted, legendized and inflated, chopped and changed to fit musical and theatrical expression. But most operas in the current repertory—including recent "common man" or antifascist works, works charged with post–World War II confusion and angst—grow out of and depend on the European past. Not to be aware of that particular past, not to know the soil out of which opera grew, is inevitably to miss a great deal of the cultural resonance of opera.

   Not knowing the basic repertory languages (Italian, German, French, perhaps a bit of Russian and Czech) is a lesser loss; even native speakers often cannot comprehend a sung text. One can always read a translation of the libretto in advance. Many houses today offer vernacular translations by way of projected "supertitles" for those who want them (and, I concede, for those who don't). If you wish to dig deeper into the world of opera, however, knowing the three chief repertory languages is, I believe, almost as important as knowing how to read music.

2. Beyond a basic fascination and familiarity with Europe, its history, art, and literature (and some of its languages), I think one is likely to get more out of current productions of opera for knowing something of

the history of opera—at least the history of operatic conventions; better still, of the history of Western music. The operas we are most likely to see and hear performed during our lifetimes will probably continue to be made up of the same 100–150 works, composed between 1600 and the present. It is beyond hoping that anyone would naturally and instinctively comprehend and appreciate the conventions of every one.

And yet old music remains, thanks to its vibrating sweetness, its widely apprehended emotional effects, and the passive way in which we are able to receive it, far more accessible and potentially enjoyable to most people than old literature or even old art. More contemporary English-speaking people, I would venture, find themselves moved readily by the music of Monteverdi or Purcell than by the verse of Spenser or Milton, by the paintings of Lorenzetti, or by the buildings of Mansart.

So it is worth trying to comprehend the conventions: making an effort to understand why and how composers once created, and audiences once expected, particular forms of music in opera. Beyond that, some awareness of the history of opera may help one to understand, tolerate, and even come to enjoy the attendant nonsense written into many standard repertory works, which may strike the first-time spectator as simply alien or foolish: da capo repeats, the cavatina (or "cantabile")-cabaletta convention, "exit" arias, inset ballets, vocal ornamentation, recitative of various sorts, "magical" stage spectacles, and those ever-popular ensembles in which characters express a whole gamut of emotions while singing over one another.

I am not pushing for flabby pluralism. To understand the origins and conventions of Metastasian opera seria (see chapter 3, "When Opera Was Still Serious") is not to accept wholeheartedly all of the tone-dead, properly neglected works of Leo, Vinci, Hasse, Porpora, Caldara, & Co. But operas still worthy of performance emerged from almost every age and tradition, and the more we try to assume the eyes and ears of their first audiences, the likelier we are to discover whatever enduring qualities they possess.

3. On the whole, I do believe that a tendency toward aesthetic pluralism and away from the position of the doctrinaire specialist is an advantage to the would-be opera lover. This is partly because of the rooted fact of the established repertory. If you can take some pleasure in *Samson et Dalila* as well as in *The Marriage of Figaro* (the two extremes of our 100-item repertory, as well as, to my eyes and ears, the bounds of tolerable

taste), you are likely to enjoy the experience of opera more often and more heartily.

Beyond as broad a tolerance for the repertory as one can reconcile with a healthy aesthetic conscience, the ideal operagoer should be endowed with a spirit of tolerance in general: a wide degree of patience, an acceptance of compromise, perhaps even a rooter's "team spirit," wishing for but not always expecting the best; an ability to wait for and then to treasure (when they come) the perfect moments and ideal realizations. Given the extraordinary demands of this multiplex art form, such moments and realizations are going to be few and far between. It helps to be able to fill in the deficiencies of a performance from one's memory and imagination, rather than to sit there squirming with discomfort at the inadequacy of it all.

4. I am taking for granted an alert musical sensibility, although not necessarily specialized musical training. One should be able to register internally significant musical patterns and motifs, changes in tonality or orchestration, even if one cannot always apply to each the appropriate technical term. The musically trained can take special pleasure in compositional ingenuity, tonal problem solving, and allusions to other music; one can certainly learn more about a score by singing or playing it oneself. (The greatest composers, like Mozart, seem to have been able to write in such a way as to please the learned and the unlearned at once.)

But there are times when expertise—to judge from the confessions of experts—seems to get in the way of enjoyment. It is possible that the world's number one authority on Verdi may get less out of a good production of *Don Carlos* than would you, or I, or George Bernard Shaw—if only because, from closely analyzing the score at home and in "unreal time," the Verdi expert has concluded how it *must* be performed, and may be dissatisfied with any interpretation but his own.

An ability to detect and respond actively to aesthetic unity would also be a help; an admiration for the artistic event in which numerous disparate elements are held together, enhanced by their juxtaposition, and converted into a single and superior thing—because that is precisely what good opera is.

5. No less important, to the person who hopes to enjoy opera on the stage as well as on record or in print, is a *theatrical* sensibility, an openness to the limitations, illusions, and potential of the living stage. In fact, the ideal operagoer should probably be endowed with a greater-than-usual theatrical sensibility, one that can relish not only fine drama well

presented but also mimed horror and madness, imagined religious rituals, elaborate spectacles and decors.

6. Along with a nostalgic traditionalism that can take delight in old Europe and its musical-dramatic conventions, the ideal operagoer would possess an openness to orchestral, vocal, and theatrical reinterpretations of old standard works that give them a new but still coherent meaning, and to altogether new operas that push the genre further, and make a new kind of sense. This qualification may be the most difficult of all to attain.

Successful new operas are likely to be rare. For a complex of cultural reasons, very few serious composers since 1920 have been able to write operas as emotionally compelling and as profoundly satisfying as the best of the preceding century and a half. However fragmented and incoherent our world grows, a good deal of our own physiological and psychological makeup still seems to crave in music the formal order of rhythm and tonality that passed for "beauty" in more apparently coherent times. Contemporary opera producers, as we have seen, often feel a serious cultural compulsion to fight against or undercut long-established traditions of performance practice.

Just as I would not want to feel so distant from and resistant to seventeenth- and eighteenth-century conventions that I could not enjoy *Poppea* or *Idomeneo*, so I would hate to be so locked into the way Wagner and Verdi wanted their works to be performed in the 1870s that I could not bear what a Patrice Chéreau or a Pier Luigi Pizzi might make of them today. Had I settled years ago for the relatively easy, sentimental-voluptuous pleasures of *Der Rosenkavalier* and *Turandot* as the limits of my tolerance for twentieth-century opera, my inner life and memories would have been impoverished, deprived of *Lear, Death in Venice, The Fiery Angel*, and *Lady Macbeth of Mtsensk*.

7. It helps, I suspect, to be a sensualist. Opera is a very sensual art. At its core are live human bodies pouring out great vibrating streams of sound. Around them flows a surfeit of instrumental pulses and vibrations, dancers, fabrics, colors, sensual appeals of every sort. There is more to opera than this, of course. Except for the odd bacchanal, and some particularly sticky moments in Wagner or Strauss, the appeal of opera is more than merely sensual, more than some Des Esseintes dream of synaesthetic self-abandon. But there's no getting away from the basic sensuality of a great deal of opera.

8. I do not want to argue, as others have done, that opera is fundamentally absurd or antirational, that you have to have a taste for insane spectacle

if you're going to like opera. (For one thing, such definitions rule out a great number of good operas.) But I do believe that an unusual ability and willingness to yield, to give in to a work of art is important: somehow to dissolve yourself and let the work include you.

In opera, for all of the power of great instrumentalists, I think this ultimately means a susceptibility to the awesome emotional power of great voices brilliantly used. This power is, I believe, potentially far greater than that of any organ or violin, any orchestra or synthesizer, more compelling than colors on canvas or words on a page. There before you is a body, like yours, with a throat and larynx, like yours, drawing out of itself (as you may dream of doing, but cannot) sounds that vibrate and seize beyond the power of any nonsinging actor. It seems to me the most captivating and beautiful thing that a human being can do on a public stage in living time.

IX

Ultimately, it is the sound of the singing human voice at its most powerful and expressive, its most carefully trained and precise that affects us in opera beyond everything else. Any aesthetic of opera, any serious attempt to explain its appeal or potential success that ignores the fact of the singer—even the often-derided star singer—will be fatally flawed. The human voice, it has been said, is "the instrument for which all others are metaphors." The *vox humana* stop on an organ, the most clever electronic synthesizer produces only the feeblest of imitations. The difference between opera and other forms of music, between opera and nonmusical drama, is that the chief performers sing.

I have read works by singers and voice teachers, by musicologists and aestheticians and opera historians; but none of them explained to my satisfaction the compelling power that great voices singing opera have over susceptible listeners like me.

Since many people remain unmoved by, even displeased by such voices, and since all human beings have at least similar bodies, I feel uncomfortable attributing this power to a physiological source. But reflecting on my experiences at good, loud, highly amplified rock concerts, where one feels that one's personal identity has been overcome by and dissolved in the sound, I wonder if the "seizing" power of great operatic singing may not have something to do with the resonant vibrations it creates in *us:* the very tangible, rapid pulses we feel in our own skulls, and sometimes deeper through our bodies, set off by the powerful vibrations of a fine singer's voice. From these inescapable vibrations inside our heads—which may lead us to feel as if *we* were making the great noise, as if it were coming from inside us—we may go on to experience the feeling of an intimate physical resonance between the singer and ourselves, between her (and sometimes his) body and our own, which gives to the experience a quality that is at once liberating and erotic.[21]

Great operatic voices do appear to "flow," in an intense and liquid outpouring, sometimes in an outburst or a jet, which then arouses *our* vital juices: in the same way that the beat, pulse, and pumping of music generally appear to engage the natural inner rhythms of our breathing or pulse, lead us irresistibly to sway, beat time, "conduct," tap our feet. As Peter Conrad—a connoisseur of voluptuous operatic sensations—once wrote, air is resonating only from the diaphragm to the head, "but the whole body sounds."

For reasons I cannot understand or explain, I sometimes find myself staring with unnatural intensity at a performer in an opera who is singing exceptionally well, as if to sharpen and focus my attention, not to miss a single pulse of his or her music; as if we were related in some intimate emotional way. I catch myself either foolishly beaming or near to tears, *not* because of the joy or plight of the character, but because I have been moved beyond any reasonable, critical response by the simple, sensual fact of the quality and vibrations of a human voice. "The singing voice," writes Conrad, "inordinate in its power and somehow miraculous as the production of a single human body, infuses the world with the vibrancy of its emotion."

Insofar as such an intimate communion is created between our body and the singer's, we may enjoy the enhanced feeling of a "better self"; we have escaped, however temporarily, the pitiable self that we know *cannot* make such sounds, or create such thrilling vibrations. We can also both marvel at and (to a degree) share the singer's sensual and dangerous self-exposure. To every live actor's risk of forgetting lines or blowing a scene is added the singer's special burden of remembering hundreds of bars of music, and performing them all musically as well as dramatically—which often involves the most extraordinary, matadorlike physical challenges to a voice going at full throttle and fully exposed. ("It's exactly like a bullfight," Luciano Pavarotti has said. "You are not allowed one mistake.")

Many public performers taking great risks, or doing difficult and admirable things (which includes acrobats as well as actors) can compel our attention and admiration. In a few cases (athletes throwing, batting, kicking, diving) our admiration is enhanced by the "body English" through which our own anatomy feels itself sharing or duplicating the gestures of the performer. (My guess is this happens more rarely with dancers and actors, unless the observer is also a dancer or

---

21. According to Hélène Seydoux, "The voice is also a sexual organ. Why? Quite simply, because it provokes physical sensations in others. We speak, quite properly, of a 'penetrating' voice, a 'potent' voice; we even say of a singer that he has 'a fine organ.' Vocal timbre is determined by the endocrinal characteristics of each individual, and more specifically by the sexual hormones. . . . A voice can be a caress, an invitation, a cry, a breath. It can be round, sensual, warm, or bitter. It can charm, attract, seduce, convince. Its power goes beyond words. . . . Nothing is sexier than the voice."

an actor.) In the case of a great opera singer, I believe that, to a person susceptible to her powers (less frequently his: tenors strive; sopranos soar), all of these characteristics combine to achieve a unique and compelling effect. To sum up what I think are the sources of a great singer's hold on us:

1. The person on stage is doing something at once extraordinarily rare and difficult (reason itself for admiration), *and* extraordinarily beautiful.

2. The source of the beauty is not a page or a painting, but a person like us.

3. This person like us is making a sound *more* beautiful than any musical instrument can do, which enhances our sense of human greatness.

4. The sound is intimately affecting, both because it comes from an organ we ourselves possess, and because it creates resonant vibrations in us.

Anyway, that's one theory. Whatever the actual reason, or reasons, for the power that great operatic voices have over people susceptible to them, it is this power that in the end provides the ultimate justification for "grand" or "international class" or "superstar" opera; opera sung by great vocal actors with one-in-a-million voices. However well performed and produced, opera done with second-class voices can never wholly justify the medium or explain its survival. "From the performative standpoint, vocal brilliance or orchestral sumptuousness must take precedence over a composer's or a performer's fidelity to the text," comments Herbert Lindenberger. As F. M. Dana says, "The experience of opera without stars has always seemed incomplete."

> Take that element [i.e., the star singer at center stage] out—the set designers will become architects, the clothes designers will become couturiers, the composer will compose beautiful music, the librettist will go off and write novels and poetry—but without the performer standing on stage, there is no reason to be in that theatre.

This is also why I believe the standard eighteenth- and nineteenth-century repertory operas (however dramatically inadequate many of them may be), operas written specifically and melodiously for the human voice at its most beautiful and expressive, will remain the standards as long as opera as we know it survives.

Although I am sure that some form of matadorlike or acrobatic—that is, exposed, difficult, dangerous—physical exhibitionism contributes to our delight in great singing, I reserve the right to say no to mere vocal display: to the notoriously "treacherous" high notes (most of them introduced as applause traps by late-nineteenth-century singers; I have come to dread the endings of many famous Italian arias); to the tricky filigree of minutely chopped runs and trills; to singers who go on and on, like underwater swimmers, without taking a breath. All of these lead the listener to wonder primarily how on earth the performer does it—the same response we have to a circus sideshow contortionist, or to those Chinese acrobats who balance asymmetrical piles of furniture and plates on their heads. The explosion of applause that inevitably follows, and that has come to seem almost a part of the music, is in large part an expression of relief that the singer made it all of the way up or all of the way through.

Peter Conrad's remarks on Maria Callas in this regard seem to me just, and to define the difference between a clever mechanical nightingale and a true singing actress.

> At every point [in *Lucia di Lammermoor*] the acrobatics are glossed as mental re-actions. During her 'Quanto rapita' monologue, Lucia ornaments the words 'eterna fe.' The gesture isn't showy; it's reflective and internal. . . . Her mad scene is an episode of recondite sonic research. . . . Singing of a 'dolce suono' in a voice which is girlishly pure, Callas lyrically retreats to a mad second childhood. When a high note on the word for altar oscillates out of control, it does so because it has taken off from the human register, and is echoing the vast vacancy within Lucia's mind. Lucia chases echoes until, in the glassy, un-physical sound Callas makes during her concert with the flute, she herself be-comes one: an acoustic specter; Orpheus insane but in tune.

I admit to being susceptible both to sheer vocalise—beautiful voices, agile, able, controlled, singing beautiful music—and great, expressive vocal *acting* of the sort Conrad here describes. If, on the whole, I tend to give higher marks to the latter, it is because it engages more of *me* in a performance.

But I see no reason to decide permanently between two such extraordinary sources of pleasure. Nor do I see any point, as many opera fans (and fanatics) insist on doing, in trying to make minute distinctions of quality between singers who are often almost equally good, or to bewail the fact that they are not Ponselles or Carusos or Flagstads. Part of the reason for attending operas as often and in as many different places as possible is to hear and see a variety of good singers performing the same roles. The experience (like that of seeing a variety of productions of the same opera) inevitably enlarges one's conception of the original work.

What *makes* a great voice is something I won't even try to address. In twenty-three years of reviewing opera performances, I have tended to steer clear of what one might consider "voice coaches' terms"—head and chest voice, *squillo* and portamento, *Fach* and tessitura, the physiological details of breath control—in trying to describe and evaluate particular voices. I have made use instead either of terms we can all clearly understand, such as "accuracy of pitch," "control of dynamics" (i.e., volume), "wobble" or "vibrato," along with metaphors by which I hope to communicate something of my own felt experience.[22] I find I use a lot of metallic metaphors (golden, silver, bronze) as well as words like "pearl" or "jewel" to convey both the "ringing" and the "precious" quality of individual sung notes. "Steely" is usually pejorative, though I have applied it to Callas, whom I admire. Words such as "dark," "mahogany," "grainy," or "nightingale" are meant to evoke other sounds and timbres. I find I use liquid references to describe a "flowing" continuity of beauty in control. Ideally, I seek out images that convey simultaneously the musical and dramatic qualities of a voice, which is, of course, the way we receive them.

Opera may have begun with politely declaiming gentleman-amateurs standing around a harpsichord or a consort of viols. But it quickly evolved into a singers-first medium, which is now the way most people perceive it. The attention paid to great singers by critics and fans, the scrupulous attention paid in reviews to vocal qualities (more attention than is given, as a rule, to dramatic, orchestral, or overall theatrical qualities) are not just star fodder for voice freaks. The singing of a great human voice, well trained and well used, can affect us, as I have tried to suggest, in an overpowering and yet intimate way, quite apart from any dramatic context. But when a combination of such voices is used as the basic vehicle for a potentially moving human drama, when each voice is given (and supported by) distinctive music that provides an opportunity for apt emotional expression, the result can create, open up, and invite us into a represented human world as no other form of narrative or expressive art can do.

Opera in general works (when it works) because (1) it tends, of theatrical necessity, to concentrate its best moments on episodes of extreme, unqualified, even essential human emotion; (2) it has a more direct, intense, and immediate means of communicating emotion (and of moving us to emotion) than nonmusical drama; (3) it has a more obvious and affecting relationship to the lives we lead (as lovers, loners, fools, romantics) than does "absolute" music, detached as the latter is from any carnal human story; and (4) it is the most complex, challenging, and demanding form of public performance. Opera has the ability to attack us with the combined power of three or four art forms (and popular spectacles) at once. A full-length play, a three-hour orchestral concert, frequently a ballet, a pageant or parade, a choral concert, and (depending on the designer) a certain amount of painting and sculpture may all be *contained* within one ordinary opera. It

---

22. Virgil Thomson, writing in 1954, expressed the wish that opera critics would stop giving voice lessons in public. "Bad pitch, gasping breath, false notes, wavering tones can be heard, and it is legitimate to mention them. It is not legitimate to tell an artist in public how to correct them."

is so difficult to pull all of this together, in fact, to pull it all off, that when the production of an opera works, or nearly works, what is "working" is something grander and more complex than any other form of public performance.

The deep and ultimately inexplicable pleasure of music—especially that of the *vox humana*—can lead to a sublime and satisfying transcendence after even the most devastating of stories. In *The Magic Mountain*, Thomas Mann describes the profound satisfaction, even ecstasy, that Hans Castorp receives from listening (on a recording) to the closing scene of *Aida*—and what operagoer can deny feeling it?—even though he was contemplating two lovers about to suffocate to death. Morally evil characters become tolerable through their music. Even though we know better, even though his own characters may belie it, an opera by Mozart can convince us (for a while) that the world is indeed a balanced, equable, humane place, where the worst of human feelings and the most extreme of human differences can find resolution and reconciliation. The subverbal, nonrational pleasure we are taking in the music itself, and the sound of singing voices, very frequently makes the world created by an opera during performance simply seem *better* than that same world depicted without music, let alone the messy, unstructured world to which we return when the curtain goes down. Peter Hall, who has very successfully directed both operas and plays, speculates that "music, because it has no literal meaning, is immediately emotional. Music immediately charges the proceedings with a sensuality and an atmosphere which is much stronger and more electric than the spoken word. . . . I think that's why people applaud for half an hour at opera, and almost never applaud for half an hour at plays. It's not that the experience of a play is any less exciting. . . . It's just that their adrenalin and emotions are high at opera."

CHAPTER TWO

Singing Greek Tragedy

From the very beginning of what we now call opera—Corsi's and Peri's lost scores for Rinuccini's *Dafne* (1594–1598), Peri's *Euridice* (1600), Monteverdi's *Orfeo* (1607)—up to the end of the eighteenth century, composers depended considerably for their plots on classical Greek legends, and often on the dramatic versions of those legends written by the three authors of early Greek tragedies whose works had survived.

From then through the nineteenth century—the years when most of the operas we still hear were performed—these ancient Greek sources were almost abandoned. They appeared to be too simple, too austere to carry the freight of a full-out romantic score, and the spectacular productions the age demanded. In the twentieth century, opera composers returned to these earliest dramatic models. Their fusion of simplicity with primal passion, their union of aesthetic purity with human experience at the edge of nightmare seemed once again attuned to the feelings and ideas that musicians wanted to express.

What little was known of Greek tragedy around 1600 led a number of Florentine humanists to experiment with various means of reviving it, or synthesizing something like it. They knew that it was sung, or chanted, or at least clearly declaimed in varying intervals and rhythms, which changed depending on the emotion expressed. The texts make clear that long set "arias" by the principal players (all of whom were men) alternated with antiphonal "duets" and more intensely poetic choral lyrics, which were sung in unison, we now believe, by an all-male chorus of fifteen. Other evidence suggests dancelike movements and instrumental accompaniment.

These and other elements of classic drama, translated through the preferred instruments and tonalities of the late sixteenth century, led to the stately, courtly, emotionally expressive earliest "operas," works intended to evoke (but in fact very different from) the fifth-century B.C. plays of Aeschylus, Sophocles, and Euripides. "It is very probable," writes the *New Oxford Companion to Music*, "that if we could hear a piece of Ancient Greek music accurately performed, we should regard it as bizarre, uncouth, and possibly barbaric."

These early Renaissance humanists, penetrated by their awe for Greek and Roman wisdom, were trying to recapture it whole. In their enlightened naïveté, they created something altogether new. As the seventeenth century progressed, the dawn freshness of this new creation became codified and regularized, and discovery gradually turned into a style. The novelty of Monteverdi's Orphic song grew into lavish, academic court entertainments: Lully's *Alceste* of 1674 is almost as extravagant as Versailles. But these entertainments were still frequently based on the prestigious texts of the Greek and Latin playwrights. The unique esteem in which *literae humaniores* (as Oxford University still calls Greek and Latin literature) were held throughout the eighteenth century helps to explain why artists like Corneille and Racine, Dryden and Pope, Lully and Gluck continued to turn to these texts for their sources and models. But the very elements in classical tragedy that had appealed to the aristocratic *camerata* of Florence rendered it unserviceable to the composers of a more popular and more spectacular form of opera, opera more dependent than theirs on elaborate vocal, orchestral, and scenic displays.

The thirty-two surviving Greek tragedies are more varied than some commentators pretend. But they did all make use of a simple, single-facade set (usually representing one place), and they played out a single action, usually the action of one day, more or less continuously. They are short—1,000 to 1,500 lines—and offer no intermission breaks. Athenian audiences could watch three of these plays, plus a comic afterpiece, in a single day. Dramatic, even horrible events occurred in them, but usually offstage. Such events were communicated to the audience after they had occurred, either by long-winded messengers or by *tableaux morts* rolled out on wheeled platforms. There were never more than three actors on stage or, for that matter, in a production. When a play called for more than three characters, the male "leads" simply changed masks and vocal tones. The fifteen chorus members, in three rows of five, chanted and danced on a level below that of the actors. Costumes were simple and traditional, all actors wore masks, and props were minimal. The entire effort was tightly focused, lucid, and direct, but in no way "realistic." Ritualized action and elevated language were designed to touch deep levels of the moral imagination, not to thrill the senses by lifelike or virtuoso effects.

Once the producers and the audiences of opera came to expect lavish period costumes and gorgeous stage settings, the fixed, flat stage houses and unity-of-action plots of the Greeks were of little more use. Mighty choruses of peasants and soldiers, onstage wars, duels, abductions, and apparitions; bel canto vocal showpieces full of trills and repeats; inset ballets; three- to five-act structures: it was impossible to draw such things out of or graft them onto classical roots.

Then the wheel turned again. The respectability of creating exotic Italo-French spectacles dwindled sometime before *Turandot*, and modern composers turned back to the Greeks. They might find what they needed in the stripped, other-worldly rituals of Aeschylus; in the balanced classical humanism of Sophocles; or in the neurotic passions and vernacular intensity of Euripides. At the same time, French and American playwrights (Cocteau, Anouilh, Giraudoux, Gide, Sartre, Jeffers, O'Neill), filmmakers (Cocteau again, Cacoyannis, Pasolini), and important stage directors in Europe and in America were rediscovering the Greek tragedians, whose work they frequently turned to novel political or psychological ends.

Most of the hundreds of classically derived operas have been dropped from the active repertory. I found reports of twenty-five operas based on the Greek tragedies performed on the world's opera stages (some on very small stages) between 1974 and 1984. Of these, four—Gluck's *Alceste*, after Euripides (1767), Cherubini's *Médée*, after Euripides (1797), Strauss's *Elektra*, after Sophocles (1909), and Stravinsky's *Oedipus Rex*, after Sophocles (1927)—lead the list. Looking at the ways these four composers and their librettists made use of their classical sources may teach us something of the flexibility and endurance of one of the oldest-known sources of human stories.

Although it's all about dying, Euripides's version of *Alcestis* is denied the title of tragedy by some commentators, because it ends happily and includes at least one semicomic scene.

Euripides's play doesn't have much of a "plot," in Aristotle's sense, or in ours. Instead, a "situation"—once established, in typical Greek-tragedy fashion, by events that occurred before the play begins—is described, demonstrated, examined, argued over, sung about, and danced about from various sequential perspectives, and then finally concluded—only to be overturned by a benevolent deity in the final scene.

The situation is the noble, magnanimous, and exemplary dying of Alcestis, queen of Thessaly, on behalf of and out of love for her husband Admetus. When the day appointed for *his* death had come, Admetus had managed to cheat the Fates and escape—but only on the condition that he come up with a substitute victim. No one else volunteering (including, to his disgust, his aged parents), his wife has offered herself in his stead. Her offer is accepted, and the day of the play is the day of her death.

Before the dying queen and grieving king even come on stage, we learn all of this from Apollo and Death, who argue out (and thereby reveal) the conclusion of the story; from a chorus of citizens, who chant about "the noblest woman alive"; and from Alcestis's servant maid, who reports in great detail the queen's sublime and pathetic preparations for her self-sacrifice. Alcestis is borne in on a litter, accompanied by her heartbroken spouse, for a magnificent death scene, which follows all of the ritual and rhythmic patterns expected of Attic tragedy. They exchange sad two-line remarks, then short six-line speeches. She has a long farewell "aria," with a choral response. He has a long answering aria, with a choral response. Then comes a sequence of line-for-line "repartee," or stichomythia, ending with broken lines, and her death. Their son recites two ten-line stanzas of grief. The body is carried inside. The chorus admonishes Admetus to be brave; he orders a year of public mourning. The chorus chants a moving four-stanza hymn to the dead.

This takes us only about halfway through the play, but it is all of Euripides's story that the operatic version uses, except for a subsequent scene of lamentation by Admetus and the "surprise" happy ending. Euripides varies and enlivens the time between Alcestis's death and the conclusion with a brilliantly bitter exchange between the king and his old father that is charged with violent hostility and rhetorical wit; and with the unexpected arrival of Heracles, en route to his fifth impossible labor. He is welcomed as a guest of the palace by a king too proud of his reputation as a host to turn him away. Heracles then proceeds to get drunk and disorderly in the house of sorrow. When he learns from an angry servant of the mourning he has interrupted, he goes to Alcestis's tomb and wrestles with Death for her body. (This we never see; we only hear of it.) Heracles then returns the body (alive) to an astonished and grateful husband.

Christoph Willibald, Ritter von Gluck (the title *Ritter*—"Count," more or less— was a papal honor, not a sign of noble birth), and his Italian librettist Raniero de' Calzabigi were obviously attracted to the potential for sad sweetness and lamentation in this story, which Gluck's pure, stately, finespun music expresses so eloquently. They cut out the father-son quarrel, and Heracles's crude intrusion, which would have clashed with their preferred texture of courtly emotions, silver-voiced airs, noble recitatives, and ritual, dancelike rhythms. To enlarge an undivided 1,100-line play into a satisfying 1767 Viennese court entertainment, they expanded backward in time, beginning their version not with Alcestis's death day, but with her husband's before hers. (Lully's seventeenth-century version takes the beginning back further still, to the battle in which her husband was wounded.) This allows for two separate sequences in which pitiful choruses sing in slow, Bach-like harmonies, repeating their woeful lines over and over. This also gives us the high drama of Alcestis's *act* of self-sacrifice on stage, proposed in her famous invocation of the spirits of hell: "Ombre, larve" in Italian, "Divinités du Styx" in the 1776 French. Gluck adds another scene in which Alcestis, alone with the infernal deities in a sacred wood, seals her vow with another gorgeous concert-piece aria, "Non vi turbate, no, pietosi dei," sad oboe breathing above, bass strings dragging like a heavy robe, treble strings singing with her, then echoing her silver-sweet coloratura repeats.

Gluck's second act opens with a joyful, major-key chorus celebrating Admetus's recovery, until his now-failing wife appears and counters his emotion-signaling music with hers. For the rest of the opera, then, we return to the single-minded sweet sadness of the opening scenes, until Apollo descends on a cloud—a genuine deus ex machina—and gives Admetus back his wife, because the gods have decided that "two such tender lovers deserve a better fate." "Oh marvel! Oh bliss!" sings the chorus. "Let us celebrate! Reign over us!" They then dance, court fashion, around their reunited and enthroned monarchs, both alive and well.

Euripides's original does have its Gluck-like speeches, its choruses full of noble generosity and all-suffusing grief. Alcestis's fears for her children's future and her tears on her marriage bed are parts of the opera as well as of the play. Responding to the emotional and theatrical needs of eighteenth-century Vienna and Paris, Gluck and Calzabigi converted Euripides's harrowing vision of death and the dark here-after into something tender, sweet, and sad. While enlarging the visible time and space of the original, they filtered out all jarring rivalries and hostilities, all comedy and crudity. Each artist wrote according to his own complex set of conventions, yet each managed to communicate a keenly felt set (although a different set) of human emotions. What the Greek playwright and the German composer have in common are a taste for artistic austerity, a sharp sense of emotional focus, and the Classical (or Neoclassical) commitment to an all-embracing formal order. If Gluck affects us more, it may only be because we can no longer hear Euripides's music.

Euripides's *Medea*, first performed seven years after his *Alcestis* (431 B.C.), is a more shocking, more astonishing, more emotionally devastating play, with a protagonist far stronger and more awesome than Alcestis. But it, too, is dramaturgically simple. It is an essentially plotless, single-minded work in which the one action—Medea's revenge-inspired murder of her enemies—is predicted, then announced, then debated, then carried out. The events that have occasioned her remorseless and bloody hatred have already occurred, and are quickly explained. Nothing delays her but (a) the need for a day's stay of her sentence of banishment to give her time to act; (b) the assurance of a safe place of refuge after she acts; and (c) the decision whether to murder her two children in order to spite their unfaithful father and save them from a miserable future. She obtains (a) from King Creon, one of her target-victims, by some ingenious role-playing and wheedling (the scene was taken over directly by Cherubini); (b) from her old friend King Aegeus of Athens, who happens by opportunely; and she resolves (c)—the decision to kill her children—by sheer power of independent womanly will, over the piteous arguments of her nurse and the chorus of her female supporters.

In one respect, *Medea* appears to offer a more promising operatic text than

Alcestis. The heroine's driving passion is more than noble, selfless, conjugal love. It is love thwarted: love, lust, and dedication (absolute, manic, lifelong), all betrayed. And the betrayed love, lust, and dedication are those of a barbarian princess who has already betrayed her own father and her homeland, murdered and chopped to pieces her own brother, and tricked other women into murdering and chopping to pieces their father. All of this Medea has done out of her passion for a man who is now casting her aside for a younger woman.

The story appealed to several opera composers of the new Italian–French, dramatic spectacle-and-aria school. One of the earliest among them was Luigi Cherubini, a Florentine who (like Lully) settled and made good in Paris. After a long lapse, his *Medea* (as its Italian version is spelled) returned to the world repertory in 1953, when Maria Callas sang the title role first in Florence, then in Milan, and, in later years, in Venice, Rome, Dallas, London, and the theatre of Epidaurus in Greece. Callas, a proud and passionate Greek-American who loved playing classic tragedy queens, also performed in Gluck's *Alceste* and his *Iphigénie en Tauride*, and in Pier-Paolo Pasolini's very free film adaptation of *Medea*.

The album notes to her recording of Cherubini's *Medea* state that "the libretto by François-Benoit Hoffmann closely follows Euripides," which is nonsense. A mid-eighteenth-century Neoclassical composer like Gluck may have expanded and sweetened Greek tragedies to suit his needs. But Cherubini, more an early Romantic than a late Classicist, together with his librettist, chopped, stuffed, sentimentalized, and theatricalized until very little is left that one can recognize from Euripides's original except the occasional fury of the protagonist and the barest events of her story. The result—especially as rewritten in 1854, when the spoken dialogue was transformed into recitative—is far more "Italian opera" than Greek tragedy. Tender sentiments (Jason's new love for Glauce, Medea's melting mother love for her treasured babes) count for at least as much musically as Euripidean lust, revenge, and hatred.

The chorus has grown far beyond Euripides's fifteen "women of Corinth" chanting and moving in sympathetic unison with their idol, far beyond Gluck's semiecclesiastical choir offering us refreshing interludes of grief, fear, or joy. It has become one of those mammoth, noisy, Italian opera mobs—in this case a mob of Corinthians all on the side of Jason, Creon, and Glauce (who is called Dirce in the 1854 Italian version), a mob that wants to tear the alien princess limb from limb. This chorus is primarily useful for Cherubini's grand-opera spectacle scenes, like the first act Procession of the Golden Fleece, or the lavish rituals in the Temple of Hera. The chorus last appears in a superspectacular finale, in which a screaming mob rushes toward the temple to murder the murderer, only to have Medea appear in the doorway, surrounded by three Furies, and brandishing over her head the knife with which she has just killed her children. "O visione d'horror!" they shout. "O terror!"

"*Barbara!*" spits Jason. "Where are my sons?"

"Their blood has avenged me!" replies the barbarous one.

"What had they done to you, *crudela?*"

"They were yours!"

"Oh ye gods. . . ."

Medea announces her departure for hell, having set fire to the temple, which bursts immediately into flame. The chorus shrieks as it flees, fortissimo: curtain.

Euripides's finale also may seem a little theatrically strained. His Medea appears suddenly on the roof of the single-set temple, with the corpses of her sons, about to escape from Athens in a chariot drawn by dragons that was given her by her grandfather the god. She and Jason parry a few final insults, the chorus throws up its hands at the unreadable will of the gods. But this still falls far short of the Paris Opera extravaganza of a temple suddenly bursting into flames, to all-out orchestral thunders.

Like Gluck and Calzabigi, Cherubini and Hoffmann had to "fill in backward," as it were, inventing new characters and episodes to expand Euripides's brief and brutal text into three acts. Their opera begins with Jason's arrival in Corinth, and his plans for a wedding with Glauce, who is never more than an unnamed presence in Euripides. In the opera, Creon, Jason, and Glauce sing and plot and fret among themselves, supported by priests, attendants, and their partisan chorus. In the play, Medea commands center stage throughout. The others exist only as reflections of her needs or as targets of her passion. Euripides's Jason makes his case against Medea so deviously and skillfully that we end up half believing him, which makes the play crackle with emotional potential. Cherubini's Jason is just a dumb romantic clod, totally alienated from and terrified of Medea, and in love with his new lyric soprano. Surprisingly, the most passionate single moment in Euripides—the messenger's 94-line description of Creon's and Glauce's ghastly deaths—has no counterpart in Cherubini. Jason and the chorus are whipped into such a musical frenzy on hearing of their deaths that no one could possibly pause for such a long descriptive aria.

Gluck's arias can still send chills up the spine, with their precise, almost organically emotional pulsing and flow. Cherubini's, despite a great deal of high-witchy coloratura, come across primarily as vocal display pieces, structured A-B-A-applause. Even the most vocally impressive of his arias, duets, and choruses sometimes make little dramatic sense—a departure from Monteverdi and Gluck that Italian/French opera was to accept for decades to come. At the conclusion of their first exchange (a searing scene in Euripides), Jason and Medea join in an emotionally meaningless duet about "the fatal golden fleece." Medea still has, in the opera, her great moments; passionate declarations that make ferocious demands on the voice. But they are inevitably followed by soft airs of maternal *tendresse*, as if no respectable eighteenth-century audience could tolerate displays of barbaric female bitchery unless they were instantly balanced by evidence of sentimental and domestic affections.

The stories are fundamentally the same, and something of Medea's primal intensity comes through. But comparing heart of work with heart of work, there is virtually nothing here of Euripides, or of the moral and artistic ideals of Greek tragedy generally. There is none of the "rage for order" that ties Gluck to his original; Cherubini's orchestra changes emotional gears with the awkward abruptness of a stick-shift learner-driver. That a few great dramatic-coloratura sopranos have found in this opera material worthy of their talents only demonstrates the great distance that separates Classical tragedy from good Romantic-declamatory early grand opera.[1]

By the time Hofmannsthal and Strauss took on Sophocles's *Electra*, they were free of the binding conventions under which both Gluck and Cherubini labored, free to ignore the presumptions of both Neoclassicism and grand opera, free to make whatever use they wished and were able to of what David Grene calls Sophocles's "best constructed and most unpleasant play." "The tightness and cogency of the plot," writes Grene (who has translated Sophocles), "go together with the absence of nobility and magnitude in the chief character in a way which never occurred again in the extant plays."

In some ways, it may appear as if, freed of conventional demands, these twentieth-century artists were able to come closer to the spirit and style of the Greeks.

---

1. Carl Dahlhaus has argued that the major differences between Euripides's original and the Cherubini-Hoffmann version of *Medea* derive from the fact that an early nineteenth-century, French bourgeois audience would never have understood the motives that drove Euripides's heroine to commit her horrible deeds. Dahlhaus sees the original Medea as driven to desperation by her exiled, expatriate, woman-without-a-country status: her (and by extension, her children's) loss of a home, a people, a polis, a political status—the worst of all calamities in the antique world. Compared to this, death was the lesser evil. Her grisly, vengeful actions would have made perfect sense to Euripides's contemporaries, Dahlhaus insists, but would have been incomprehensible to Cherubini's auditors in 1797 Paris without some form of psychological elaboration.

"To render comprehensible to a postrevolutionary public an intrigue whose historico-social grounding had long ceased to subsist, Hoffmann, Cherubini's librettist, performed a *psicologizzazione* totally alien to the Euripidean world, a psychological elaboration—and this is crucial—that was structurally dialectical, and which could therefore give life to the drama." This he did, writes Dahlhaus, primarily by building up the wedding preparations (and the actual wedding) of Creusa/Dirce and Jason as a counterplot to the omnipresent threat that Medea represents and by enriching the "human" natures of both Jason and Medea, thereby infusing the action with a "tragic irony" unknown in the original.

The great instrumental *concertati*, the introduction of Dirce and her attendants, the march and chorus of the Argonauts, the prayer scene of Act I, the trio and above all the wedding scene of Act II might all, taken by themselves, seem little more than the standard requisites of French opera tradition. But the dark shadow that the terror evoked by Medea throws over them creates a *gepresste Stimmung*, a "feeling of anguish" that Richard Hohenemser (Cherubini's first German biographer) thought he could hear in the music itself—but which, to tell the truth, is not really there.

Like Sophocles, they could present a single unbroken action set in a single place; no intermissions, no set changes, no subplots, no dramatized past action: total unity of time, place, and action. The opera, like the play, represents an awful, inexorable, arrow-straight progress from will to deed, the horrifying climax of Electra's many years of wretchedness and waiting.

She is here, as in Sophocles, unquestionably the protagonist. Every scene in the opera, like every scene in the play, is focused on or manipulated by her. In proper Greek fashion, the key episodes take the form of carefully crafted confrontations: Electra and her weakfish sister, Electra and her hated mother, Electra and her long-lost brother. The chorus, although individuated into separate characters (an effect the Greeks also achieved at times), is reduced once again to a small, coherent band of worried observers, the serving maids at Aegisthus's palace.

It cannot be denied that Hugo von Hofmannsthal (who wrote his German adaptation of the play first) and Richard Strauss (who then collaborated with him to transform it into an opera) follow closely Sophocles's scheme and action. What they did in addition is to "open it up," as other twentieth-century artists have done with other Greek tragedies, by trying to provide the characters with psychological motivations far in excess of anything Sophocles thought necessary. This enabled them to transform a supreme morality play into a hyper-Freudian horror story, communicated on heated currents of imagery, diction, and (especially) music far more willfully voluptuous and discordant than anything a fifth-century B.C. Greek artist, however inspired or demented, would have dreamed possible or useful.

Every element of Sophocles's tragedy that has led commentators to find it "unpleasant" or "ignoble" has been tightened by Hofmannsthal and Strauss to a pitch of intensity that renders their version far more ugly and shrill. Almost every element of formal control or ritual order that gives a bearable shape, a possibly salutary meaning to the Greek original has been dropped. What has been added in the way of language, characterization, and music only stresses the new sense of chaos and uncontrol.

The Electra of legend—like Sophocles's Antigone or Shakespeare's Hamlet— begins as a child burdened and obsessed by a sacred duty. She feels she must avenge her father's murder by punishing her guilty mother and her mother's sinful consort. Although she hopes to obtain the aid and support of her sister and her brother in the act, she feels strong-willed enough to kill the two elders herself if she must. "Necessary" as the deed may ritually be, all of the reasonable people around her (notably, in Sophocles, her sister and the chorus) beg her to calm down, to cast off her excess of grief, and to accept the existing order. Alas, she replies, she cannot. She is just lucid enough to know that she's obsessed. She takes her filial obligations with supreme seriousness, and regards Clytemnestra's and Aegisthus's sins as too mortal to be forgiven. As she answers the "reasonable" chorus:

In such a state, my friends, one cannot
be moderate and restrained nor pious either.
Evil is all around me, evil
is what I am compelled to practice.

Strauss's Elektra takes this obsession several steps further, to a point that may
well seem pathological. She lives with the dogs, digs in the ground with her
fingers for an axe, lewdly lusts for her young sister's flesh, and torments her
mother near to madness with detailed and grisly images of the death that awaits
her. Even Elektra's brother, Orest, when he finally recognizes her beneath her
rags, sunken cheeks, and filthy hair, sees that she is hopelessly far gone. In Strauss,
then, the drama begins not with a passionate agent of moral vengeance, but with a
madwoman.

In Sophocles, the surrounding characters are varied and personalized only insofar as the legend requires. Sophocles never individuates his characters very deeply,
but he usually allows to each a degree of self-justification sufficient to keep the
moral combat tense and alive. Chrysothemis is less vengeful and dedicated than
her sister but, in compensation, is more sweet, more sane, more sensible. In their
line-for-line exchanges in the play, it is impossible to say for certain which sister
makes the stronger case. Clytemnestra and Aegisthus *did* kill Agamemnon, but
they can offer good reasons for their deed. In her great showdown scene with
Electra, Clytemnestra comes off as neither a villain nor a fool. Both Orestes and
Aegisthus seem strong and reasonably noble, trapped by their roles in the legend.

Each of these in the opera is twisted into something neurotic or morally weak or
both. Orest seems at first frightened of his mad sister (as who would not be?) and
unwilling to act; later, he is a melting Tristan to her rapturous Isolde. Aegisth is
explicitly called a "woman" and shown as a blustering fool. Chrysothemis is
obsessed by her barrenness and desperately envies "normal," childbearing women.
Klytemnestra is transformed into a manic hag, bloated, diseased, and insanely
superstitious. She hangs her sick body with magic stones, and slaughters fields full
of beasts in the vain hope of dispelling the incubus that rides her in sleep.

The poetry of Sophocles is rich, varied, worldly, and expressive: dawning bird
song, blazing stars, and well-bred horses fill and broaden the lines. Even Electra
cries and laments in terms of Niobe and robbed nightingales, as well as axes and
blood and beds. The chorus offers her what is meant to be genuine and heartfelt
consolation:

Take heart, take heart, my child.
Still great above is Zeus,
who oversees all things in sovereign power.
Confide to him your overbitter wrath.

STRAUSS, *Elektra*, Danila Mastilovic (left) and Martha Mödl,
Berlin Staatsoper, 1964. Photograph by Marion Schöne.

The greatest "set piece" in the play is a pretend-messenger's fictional account of
Orestes's death in a chariot race, as brilliant and compelling as the comparable
accounts in Homer or Racine.

Hofmannsthal's verbal texture, by contrast, could not be more relentlessly
repulsive—particularly the language of his two madwomen. We are fed carrion,
blowflies, corpses, breeding vultures, hanged bodies, dog's slop—all in the early
lines of the first scene. Klytemnestra's similes are as grotesque as she is: "I will open
up my soul, as sick people do when, sitting by the pool in the evening, they expose
their ulcers and their suppurating wounds to the cool evening air." Elektra's lesbian
love song to her sister is a piece of overripe, *commencement de siècle* Viennese fruit.
Characters reach beyond language to laugh hysterically, whimper like wounded
animals, shriek in agony, far beyond the limits of Attic decorum. Elektra visualizes
her father's death, then her mother's and her other enemies', in scenes and lines
overflowing with blood, Blood, *Blut*, a hundred throats gushing with it, pouring
it out like pitchers, a surging wave of blood, a swollen stream of blood; kill the
horses, slaughter the hounds, purple fumes will rise in the air, and I will dance

around the pile of bodies! Meanwhile the music sweeps and surges and screams around her, every bit as hysterical as she is.

For all of the bare-bones similarities between their two *Electra*s, therefore, it is obvious that the imagination and moral vision of Hofmannsthal and Strauss are worlds removed from those of Sophocles. Virtually from start to finish, the unfettered music proves this more clearly than any verbal demonstration could do. The moral and physical horrors of Sophocles's "unpleasant" play are controlled and contained by a taut, shapely structure of strophe and antistrophe, answering lines and choral intervals, precise and complex rhythms small and large. The far more explicit horrors of the German opera are blasted and blatted, shrieked and squealed by voices and instruments meant (despite their underlying structures) to seem mad themselves, on the edge of splitting and bursting. Voluptuous waves of strings keep rolling up to manic bursts and fortissimo crescendos; then melting into sour-honey streams, punctuated by axe blows and whiplashes and clubfooted waltzes as called for by the text. Impelled by the pressures and insights of his own time, Hofmannsthal, like Freud, leapt willingly into the realm of the irrational. His nightmarish text, seconded by Strauss's nightmarish music, twisted Sophocles's mad heroine and her world into an unearthly (and riveting) case study in *psychopathia sexualis*.[2]

With Stravinsky's *Oedipus Rex*, we almost come home. Stravinsky, like Strauss, felt free of earlier operatic conventions. He *was* in fact far freer than Strauss (whose operas he despised), since Strauss was still very much a child of Wagner, and of post-Hapsburg Vienna. Igor Stravinsky was an international exile and wanderer, the supreme eclectic of Modern music, a man of broad and extraordinary culture

---

2. Of the 1910 London première of Strauss's *Elektra*, Ernest Newman wrote:

> If it were not for this strain of coarseness and thoughtlessness in him, he would never have taken up so crude a perversion of the old Greek story as that of Hugo von Hofmannsthal. . . . To make a play a study of human madness, and then to lay such excessive stress upon the merely physical concomitants of madness, is to ask us to tune our notions of dramatic terror and horror down to too low a pitch. Strauss, of course, revels in this physical, and therefore more superficial, side of the madness. . .
>
> Much of the music is as abominably ugly as it is noisy. . . . The talk about complexity is wide of the mark. The real term for it is incoherence, discontinuity of thinking.

Returning to his attack after some contemptuous taunting in print by George Bernard Shaw, who admired *Elektra* (their exchange on the subject ran through seven published letters and was taken up again two years later), Newman further defined what he saw as the weaknesses of *Elektra*: on Strauss's side, "ugly, slap-dash vocal writing, which he attempts to carry through by means of orchestral bravado, a crude pictorialism, ineffective violence simulating strength, a general coarsening of the tissue of the music, a steady deterioration in invention"; on Hofmannsthal's, "a most unpleasant specimen of that crudity and physical violence that a certain school of modern German artists mistake for intellectual and emotional power."

The Newman-Shaw exchange was largely a trading of personal insults between two self-assured and influential critics, which readers of the time no doubt relished. On the whole, I believe that Newman had the better of it, but that may only be because I share his response to the opera.

who could put his hand to almost any text or idea and find a way to turn it into "pure" and yet highly expressive music—music that in the end often seems almost unlocatable in time or place. Sublimely self-confident, he worried as little as have most Modernist masters about appealing to the popular majority; making an exception for his exciting early ballet music, the popular majority has returned the favor. *Oedipus Rex*, which he calls an "opera-oratorio," is defiantly static, antitheatrical, and unspectacular, by opera house standards; which may be one reason few operagoers get a chance to see and hear it.

This is a pity, because in it Stravinsky forces us back very close to what I believe was the bone-and-blood appeal (and the terror) involved in the original, fifth-century B.C. experience of a major Greek tragedy. In *Oedipus Rex*, wrote Virgil Thomson, Stravinsky was able to "produce an oratorio about a Greek tragedy that is closer to the original aims of opera than anything else written. . . . The whole does exactly what the inventors of opera in Florence (around the year 1600) had hoped opera would do. It revives a Greek tragedy convincingly."

Stravinsky does everything he can to distance and ritualize the action, or non-action. He asks the singers to wear masks, and to stand rigidly on little individual podiums ("I abhor verismo"). The chorus is to sit cowled and faceless in a semicircle behind them, reading from scrolls. He had Jean Cocteau write (and rewrite) a much-shortened French version of Sophocles's play, which he then shortened some more, and had translated back—into classical Latin! In exile from Russia, he still felt the other Western languages were too alien for him to use. Ciceronian Latin seemed pure and universal, and gave him a wonderfully clear structure of sounds and syllables to set to music. Stravinsky's antirealistic "distancing" devices are not those of fifth-century B.C. Athens. But his end result may come closer to its intent (as Virgil Thomson claimed) than that of any of the other composers I have discussed. He was, at the time he wrote *Oedipus Rex*, committed to an orthodox Christian faith and a Classical aesthetic, and he chose the play, the form, and the language in the hope of making a universal and archetypal musical statement.

There is no need to discuss what Stravinsky and Cocteau added, because they added nothing. The entire work (performed unbroken) takes about fifty minutes, and gains in urgency and impact from its concentration. Stravinsky was persuaded to add a vernacular "narrator," who breaks in between episodes to sum up the plot ahead in the audience's own language. The role—originally played by Cocteau himself—has been attempted by a number of distinguished stage actors, from Ralph Richardson and Michael Hordern to Michel Piccoli and Maria Casarès. Stravinsky later professed to hate the device, and I prefer the work without it. No matter how stately and sonorous the speaker, these little "subtitles" have the momentum-killing effect of television commercials interrupting a great late-night movie.

The episodes occur in the same order as they do in the play: the chorus's plea and Oedipus's promise concerning the plague; Creon's report on the oracle and Oedipus's fatal vow; Tiresias's rejected revelation of the truth; Jocasta's unintended "leak" concerning the murder at the crossroads (a climactic moment in Stravinsky's opera); the messenger's and the shepherd's subsequent revelations (delivered simultaneously in the opera); the chorus's report of Jocasta's and Oedipus's respective fates, and its farewell to the blinded king. Each contains far fewer words than the dramatic original; details, arguments, explanations, and imagery have been cut, so that the music can work its own emotional effects. In a few cases, the cuts are so extreme that the speakers make little sense—the Messenger, for no apparent reason, adds to his message of Polybus's death, "He was not Oedipus's father." What the chorus declaims may be, in this shorthand form, more "obvious" than in the original, especially when they repeat it over and over. Most of the texts, however reduced, do seem to convey the essence of the play, and they seem, when sung, no less awesome and terrible.

Whether Stravinsky's opera-oratorio is an adequate "substitute" for Sophocles's play is for the listener to decide. However eclectic, Stravinsky still works in a recognizable and highly individual musical idiom, which may seem to some admirers of Greek tragedy too cleverly "modern" and formulaic, or too mock-barbaric, or simply too loud and insistent to equal, represent, or do justice to the famous original.

I find the modern musical version apt, direct, and powerful. Words that matter most (*sciam:* "I will know!") are hammered in mounting repetition over Stravinsky's inexorable drumbeats. Key verbs in particular—*ulciscere*, "avenge" (Laius); *reperere*, "discover" (the murderer); *luere*, "purge" (Thebes)—are driven in like steel nails. The dreaded words of discovery are uttered like the crucial verse in a Holy Week Passion:

Natus sum, quo nefastum est;
Concubi cui nefastum est;
Cecidi quem nefastum est;
Lux facta est.

Accursed was I born;
Accursed was my marriage;
Accursed was my shedding of blood;
Now comes the light.

The last words are declaimed to a descending, crazed clarinet fanfare. There is something ecclesiastical, like a baroque cathedral service with organ, chorus, and soloists, about the wavelike rise to crucial lines over an irresistible, almost primitive ostinato of chorus and percussion:

Rex rex rex, peremptor regis est!

A king, a king, a king is the murderer of the king!

To rivet in our minds the importance of a line or phrase, Stravinsky takes it and plays with it; has it chanted, rising and falling, to "scary" harmonies and strange, spidery, noodling instrumental overlays; then drops to a white, eloquently speaking silence. Oedipus, Jocasta, Tiresias, and Creon all speak-sing in free semirecitative (different for each character) that is at once "operatically" compelling and dramatically precise.

When Jocasta lets slip the "crossroads" clue—Laius was killed at a crossroads; "Laius in trivio mortuuos"—the music slows down creepily, and the chorus picks up "trivium, trivium," "crossroads, crossroads," like the beat of Oedipus's own conscience. It then plays it against Jocasta's insistent line, "Oracles always lie," over and over and over. The pace slows down, grows more ominous, the drums become more threatening. Oedipus, urgent and frightened, admits in short gasps that he *did* once kill an old man at a crossroads. Jocasta, now wild and shrill, much too fast, begs him to come home at once. Their duet, over the now near-maddening death-drums, the calling horns and lower brass, is a capital instance of Stravinsky's ability to achieve with his musical means much of the moral anxiety and mortal terror of Sophocles's 2,400-year-old verbal structure.

(1984)

CHAPTER THREE

When Opera Was Still Serious

Opera seria is something today's average operagoer is more likely to read about than to hear or see. The exceptions—all of which have benefited from revivals in recent years—are the operas of Handel; Mozart's *Idomeneo* and *La clemenza di Tito;* and, insofar as the term can be legitimately extended into the nineteenth century, Rossini operas like *Tancredi*, *Maometto II* (later rewritten as *The Siege of Corinth*), and *Semiramide*. In the past twenty years, British and American audiences have had the opportunity to see all of these works, including a broad sampling of Handel's operas and (in a few places, at least) Vivaldi's *Orlando furioso*. We may finally be developing a clearer sense than our parents and grandparents could have had of the peculiar nature and mixed attractions of this old-fashioned, once incredibly popular form.

For the better part of the eighteenth century, opera seria *was* opera, for all of the world (except France) that knew opera existed. Thousands of ad hoc recitative-and-aria constructions were hammered together for court and commercial theatres all over Europe, most of them named after and dealing with kings, queens, princes, or princesses of ancient or legendary realms, their dynastic rivalries, and their tangled loves.

All of these were performed in Italian, no matter what the local language. They were built around action-stopping, stand-and-deliver solo vocal showpieces of the sort we now call "da capo" arias—arias in which the first of two short stanzas, usually made up of four lines sung several times each and repeated, is then repeated again "from the top," or da capo, at the end of the song, in a frequently spectacular display of whatever grace notes, trills, scale runs, shakes, and unbelievably long-held breaths the singer can manage.

"The secret of this stupefying popularity tends to elude us," one modern music historian has written. Why, for the better part of a hundred years, did people in

London, Vienna, and Prague, let alone every city in Italy, apparently so crave this form of entertainment that they often went to see it two or three times a week? Why did they expect *new* opera seria every year (which is the reason so many of them had to be written), but then sit through the same ones night after night? And why, with relatively few exceptions (such as the operas just noted), have most of them disappeared?

It's easier to talk about opera seria than it is to define it. In *Handel and the Opera Seria*, Winton Dean uses the term to mean "all Italian opera other than opera buffa during Handel's lifetime [i.e., 1685–1759]." But you can get by with that only if you're writing about Handel. The poets and composers who wrote opera seria didn't even start calling it that until sometime around 1785. I'm using the term to mean all totally noncomic operas with Italian texts between the first by Alessandro Scarlatti and Handel (1705–1707) and the late-blooming "heroic" operas of Rossini (1813–1823).

One man's name so dominates every discussion of opera seria that one is tempted to use him as a guide, and build a definition around his life and work. Pietro Metastasio, né Trapassi, was a clever grocer's son born in Rome in 1698. From the age of eleven, he was adopted and carefully educated by a learned humanist who (correctly) saw in him the promise of a major poet. After writing for Italian theatres seven immensely successful *melodramme*, or *dramme per musica*—plays in verse *intended* to be set to music—Metastasio was appointed court poet to Emperor Charles VI at Vienna in 1730. Particularly admired by Charles's daughter, Empress Maria Theresa, Metastasio lived in Vienna in fame and comfort until his death in 1782. In Vienna, he wrote twenty more plays-for-opera, as well as poems, texts for cantatas, oratorios or *azione teatrale*, 2,500-plus letters, and essays on Aristotle and the Italian epic poets.

Alfred Loewenberg, in *Annals of Opera*, cites 107 surviving operas written to Metastasio's texts. But Loewenberg estimates that Metastasio's 27 plays (it is demeaning and imprecise to refer to them simply as librettos) were set to music "far more than a thousand times." Between 70 and 100 operas (authorities differ) made use of his best play, *Artaserse*, as a text; perhaps 80 more of *Alessandro in India;* at least 60 of his first original play, *Didone abbandonata*, of 1724; and at least 50 of *L'Olimpiade* (*The Olympic Games*).

The odds are that you've never heard, perhaps never even heard of, any of these operas—although a decent Hungarian recording of Antonio Vivaldi's setting of *L'Olimpiade* (Venice, 1734) was made for the tricentennial of the composer's birth in 1978, when the opera was also performed in Turin. The one Metastasio title you may know is *La clemenza di Tito*, which was first set to music by Antonio Caldara for Vienna in 1734 and later by forty to sixty others—including Mozart, whose version was first performed in Prague in 1791, just three months before he died.

Mozart also made use of Metastasio's text for *Il re pastore*, and of his alterations to Giovanni da Gamerra's *Lucio Silla* (composed when Mozart was sixteen). He set to music a serenata and an oratorio by Metastasio and, as single songs or vocal ensembles, more than twenty of his poems, most of them taken from his plays. Vivaldi wrote music for three of Metastasio's plays. Handel also wrote music for three, and new arrangements for the scores of four others. Gluck, who is supposed to have led a rebellion against Metastasio, set a total of fifteen. His plays have been "musicked" into operas by Haydn, Cherubini, Cimarosa, J. C. Bach (who used eight of them), Pergolesi, Nicola Piccinni, Baldassare Galuppi, and Thomas Alexander Arne.

These are the better known. Most of the Italian and German opera composers who spread Metastasio's characters, plots, and poetry all over Europe have passed into the quiet possession of music historians: Antonio Caldara, Leonardo Vinci, Leonardo Leo, Johann Adolf Hasse, Niccolò Jommelli, Tommaso Traetta.

As someone tends to do at least once a generation, Metastasio and his fellow "Arcadians"—notably Apostolo Zeno, the man who preceded him as court poet at Vienna—set out in the years around 1700 to reform opera of its more egregious and irrational abuses. What these reformers found distasteful in Italian opera of the generation before theirs was the great distance it had sunk from the literary-humanist, Neoclassical ideals of the Florentine gentlemen who had invented opera just a century before.

The reformers, originally a group of Rome-based literati, objected to the casual infusion of comic characters into tragic or heroic plots, which could swell casts to twenty or more. They objected to the excessive dependence on "miraculous" events—sea monsters rising out of the waves, gods descending in four-horse chariots, distant planets, transformation scenes, sets that rose and fell at the whim of sorcerers. They objected to five-hour-long spectacles containing forty to sixty arias. They denounced the wild and tangled plots of bastardized classic stories, which sometimes sound less like opera than like the extravagant and facetious rewritings of fairy tales still popular as Christmas "pantomimes" in England. (The "corrupt," crowd-pleasing style is still visible in the operas of Handel, who tended to ignore dramatic reforms.)

But what had the reformers to offer in place of Italian Baroque opera—what one critic of 1706 called this "monstrous union of a thousand improbabilities"?

You can learn what most opera seria plots are like by reading the collected works of Pietro Metastasio; I stopped, I confess, after fifteen plays. In each of these, five or six characters are royal, noble, or at least heroic. The sixth or seventh—there are never more than seven named parts—may be a confidant(e), who is there to permit his or her master or mistress to express intimate emotions, as Desdemona does to Emilia. Occasionally one has need of a messenger to report offstage horrors ("É morto?" "É morto!").

The lead singers—who usually numbered, in those days, two male (i.e., castrato) sopranos and two females—had to include at least four royal-type lovers. (High vocal ranges equal love.) These characters are either *not* in love with the people who love them, or are prevented from consummating their love by affairs of state, disguises, promises previously made, or the edicts of unfeeling royal fathers. This permits plots of sustained tension and complication, and numerous occasions for "broken-heart" arias—arias of sensual torment and self-pity that display soprano voices so well. The addition of a fifth or even a sixth unhappy secret admirer, or *amanta occulta* (who may also be the confidant or messenger), can add to the intrigue, and provide more opportunity for poignant vocal confessions of unrequited love.

Lower vocal ranges are reserved for royal fathers, secondary generals, and villains. Their job is to stir up the nonamatory portions of the plot (palace coups, wars with rival kingdoms, threats of tyrannicide—although a great many arias are about death, no major character should actually *die* in an opera seria, because we want them all on stage for the finale); and to do all they can to keep the proper lovers from pairing off before the *ultima scena*, when (as a rule) everything comes out all right.

In three of Metastasio's twenty-seven *melodramme*, good people *do* die before the end, although for noble and heroic reasons. Far more often, some sudden revelation ("Ecco tuo figlio!" "Ecco mio padre!") dissolves the barriers that have separated the two sets of lovers for three stressful, music-filled acts. The villain, smitten by the sublime goodness of everyone on stage, instantly reforms. The tyrant-king or emperor now finds himself obliged by his own laws to order the death of the malefactors—frequently including his best-beloved friend, even his own son. Instead, he has a last-moment inspiration of *superlative* goodness (hence, "The Clemency of Titus"—or of Hadrian, Caesar, Cyrus, Alexander, or Arta-xerxes), forgives everybody, and is praised in a quick closing chorus.

Metastasio does not, however, just write the same plot over twenty-seven times, as his detractors have claimed. In each of his best plays, he rethinks the conventions, comes up with a new and provocative set of circumstances, and works hard to make us *care* about his highminded, overemotional, melodrama-trapped characters.

Since the mid-nineteenth century, it has been de rigueur to sneer at the simplistic, plot-complicating recitatives of opera seria. But I found many of these sequences (some of which are set in elaborate verse forms, for composers to make the most of) to be impressively dramatic. In *Alessandro nell'Indie*, for example, Metastasio's second most popular text, a king and a queen of rival Indian kingdoms—both under heavy pressure from Alexander the Great—share scenes of tender, then bitter verses, love/hate exchanges that cry out for the melodies and orchestral commentaries of a master musical dramatist. Caesar's confrontation with Cato in *Catone in Utica* is great theatre by any standard, musical or not.

The most challenging set of rules for the poet of an opera seria dealt with the arias. Every lead singer had to have at least four of these, properly spaced throughout the opera; secondary singers got one to three. (There were few duets or ensembles; star singers of the time did not like sharing.) Each aria—though this was frequently not the case—was supposed to convey a different, set, single emotion (rage, jealousy, grief), which exploded out of the foregoing recitative. No two arias in a row were to express similar emotions. Each aria was to be followed at once by the *exit* of its singer, to avoid breaking up the recitative and to encourage maximum applause. Before the end of the century, frustrated composers were breaking many of these rules.

You can understand why. Try to write a serious, rational, didactic (and entertaining) Neoclassical happy-ending verse drama, containing between twenty and twenty-five passionate exit speeches (each of these speeches running to eight rhyming lines of seven to ten syllables each); make those lines dramatically meaningful; and somehow keep the action surrounding them continuous and gripping. "Quel labirinto!" as one character in *L'Olimpiade* remarks on the plot he finds himself in.

One further bend to the labyrinth: just after being condemned to death, rejected by your lover, or betrayed by your best friend—all good motives for a passionate exit-aria explosion—you must sing four lines (sometimes five or three; even two, in Handel) expressing your plight; sing them again, modulating to the dominant or the relative minor; and then sing them a third time, back to the tonic. Then sing a second stanza, in a related rhythm or key, perhaps taking back, qualifying, or reflecting on your original four lines. And then assert (da capo) your original outburst more passionately than ever, over and over and (singing your poor heart out) over again. In this way, eight short lines can be made to fill up five to ten minutes of vocalizing on stage—which is what people came to hear.

In one of Cleopatra's best-known arias in Handel's *Giulio Cesare*, what she is saying in her first two-line stanza is "Unless you show me pity, just heaven, I will die." What she *sings* is "Se pietà di me non senta, giusto ciel, io morirò, giusto ciel io morirò, io morirò giusto ciel, giusto ciel io morirò, se pietà di me non senta, giusto ciel il morirò, giusto ciel io morirò, giusto ciel io morirò, se pietà di me non senta, giusto ciel, giusto ciel io morirò, giusto ciel, giusto ciel io morirò, giusto ciel io morirò." After a short break for two other lines and ritornellos, she sings these same words again.[1]

Some aria texts are purposely broken up into stuttering, schizophrenic frag-

---

1. Mozart—at least the teenaged Mozart—was not above such "relentless" repetitions, as a recent biographer has called them. "Cinna's B-flat aria in *Lucio Silla* . . ." writes Wolfgang Hildesheimer, "has 281 bars of music for eight dreary lines of text. . . . Tamiri [in *Il rè pastore*] in her A-major aria 'Se tu di me fai dono' (No. 11), asks the same question, 'Perchè son'io crudele?' fully eighteen times."

ments. Others take the form of a "simile" aria, or *aria di paragone*, in which a confused, tormented, or ecstatic actor compares his or her emotional state to that of a river, a raging sea, a mother tiger, a serpent, or a drifting, abandoned ship. Other verses for arias are written to encourage picturesque or coloristic musical effects by including words for nightingales, zephyrs, trumpets, or death. Clever analysts like Eric Weimer have studied closely the musical settings of these supposedly formula-bound arias, to demonstrate how well their mellifluous syllables and translatable images lend themselves to musical composition, and how well certain composers rose to the challenge. "Metastasio's measures," wrote Dr. Burney, the eighteenth-century music historian and critic, "in the songs with which he terminates the scenes of his dramas, are so sweet and varied, that they have often suggested to musical composers, by the mere perusal, melodies of every kind."

Even though most of them have been lost, there are still far too many opera seria scores around for one to generalize safely about their music. Some of their basic features (the number and length of arias, the da capo form itself, the nature and degree of orchestral participation, the use of ensembles, the role of chorus and ballet) changed considerably as the eighteenth century drew to a close. *Idomeneo* (1781) has only twelve arias, but it has nine choral numbers, three marches, a ballet, and three ensembles. By *La clemenza di Tito* (1791), Mozart had cut the arias down to ten, half of them *senza da capo*, all with minimal word repeats or superfluous decorations. He added three duets, three trios, five choral numbers, and a march. Both operas include subtly scored and richly accompanied recitatives. In both, the orchestra plays a major dramatic role.

Before Mozart, few opera seria composers attempted to organize their chains of jewel-like arias and linking recitatives into musically unified wholes, or even to tie together series of numbers or scenes. Their operas were, as one critic puts it, the sum of their parts: nothing more and nothing less. What distinguishes them musically is what Donald Grout calls "that instinctive adaptation to the qualities and limitations of the voice which is the gift of nearly all Italian composers."

At the time they were written, no one regarded these particular combinations of words and music as holy works of art. The words inevitably came first—*prima le parole, e poi la musica*, to reverse the title of Salieri's buffa—and were regarded as more important and lasting than the scores, which might vary for every new production. Almost every opera composer of the century recycled old tunes (his own or others') into new operas. Handel's 1732 pasticcio arrangement of Leonardo Leo's *Catone in Utica* includes a few arias by the composer of record, but even more by Hasse, Porpora, Vivaldi, and Vinci, borrowed from a dozen different operas.

The texts would be altered as well, to suit the special conditions of any new performance. Even the great Metastasio agreed, under protest, to rewrite four of his early hits to satisfy the demands of a celebrated castrato who insisted on fewer but longer arias. Our painstaking researches in quest of authentic or "definitive" scores would have made no sense to eighteenth-century opera composers, whose work was often seen as no more important than that of the set designer, and considerably less important than that of the singers. Their music was often regarded by its audiences as people today might regard the music at a circus or a film, which is one reason so relatively little of it has survived.

In fact, the expectations and behavior of audiences explain some of the stranger features of opera seria. In Italy during the eighteenth century, and probably in most other countries as well, going to the opera was regarded as a social, rather than an aesthetic, experience. (What's that? You say the same is true today?) Well-to-do patrons could rent boxes for a whole season, decorate them to their own taste, and turn them into small private living rooms where they could receive friends, chat, play cards, eat, and drink—all *during the performance*. "Chess is marvellously well adapted to filling in the monotony of the recitatives," observed a French visitor to Naples, "and the arias are equally good for interrupting a too assiduous concentration on chess." Because they knew the plots already, and weren't there for the story in any case, operagoers tended to talk through the recitatives (which grew shorter and shorter as the century progressed), and might turn toward the stage only to hear one of their favorite singers performing a big number. The whole experience was probably closer to an evening at Vauxhall Gardens, or a café concert in Paris (with occasional turns by a visiting celebrity singer) than to an evening at most opera houses today.

Under these circumstances, it was ultimately the celebrity singers, the *primi uomini* and *prime donne*, who called the shots. Paid ten times as much as the poet or composer, they were what people had come to see and hear. These celebrities were expected to add their own vocal ornaments to the written score, pull out all stops for the da capo repeats, and improvise display pieces for the breaks, or cadenzas— which might include intricate note-for-note "duels" with a virtuoso flautist or trumpeter.

Throughout the century, angry poets, composers, and critics complained about the cavalier ways in which singers treated would-be serious operas. During the orchestral ritornellos between stanzas of their arias, singers might walk about, chat, adjust their costumes, or take snuff. They might bow to or joke with their friends in the audience. They sometimes interjected favorite arias of their own, totally irrelevant to the plot. It was the star singers, not the composer-conductor, who set the pace of an aria. It was for them that new music had to be written each season, for them that composers had to come up with music carefully adapted to their individual vocal ranges, skills, and idiosyncrasies. It was the singers who insisted on shorter and shorter recitatives, longer and longer da capo sections, and the extravagant multiplication of repeats, in order to have maximum opportunity to display their vocal prowess.

This short summary of what opera seria was, on the page and on the stage, may begin to suggest some of the reasons its silvery bubble burst. Not surprisingly, the aesthetically detached, primarily social, canary-fancier or café-concert relationship of upper-class audiences to opera seria gradually diminished: a vogue, briefly a craze, spectators tired of its growing extravagance, the old-fashioned sameness of it all, and turned to other amusements. Even the better late-Metastasian composers, like Jommelli and Traetta, began to protest against the everlasting obligation to set the same old texts again and again—texts that seemed less and less suitable for the kind of music they wanted to write.

Although they were back by Rossini's time, castrati were banned after Napoleon invaded Italy in 1796. But it was generally agreed by those in a position to compare that none of their successors had measured up to the incredibly gifted male sopranos of 1720–1760, like Senesino and Farinelli. Without virtuosi castrati (who made the works seem freakish to the nineteenth century in any case), most opera seria was long regarded as unperformable.

Other changes, external and internal, helped bring about the demise of opera seria, or at least its transformation into something else. Italian opera buffa kept increasing in quality and popularity throughout the century, cresting with works by Paisiello, Haydn, Cimarosa, and, of course, Mozart and Rossini. Spared the need for classical, moralizing plots and sheer vocal display, comic operas grew to be more recognizably "human" and audience-involving than opera seria. This led to a serious split in the Italian theatregoing public. (A whole subgenre of comic opera was devoted to parodying opera seria—a tendency still audible in *Così fan tutte*.)

The rise of the symphony and the oratorio, and a growing preference for works in their own language, began to alienate German and English audiences from the long-dominant "Italian opera" mode. Paris, and French taste generally (which involved, among other things, greater use of chorus and ballet, and less dependence on vocal virtuosity), gradually took over the cultural center stage. After the French Revolution, the court theatres and aristocratic patronage that had supported opera seria began to wane. And the radically new works of Gluck and Mozart let people know that something better was possible.

After almost a century of neglect, the revival of opera seria began in Germany with seven performances of Handel operas at the Göttingen Festival in the 1920s, and with the efforts of the Halle Festival, another Handel shrine. Winton Dean traces the British rediscovery of Handel's operas to an "almost accidental" production in 1955, which led to the creation of the Handel Opera Society in London. Both Halle and the Handel Opera Society are now apparently committed to mounting all of Handel's thirty-nine surviving operas, and to "operatizing" as many of his oratorios as they can.

For the two hundred years before 1955, Dean noted, there had been only three English stage revivals of Handel's operas. Thirty years later, during the Handel bicentennial year of 1985, one could (with a little traveling) have seen at least sixty-seven fully staged professional productions of twenty-two Handel operas—including nine different versions of *Giulio Cesare*—as well as operatic stagings of twelve of his odes and oratorios. Companies around the world now perform Handel's operas every year, which has done more than anything else to accustom modern audiences to the conventions of opera seria. Although no threat yet to *Aida*, *Bohème*, or *Carmen*, Handel's *Giulio Cesare* and *Orlando* are inching up to the status of "repertory staples."

The summer festivals at Salzburg in Austria and Glyndebourne in England helped open the floodgates, before and during the bicentennial celebrations of Mozart's birth in 1956, to a worldwide deluge of his operas that has not yet diminished. His two best serious operas, *Idomeneo* (which tends to be called either "the best opera seria ever written," or a work so innovative it falls outside the genre altogether) and *La clemenza di Tito*, only returned to the regular repertory lists after revivals at these two festivals in 1949–1952. Since then, each of these operas has been recorded several times. Each is now produced by several companies or festivals a year—since 1970, in more or less accurate versions. (The United States tends to catch on to these rediscoveries a decade or so late.) The teenaged Mozart's lesser opere serie also get an occasional hearing nowadays, but then so does almost anything he wrote.

Gluck, whose most commonly performed works *do* fall outside the opera seria tradition, has been a persistent, if minor, repertory regular in France and Germany and, to a lesser degree, in other countries as well. Rossini's "historical romantic" operas, such as *William Tell*, have never quite fallen out of the repertory, but his early-nineteenth-century "heroic" operas (*Semiramide, Tancredi*, etc.) only began to reappear in the mid-1960s, when people like Joan Sutherland and Marilyn Horne—prime movers in the Handel opera revival as well—decided to risk singing them.

Until such singers appeared, one commentator after another had declared that opera seria was hopelessly beyond resurrection. Fifty years ago, it was simply taken for granted, by critics like E. J. Dent, that twentieth-century audiences would not tolerate "soprano heroes" of either sex. Even if they would, wrote another critic as late as 1955, "we haven't the singers able to satisfy the demands of ability, span, and expressiveness, not to mention the improvised embellishments."

So far, the opera seria revival hasn't moved very far beyond Handel, Mozart, Gluck, and Rossini. Other eighteenth-century composers—Piccinni, Galuppi,

Pergolesi, Cimarosa, and Paisiello—are well represented on the production lists, but almost exclusively by their comic operas. Since 1950, the opere serie of Vivaldi (ten productions of eight operas, according to *Opera* magazine) and of Haydn (seventeen productions of four operas) have attracted the most revivalist attention. Four of Alessandro Scarlatti's opere serie have been produced a total of nine times. In all three of these cases, I suspect that the popularity of the composer's non-dramatic work had something to do with the choice.

Jommelli's *Fetonte* was given at Stuttgart in 1986 and at La Scala in 1988, his *La schiava liberata* at Amsterdam, Naples, and Berkeley. Traetta's *Antigone* was given at Florence, Mannheim, Valle d'Istria, and Spoleto; his *Ifigenia in Tauride*, at Valle d'Istria. J. C. Bach's *Amadis de Gaule* (perhaps more a French opera than an Italian) has had three revivals; his *Temistocle*, two; his *Lucio Silla*, one. Two of Hasse's operas have had staged revivals since 1975; a third was done in concert, a fourth on the BBC. Salieri's grandiose, Gluckian *Les Danaïdes* had a bicentenary revival in Perugia in 1984. Carl Heinrich Graun's *Montezuma* was brought back by the Berlin State Opera in 1982 and 1989, and performed at Menotti's Spoleto/Charleston Festivals in 1986–1987. Add two Giovanni Bononcinis, one each by Leo, Gasparini, Piccinni, and Sacchini, and a couple of early serious works by Cherubini and Pergolesi. Published scores of such works are becoming increasingly available, but the record of modern performance is still very thin.

When reviewing these rare revivals, critics often feel compelled to comment on how tedious and uninspired most opera seria seems to be, how far short of Handel, Gluck, and Mozart these lesser men fall: "A 20th Century audience cannot be expected to take an early opera seria [like Scarlatti's *Mitridate*] quite seriously." "Taken as a whole, they [the arias of Hasse's *Attilio regolo*] only revealed the incomparably finer and more subtle evocation of drama, the instrumental and vocal variety of Handel." "The value of the evening [J. C. Bach's *Temistocle*] lay in the opportunity to glimpse an operatic epoch almost forgotten due to the later splendour of Mozart."

The conventions of any art form grow out of or in response to the ruling ideas and social conditions of its time and place. Depending on our distance from that time and place, these conventions may seem to us puzzling, alien, freakish, even disgusting. Piled one on another, they can create a wall between us and the work we find impossible, or at least not worth the effort, to scale.

The chief conventions that still block access for many people to eighteenth-century opera seria are (1) the use of female-quality voices (whether women's or countertenors', castrati being no longer with us) for mature and manly heroes like Caesar and Titus, Achilles and Alexander; (2) the action-halting effect of so many long set-piece arias, which tend to kill the pace and continuity of a drama, and turn operas into concerts; (3) the vapidity of many of the aria texts, which become all the more threadbare as the same words are repeated eight, ten, or twelve times, and as their vowels are stretched out for dramatically meaningless melismas; and (4) the foreign-language recitatives, which are often of minimal musical or dramatic interest.

The plots, I think, for all of their highmindedness and complexity, are rarely a problem. Any operagoer who can tolerate the plots of most works in the current repertory—*Turandot*, let us say, *Parsifal*, or *Die Frau ohne Schatten*—should have no trouble with Metastasio's. Some of Handel's plots, I concede, can be more than usually silly, even for opera. But most opera fans, today as in 1730, are willing to put up with silly plots in exchange for good music, well sung and well played, combined with impressive and appropriate staging.

The walls of convention that surround opera seria can be surmounted with the right kind of support from the people who produce it. Correct orchestration, performance style, and vocal ranges, I think, are the right way to start—within the limits of what is possible, and the freedoms the eighteenth century granted itself. There's no point in trying to sell eighteenth-century opera by trying to make it sound nineteenth century. When the acting, singing, and staging are coherent, strong, and full of conviction—whatever the chosen imagery or theatrical style—I find I can quite easily accept a Janet Baker or a Marilyn Horne impersonating a Roman emperor or a medieval general. A few countertenors (Jeffrey Gall leaps to mind) have managed to overcome my resistance to that unearthly vocal range. The Italian language, I believe, is essential. The music is written to slip onto already lyrical vowel sounds like a fine glove onto flawless fingers, and can be made to fit no other language so suavely. There are often—almost always in Handel—spectacular possibilities for costume and spectacle. Even Metastasio, for all of his clucking about seventeenth-century Venetian excesses, wasn't above writing in queens who hurl themselves into burning cities, which are in turn swallowed up by oceans out of which rise divine kingdoms, *ricca e luminosa;* or Alexander's army encampment in India, "with elephants, towers, covered wagons, and war machines," within which a bloody battle takes place and a major bridge collapses.

Much of the recitative of opera seria *can* be acted, or at least musically declaimed, with something resembling the passion and conviction of a good Comédie-Française production of Racine. Lines that are certifiably brain dead can always be cut. But one must be very sure they're dead, and not carrying forward some essential current of action or music.

As for the five- to ten-minute tralalalalalala arias—I don't know what to say. I have serious problems with emotionally empty, musically dull, and dramatically meaningless da capo arias, which the opera seria tradition (including Handel) includes more of than one might wish. When florid singing is devoid of drama, I find myself counting the repeats, not rising on wings of song. In neither ballet nor

HANDEL, *Rinaldo*, Marilyn Horne, Metropolitan Opera, 1984.
Photograph by Winnie Klotz.

opera am I a fan of "circus turn" acrobatics, the kind of spectator who can admire and applaud mere physical feats—super-rapid scales, trills, and shakes; a dozen bars sung without a breath; the single astonishing high note.

But accuracy, precision, notes hit dead center from distant leaps, tonal nuance and shading, and expression through the voice—these are something else, especially if the voice is beautiful to begin with and under total and artful control. A few da capo arias *do* work dramatically: when a character, like Orlando in his *furioso* phase, has clearly gone out of his mind, or when the words of the A-B-A sections have been musically converted into a credible sequence of evolving and contradictory emotions. But there is no way, logically, or even dramatico-irrationally, to "act" lines such as "I have a hundred phantoms [zombies, serpents: *larve*] inside me, I have a thousand furies in my breast" (from *L'Olimpiade*) eleven times over.

The 1981 San Francisco Opera production of Rossini's *Semiramide*, with Montserrat Caballé and Marilyn Horne, and the San Francisco Opera Center's production of Handel's *Giustino* in 1989 adopted what seemed to me very sensible approaches. The first round of an aria, about to explode into vocalise (the A-A'-B sections for Handel, the cavatina for Rossini), was sung "normally" on stage by a singer either soliloquizing alone or dramatically facing his or her lover/antagonist/confidant(e). For the second round, the singer then stepped to the front of the stage—on little peninsulas built out over the orchestra in *Semiramide*, before a painted curtain in *Giustino*—and sang the embellished A-A' repeats or cabalettas to *us*. We applauded; the curtain rose, or the actor moved back downstage; and the action continued. Directorial ideas like these seem to deal honestly with the knotty problem of "how to act repeats," and to acknowledge that Italian opere serie will always be half music-drama, half concert-in-costume.

The fundamental weakness of opera seria was the near-total separation of the dramatist (with his own literary pretensions, his nonmusical ideals) from the composer. Only when the two work together as one, or at least as a working partnership—with the composer clearly in charge—do we appear to have any chance of achieving operas of genuine and lasting dramatic force. Mozart and Gluck understood this perfectly. So did Monteverdi. So has every important composer since 1800.

How, then, are modern audiences to enjoy all of the serious Italian operas written between Monteverdi and Mozart? One way may be to pretend that we're in our own private box in Venice or Vienna, surrounded by food and drink and friends and the glow of a thousand candles, happily hearing it all for the first—or the twenty-first—time.

(1989)

CHAPTER FOUR

Ariosto and His Children

A work of literature may be considered a classic—a unique, enriching, enduring masterpiece—even if very few people read it any more. Durability need not mean immortality. It's enough that a book *was* enjoyed by many generations of readers past for it to have earned classical status, even if most modern readers have lost the ability to enjoy it. One might also measure the originality, the capaciousness, and the fertility of a book—all possible marks of a classic—by the number and quality of the *other* works of art it has directly or indirectly inspired.

By either test, Ludovico Ariosto's *Orlando furioso*—a 38,736-line Italian poem first printed in its complete form in 1532—must be judged one of the most enduring and fruitful works of literature ever written. It is also, for those who are still able and willing to enter it, one of the most captivating. Lost in its dark forests, stormy seas, desert islands, and enchanted castles; entangled in its bloody combats, its passionate love affairs, and its vile and heroic deeds; guided throughout by one of the most engaging narrators in all literature, I find myself wanting the book never to end.

Over three hundred years, *Orlando furioso* spawned an extraordinary progeny of other works in literature, music, and art. But (with the possible exception of Cervantes's *Don Quixote*), I think it remains richer, more humane, and more valuable than any of the paintings, poems, plays, novels, songs, and operas it engendered.

The first version of *Orlando* (or the *Furioso*, as Italians familiarly call it) was published in 1516 in an edition of 1,200 copies partly subsidized by Cardinal Ippolito I D'Este of Ferrara, to whom it was dedicated. Ariosto (born in 1474) had served in the worldly cardinal's household as a courtier/diplomat from 1503 to 1517; he had traveled for the cardinal on missions to King Louis XII of France and Pope Julius II. Although Ariosto had worked steadily on the poem since about 1505, it was only after he quit the cardinal's service and went to work for his brother Alfonso I D'Este, duke of Ferrara, that the poet was able to devote most of his time to his writing. He published a second and enlarged version of the *Furioso* in 1521 and (after a three years' break governing an unruly province of the duke's) the final version eleven years later. In October 1531, he was granted a pension of 100 gold ducats a year for the rest of his life—which, unfortunately, ended twenty-one months later.

By 1600, *Orlando furioso* had gone through 154 editions, some quite elegant and costly, others "popular" and relatively inexpensive, and had been translated into all of the major European languages. Some of the translations, like John Harington's into English of 1591, were regarded as important creative accomplishments in their own right. It has been estimated that 25,000 copies were printed during the century—more than any other work of its time. Ariosto was the first writer in history to win an international reputation during his lifetime through published versions of his work.

Books have been written about the influence of *Orlando furioso* in Spain, France, England, and Germany. Scholars have tried to measure its impact in Russia, Poland, Hungary, and Latin America. After the translators came the imitators, the sequels, the parodies. The most notable successor in Italy was Torquato Tasso's *Gerusalemme liberata* of 1581, a more orderly, moralistic, and quasi-historical work of some 15,000 lines, whose author—another courtier of the Duke of Ferrara—very specifically set out to rival the "Ferrarese Homer." Spanish writers kept turning out *Orlando III*s and *IV*s and *V*s, inventing new adventures for Ariosto's characters in order to cash in on the "knight errant" craze. This phenomenon was in turn seized on, and turned into an even more popular and enduring masterpiece, by Miguel de Cervantes in 1604.

The influence on other writers of so comprehensive, so multiplex, so richly imagined a work as the *Furioso* is, in the long run, impossible to trace. But for three hundred years, scores of important authors all over Europe acknowledged their admiration and affection for Ariosto's poem. Many eighteenth-century writers and critics were dismayed by his paganism and profanity, his "irregularity" and love of the fantastic. But even Voltaire, who started out hostile, ended up regarding Ariosto as one of the consummate masters. Revising an earlier negative opinion, Voltaire called the poem in 1764 "so extensive, so full of variety, so fruitful in every kind of beauty that after having perused it, I have, more than once found my appetite excited to begin it again. . . . The Orlando Furioso is at once the Iliad, the Odyssey, and the Don Quixote." "For God's sake," the British statesman Charles James Fox wrote to a friend, "learn Italian as fast as you can in order to read Ariosto."

Historians of the novel (the growing popularity of which, in the end, helped kill the audience for poetic epics) frequently begin with *Don Quixote;* but *Don Quixote* depends crucially on *Orlando furioso*. Cervantes refers to Ariosto and his characters eighty-three times in his text. Readers of Cervantes will recall Don Quixote's christening a barber's basin "Mambrino's helmet"—the enchanted helmet, in Ariosto, that Rinaldo wears. Examining the demented knight's library, his rational friends discover a copy of Ariosto and decide to save it from the bonfire. At one point, concerned that his Lady Dulcinea will think him insufficiently in love, Don Quixote decides to strip himself naked and cut a few capers in the manner of Orlando-gone-mad, so that Sancho can report back to her his master's amorous antics.

> With that, slipping off his Breeches and stripping himself naked to the Waist, he gave two or three Frisks in the Air, and then pitching on his Hands, he fetch'd his Heels over his Head twice together; and as he tumbled with his Legs aloft, discover'd such Rarities, that *Sancho* e'en made Haste to turn his Horse's Head, that he might no longer see 'em, and rode away full satisfy'd, that he might swear his Master was mad.

Another landmark of Western literature that could not have existed without Ariosto's is *The Faerie Queene* of 1596—a suave, stately, allegorical (and utterly humorless) 35,000-line poem. Edmund Spenser acknowledged in his letter-preface to Sir Walter Raleigh that he had intentionally "followed" Ariosto. In another letter, he confessed his hope to "outgo" his Italian master. He did not.

Tasso, Cervantes, and Spenser are the major authors most directly and obviously indebted to Ariosto's poem. But the nationalist-romantic epics of Portugal and France (Camões's *Os Lusíadas* and Ronsard's *La Franciade*) also clearly depend on the *Furioso*. The French poets Du Bellay and La Fontaine, both great admirers, borrowed from it considerably. Sidney, Jonson, and Marlowe made use of or reference to it. Molière collaborated with the composer Lully on an extravagant three-day spectacle at Versailles in 1664 based very freely on the episodes of Alcina's enchanted island, in which young Louis XIV himself played Ruggiero and noblemen of his court the other paladins of France. Milton, a great fan of Italian literature, referred frequently to Ariosto in his early works and notebooks and (to Dr. Johnson's dismay) borrowed Ariosto's "depraved" and manic style for the portrait of Limbo in *Paradise Lost*. Part of the serious plot of Shakespeare's *Much Ado About Nothing* was derived (perhaps at second hand) from the inset Ginevra/Ariodante story of Cantos IV–VI. Orlando in *As You Like It* (though in no way comparable to his heroic namesake), carving his lady-love's name on the bark of every tree in the Forest of Arden, probably owes something to the notorious tree carving of Angelica and Medoro—the discovery of which, in fact, drove the original Orlando *furioso*.

Run, run Orlando, carve on every tree
The fair, the chaste, and inexpressive she.

Several Italian playwrights staged adaptations of episodes from the *Furioso* during the seventeenth and eighteenth centuries, not unlike those set to music as operas. Byron's *Don Juan* is demonstrably *ariostesco*. He praised the Italian poet in his own works ("His fancy like a rainbow, and his Fire / Like that of Heaven, immortal"), as did Goethe in a play he wrote based on the tragic life of Tasso. Pushkin very clearly followed Ariosto's model in his own romantic epic *Ruslan and Ludmilla* (1820), the source of Glinka's opera. Sir Walter Scott (once called the "Scottish Ariosto") was a fanatic devotee of the Italian poet.

Although "people stopped reading" Ariosto, we are told, more than a century ago, substantial chunks of *Orlando furioso* are still required reading in most Italian schools, which explains why most Italian editions in print are considerably shorter than the original, and are equipped with explanatory footnotes and introductions. The ever-growing, ever-thirsty international literary-academic establishment has absorbed Ariosto like a sponge, and squeezed out thousands of articles and books analyzing and explaining his great work. One American professor, who is trying to get *Orlando furioso* onto college reading lists in his own country, compares it to Tolkien's *Lord of the Rings*, and cites episodes from "Star Trek" that sound to him like borrowings from Ariosto.

More interesting to me than all of these are the responses of two of the most wonderfully imaginative fiction writers of our time, the Argentine Jorge Luis Borges and the Italian Italo Calvino. Borges, a self-proclaimed "reader and rereader of Dante and Ariosto," wrote a poem entitled "Ariosto and the Arabs." Calvino, who published his own witty condensation of *Orlando furioso* in 1970, frequently credited Ariosto as a major influence on his work. Three of his marvelous novels—*The Nonexistent Knight*, *The Cloven Viscount*, and *The Castle of Crossed Destinies*—come very close to modern-day versions of Ariosto. Both Borges and Calvino have tried to recapture for our time the absolute, unbound freedom of the *Furioso* by creating magical other worlds in which anything can happen.

Partly because of the time and place at which he wrote, Ariosto and his epic were from the start identified with the visual arts. The poem itself is full of elaborate descriptions of architecture—mostly enchanted palaces of a fantastic, superluxurious sort. Sculpture and painting are called on to offer prophetic tributes to Ariosto's patrons, the D'Este family of Ferrara. (The spectacular water gardens of the Villa D'Este at Tivoli outside of Rome were built by Cardinal Ippolito II, the nephew of Ariosto's first patron.)

Working at a sophisticated early-sixteenth-century Italian court, moreover— one with close family ties to the no less sophisticated courts of Mantua, Milan, and

Urbino, a dynamic rivalry with Venice, and a nagging dependence on Rome (all of which places Ariosto knew)—the poet could not help but meet and become acquainted with celebrated Renaissance painters. Many of them, like him, lived as courtier-dependents, and devoted much of their creative effort to the commissions or the celebration of their noble or clerical patrons. Ariosto knew Titian personally, and praised him (along with Leonardo, Mantegna, Giovanni Bellini, Michelangelo, Sebastiano del Piombo, Raphael, and the two Dossi brothers of Ferrara) at the start of Canto XXXII. Dosso Dossi, Giovanni Bellini, and Titian were all commissioned by Duke Alfonso to do Ovidian paintings for his palace in Ferrara, at the same time that Ariosto was working on his second edition. Titian painted a portrait of the poet—a bearded, balding, hook-nosed, tired-eyed gentleman in profile—reproduced in an engraving for the 1532 edition.

The first works of visual art "inspired" by *Orlando furioso* in fact were the woodcuts that were printed—one for each of the forty-six cantos—in the Venetian editions of 1542, 1553, 1556, and 1584. In the latter two editions, the engravers packed extensive stretches of geography with agitated little figures (helpfully captioned by their names) fighting or weeping or making love or dying or going mad in overlapping, picturesque, and crudely drawn settings. Most of them show several episodes of a canto taking place within the same frame, in a sort of comic-strip fashion. For his 1591 English translation, Sir John Harington's publishers had the Venetian engravings redrawn (adding, in one case, pornographic details) and cut on copper.

Although it never achieved the popularity in this respect of Ovid or the Bible, Ariosto's poem was drawn on frequently after 1532 as a sourcebook for visual artists. Before 1600, Nicolò dell'Abate had decorated a palace in Bologna with a whole series of dramatic frescoes depicting Ruggiero's adventures on Alcina's island. In the seventeenth century, several painters of the Bolognese school (Guido Reni, Albani, Domenichino, Guercino) rendered episodes from the *Furioso*—mainly the love idyll of Angelica and Medoro. In 1641, Duke Francesco I D'Este had his villa at Sassuolo decorated with a series of self-celebrating frescoes from the book. Rubens painted a particularly salacious view of a dirty-minded old hermit (the story is from Canto VIII) staring at a sleeping, nude, and remarkably fleshy Angelica. In 1757, G. B. Tiepolo did a wonderfully "operatic" series of frescoes on the walls of Palladio's Villa Valmarana outside of Vicenza, including four rich and sensuous scenes from Ariosto; his son G. D. drew many episodes out of the *Furioso*. In a recent book devoted *entirely* to renderings of the Angelica-Medoro tree-carving motif, the author describes and illustrates twenty-five different versions of this one scene made between 1577 and 1825.

Boucher executed some ripely erotic scenes from the poem. Fragonard, working toward an edition de luxe that was never published, made a total of 150 drawings after Ariosto, which include some of his most deft and evocative work. At the

Paris salons between 1806 and 1827, twenty-one scenes from *Orlando furioso* (mostly Angelicas and Medoros) were displayed—more decorous and sentimental than erotic, with the one wild exception of Ingres's *Ruggiero Saving Angelica* of 1819, a voluptuous subject he painted several times. In 1826, a German artist named Julius Schnorr von Carolsfeld (the father of Wagner's first Tristan) covered the walls and ceiling of the Ariosto Room of the Cassino Massimi in Rome with ten scenes from the poem. Between 1830 and 1920, forty more Ariostan subjects were displayed at the Paris salons, including one painting and three sketches by Delacroix. By midcentury, Ruggieros in full armor saving chained and naked Angelicas had displaced the tree-carving idyll for first place, which may say something about Second Empire tastes.

With very few exceptions, these painted, drawn, engraved, and sculpted versions concentrate on two episodes, out of the hundreds in the poem: the love affair between Angelica and Medoro (usually showing one or the other inscribing their names on a tree, as they loll naked in a verdant landscape) and Ruggiero on his winged horse saving poor Angelica from the horrible orc. This process of selection, in which one artist tended to repeat the motifs chosen by his predecessors, resulted in a considerable shrinking of the bounty of the *Furioso*. In the hands of four centuries of visual artists, the poem was all too often reduced to one vaguely sadomasochistic male fantasy scene (once he has saved Angelica, Ruggiero is eager to rape her), and to an image taken from the one idyllic romance in the whole book, which occupies twenty stanzas (of 4,844) in the middle of Canto XIX.

To a substantial degree, the same process of sentimental reductionism took place in the music that drew on Ariosto's great poem. Non-Italians today are likely to know of the *Furioso* only by way of a handful of eighteenth-century operas more or less based on it, operas that are still occasionally performed: Handel's *Orlando, Alcina,* and *Ariodante;* Vivaldi's *Orlando furioso;* Haydn's *Orlando paladino;* and Donizetti's *Il furioso all'isola di San Domingo.*

Ariosto's first translation into music, however, took place a century or two earlier, when individual eight-line stanzas of *Orlando furioso,* or groups and "cycles" of stanzas, were converted into two- to six-voice madrigals for performance before aristocratic gatherings. Parts of the poem were also recited, to stock guitar accompaniments, by traveling minstrels or *cantastorie* (story-singers) before working-class crowds in piazzas all over Italy. "It is sung not only by the people in taverns and in barber shops," wrote Giovanni de' Bardi in 1583, "but also by noblemen and men of great learning. It is so full of harmony and rhythm that everyone learns its verses with great facility."

The emotionally expressive, musically sophisticated madrigal form was one more of the artistic triumphs of the D'Este court of Ferrara, primarily in the generation after Ariosto's death. Bartolomeo Tromboncino first set to music a portion of the *Furioso* (still unpublished at the time) in 1512 for Isabella D'Este Gonzaga, marchesa of Mantua, patron of Mantegna and Perugino, sister of Ariosto's cardinal-padrone, and "probably the most learned woman of her time." Between then and 1623—primarily between 1540 and 1580—a total of 226 different stanzas of the *Furioso* served as texts for at least 730 published madrigals, composed by people such as Orlando [!] di Lasso, Andrea Gabrieli, William Byrd, and Palestrina. In 1561, a Flemish composer named Jaquet de Berchem published a cycle of ninety-one stanzas of the *Furioso* set to music, with connecting plot summaries, forming a deft condensation of its more passionate and famous episodes. This was dedicated to (and commissioned by) Alfonso II D'Este, the son and successor of Ariosto's second patron.

"One of the reasons for the immense popularity of Ariosto's epic poem," James Haar writes, "was that it not only read well, but 'sang well'—with favorite stanzas or preferred episodes (formed of several stanzas) declaimed or sung—sung as madrigals, naturally." By studying these favorite stanzas or preferred episodes, one can learn what image of its almost infinitely varied whole Renaissance composers chose to harmonize and thus to pass on. Of the twenty-one stanzas set to music ten times or more, eight were taken from the longing outbursts of Bradamante (a tender-hearted woman warrior) for her unusually errant knight-lover, Ruggiero. Three are similar expressions of anxious longing by two of Angelica's many spurned lovers. In all eleven of these, the speaker is tormented by jealousy of a possible rival—the very emotion that drove Orlando mad. The stanza in which Orlando first begins to crack, XVIII, 127, was set to music sixteen times, making it third in popularity after VIII, 26 (Orlando longing for his lost Angelica) and I, 42. With nineteen musical settings, I, 42—which forms part of another of Angelica's suitors' laments—was the all-time hit musical stanza:

La verginella è simile alla rosa
ch'in bel giardin su la nativa spina
mentre sola e sicura si riposa,
né gregge né pastor se le avicina;
l'aura soave e l'alba rugiadosa,
l'acqua, la terra al suo favor s'inchina:
gioveni vaghi e donne inamorate
amano averne e seni e tempie ornate.

A virgin is like a rose: while she reposes on her native thorns, alone and safe in a lovely garden, neither flocks nor shepherd comes near. The gentle breeze and the morning dew, the rain, the earth, bend to do her homage. Young lovers like to wear her on their breasts and brows.

In the next stanza, the speaker goes on—like most male lovers in the poem—to express his mortal terror that someone else has "plucked his rose" (i.e., deflowered the virginal Angelica) before he has had the chance. A kind of rabid lust and sexual possessiveness permeates the poem, if not the stanzas favored by composers.

Four of the twenty-one most popular stanzas are taken from the opening lines, or *proemi*, of cantos. In three of these, the poet is declaiming passionately, in his own voice, against love—personalized as the cruel god Amor—for the wretched things it does to males and females alike, but mostly to males. One stanza is from a long letter of Bradamante's to her wandering lover, insisting on *her* rocklike fidelity.

Of the remaining four stanzas most favored by Renaissance composers, two are pure (and magnificent) pieces of landscape painting: one of Alcina's enchanted island, as seen from the back of a flying horse; the other of the earthly Garden of Paradise. A third is a famous portrait in words of the beauties of the naked virgin Olimpia, who has just been saved from being devoured by another horrible monster. Fifteen composers set to music Ariosto's splendid image of her face smiling through tears after her recovery. Five of them went on to musick the next stanza as well, in which the poet describes the impact made by her eyes and hair on a young man standing nearby. No composer took on the challenge of the next three stanzas, in which Ariosto describes in tactile, glowing detail Olimpia's bare breasts, her hips, her belly, her thighs, and her private parts. In Italian, on the printed page, these three stanzas are art and music already, thanks to the sheer beauty of their images and sounds.

Not all of the love affairs in the *Furioso* end in maddening frustration, like Orlando's. Stanza XXV, 68 gives a hint of the joyful, Mediterranean eroticism with which the poem is packed, like a green plant in spring full of sap. In this instance, Ricciardetto has cleverly tricked Fiordespina into bed by pretending to be his twin sister Bradamante (whom she adores)—but a Bradamante suddenly enchanted into male shape to satisfy the surprised girl's needs. "She could not believe her eyes, or her fingers. . . . She needed solid proof to convince her that what she was actually feeling was what she thought she felt."

Non rumor di tamburi o suon di trombe
furon principio all'amoroso assalto,
ma baci ch'imitavan le colombe,
devan segno or di gire, or di far alto.
Usammo alti'armi che saette o frombe.
Io senza scale in su la ròcca salto
e lo stendardo piantovi di botto,
e la nimica mia mi caccio sotto.

No roll of drums, no trumpets' peal gave warning of the amorous assault.
[Sixteenth-century madrigalists, like Handel later on, loved setting lines like

that to music.] Instead, dovelike kisses gave the signal whether to advance or stand firm. We used other weapons than arrows and catapults. I leapt on the battlements without a ladder and planted my standard there at one jab, and buried my enemy beneath me.

In the hands of the madrigalists, the immense and tangled world of Ariosto's *Orlando furioso* was reduced to a sequence of songs of sad love-longing, fearful jealousy, lust thwarted or (more rarely) satisfied, gorgeous spring gardens, and voluptuous nudes. The longer sequences that were most often turned into song cycles were the extended longing-laments of Bradamante for Ruggiero and of Orlando for Angelica, the heartbreaking plaints of Olimpia left alone on a desert island by her faithless spouse, the piteous grieving of Isabella as her lover dies in her arms, and the wild outburst of Orlando when he realizes that Angelica has fallen in love with Medoro.

As converted into opera, *Orlando furioso* emerges no less dominated by *Amor*, no less tender pathetic, no less a poem almost exclusively about the sweet sadness and cruel suffering of love—which represents perhaps one-fifth of the poem that Ariosto wrote. Because opera libretti in the seventeenth and eighteenth centuries were frequently recycled from composer to composer, even from performance to performance, and were rather liberally revised; and because only a small fraction of the many operas performed during those centuries have survived, it's impossible to estimate how many different operas using the characters and events of Ariosto's epic were actually composed. Scanning several sources, I turned up a total of forty produced between 1619 and 1801. Almost all of them take their titles from one of the characters. Orlando, Angelica, Medoro, Bradamante, Ruggiero, Alcina, Ginevra, Ariodante, Atlante, Olimpia, and Rodomonte all turn up, alone or in pairs, as titular heroes of their own operas, which gives some idea of what a huge department store full of plots composers and librettists found in the *Furioso*.

The original poem is obviously much too long, too cosmic, too busy, and too multiple in its effects and intentions to be reduced to one evening of opera. Something along the lines of the Barraults' circuslike *Rabelais*, or Ariane Mnouchkine's wild French Revolutionary pageant-dramas might suit it better. The Italian director Luca Ronconi staged a successful nonmusical *Orlando furioso* of this sort in 1970, and produced a film version in 1974.

In his preface to the 1713 version of *Orlando furioso*, Vivaldi's librettist Grazio Braccioli wrote, "The numerous exploits of the vast epic involve half the world, so to speak. Such actions have been limited by us in this drama to one. At its beginning, middle, and end are the love, madness, and recovery of Orlando." The operatic versions of *Orlando furioso* tend to concentrate on one of three broad areas of action.

1. Most often (like Braccioli's), they focus on Orlando's passionate love for Angelica, the madness to which it leads him, and (sometimes) his eventual cure; along with the love of Angelica for his rival Medoro. This is essentially the substance of Handel's *Orlando*. Some "pastoral" versions concentrate almost exclusively on Angelica and Medoro—even on what happens to them after they disappear from Ariosto's plot.

2. Several of the *Furioso* operas are set entirely on the enchanted, lotus-land island of Alcina, a sorcerer who (in Cantos VI–VII) tempts brave knights to become her lovers, then discards them and turns them into rocks or trees. Ruggiero, the Saracen superhero, is the most notable of her conquests. In some operatic versions (like Vivaldi's *Orlando furioso* or Handel's *Alcina*), his beloved Bradamante goes to the island to save him; in the original, this was accomplished by the "good witch" Melissa. Librettists like Braccioli sometimes tried to combine a number of Ariosto's plots by setting them all on Alcina's island or by conflating her enchanted castle with Atlante's.

3. Canto V and parts of Cantos IV and VI (Ariosto skips around a lot) tell the wholly independent story of Ginevra and Ariodante, a tale of lust, romance, and chivalry in Arthurian Scotland, which became a popular opera plot in its own right. The best known of these is Handel's *Ariodante* of 1735.

After selecting one of these three basic areas of action, most opera librettists proceeded to "improve" on the original by adding new magical scenes, comic characters, or pathetic events of their own.

Wandering through Ariosto's epic are about twenty major and twenty signifi-cant minor characters, along with several thousand extras. There are at least as many separate stories, or fresh adventures, as there are cantos, many of which Ariosto keeps moving simultaneously. When any one of these—beyond the basic three situations—is introduced into an opera, it is usually in glancing, comic, or irrelevant ways. The Saracen giant Rodomonte, for example, a magnificent oppo-nent for Charlemagne's forces, slaughters hundreds of people with a few swipes of his sword, and comes near to destroying all of Paris single-handedly. In Haydn's *Orlando paladino*, Rodomonte is simply a great oversized clown who frightens people by talking (or singing) in the style his name has given to the English language ("rodomontade: vainglorious boasting or bragging; pretentious, bluster-ing talk").

I do not mean to belittle the achievements of the many writers, artists, and musicians who have drawn their characters, ideas, and incidents from the bottom-

HANDEL, *Orlando*, Jeffrey Gall and Valerie Masterson, San
Francisco Opera, 1985. Photograph by Marty Sohl.

less well of Ariosto's epic. But it is important to remember—especially at a time when people are likely to know the children better than the parent—how vastly much more there is in the poem than in any of the works it inspired.

All of the sex and violence are gone, for one thing: great, wholehearted Boccaccian sex (Ariosto drops lust from his list of the Seven Deadly Sins, and writes two eloquent defenses of fornication) and spectacular violence, by which heads and limbs are lopped off right and left. All of the Handelian stage machinery in the world, the most lavish sets money can buy, can never duplicate the mind-boggling magic, the fluid geography, the warm sensuality of the original. Nothing is left of the grim and vicious world of early sixteenth-century Italy (this is the age of Machiavelli as well as of Castiglione), which forms so constant and so oppressive a presence in the book.

And all of Ariosto's theatrical "adaptors" have had to cut out the most appealing, most sympathetic character in the epic—the narrator. There is no place for Ariosto's alter ego in an eighteenth-century opera. But in taking him out, they have surgically extracted the generous, worldly-wise, pretension-deflating intelligence through which we observe all of these adventures, all of the cosmological travel, the killer-women and man-eating monsters, the bloody battle scenes and hand-to-hand combats, the impossible marvels and derring-do.

His skeptical, tolerant, self-implicating perspective aligns him with contemporaries like Erasmus and successors like Montaigne. According to Thomas M. Greene, "In his [the narrator's] critical sense, his artistic independence, his freedom from any tradition, Ariosto stands as a more modern figure than any of the men who attempted after him to write epic poetry. . . . In his sensibility we encounter, astonishingly early, the blurred edge of consciousness, the reflexive irony, the unwillingness to see quite whole and clear, the capacity to entertain simultaneously more than one thought."

Before he became president of Yale, before he became commissioner of baseball, the late A. Bartlett Giamatti was best known as an eminent scholar and eloquent defender of Ludovico Ariosto. No doubt Giamatti's Italian heritage had something to do with this. But his deep-lying affection for *Orlando furioso* was also a good indication that this latter-day "Renaissance man" had his priorities straight, as can be seen in this passage from Giamatti's introduction to a 1968 edition of the poem:

> There is more to an epic than simply length. It must also define a world; it must communicate the immensity of the universe both without and within its characters. Nobility, bravery, a sense of high purpose, the love of ideals and objects worth the highest devotion of man—all these, through careful accumulation of detail and incident, must be part of the world of a poem if it is to deserve the name epic. But, above all . . . there must be space and there must be energy; the epic hero must have horizons at his disposal, and he must have the strength and the will to conquer them. . . .

The *Orlando Furioso* contains far more than a shimmering, translucent vision of the chivalric world; it also conveys a clear, acute sense of the shortcomings, the limitations, the horrors, and the follies of that world. Within the harmonious, ordered universe of the poem—perpetual in its perfection—Ariosto gives us an image of a world which is changing and in decay. We are exposed to the beautiful surface, and also to the brutal realities of life. . . . In the solitary figure of Orlando, we see the extremes to which a man's folly can bring him, and we have an insight into all the power latent in the delightful world of the poem, and into all the despair.

Whatever the pleasures I may derive from Spenser or Calvino, from Tiepolo or Fragonard, from Handel or Vivaldi, I would rather live in a world without their imitations of and derivations from Ariosto than in a world that did not contain the original poem. "When you are tired of Ariosto," C. S. Lewis once wrote, "you must be tired of this world."

(1989)

CHAPTER FIVE

Don Giovanni: The Impossible Opera

Even if you know no Italian and are unblessed with supertitles, a staged version of Da Ponte and Mozart's *Don Giovanni* is likely to be comprehensible. This is partly because its story has remained part of popular mythology. We continue to call a man who shares its hero's style and obsessions a "Don Juan." If you are the least bit aware of the myth, you will expect to see a heartless, dashing womanizer who, after plowing his way through hundreds of females, gets his comeuppance at the cold hand of a stone statue—the murdered father of one of his females—which drags him off to hell.

Beyond that, much of the opera's action is likely to be fairly clear on stage: the opening duel and death, the villain's flight, the daughter's bereavement and vow to revenge. Even the first-time viewer will probably figure out that Donna Elvira is one of Giovanni's previous conquests, now discarded and bitter. And the explanation his servant provides of her insignificant place in his master's "catalogue" is as easy to translate as anything in foreign-language opera:

> In Italia, sei cento e quaranta,
> In Almagna [Germany], due cento e trent'una,
> Cento in Francia,
> In Turchia novant'una;
> Mà in Ispagna . . . mà, in Ispagna son già mille e trè!
> [640 + 231 + 100 + 91 + 1003 = 2065]
> . . . cameriere, cittadine . . . contesse, baronesse,
> marchesane, principesse . . .
> d'ogni grado, d'ogni forma, d'ogni età . . .

The seduction of the young peasant maid ("of any rank, of any shape, of any age") and the jealousy of her fiancé follow logically. This is Don Juan in action, going for number 2066. A few of the scenes that follow may be somewhat bewildering: the costume-changing bit with Leporello, the entry of three masked people in long capes and hoods, the lengthy sextet. But Giovanni's own music— his honeyed tempting of Zerlina, his mandolin serenade, his energetic song about drinking and dancing—all seem perfectly in character with his myth. Once we realize who the statue is, the cemetery scene, with its challenge and invitation, and the final supper and damnation (with all of Leporello's frightened and comic asides) make good dramatic sense.

This is not to say that *Don Giovanni* rolls along as smoothly as a well-made play. Not many operas do. Fans usually attribute this defect, if it is one, to what one might call "lyrical interruptions." However refined their interest in drama, most opera lovers still enjoy gorgeous singing, all by itself, enough to put up with numerous interruptions in the plot. And *Don Giovanni* has what may be the greatest number of sublime lyrical interruptions per hour of opera of any major repertory work.

Some of these interruptions result from the fact that the company Mozart was writing for in Prague had three sopranos of almost equal importance, all of whom expected two star-turn solos (his Donna Elvira in Vienna demanded a third) as well as a decent share in the ensembles. For the Prague Don Ottavio, Mozart composed the opera's single most demanding stretch of show-off vocalise: Baglioni was obliged to sing one five-bar, sixty-note roulade in a single breath. When that proved too much for Morella, the tenor in Vienna, Mozart wrote for him an equally lovely alternative that was easier to sing. Nowadays, when no self-respecting tenor would admit to being unable to manipulate the Big Dipper runs of "Il mio tesoro," or agree to relinquish the melting intervals of "Dalla sua pace," the action stops dead twice while this stiff, handsome dummy in black velvet and Spanish lace struts his stage-center stuff and wins his expected bravos.

Not all of the lyrical interruptions are as antidramatic as Don Ottavio's. Some of the showstoppers—Leporello's catalogue aria, his master's "Deh vieni" serenade and "Finch'han dal vino" (the so-called champagne aria), Zerlina's two plangent appeals to her mate, Masetto's brief outburst of defiance—are well integrated into the action. With the exception of the tedious sextets, most of the songs Mozart and Da Ponte write for more than one person further and enrich the drama, rather than stop it in its tracks.

The lovely A-major *duettino* in which Don Giovanni wins Zerlina is a little drama all by itself. It starts with the achingly sweet intervals of his first appeal, which are answered about an octave higher in a charming expression of Zerlina's internal confusion ("Vorrei, e non vorrei"—"I want it, and I don't want it"). After a coy transition, and some twists on the fiddles, come faster and faster exchanges as the two grow closer and more heated. Her notes descend; the woodwinds press as she weakens ("Non son più forte!") until finally, after a last pause of dying conscience, she is pulled into breathless 6/8 harmony and cries along with him, "Andiam!"—"Let's go!"

The intercutting and blending of the musical lines, the very repeats and progresses duplicate the irresistible—and clearly sexual—movement from his to hers to theirs. Much as I abhor heartless seducers, and suffer for poor Masetto, so emotionally persuasive is this duet that I find myself wanting the seduction to succeed, and I feel as frustrated as Don Giovanni must feel when the ubiquitous Elvira interrupts his tender designs.

The cemetery duet (Act II, Scene 9—briefly a trio), called "O statua gentilissima," is so vividly theatrical that one tends to forget it's a vocal "number" at all. Leporello starts to address the statue, but keeps interrupting his own lines in shudders of sheer fright. Each time he stops, he is threatened by Don Giovanni and returns to his terrifying chore. When the statue does finally reply (with his customary consort of woodwinds and brass), Leporello nearly goes out of his mind. When both men notice the statue's nod, they acknowledge it by singing together. When they quit the scene, they are rhyming verbally, and musically in harmony, but their emotions are at opposite ends of the world.

Were it not for the extraordinary reputation of the three Mozart–Da Ponte operas (since the prewar Glyndebourne performances, most of the opera world has taken to writing of them as if they were flawlessly unified musical-dramatic wholes), this distinction between vocal numbers that sustain dramatic progress and those that simply and beautifully interrupt it might not be worth making. It is possible that *Don Giovanni* benefits from a reputation earned primarily by the other two. The text and plot of *Così fan tutte* (1790) are set up to be so lucidly symmetrical that Mozart's beautiful, bittersweet score can match Da Ponte's libretto with a mirror-image precision. (In fact, as Joseph Kerman points out in *Opera as Drama*, Mozart takes the lovers' emotions a good deal more seriously than Da Ponte does.) Every producer takes advantage of this apparent symmetry; every listener adores it. The characterizations and intrigue of *The Marriage of Figaro* (1786) are far more complex than *Così*'s. But the miraculous working out of all its complexity, in which music at once creates the eleven characters and their world, tangles and untangles the plot, and englobes the whole in a glow of heavenly harmonies and melodies, is probably responsible for the fact that this, the earliest of the Mozart–Da Ponte collaborations, usually inspires the warmest affection today.

If these two operas are not easy to realize satisfactorily in performance, it is because of the purity, sympathy, and musicianship they require. With *Don Giovanni* (1787), there are problems so deeply rooted in the text and scores that one of Mozart's most dedicated modern commentators, Georges de St.-Foix, wrote of "the near impossibility of giving to this *dramma giocoso* a representation absolutely adequate to the original." E. J. Dent, an early and ardent Mozartean, called *Don*

MOZART, *Don Giovanni*, Berndt Weikl, Hamburg Opera, 1973.
Photograph by Fritz Peyer.

Giovanni "a work containing moments of the most overwhelming beauty and the greatest dramatic power, along with curiously incongruous lapses into the mannerisms of an old fashioned style, the whole being to some extent disfigured by a general vagueness and confusion of plan." Harold Rosenthal, former editor of *Opera*, called it "one of the most difficult operas to bring off successfully."[1]

Perhaps for these very reasons, almost every distinguished opera producer of the past fifteen years, and several from other fields, have tried, often by novel and radical means, to iron out the inconsistencies of *Don Giovanni*. Walter Felsenstein, Jean-Pierre Ponnelle, Günther Rennert, Franco Zeffirelli, John Copley, August Everding, Peter Hall, Götz Friedrich, Maurice Béjart, and Joseph Losey (I list them chronologically) are among the many celebrated producers who ventured new versions of this problematic work between 1966 and 1981.

Because it is always taken for granted that Mozart is one of the supreme geniuses of human history, much of the blame for the "problems" of *Don Giovanni* is often visited on Lorenzo Da Ponte, the failed priest from Venice who wrote Mozart's librettos. ("The speed with which the piece had to be written explains certain of its crudities," writes Kerman. "The libretto is full of improbabilities . . . [which] are fortuitous and clumsy. . . . Da Ponte is mostly responsible for the weakness.")

Da Ponte *does* have a few things to answer for. By his own account, he was working on two other librettos at the same time he was putting together *Don Giovanni*, and the available evidence suggests that he may not have devoted to it the fullness of his powers. A good chunk of it, in fact, was lifted directly from a contemporary version by one of his rivals, Giuseppe Gazzaniga. Like most operas, Da Ponte's has its logical gaps. How, for example, does Donna Elvira manage to keep showing up just where Don Giovanni happens to be, at just the wrong time? And what on earth are Masetto and Zerlina doing walking in the door to Donna

---

1. There is no end to this sort of commentary. Interviewing producers of several recent German *Don Giovanni*s for his compendious book on opera production, Rudolf Hartmann received responses like these:

> *Don Giovanni* presents the producer with one of the most fascinating operatic tasks of all—and one of the most mortifying. There is probably no way of finding an answer that satisfies beyond the evening of the première. Countless questions must be answered by any producer. Why does Don Giovanni kill the Commendatore? . . . It now seems incomprehensible that Don Giovanni should have been depicted as an indefatigable philanderer in his prime, when in fact the opera deals with the twenty-four hours of a man whose life is in a state of pathological decay. . . . *Don Giovanni* offers a surfeit of problems. . . . How are we to cope with the problem of the Commendatore's statue? . . . We must assume that the alleged identification of the statue in the churchyard and its appearance in Giovanni's palace were the hallucinations of a disintegrating mind. (Peter Ebert)

> The inscription on the plinth of the statue is of Leporello's own invention, a ruse to coax his master away from the cemetery. . . . And yet the product of Leporello's terrified imagination was so preposterous that even Giovanni would surely have dismissed it, had not his head been befuddled by feasting and wining. [Leporello's] dubious response deluded Don Giovanni into believing that he was standing by the Commendatore's grave. (Rudolf Noelte)

Anna's courtyard just as Leporello is trying to escape? How and when did the trio of masked avengers get together to form their conspiracy? How did the Commendatore's statue (its inscription proves it a recent one) get put in place such a short time after his death? What did Zerlina expect to happen in the antechamber? Could everyone in Seville really confuse Don Giovanni with his servant just because they exchanged cloaks and hats? Where *are* we, most of the time? What *time* is it?

Questions like these have bedeviled commentators for nearly two hundred years. But most of them don't bother me much. Whatever world Don Giovanni and his fellows may inhabit, it is obviously built in great part of conventional theatrical artifice. This is a world where the best jokes and the most spontaneous cries of passion are inevitably repeated four bars later for reasons of musical symmetry. Looking in on such a place, the sympathetic operagoer will accept coincidental encounters, warped time frames, and transparent disguises (by which everyone is deceived) as traditional and expected furniture.

One of my difficulties with Joseph Losey's 1979 film version of *Don Giovanni* arises from his attempt to ignore or deny the native unrealisms of the Mozart–Da Ponte world. By having his cameras close in on real faces in real places, Losey tries to win our conviction through naturalistic characterization. But the effort dissolves in futility every time a character has to sing the same lines six or eight times over ("Morte mi da, morte, morte mi da, morte mi da," and so on). Losey's Commendatore is really killed, gushes real blood in a rain-soaked Palladian piazza in Vicenza. And then we stare into the tormented, "real" face of his daughter as she utters her stock-tragic "Io manco! Io moro!" etc., and try not to giggle. *Everyone* keeps threatening to die of grief (or unrequited love) in this opera. It's a literary conceit that was already tired by the early Renaissance, and one that cannot be resuscitated into realism today.

Other producers, avoiding the naturalistic trap, have taken different directions in their attempts to find a unifying style for this "most difficult" of operas. Throughout most of the nineteenth century, the Faustian-Romantic elements were stressed, even exaggerated. Additional deaths and horrors were sometimes added to those of the original. The flames and demons were enlarged; the "comic" finale was cut. (Jean-Pierre Ponnelle recently found an ingenious means of achieving something of the same effect, while retaining the jaunty final chorus. He had it sung by six terror-stricken people staring down at Don Giovanni's corpse.) All sorts of great stage "effects"—collapsing ceilings, closing-in walls—have served to represent Don Giovanni's doom.

Some of the more celebrated recent versions have made Don Giovanni a total antihero, a creature of the most sinister evil. He becomes a cold, calculating rapist and murderer in a world almost unrelievedly dark—a character infinitely distant from Ezio Pinza's endearing swashbuckler-sensualist. Others have shown him as an old roué well past his prime, a near-dotard unable to score, surrounded by degenerate servants. (Mozart's first Don Giovanni was twenty-two. He must have started early and worked efficiently to attain his tally of 2,065 names.)

Many productions in the 1960s and 1970s went all out for sex, even beyond the heavily erotic implications of text, score, and stage directions. Don Giovanni's palace was stocked with sated, near-naked females, like a Fellini fantasy or Hugh Hefner's Playboy mansion. In one Australian production, Don Giovanni sang "Finch'han dal vino" in his underpants. Götz Friedrich's drunken peasants rolled about in lustful abandon. Joseph Losey illustrated several suggestive lines with nude female flesh, and so heated up Masetto during Zerlina's "Vedrai, carino" (when Teresa Berganza kept repeating, "Toccami qui"—"Touch me here"—in the movie, she was *not* pointing to her heart) that he proceeds to have her up against the nearest wall. Surprisingly, no feminist producer has yet seen fit to resurrect the "comic" episode Mozart added for Vienna, in which Zerlina ties Leporello to a chair and threatens to mutilate him with a razor.[2]

"Proletarian" productions have turned Masetto and Leporello into heroes of the people and the peasant mob into an avenging chorus. In these, Don Giovanni—*un nobil Cavalier*—is punished more for the injustices of his class than for his lechery or disrespect for the dead.

To Freudianize the opera, the stone guest sometimes disappears altogether. The Commendatore's offstage cries become the voice of Giovanni's tortured conscience, and he either kills himself or dies of convulsions. Both Donna Elvira and Donna Anna have been portrayed as over-the-edge neurotics or worse.[3] The Copley/Davis/Lazaridis production of 1973 backed the stage with giant mirrors, so the Covent Garden audience kept seeing itself implicated in these unsavory goings on, and the Don Giovanni images kept multiplying. Maurice Béjart, in Geneva (1980), carried this idea one step further, and had up to ten live alter-ego Giovannis on stage at the same time.

Each of these interpretations may teach us something new about the potential meanings of this opera that others neglect. But each also appears to sacrifice some part of the fullness of *Don Giovanni* in the interests of a unified concept or style. As if determined to prove their seriousness and depth, many producers are willing to forego the lighter, more comic aspects of what Da Ponte specifically labels a *dramma giocoso*—aspects I would have thought unavoidable, given the text and the score. But any jest may be snarled and turned nasty: Zerlina's pliancy, Masetto's jealousy,

2. The scene was reinstated in Peter Sellars's profoundly bleak production at Purchase, New York, in 1989, which is set among drug addicts in a contemporary New York slum.

3. At Purchase, Donna Anna was portrayed as a heroin addict dependent on Don Giovanni for her supply of the drug. She injects herself with a hypodermic needle just before singing the coloratura section of "Non mi dir." Many critics, beginning with Berlioz, have found this section undramatic, to say the least (she has to sing nine and a half bars on the syllable *a* in "sentirà"), inexplicable except as Mozart's concession to a demanding soprano. A drug-induced fit at least provides a new explanation.

his beating, Giovanni's remarks about women, Leporello's greed and envy—all of these may be played either for laughs, or for their vicious implications. Conductors like Otto Klemperer and Karl Böhm can turn the brightest song dark with slow, fateful tempos and a heaviness of orchestral tone. After seeing what Copley, Hall, Ponnelle, and Losey, respectively, had made of *Don Giovanni*, I began to find myself thinking it a mean, amoral, unlovable opera at which one could not possibly laugh long, or take much free-hearted pleasure.

And yet, reading the score or listening to a successful recording (my favorite is still the Giulini version of 1960, with its unsurpassed trio of sopranos), I remain convinced that Mozart and his librettist *did* intend the light aspects of this opera to coexist with, even to dominate, the dark. The brash, iconoclastic, even jolly scenes with which the opera opens and closes strike me as hints from the composer not to take the whole affair too seriously. Minutes before his damnation, over Donna Elvira's moralizing and Leporello's sentimentalizing, Don Giovanni offers a toast to his own hedonist's ideal. His proud, defiant leaps up to D on the accented syllables persuade me that Mozart doesn't entirely disagree:

> Vivan le *fem*mina!
> Viva il buon *vino*,
> So*stegno e gloria d'umanità!*

> Long live women!
> Long live good wine,
> the support and the glory of humankind!

One way of describing the *Don Giovanni* "problem" is to say that Mozart and Da Ponte seem, by turns, to take their story very seriously, and then not to take it seriously at all. The clear-cut tragedy of the Commendatore's murder is instantly deflated by Leporello's "Goon Show" question—"Which one is dead? You or the old man?"—and is then reinflated by the opera seria pathos of Donna Anna and Don Ottavio. The greatest womanizer of all time is frustrated at every step an opera on the theme of coitus interruptus?—and then dragged off to hell for his sins. The astonishing episode of his damnation, with its marble avenger, its chorus of demons, its blaring D-minor trombones, its fortissimo basses and drums, its shrieking scales and tortured harmonics, is preceded by one silly scene—a trivial exchange about piggish mouthfuls of food, sung to self-mocking echoes of the authors' latest hit—and followed by another, a bouncy D-major sextet that seems to mock the whole heavy-breathing effect.

T. S. Eliot tries to explain the problems inherent in *Hamlet*—a work with which *Don Giovanni* is often compared—as the result of Shakespeare's problems in writing it. Given the basic plot he inherited, Shakespeare was obliged to write about supernatural beings, obligations, and punishments (what Eliot calls "the 'intractable' material of the old play") he personally didn't believe in. Something like that may be happening here. Child, to some degree defender of the Enlightenment that he was, Wolfgang Amadeus Mozart couldn't have invested much credibility in the stony guest he had to make use of—this noisy, echoey spectre out of *A Christmas Carol* who now lives somewhere down with Proserpine and Pluto, and takes it on himself to play a sort of selfish revenge god to end Don Giovanni's fun, and ours. Mozart was stuck with the marble Commendatore, and was too tightly placed in cultural history to mock the old legend altogether, in the cynical manner of an Offenbach or a Giraudoux. So we're stuck with him, too.

If the Commendatore walks into this opera from another world, Donna Anna and Don Ottavio walk into it from at least another century. Producers and performers have tried every which way to make them fit, but none of these three seems to breathe the same air as the rest of the cast. Not being a producer, I don't have to resolve these dilemmas—any more than I have to come up with a way to render "dramatic" a static, 209-bar sextet in which the same line ("Che impensata novità!" "What an unexpected development!") is repeated twenty-one times by five people.

Critics have tried to define an overarching unity for *Don Giovanni* in many ways: in the innumerable references (comic and tragic) to death and mortality; in Don Giovanni's own occult influence over all concerned; in the complex algebra of key changes; in the fact that life is made of contradictions, that comic gravediggers do in fact follow hard on tragic suicides. What we may be up against is a composer who was far less troubled by all of these "irreconcilables" than we are—provided he could contain them in music that seemed to him all of a piece.

In general, I think, Mozart *was* able to keep his score coherent and continuous, by finding musical structures that could contain both comic realism and romantic tragedy. The celebrated "Tanzscene" of the Act I finale is just one instance of his "ability to hold two opposed ideas in the mind at the same time," as Scott Fitzgerald puts it, "and still retain the ability to function." Don Giovanni dances away a reluctant Zerlina to one melody (a contredanse), while Leporello waltzes an angry Masetto out of earshot to another, and the noble masquers watch in horror, while pacing a stately minuet. For fourteen of the minuet's bars at least—until Zerlina cries out for help—all three dances, in three different times (3/4, 2/4, 3/8) fit exquisitely into one another, and are somehow able to contain six different sets of emotions.[4]

---

4. In *Mozart's Operas*, Daniel Heartz points out that simultaneous performances of such different dances actually took place in the ballrooms of Vienna, Bonn, Florence, and Prague during Mozart's lifetime. The descriptions and illustrations he discovers "unite to suggest that Mozart did not invent the idea of contrasting dances both successively and in combination with each other, simultaneously. He had observed such phenomena in the world about him."

According to J. C. Robbins Landon in *1791: Mozart's Last Year*, at the grand coronation ball held in

Nearly as impressive is a triple-emotion *terzetto* at the start of Act II. First Giovanni, in "amorous C major," swears he has repented ("Believe me or I'll kill myself"), while Donna Elvira, at the window, tries hard not to believe him, and Leporello tries hard not to laugh. Then, back in A major, Don Giovanni gloats cynically at the success of his ruse, Donna Elvira agonizes over whether to yield, and Leporello marvels at his master's wiles. This three-minded blend is effortlessly sustained. With the voices in harmony, alluring woodwinds and strings weave in and out. Soaring waves of blissful vocalism float in the air, understruck by a moving bass line, until Elvira's yielding soprano lilts lyrically over the rest in descending 32nds, and gives over to the strings as she falls.

If this opera does not "hang together" entirely, it is full of dozens of such instances of this near-miraculous capaciousness, this "yoking of disparates" in a common musical world. The accents of brittle recitatives fall precisely on the up notes of a lyrical melody they undercut. Donna Elvira rages in the most exquisite way. In one moment I love, Giovanni and Elvira are having it out like an angry old married couple, trading patter-pace insults back and forth, while Ottavio and Anna soar on above in their typically long, sweet, old-fashioned lines, wondering which of the two to believe. And each syllable, each note, matches every other on its vertical line.

Da Ponte's stage directions are fairly sparse, and can't provide much help for bewildered producers. Although Mozart conducted his own operas frequently, and we presume that Da Ponte instructed the performers, stage action in their day was still more or less improvised and ad hoc. Mozart may never have seen a live version of *Don Giovanni* as coherent as the opera in his head.

The extraordinary fusion of worlds, characters, and emotions Mozart has wrought in the score of *Don Giovanni* asserts a faith in the unity of human nature and human activity that the plot itself belies. The challenge to any producer is to find a theatrical style as capacious, as capable of embracing absolute contradiction, and yet as graceful and as classically coherent as the style of the notes on the staves of the score.

(1981)

Prague on September 12, 1791 (when the Mozarts were in town for his *La clemenza di Tito* première), "three orchestras in the new room and two in that which connects to the National Theatre were manned by some 300 musicians. . . . It is certain that much of the music of this gala was from Mozart's pen," Landon asserts, "including some of those minuets and German dances which the Prague public so dearly loved."

The Prague public also dearly loved *Don Giovanni*, which had premiered there in 1787. The opera was performed, by imperial command, September 2 of coronation week at the National Theatre, with Mozart present, and as table music at the palace the day before.

Is it altogether fantastic to imagine those three orchestras in the new ballroom at Prague, just three months before Mozart's death, playing, simultaneously, three of his dances?

CHAPTER SIX

What Peter Sellars Did to Mozart

Since the beginning of the 1980s, Peter Sellars (born in Pittsburgh in 1958) has become the most written-about director in the American theatre. Unique among the more creative and venturesome American stage directors, he has focused most of his attention on opera, specifically, since 1980, on the three operas Mozart wrote in collaboration with Lorenzo Da Ponte.

By the age of twelve, Sellars was familiar with Andrei Serban's version of Brecht's *The Good Woman of Setzuan*, knew the theatre work of Cocteau and Josef Svoboda, and was running his own experimental puppet theatre. While in prep school, he outraged the drama instructor (who called him "a glib, exasperating, and bullheaded young man interested only in boosting his own ego") by directing offbeat productions of twentieth-century classics, instead of the safe Broadway standards the department preferred. After graduating from Phillips Academy at Andover, he spent a year in Paris, where he so immersed himself in experimental, anti-Boulevard theatre that he came to regard Samuel Beckett as the norm, Arthur Miller as the aberration. In effect, in his education as in his career, Sellars skipped completely over traditional theatre and theatre practice, and began at the adventurous cutting edge.

As an undergraduate at Harvard (1976–1980), he established his reputation as a theatricalist innovator. He was interested primarily not in new plays, but in unprecedented, challenging, and often slightly mad interpretations of the classics, both modern and historical—an interest later demonstrated in his radically revisionist interpretations of Handel, Mozart, and other opera composers. Soon after he arrived at Harvard, Sellars mounted a production of Shakespeare's *Coriolanus* in which the audience was led down from the balcony to the lobby of the theatre at intermission, where it was taunted by an angry Roman mob. While still a freshman, he produced a gaga version of the Edith Sitwell/William Walton *Facade*

(1922) on the Loeb Theatre main stage and made an unsuccessful proposal to the Harvard-Radcliffe Gilbert and Sullivan Players for a *Gondoliers* dealing with South African divestment. Rejected by (and rejecting) the Harvard theatre establishment, he formed his own "cabaret theatre" in a basement room of Adams House, his residential college. He proceeded to direct more than thirty plays there and elsewhere during his remaining years at Cambridge. "I was incredibly obnoxious," he has said of his Harvard years. "Even more obnoxious than I am now."

Among his Harvard productions were Mayakovsky's *The Bedbug* (based on the 1929 production by Vsevolod Meyerhold, the Russian experimental director on whom Sellars wrote his senior thesis),[1] which he set in the contemporary United States, with shopping carts and Muzak; and Pushkin's *Boris Godunov*, for which the audience was led in procession through the streets and tunnels of Cambridge, to find Boris's body lying in state in the basement of Adams House. The lead in his production of Ibsen's *When We Dead Awaken* was played by a pile of newspapers. He did a four-hour condensation of Wagner's *Ring* with puppets, real people, recorded music, and his own spoken plot summaries. His *Macbeth* was played by a total of three actors in a long, thin corridor; the audience lined the walls. His *Anthony and Cleopatra* was performed around (and in) the Adams House swimming pool—a concept he was to return to later, with a different Cleopatra, in directing Handel's *Giulio Cesare*. The Loeb—Harvard's well-equipped, semiprofessional theatre—invited him back the summer of his junior year to repeat *The Bedbug*, and also to direct Chekhov's *The Three Sisters* (with long silences and Chopin nocturnes between the scenes) and an unusually bloody version of Wedekind's *Lulu*.

He climaxed his Harvard career with an outrageous, four-hour-long *King Lear*

---

1. The ideas of Vsevolod Meyerhold have continued to rule over Sellars's career. Oscar Brockett describes some of the ideas in *The Theatre: An Introduction:*

> To Meyerhold the director was the only true artist of the theatre. He rewrote or adapted plays to fit his own conceptions and shaped every element in accordance with his own vision. His was a director's theatre. . . .
>
> Not interested in psychological realism, Meyerhold wished each of his actors to have a body as efficient as a machine in carrying out the orders of its operator. The actors, therefore, were trained in ballet, gymnastics, and circus techniques until they were capable of responding instantly to the needs of the director. . . .
>
> Meyerhold wished to achieve *theatricalism*. Instead of striving for the illusion of real life, he wished the audience to remain conscious that it was in the theatre. He believed that, since the theatre was an art, all its means should be used self-consciously and to their fullest capabilities. Consequently, he removed the front curtain from the stage, placed lighting instruments in full view of the audience, used a 'gymnastic' approach to acting, juxtaposed many constrasting dramatic elements, and used totally abstract settings called *constructions*. . . . Ultimately, the stage, the actor, and all theatrical elements were viewed by Meyerhold as a single, complex machine to be used by the director. His was a dictatorial approach."

In *The Empty Space*, Peter Brook writes, "In America today, the time is ripe for a Meyerhold to appear, since naturalistic representations of life no longer seem to Americans adequate to explore the forces that drive them."

on the Loeb main stage in February 1980 ("an interminable mired melodrama set in a tempest of technology," wrote the *Harvard Crimson*), in which he played the lead himself, after the black street performer he had originally cast for the role froze during rehearsals. (Sellars is a boyish, impish-looking fellow five feet, four inches tall: not one's standard image of a Lear.) The production included a stage covered with sheet metal, which reflected the overhead lights into the blinded eyes of the audience; screeching music performed on steel cellos, which drowned out many of the lines; an hour-long high-tech storm scene; four working TV sets; an onstage Lincoln Continental (Lear's castle), which each night was stripped down to its frame. (Eight years later, Sellars was to play Shakespeare in Jean-Luc Godard's bizarre film "version" of *King Lear*.)

Even before Sellars graduated, Robert Brustein, artistic director of the American Repertory Theatre (which uses the Loeb Theatre as its home), hired him to direct Gogol's *The Inspector General*—another Meyerhold classic. The production involved giggling Russian ladies dressed in 1950s U.S. prom gowns, who were affixed to a sofa that wheeled in and out, a giant hanging fish, trapdoor entries and exits, music for kitchen pans and kazoo, and a fourteen-foot pineapple that rolled back and forth across the stage.

In 1983, he was engaged as director of the Broadway musical *My One and Only* (based on the 1927 George Gershwin/Busby Berkeley original), intended primarily as a vehicle for Twiggy and Tommy Tune. But his ideas ("*Pajama Game* meets Bertolt Brecht," as one critic characterized them) were rejected as unperformable, or at least uncommercial, before the first out-of-town tryouts. About the same time, Sellars was awarded a five-year "genius grant" from the MacArthur Foundation. The grant (which typically offers the recipient a $1,000 stipend annually for each year of his age), Sellars says, changed the whole nature of his work. "Without the money, I might have given up directing." With it, he felt he could accept whatever projects seemed to him "important and interesting to do." He accepted a three-year contract as artistic director of the Boston Shakespeare Company, where he directed a few unusual productions (of Beckett and Chekhov as well as Shakespeare), but broke his contract after one season. He also directed a Brecht play for the new La Jolla Playhouse in California, in which actors were sent into the farthest reaches of the stripped stage house. For the Guthrie Theatre in Minneapolis, he concocted a bizarre four-hour pastiche called *Hang on to Me*, in which sixteen Gershwin songs were interpolated into a 1904 Maxim Gorki drama of Russian ennui.

The reason Sellars quit Boston in 1984 was that he had been offered, at twenty-six, the job of artistic director of what was to be America's own National Theatre, based at the Kennedy Center in Washington, D.C. His appointment generated a great deal of publicity and no little controversy. After less than two years, he withdrew from the post for what he called "a year's sabbatical." In fact, he never returned, and the American National Theatre (ANT) project collapsed. Under Sellars's slightly frantic direction, the company had been spending from six to eight million dollars each year, instead of the projected two million. Several key productions (out of a total of twenty-four) had to shut down before the end of their scheduled runs. The last work to be performed played to 20 percent capacity houses.

Peter Sellars's own productions during the ANT's eighteen-month lifetime included a version of Sophocles's *Ajax* (repeated in La Jolla) set at the Pentagon after a Latin American war, in which the lead—a "signing" deaf actor—appeared first in a glass booth half-full of blood; Chekhov's *A Seagull*, with Colleen Dewhurst; Robert Sherwood's *Idiot's Delight*, with Stacey Keach and JoBeth Williams; and, in June 1985, a dazzlingly theatricalist, occasionally surrealist version of *The Count of Monte Cristo*, the popular nineteenth-century American melodrama based on Dumas's novel, which James O'Neill (Eugene's father) concocted and then toured in successfully for thirty years. Like some of Sellars's Harvard and Boston Shakespeare productions, *The Count of Monte Cristo* made use of devices (many of them championed by Meyerhold) Sellars has since incorporated into his versions of classic operas: the use of visible stage machinery as a part of the set; dramatic shifts from brilliant light to near-total darkness; circuslike coups de theatre; politically conscious interracial casting and contemporary references; the use of large symbolic objects, giddy clowning, and precisely choreographed movement; heads sticking out of trapdoor dungeons; and, overall, a wild intensity of directorial invention that frequently masked, submerged, or subverted the text from which it was supposedly drawn—no great matter, some critics conceded, for a text as essentially thin as that of *Monte Cristo*.

When he accepted the ANT job in 1984, he told an interviewer that, should the enterprise fail, "at any point I can go back and do Mozart operas in Boston. I don't have this need for everyone to love me." Since the summer of 1986, Sellars has devoted himself almost entirely to opera production, with the exception of a 1922 Soviet "epic" drama (Velimir Khlebnikov's *Zanzegi*) he directed in Los Angeles and Brooklyn in 1986, and an aborted collaboration with the radically innovative Wooster Group of New York in 1987. In the latter year, he was appointed artistic director of the Los Angeles Festival. The first Los Angeles season under his direction, devoted almost entirely to little-known performers and other artists of non-European origin, took place in September 1990.

Peter Sellars's first production of a Mozart opera was a *Don Giovanni* he staged in September 1980 (at the age of twenty-two) for a festival at Manchester, New Hampshire. It was similar in many respects to the darkly contemporary versions he was to offer at the PepsiCo Summerfare in Purchase, New York, in 1987 and 1989. In the cast were James Maddalena and Susan Larson, who have remained part of Sellars's "floating opera repertory company" ever since. His first *Così fan tutte*—closely resembling in concept the 1986, 1987, and 1989 Purchase versions, which featured four of the original six singers, the original conductor, and the original costume designs—was staged for the outdoor Castle Hill Festival in Ipswich, Massachusetts, in August 1984; it was also staged at the Theater der Welt festival in Stuttgart in June 1987. Sellars's version of *The Marriage of Figaro* was first performed at Purchase in the summer of 1988 and repeated there, along with the other two Da Ponte operas, the following summer. *Don Giovanni* and *Figaro* were performed in November and December 1989 at the Maison de Culture at Bobigny, northeast of Paris. All three were videotaped in Vienna in 1989 and telecast internationally during 1991, the bicentennial of Mozart's death.

In addition to the three Mozart–Da Ponte operas, Peter Sellars has also produced Handel's *Saul* and *Orlando* (the latter at the American Repertory Theatre, Cambridge, Massachusetts, 1981); Haydn's *Armida* (Keene State College, New Hampshire, 1981); Gilbert and Sullivan's *The Mikado* (Lyric Opera, Chicago, 1983); Peter Maxwell Davies's *The Lighthouse* (Boston Shakespeare Company, 1983); Handel's *Giulio Cesare* (PepsiCo Summerfare, Purchase, New York, 1985; Opera Company of Boston, 1987; Théâtre Royale de la Monnaie, Brussels, 1988; and Théâtre des Amandiers, Nanterre, 1990, videotaped in 1990); Brecht/Weill's *Das kleine Mahagonny*, on a double bill with staged movements from several Bach cantatas (PepsiCo Summerfare, 1985; and Brooklyn Academy of Music, 1989); Nigel Osborne's *The Electrification of the Soviet Union* (Glyndebourne Touring Opera, Great Britain, 1987); John Adams's *Nixon in China* (Houston Grand Opera, November 1987; subsequently at Brooklyn, Washington, Amsterdam, Edinburgh, and Los Angeles); Wagner's *Tannhäuser* (Lyric Opera, Chicago, 1988); and Mozart's *The Magic Flute* (Glyndebourne Festival, 1990). His production of John Adams's new opera, *The Death of Klinghoffer*, opened in Brussels in March 1991, and was scheduled to be performed after that in five other cities in Europe and the United States.

I want to concentrate my discussion on Peter Sellars's productions of the three Mozart–Da Ponte works at Purchase, New York, in 1989. So I will point out only a few aspects of his other operatic ventures that seem pertinent to what he has chosen to do with Mozart.

The new operas he has produced, Nigel Osborne's *The Electrification of the Soviet Union* (based on a Pasternak novel) and John Adams's *Nixon in China* and *The Death of Klinghoffer*, tend to begin with Sellars's ideas, rather than those of the composer or librettist. On the evidence of such work, it is obvious that he is committed to bringing to the opera stage contemporary (and controversial) political and social issues and events.

But he is no less committed to doing this in his productions of eighteenth- and nineteenth-century works. These are not simply "updatings," like Jonathan Miller's *Rigoletto* set among New York Mafiosi, or a turn-of-this-century *Tosca*. They are insistently, defiantly about today. His version of Handel's *Orlando* (composed in 1724) is set at Cape Canaveral mission control, with Handel's eighth-century hero as an astronaut in a bright orange jumpsuit, and the high priest Zoroastro as a space scientist who studies the stars on his video screen. Handel's *Giulio Cesare* (1711) is set by Sellars in the contemporary Middle East, alongside the swimming pool of an unfinished, terrorist-bombed Cairo hotel, where Cleopatra is working as a cocktail waitress. Caesar is played as a manic Western leader who is visiting Egypt for a summit conference, and threatening nuclear war. Handel's *Saul* (1739) Sellars restages as a Watergate drama; Haydn's *Armida* (1783) he sets in Vietnam, with local children playing the armies, both living and dead.

For the Lyric Opera's *Tannhäuser* (1845), the medieval German knight is turned into a popular modern American TV evangelist of the Jimmy Swaggart sort, teased into sin by the provocative, seminude nymphs of the Venusberg Motel. The song competition takes place in a replica of the Crystal Cathedral in Garden Grove, California, complete with microphones and TV cameras. The "gentlemen of Japan" in Sellars's Chicago *Mikado* (1885) are international business tycoons seated around a boardroom table, with a view out their window of the skyscrapers and neon of Tokyo today. Nanki Poo is a punk rocker who zooms in on a motorcycle; Yum Yum, a miniskirted twit.

Beyond his radical conversion of music dramas originally set in far different times and places into visible tracts for our times, Peter Sellars also introduces a great many individual modern-world artifacts and ideas, usually by way of costumes, props, or dances, like the Lincoln Continental in the Harvard *King Lear*. The shepherd Dorinda in Handel's *Orlando* wears Levi's cutoffs and lives in an Airstream trailer. During the overture to *The Mikado*, Japanese airline hostesses demonstrate to the audience the use of their overhead oxygen masks. The Mikado himself drives on stage in a red Datsun, surrounded by security guards. A chartered jet is ready to fly the pilgrims of *Tannhäuser* to Rome. (Some critics thought Rome an odd place for a lapsed American TV evangelist to go for his pardon.) Lipsticks, machine guns, ballpoint pens, plastic toys, jeeps, Big Macs, and other bits of the detritus of contemporary civilization take on, in Peter Sellars's operas, a heightened symbolic importance. Characters in kicky-current clothes perform modern chorus-line steps, twitchy rock dances, or vaudeville buck-and-wings to eighteenth-century music.

The mock-tangos and Mark Morris–designed dances are only the most explicit forms of choreography in Peter Sellars's operas. Since his earliest musical productions, Sellars has made use of an intricately stylized form of stage movement in which characters blend, writhe, roll, wave their fingers, and twist their torsos in patterns that not only follow, but also seem to "shape" or capture the music of the score. In this, even more than in his elaborate structures of contemporary (and usually American) reference, Sellars reveals himself as a citizen less of the world of opera than of the Western theatrical avant-garde—a phrase, I should add, he professes to hate. In the hands of people like Robert Wilson, Peter Brook, Lee Breuer, Richard Foreman, Andrei Serban, Jerzy Grotowski, Yuri Lyubimov, Laurie Anderson, and Bill Irwin—the men and women who, more than most residents of the opera world, are Sellars's true kindred spirits—this antitraditional, all-embracing, and highly gestural branch of modern theatre has incorporated every possible form of expressive stage movement and effect: Noh and Kabuki, traditional mime, modern ballet, Javanese puppet theatre, vaudeville and burlesque, TV sitcom, American Sign Language, martial arts, commedia dell'arte, Broadway, pop, and folk dance.

Andrew Porter, writing in *The New Yorker*, has been especially impressed by this aspect of Peter Sellars's opera productions. Of *Orlando*, he has written, "In the trio, the three singers move through intricate, mazy patterns that seem not a gloss on the music but a marvelous, living enactment of it. Mr. Sellars' control of the long phrase, of stillness, of sudden shifts of direction, of musical and emotional counterpoints struck me as near-miraculous." Of *Giulio Cesare*: "Sellars hears Handel's music kinetically and realizes it in stage movement suggested by its flow, its tensions, its melodies, rhythms, and dynamic shapes. At its best, his 'choreography' is as subtle, musical, and revealing as Balanchine's."

What success Sellars has achieved in his opera productions so far depends to a very large degree on his having had at his disposal, for the past ten years, a coherent, continuous, and highly disciplined group of singing actors, musicians, and theatre technicians. The very intricacy of his patterns of stage movement, the frequently outrageous things he asks his singers to do (e.g., strip to their underwear, then sing complex eighteenth-century music while rolling on the floor), the circuslike tricks they must perform, and the intensity of certain characterizations could have been achieved only with extensive rehearsals with a unified and willing troupe of performers. The discipline of his company recalls that of Walter Felsenstein at the Komische Oper in East Berlin or Giorgio Strehler at the Piccolo Teatro di Milano, in the years after 1947—two earlier theatricalist innovators in opera with whom Peter Sellars might reasonably be compared.

Craig Smith has conducted most of Peter Sellars's opera productions, except those at the Chicago Lyric and some of the John Adams operas, with a friendly ensemble of Boston-based musicians. (In 1991, Sellars and Smith created a new opera company of their own, based in Boston.) The "company regulars" among his singers are also Boston based, many of them members of the Emmanuel Church music group of which Craig Smith has been musical director since 1970. If Peter Sellars has never worked with opera conductors, orchestras, or singers of the very highest level (he backed out of a scheduled triple bill at the Metropolitan in

1989, planned for Jessye Norman and Samuel Ramey), he has been exceptionally fortunate in his production team—set designers Adrianne Lobel and George Tsypin, costume designer Dunya Ramicova, and lighting wizard James Ingalls—who have been able to realize, perhaps even to inspire, his most unusual and provocative fantasies.

Strange things happened to the expected actions, characterizations, and settings of the Mozart–Da Ponte operas when they fell into Peter Sellars's hands. His versions of all three take place in the United States (apparently in or around New York) and in the present time. In fact, certain political references in *Così fan tutte* were updated between the 1987 and 1989 productions to account for the results of the U.S. presidential election of 1988.

The Marriage of Figaro takes place entirely within a modern fifty-two-story apartment building in Manhattan, specifically identified in Sellars's program notes as the Trump Tower. The Count and Countess Almaviva occupy a lavish two-story penthouse apartment, with vast views in two directions, a large imitation Frank Stella painting on the living room wall, and a landscaped terrace on the lower level (onto which Cherubino leaps, destroying a potted poinsettia). Figaro is the Count's chauffeur, and Susanna is the Countess's maid; the Act I chorus is made up of other service personnel from the building, who come in bearing little Christmas gifts for the Count.

Cherubino, who is called "the neighbor's kid" in the program, is a moody modern teenager who wears jeans and gym shoes with his hockey jersey and shoulder pads, and tends to hang around the Almavivas' laundry room (which is to serve as Figaro's and Susanna's bedroom after their marriage). The boy is surprisingly familiar with both Susanna and the Countess. The wealthy, Manhattan-based Count somehow has the power to order Cherubino into the U.S. Army when he grows impatient with the boy's amorous antics.

Dr. Bartolo and Marcellina are dressed as fashionable upper-middle-class New Yorkers. Sellars tells us that Bartolo is now a professor and that Marcellina, the Count's "executive assistant," has started her own small business. The strained bitterness of their onstage deportment is explained by another of the director's program notes, in which he declares that Marcellina and Bartolo have been carrying on a less-than-happy love affair for more than twenty years. Marcellina, suddenly desperate to be married, decides to force the issue with Bartolo by pretending to "cash in" on an old promise of Figaro's: he must either repay her a considerable debt, or marry her himself. (As it turns out, of course, Figaro is Marcellina's and Bartolo's illegitimate son, although all three appear to be about the same age.) She does this, Sellars tells us, in the hope of eliciting the long-awaited proposal of marriage from Bartolo. He is made miserable by her decision, but offers no proposal. In turn, she is made miserable (we are told) by the trap she now finds herself in, but proceeds with her nasty scheme. As none of these intentions or motivations can be deduced from the libretto, one must intuit them from a combination of the actors' facial and vocal expressions and the director's highly original synopses.

Don Basilio is some sort of devious, greedy pimp or underworld operator, who wears a trendy leather jacket and is identified simply as being "in the music business." It's unclear what his connection is with the Count or, for that matter, with Marcellina and Bartolo, whom he aids in their design to trap Figaro into marriage. Don Curzio, the Count's attorney, carries a cellular phone in his attaché case.

Barbarina is the punkish, pouty, teenaged daughter of the building superintendent. She is in love with Cherubino, but has also (like Susanna) been propositioned by the Count. Figaro, Cherubino, and Susanna all appear to be on terms of casual equality with the Countess. The Countess, depicted as a neurotic, love-starved society woman, very sensually undresses, caresses, tickles, and kisses the nervous Cherubino in Act II and lustily embraces him in Act III. (In the third play of his "Figaro" trilogy—Da Ponte's text is based on the second—Beaumarchais deals with the illegitimate child of the Countess and Cherubino. One could fall back on the French playwright, perhaps, to explain this novel characterization.) When the Count enters her bedroom unexpectedly, he is dressed in Abercrombie & Fitch hunting clothes and carries a rifle, which is a bit puzzling in midtown Manhattan. When his suspicions are aroused, he hurls his wife to the floor, kicks her cruelly, and points a pistol at her head.

For the double wedding, Figaro wheels in a CD player for the march. A crowd of Barbarina's punkish friends dances a sort of erotic, pop-ethnic fandango, choreographed by Mark Morris. Basilio records all the campy carryings-on with a portable video camera. Act IV becomes a decadent indoor/outdoor house party in the manner of Antonioni's *La Notte*, at which both Figaro and Marcellina threaten to kill themselves by jumping from the terrace. Throughout the opera, the emotions and passions (lust, jealousy, vengeance, depression) of almost everyone involved are screwed up to a frantic and destructive or self-destructive pitch.

Don Giovanni, in Peter Sellars's 1989 version, is a feared and brutal young drug addict/rapist in a run-down New York neighborhood, identified by some critics as Spanish Harlem. He and his greedy sidekick/dependent Leporello were played at Purchase in July–August 1989 by black twin brothers, Eugene and Herbert Perry. They dressed almost identically in jeans, black shirts, and dark leather jackets, which added a metaphysical, doppelgänger quality to their role switch in Act II. Whatever the precise locale, the population is racially mixed—and not simply as a result of what is called "open casting."

Giovanni is, of course, a notorious seducer, with (Sellars tells us) "a preference for 12- and 13-year-old girls." Donna Anna, a white woman from a higher class and a better part of town, comes to his neighborhood (the whole opera takes place on the same shabby street) for her heroin. She "shoots up" on stage midway in "Non mi dir" (as does Giovanni during "Finch'han del vino"), and appalls Don Ottavio by showing him the needle tracks on her arm. The *quattro doppie* that Giovanni offers Leporello at the start of Act II are lines of cocaine.

The opera begins with Giovanni's attempted onstage rape of Donna Anna, from which she escapes into an abandoned four-story apartment house that fills the rear of the stage. Her father, a distinguished-looking gentleman in evening dress, happens to arrive on the scene in search of his daughter at that very moment, which is where Giovanni shoots him dead. Anna, "traumatized" by the attempted rape, forces her pathetically confused fiancé Ottavio (a local police officer) to a vow of revenge, repeatedly dipping their hands in her slain father's blood during the repeats of their duet. Ottavio radios for an ambulance, and a team of paramedics carries off the corpse. (Anna's later explanation to her fiancé of what took place is considerably at odds with what we have seen, but Sellars simply tells us that she is lying.)

Donna Elvira, one of Giovanni's 2,065 former conquests, now arrives "from the bus station," a tarty-looking woman in red tights, black boots, a striped miniskirt, and a gold-spangled black jacket. Masetto is a tall local black man given to violence; his new bride Zerlina, in the summer 1989 production, is a fickle young Chinese girl easily tempted by Giovanni. "The palace" Giovanni invites the wedding company to is (we read, although we never see it) a nearby all-night disco. Giovanni's dominion over other members of the cast appears to derive from his reputation as a dangerous criminal entrepreneur, a kind of Mafia *padrone* offering *protezione*—two words of the Italian text that come close to fitting the action.

As there is no real palace (Sellars's Giovanni and Leporello appear to live on, and off, the streets), Giovanni gets Masetto drunk (we are told) at a local bar. Provisions for Giovanni's street party come from the looting of a neighborhood grocery by a menacing gang of blacks, which may or may not be under his control. Masetto actually does beat Zerlina (we hear the blows coming from inside their flat) before she sings, "Batti, batti," which makes her seem more a masochistic "codependent" than a clever Mozartean flirt.

Anna, Ottavio, and Elvira emerge from the abandoned apartment house in jazzy party clothes (but unmasked) to join Giovanni's increasingly wild street dance, in the course of which their host strips down to his underwear ("Viva la libertà!"); some of the guests follow his example. After his second rape attempt in the opera (of Zerlina—inside, it would appear, the neon-crossed church where she was just married), he is surrounded by the three "maskers," plus Masetto, who hold guns to his head and threaten to kill him, but do not.

Midway in Act II, a funeral procession comes on stage carrying the coffin of Anna's father, which is dumped in a gas-workers' hole in the road that has been there all along. Later, her dead father walks, red-eyed, onto a platform above the church facade at left—a platform that had earlier held a different, religious statue, until Don Ottavio yanked it down by a convenient rope.

After parleying with the new statue, Giovanni and Leporello share a final feast—milkshake, hamburger, french fries, Chicken McNuggets—on the front steps of the apartment, while Leporello plays his master's musical requests on a giant "boom box," or portable cassette player. Elvira, a suddenly born-again Christian, arrives bearing a Bible and haranguing Giovanni to repent. He throws his french fries at her. Anna's father's "ghost" rises up, green-lit, inside the apartment lobby behind them. Once again Giovanni strips to his pale blue briefs and follows on his knees a prepubescent girl (a symbol of his vilest vice?) who leads him down a glowing manhole in the torn-up street. Suddenly the nude torsos of sixteen chorus members (souls in hell, perhaps) pop out of trapdoors in the floor like jack-in-the-boxes. Next, Giovanni's five adversaries, wearing shroudlike gowns, pop in and out of similar trapdoors to sing a reduced version of the finale, while Leporello, surrounded by four menacing black thugs, slouches on the darkened stage. The apartment house facade flies apart, red lights appear under the trap doors, and an ashcan bursts into flames. End of opera.

In *Così fan tutte*, Don Alfonso (one learns from Sellars's program notes) is "a Vietnam vet who is having trouble hanging on": alcoholic, embittered, something of a burnt-out case. He has bought his sassy, hard-boiled girlfriend Despina a classic 1930s-style chrome-lined American seaside diner, which they run together and in which most of the action takes place. Theirs is an emotionally exhausting, on-again, off-again relationship, somewhere between Stanley and Stella Kowalski's and Ralph and Alice Kramden's, in which each by turns torments and then makes up to the other. Alfonso's denunciation of women in "Nel mare solca" is violent and deeply personal; Despina's "In uomine, in soldati" and "Una donna a quindice anni" are both sung as the autobiographical accounts of a bitter and brutalized woman.

The relationships among the two other pairs of lovers, who are dressed to suit this contemporary working-class milieu, are not easy to puzzle out in this production, except insofar as all of them seem quite miserable, and grow increasingly disoriented and unhappy as the action progresses. We are told in the program, and to some degree shown on stage, (1) that the two original pairs aren't getting along, and that the men's response to Don Alfonso's challenge is the result of insecure bravado; (2) that the two women are admiring and praising, not their own boyfriends' portraits, but photographs of handsome celebrities in a magazine, and that marriage is the last thing they want; (3) that their violent professions of

affection are really dangerous signs of mental distress; and (4) that they immediately see through the transparent "disguises" of Guglielmo and Ferrando, but
eventually decide (while continuing to reject their "own" fiancés) to go along with
the dangerous mate-swapping game. Meanwhile, the two men "as Albanians"—
costumed and performing exactly like the two klutzy Czech swingers (the "wild
and crazy guys") created by Steve Martin and Dan Ackroyd on TV's "Saturday
Night Live"—grow increasingly pushy and gross, as if their "disguises" allowed
them freedoms they would not have otherwise taken. Much of the action throughout the opera seems to be prompted or directed by Don Alfonso and Despina.

Sellars's version of the mock-suicide scene is played mainly for low-comic laughs.
The "poison" the men take comes from the diner's plastic catsup and mustard
containers. The mesmeric doctor Despina impersonates is modeled on the movie
actress Shirley MacLaine, in her recent incarnation as a psychic medium. (In earlier
productions, the part was modeled after Dr. Ruth Westheimer, the popular American TV sex counselor.) Dr. Despina wheels in a huge "Die-Hard" brand, German-
made battery, which she attaches by jumper cables to the dead men's crotches. Their
penises spring to life independently of the rest of their bodies.

In the second half of the bitter game, Dorabella and Guglielmo *do* in fact appear
to fall hopelessly in love with each other, while Fiordiligi goes nearly out of her
mind trying to reject the advances of her sister's old sweetheart. The men's mutual
confessions (of erotic victory and defeat) lead Guglielmo first to drink, then
(during "Donne mie") to a frantic, abusive tour through the theatre with a hand
microphone, during which he pulls up women from the audience in the manner of
a Donahue-like TV talk-show host to denounce the unfaithfulness of all of their
sex. The result for Ferrando is an implacable self-disgust and a hatred that continue
into the final, profoundly bleak wedding scene (at which the "guests," unaccount-
ably, appear half-asleep in their nightclothes) and the "return" of the undisguised
men. Because, as I say, the disguises never fooled anyone on stage for a moment, it
is sometimes difficult to know what to make of the hysterical outbursts and
distraught behavior of everyone concerned.

In the past twenty or thirty years, there have been hundreds of productions of
standard repertory operas, from Monteverdi through Puccini, set in times and
places other than those indicated in the texts or favored by their original creators.
In addition to the abstract, symbolist, or otherworldly settings frequently used for
Wagner, opera seria, and other legendary or expressionist operas (*The Magic Flute*,
Pélleas et Mélisande, *Elektra*, *Jenůfa*, *Lulu*), we have had *La forza del destino* set during
the Spanish Civil War, 1930s *Don Pasquales*, Norma singing "Casta diva" from the
turret of a tank (or as a survivor of the Nazi Holocaust), Rigoletto as a bartender in
1950s New York, Carmen as a modern guerrilla, Aida pushing a mop, Madame
Butterfly living through World War II in Nagasaki (and killing herself just as the

atom bomb explodes), Gluck's leather-jacketed Orfeo losing his Euridice in a car crash, and a *Ritorno d'Ulisse in patria* in which the war Ulysses is returning from is the war in Vietnam. A favorite device is to stage an old opera not in the era in which the author intended it, but in the year in which it was first produced: hence all the 1876 Wagner *Rings*, and Strauss operas set in the 1910s and 1920s. The French Riviera (for comedies) and the Fascist dictatorships (for tragedies) have been especially popular for such updatings, in which producers often use the earlier work to "make a statement" about the modern world. Confined mainly to German opera houses in the 1960s and early 1970s, such productions are now as likely to turn up at Cardiff or Long Beach as Kassel.

Peter Sellars insists he has no patience with such restagings. "I *hate* updatings as a gambit," he says. "I resent it actively—it's cheap and vulgar and obnoxious and not to the point. My productions are never updated." Instead, he declares, he is juxtaposing cultures, setting up a "visual counterpoint" to the music to stimulate the greatest possible intensity and range of response. To recreate the novelty and shock of the Mozart–Da Ponte operas at their première performances, without obliging either modern actors or modern audiences to imagine their way into another century, he recasts them in the "image language" or "systems of reference" of the contemporary United States. In this way, he insists, he is trying not to update great works of the past, but to "test the present against them," not to make some specific comment about U.S. society today, but to get at the heart and core of the work: the characters' emotional plights as revealed in the score. Powdered wigs and satin breeches, sabers and candelabra and rococo garden sets are all, he believes, inessential trappings that get in the way of Mozart's essential meanings and drama. "I believe very strongly," he was quoted as saying while still at Harvard, "that the point of the theater is to make people notice the present. Most people go to the theater to escape the present."

Critics favorably disposed to Sellars's versions of Mozart admit to being unhappy with some of his grosser inconsistencies, and with his dark and narrow visions of the Mozart–Da Ponte worlds. But they have little or no trouble with his contemporary American restagings, which they regard (I am paraphrasing) as viable starting points for explorations of the emotional life of these operas in overtly modern terms. They praise the operas' cultural immediacy and passionate vitality. In general, his defenders argue, every movement in these operas, every gesture, every invention, every response, springs directly from the score, which Sellars and his conductor-partner Craig Smith have obviously studied very closely. Above all, they praise the theatricalism, the high-spirited intensity, and the ensemble finesse. However many faults they may find in his rewritings and interpretations, they insist—comparing his productions with international-style Mozart, for which well-known singers are flown into traditional stagings—on Sellars's greater theatrical brilliance and power to seize. Like the operas or not, the Sellars advocates insist, you will find them "stimulating," "engrossing," "gripping," "vibrant," "immediate," "shocking," "vivid," and "wildly imaginative."

Sellars's own explications and defenses of his stagings of the Mozart operas appear in the casual, quirky, and apparently unedited introductions to and plot summaries of each opera he has written, which are distributed to audiences at productions. (The summaries are of *Sellars*'s operas, rather than the simpler, earlier versions of Mozart and Da Ponte.)

In a recent interview for *American Theatre*, Sellars belittles the theoretical writings of Bertolt Brecht (whose plays and poems he greatly admires). "I should know, I put out a fair amount of that stuff—you know, stuff that's designed to annoy people or provoke." He was referring, I suspect, to things like his program notes for the Mozart–Da Ponte operas, which are clearly designed to be "outrageous." Because these operas were presented in contemporary sets and costumes during the 1780s and 1790s, he insists, they should be presented in contemporary sets and costumes today. Because they were full of notoriously topical references for eighteenth-century audiences, they should be full of modern topical references today. He cites the U.S. drug traffic (for *Don Giovanni*) and the Leona Helmsley trial (for *The Marriage of Figaro*) to prove that "the oppressive class structure that Mozart depicted is alive and well 200 years later in The United States of America." He refers to an unusually promiscuous AIDS patient to demonstrate that the totals in Leporello's catalogue are more realistic than fantastic. "The Count has a severe Ed Meese–type memory lapse" regarding his sexual overtures to Barbarina. "Bush has decided to invade Panama" is his explanation for Ferrando's and Guglielmo's being recalled to active duty.

It is in these program notes that we first learn of the unusual motivations and relationships Sellars has decided to attribute to Marcellina and Bartolo, Don Ottavio and Donna Anna, Don Alfonso and Despina, the four lovers of *Così fan tutte*; of Don Giovanni's pedophilia, Donna Anna's drug addiction, and Ottavio's antifeminist disgust with his rape-victim fiancée. It is here we learn that Ferrando in *Così* is "the composer's own tortured self-portrait"—a way of reading Mozart's music I thought had been discredited some years ago. Sellars imposes new moralistic readings, or patches over inconsistencies (like the unmasked maskers), simply by adding a few lines to these notes. In them, he alternates slangy gags and winking asides with paragraphs of philosophizing. Here is his gloss on the difficult-to-stage ensemble that concludes "Che impensata novità!" (What an unexpected development!: the line has to be repeated twenty-one times by five people through sixty-one bars) in Act II, Scene 8 of *Don Giovanni*. The disguised Leporello has just revealed his true identity in order to escape being killed by Giovanni's enemies.

In the terrifying presumption of appointing themselves instruments of God's divine wrath, they have omitted to consider the unknowability of the world and the frailty of human certainty. And they have failed to reckon with God, who is certainly working in mysterious ways. A thousand murky thoughts course through everyone's head as they pass through their own personal dry run for the Last Judgement, suddenly forced to examine their own motives as their attempt to cast the first stone is thwarted. In the whirlwind of high anxiety and private doubt each character is confronted by an intimation that there is nothing hidden that shall not be revealed. "Che impensata novita" what unexpected news the characters keep repeating. After a while those words are transfigured into a meditation on the un-thought-of New Life.

As a writer, rather than a theatre professional, I admit to being almost as put off by these turgid, pushy, and ill-written exercises in specious self-defense (which many critics quote uncritically, as if they did indeed justify what is happening on stage) as I am by the excesses of the productions themselves. But perhaps the author intends them to elicit precisely my reaction.

In his notes for *Don Giovanni*, Peter Sellars writes, "To those who object to the absence or alteration of certain details of the setting, I would rather like to say, with the spirit of the Commendatore, 'Non si pasce di cibo mortale chi si pasce di cibo celeste; altri cure, piu gravi di queste, altra brama quaggiu mi guido [He who has fed on the bread of heaven has no need of earthly bread; I am guided by a greater purpose, a different mission than this].'" In the handout, Sellars leaves this quotation untranslated, perhaps hoping that "those who object" will pass over the celestial arrogance of his response.

To people who have wondered why productions so visibly modern and American are sung in Italian, Sellars has replied that none of the available English translations is good enough. One may well agree, but the response appears disingenuous. Were his singers to perform in the language of the audience (or with accurate supertitles), non-Italian speakers would very quickly realize that a great deal of Sellars's stage action is utterly at odds with Da Ponte's texts. People are often saying things that make no sense.

Andrew Porter, since 1984 one of Sellars's most ardent advocates among American music critics, defends this textual nonsense on the rather tired argument that *all* opera is antinaturalistic (real people don't converse in song, with an orchestra present, etc.), and that Sellars's stagings are just more patently antirealistic than most others: why not tolerate one layer of nonsense more? ("Among so many conventions, it is easy to accept another: that an eighteenth century text is being sung, in Italian, to eighteenth century music, in a modern New York setting.") He finds the discordance between the words Sellars's actors are singing and the things they are doing to be "undisturbing, even piquant," and he mocks the "literal-minded" who object.

And yet Porter has also written, "Sellars pays keenest attention to what the characters say and sing." One's response to this issue may depend on how well one knows the original text (or can understand sung Italian); and on just how much nonsense (or "antinaturalist convention") one is prepared to tolerate, even in opera.

That Sellars ignores many of Da Ponte's cast descriptions and stage directions and substitutes his own bothers me not at all, as long as the music and sung text do not demand the original versions. Characterizations and stage directions in the theatre range from the minimal (Greek tragedy, Shakespeare) to the maximal (Shaw, O'Neill), and directors have long felt free to improvise their own. In *Così fan tutte*, for example, we "should" be, by turns, in a garden overlooking the Bay of Naples, the ladies' boudoir, a garden at the seashore with grass seats and two small tables, a room in the sisters' house, and a large richly bedecked room with a table set for four. Instead, we spend the whole opera in and outside of a streamlined American diner, or in artificial garden flats along the side walls of the theatre. Boats are supposed to arrive on stage to carry the two men off to war, or to bear on singers and musicians. Instead, Alfonso plays with a model warship behind the counter that is "bombarded" by toy planes; the chorus is made up of townspeople protesting current U.S. political acts. Instead of drawing their swords, the men pick up table knives; instead of poison vials, they drink from condiment jars. The "well-bred ladies," who obviously aren't, and their equally lowbrow swains refer to hydras, basilisks, phoenixes, Penelope, Artemisia, Cupid, Venus, Mars, the Eumenides, Cythera, Jove, Mercury, Pallas, Narcissus, and Charon—an example, perhaps, of the "cultural juxtaposition" that Sellars and Porter find so piquant.

Locations in classic opera (like Shakespeare's "seacoast of Bohemia") are often little more than conventions—although some aspects of Italy and Spain are written into Mozart's music. I can accept Dorabella lamenting, from somewhere in Westchester County, that her lover has "left Naples"; references to nearby Burgos in a New York–set *Don Giovanni;* and references to nearby Seville in a New York–set *Figaro*. Innovative and still credible productions of Shakespeare plays have accustomed us to kings, counts, and emperors, who are visibly *not* kings, counts, or emperors but rather their latter-day counterparts as heads of state or men of power. I balk at "royal edicts" cited in modern American settings (and have never grown completely comfortable with a Harlem crook being addressed as *cavaliere* or *sua eccelenza*). But in the end I concede that, if Donald Trump's tower can be owned by a count, then New York can have a king.

The trappings, rituals, and attitudes of a genuine aristocracy, however, the elaborately class-structured society on which so much of Mozart's and Da Ponte's

MOZART, *Così fan tutte*, Susan Larson (left) and Janice Felty,
PepsiCo Summerfare, 1989. Photograph by Peter Krupenye.

dramas depend, can seem ludicrous in modern-day American settings. Don Giovanni's seduction of Zerlina hinges on his insisting (and her credulously accepting)
that the morals of noblemen like him have been slandered by plebeians like her.
But look at the two people who are singing the lines! Don Ottavio, an undercover
cop, has trouble believing that a "fellow aristocrat" like Giovanni (visibly a drug
addict and a criminal) could possibly have dishonored a woman. Don Giovanni
has no palazzo; a New York penthouse is not a *castello*. Although the Count refers
to Figaro as his vassal, and Cherubino as his page, it is inconceivable that a New
York socialite could order a neighbor's son off to war. All the lines and verses about
the Count's having (it is hoped) abolished the droit de seigneur (itself a fabrication
of Beaumarchais, according to Daniel Heartz) make no sense. Quite apart from the
more serious inconsistencies in the character of Marcellina as conceived by Peter

Sellars, it is a little silly to hear her addressed by Susanna as "la dama d'onore, di Spagna l'amore."

Peter Sellars's *Don Giovanni* traduces dozens of individual lines, from the condemned man's feast—Giovanni and Leporello sing of their pheasant and fine wine while eating Big Macs and sipping milkshakes through a straw—to Leporello's "fat little book" (in fact, a porno slide show) of all the noblewomen and commoners his young New York padrone had somehow seduced throughout Europe. Giovanni orders Leporello to show his guests through the garden, the gallery, the apartments, and the ballroom of his palace, to offer them chocolate and coffee, wine and prosciutto; instead, they mill about a dirty street and drink stolen beer.

When I arrived home from Purchase in the summer of 1989, suffering under the pressure of these conceptual muddles, one of the first things I did was to reread the librettos and note every line in these operas that had belied its own visible incarnation. These varied from the trivial (seven references to Seville in *Figaro*, the costumes supposedly worn by Cherubino and Leporello, smashed poinsettias instead of carnations in *Don Giovanni*), through the annoyingly nonsensical (any number of objects referred to that simply weren't there: trees, muskets, swords, masks, torches, cloaks, chocolate and sorbet, a casino, a night cap, arsenic, mustachios, poor peasant girls), to the dramatically substantial.

Peter Sellars's claim that he is simply trying to juxtapose alien cultural imagery in the hope of provoking new ideas is all very well. But what are the members of a chorus impersonating modern American employees supposed to think or mean, and what are we supposed to think as we listen to them, when they sing the praises of their employer for not claiming his medieval "right" to deflower any bride-to-be in his employ? For all the garbage Figaro overturns and the fresh eggs he hurls against the wall, his "Non più andrai," addressed to this particular Cherubino, simply makes no sense. Anna, Elvira, and Ottavio wear no masks at Giovanni's street party. Sellars explains this away casually in his notes. But Giovanni has lines that indicate shock and surprise when he "recognizes" the three later, after they "unmask." Giovanni serenades an empty window; the Elvira represented here obviously has no maidservant.

In *Così*, at a time when Despina and Alfonso are on stage together in their diner, he supposedly "knocks at her door," and she asks, "Who's there?" Despina is called a chambermaid, and the two sisters her employers, which they visibly are not. While Dorabella and Fiordiligi are loudly proclaiming their outraged refusal to grant their Albanian suitors a kiss, the four of them are writhing in sensual couplings all over the floor.

Does *none* of this matter? I think it does. I cannot conceive of serious singing actors, attempting to incarnate created characters, so frequently having to say things that belie the very characters they are playing, and the world they are pretending to inhabit. What fruitful frisson an audience is to receive from this nonsense-making "juxtaposition of cultures" I cannot imagine. What it frequently produced at Purchase were giggles and guffaws.

Acting "against the text"—and, in the case of opera, against the music—is another matter, and clearly one in which a director's creative liberty may prevail. It is one thing (and an awkward thing) for an actor to refer to his sword and then pull out his gun; it is quite another for a woman to profess her hatred for a man she secretly loves. All three of the Mozart–Da Ponte operas are full of scenes of conscious and semiconscious deceit, self-deception, uncertain motives, and the like. There is no reason a director may not, within a coherent scheme (which need not be naturalistic), discover others still.

I cannot bring myself to accept Peter Sellars's novel readings of Marcellina and Donna Anna. But I grant that they *can* be made to fit the text and score by the application of a little pressure to the way in which lines are acted and notes are sung. A Marcellina who breaks into frustrated tears at the end of her Act I duet with Susanna (a duet I always thought was meant to be funny), a Donna Anna whose coloratura outburst at the end of "Non mi dir" is explained as the result of a heroin injection are possible, perhaps, but they are certainly strained directorial conceits.

Others of Sellars's original interpretations of characters (and, hence, of their music) are more persuasive—occasionally, in fact, quite moving—enlargements of the roles. The wrenching moral confusion of his Don Ottavio—totally uncertain whether to trust his demented fiancée—yields a perversely twisted reading of "Dalla sua pace," ugly but honest, operatic but sordid, in which the lyric line is totally ravaged. Evil as the whole idea seems, and utterly at odds with the music, it does provide a real "action" for what is usually a mere tenor showpiece. The heavily erotic, beautifully choreographed undressing (rather than dressing) of Cherubino by Susanna and the Countess is breathtaking in the way in which it seems to grow entirely out of the three spiring and intertwining vocal lines. Sellars's sublime staging of "Dove sono," with the Countess posed on a mezzanine balcony against a giant picture window—at times clutching at the glass, her back to us, as a magenta-orange sunset fades over Manhattan—is one of the unforgettable sound-and-sight moments of opera. Almost everything that Don Alfonso and Despina sing in the presence of each other takes a new and poignant depth from Sellars's conception of them as battle-scarred lovers—most notably, their "school for lovers" mime, where the two of them teach their inept charges how to make love, how to woo and be wooed. Two different plays are going on at once: their "act" for the confused young lovers, and the much darker, more deadly serious act they are playing for each other. "Una donna a quindici anni" is sung to a cruel, mimed restaging of their entire relationship. One may never have expected to hear

Despina singing "Viva Despina che sa servir" while cringing, shaking, and near to tears—singing the words, in effect, against the obvious line of music and text; but given the character Sellars has developed, this makes fine and pathetic sense.

Singing, acting, and moving against the music—or at least against the apparent emotional direction of music and text—can be a dangerous game for a director to play. One memorably jarring, and in the end half-convincing example is Fior-diligi's "Come scoglio," in which she goes off her head in the course of the song—proving that she is anything *but* "like a rock"—and ends up collapsed on the floor, tickled by the others, which encourages us to envision her greater collapse to come. Sellars, who has expressed his disdain for traditional, beautiful showcase arias (and who rarely works with singers who could do them total justice in any case), often seems eager to contradict or "de-beautify" such arias by having the singers spit out their words in a spitefully ironic fashion; by forcing them through weird and wild movements during their songs; or simply by following their final notes immediately by some jarring new action (Despina drops a pile of dishes just as "Soave sia il vento" whispers to its close)—which, of course, also inhibits applause.

This kind of criticism may seem unfair to a producer who has, one often reads, the most impeccable respect for Mozart's scores. Peter Sellars and Craig Smith have been at once generous and careful about appoggiaturas, vocal embellishments, the music of recitatives, and the overall integrity of the published scores. But a number of their decisions may lead one to question the quality and depth of that respect.

Adding, subtracting, and moving numbers (even whole scenes) in the Mozart–Da Ponte operas was standard practice even before Mozart's death in 1791. Of itself, this is certainly no sign of disrespect. One is always curious, however, about why a producer or conductor makes such decisions. One of the more unusual Sellars/Smith choices is to replace Dorabella's lovely "È amore un ladroncello" (Love is a little thief) in Act II, Scene 10 of *Così* with the troubled "Vado, ma dove?" (I go, but where am I going?)—an aria Mozart composed for a completely different opera.[2] Sellars does this, I presume, because the sentiments and music of "È amore" are too frivolous for his conception of Dorabella's near-psychotic mental state at this point, while "Vado, ma dove?" fits it very neatly. He also imports a tender musical interlude (an arrangement for fortepiano from the first movement of Mozart's G-major piano concerto, K. 453) to accompany Guglielmo's and Dorabella's stroll in the garden before their duet.

In *The Marriage of Figaro*, the adagio from the E-flat Serenade for Winds (K. 375)

2. Martin y Soler, *Il burbero de buon cuore*. (The Mozart aria, written for his first Dorabella, is K. 583.)

is performed to close up the gap between Acts I and II, where it also serves as a prelude to the Countess's sad and self-pitying "Porgi, amor." The usually cut final-act arias for Marcellina and Basilio are retained. Both are interpreted in the harrowing, neurotic style that dominates Sellars's version of this opera. Sellars characterizes Basilio's "In quegli anni" as "an aria of unbearable self-loathing." The second half of Marcellina's "Il capro e la capretta" is turned into a violent feminist outburst, which ends with her contemplating suicide.

In *Don Giovanni*, Sellars restores the awkward and disagreeable Scene 10b of Act II, which is rarely performed in the theatre. (In thirty years of *Giovanni*s, I had never before seen it staged.) In this scene, which Sellars calls "wonderfully comic," Zerlina traps Leporello, ties him to a chair, and whirls about a great kitchen cleaver with which she threatens to cut off various parts of his body.

Even more interestingly, Sellars decided to cut the sixty-one bars of "reconciliation" music and text for the puzzled survivors that follow Don Giovanni's damnation. "We are making this cut," he writes in his notes, "because we feel it reflects a much more accurate picture of Mozart's last thought on the subject and shows greater insight in the inability of these characters to find easy solutions to their situations." In this opinion, Sellars is rejecting the judgment of virtually all twentieth-century Mozart scholars.[3] The "insight" shown in cutting the next-to-last lines of the opera is really more Peter Sellars's than Mozart's and, like most of the producer's textual decisions, seems intended to strengthen, even to force, an unrelievedly dark interpretation.

3. In his program notes, Peter Sellars asserts that Mozart himself chose to cut bars 689–749 for the Vienna production of 1788, as an indication of the composer's final and considered artistic opinion. Others disagree.

In *Mozart*, Wolfgang Hildesheimer writes:

It is highly debatable whether Mozart "approved" the cut of this scene in the Vienna production, or whether he was accommodating some wish from above or below. It would not have been the only time. Wolfgang Plath and Wolfgang Rehm, the editors of *Don Giovanni* in the *Neue Mozart-Ausgabe*, write, "Strictly speaking, there is only one version of *Don Giovanni* which has an absolute claim to authenticity; that is the opera as it was composed for Prague and performed there on October 29, 1787, with unparalleled success. Likewise, this is the only version which can be called definitive. The so-called Viennese Version, after all we can conclude from the source material unearthed, is anything but clear; rather it is by nature variable, experimental, open-ended." Right. Strictly speaking, the Viennese adaptation is no version at all but something produced ad hoc to which Mozart had to accommodate himself.

Julian Rushton contends in *W. A. Mozart: Don Giovanni*: "Unfortunately, we do not know which form of *Don Giovanni* Mozart preferred, although it was probably the original version [i.e., with the final scene uncut] that he directed, the last time he heard it, in Prague on 2 September 1791. . . . In default of further evidence the chronology of these cuts must remain uncertain; possibly various ways of ending the opera were tried out during 1788. There is no way of knowing which the authors finally preferred." Similar opinions are expressed in Hermann Abert, *Mozart's Don Giovanni*; Alfred Einstein, ed., *Don Giovanni* (Eulenberg miniature score); Georges de Saint-Foix, *W. A. Mozart*; Christof Bitter, "*Don Giovanni* in Wien, 1788"; James Liebner, *Mozart on the Stage*; William Mann, *The Operas of Mozart*; Jean Victor Hocquard, *Le Don Giovanni de Mozart*; and *Mozart: Don Juan*, *L'Avant-scène opéra*, no. 24, notes by Jean Victor Hocquard and Pierre Malbos.

Two other aspects of Sellars's productions may be troubling to viewers who believe (as I do) that most of the potentially deepest meanings of these operas are conveyed by Mozart's vocal lines. The first is a maddening tendency to stop all music and action dead for ten, fifteen, even twenty seconds, in order to achieve what I presume are meant to be "meaningful" dramatic pauses. These occur just before (or after) a character's unexpected arrival; before lines or verses the director wants to underline (e.g., the last chorus of "Se vuol ballare"); or whenever the director wants to leave time for deep thoughts or comic doubletakes. *Figaro*'s "Sua madre" ensemble is riddled with these vaudevillian holes. There are more than a dozen major breaks in *The Marriage of Figaro* alone, including a barbarously long pause between the andante and allegro of "Dove sono." An equally long and musically disruptive pause separates the final repeat of Ferrando's "Un'aura amorosa" from the rest of the song. Sellars seems unwilling to trust an audience to get Mozart's musical points, just as he seems unwilling to trust Mozart's music to convey the composer's dramatic intentions, without his own heavy-handed and melodramatic punctuation.

A second antimusical innovation involves the poses and postures in which Sellars's actors have to sing. In all three operas, magnificent arias are sung by people facing away from us, pressing their heads against a wall, lying on their stomachs or their backs, falling repeatedly to the floor, writhing on their spines, fighting, making love, crawling, or rolling over and over. The stage pictures that result may be powerful, handsome, and apt. But there goes the music. For the singer, accuracy and purity of tone are bound to be lost. For the listener, whole notes are muffled, or disappear completely. Cherubino lies prone on Figaro's and Susanna's sofa bed while singing "Non so più," humping the mattress as if masturbating ("Ogni donna mi fa palpitar"). The action is as tawdry as a scene from any horny-teenager movie; more seriously, it kills the music. The point and poignancy of "Non so più" lie wholly in its vocal line. By forcing the singer into this ludicrous mime, the vocal line is shot.

Sellars has frequently been praised for another kind of movement-to-music: his unique and intricate weaving of many stage traditions into an antinaturalistic and musically expressive choreography for his singers to use during their arias and (especially) ensembles. "Deeds of music made visible," Andrew Porter has called these movements, adopting Wagner's description of his own theatrical ideal. For these I have nothing but admiration. Sellars has devised apt, expressive, and "musiclike" movements, which his actor-singers (become dancers) enact with consummate skill.

The great Act II finale of *Figaro* is transformed into a sung dance of four against three, in which each member of each team moves hands and feet to the line of his or her own music. "Sua madre / suo padre" is set to a similarly clever dance of good guys versus bad guys. After the first, "acted" line of the Act III Letter Duet,

Susanna and the Countess begin twirling about slowly like ancient Chinese dancers, turning as if on ice skates (each move a visual counterpart of their sung notes). They fall softly to their knees, then to the floor, roll over, kneel up, roll back, shaping with their paired, bent bodies the suave and subtle music of this most tender of duets.

When Donna Elvira is declaiming against Don Giovanni, he is insisting she is mad ("La povera ragazza è pazza"), and Ottavio and Anna are wondering which of the two to believe, the director has the three others wall Elvira in by walking around her in a tight triangle, each singing a line as he or she steps to stage front. The minuet of the three conspirators is performed as a nearly static step-side, step-back dance, the offbeats accented with finger snaps.

Così fan tutte is almost "through-choreographed," perhaps because Sellars and company have been working on it so long and so consistently. Whole numbers are mimed by hands waving like swimming fish, twisting and clutching in pairs, rising high for individual high notes, shaking wildly on insecure trills. The more emotional arias and ensembles are sung by people dropping to their knees, writhing on their backs, or rolling in gentle waves on the floor. Erotic duets are sung by couples kneeling front to front, then back to back, moving in slow mirror images, cringing, crawling, grasping, their locked hands dancing separately from their bodies. The "Albanians" dance a kind of twitching comic soft-shoe, with their index fingers lifted. Despina and Don Alfonso tango as they sing, with the intimate violence of experienced sexual partners. To military music, the two officers move sharply (first one, then the other) right, left, about, hands up, hands out. Their girlfriends join them, twirling and singing to their eighth notes, while the men move and sing to their quarter notes, each following a separate line of music. *In actual fact*, they make the music visible. At one chilling moment in the Act I farewell, the "wrong" couple crosses from their hand-holding circle dance. Passing a bit too closely, they exchange a dangerous glance, like a moment from José Limon's *Othello*-based ballet, *The Moor's Pavane*. Both finales are shaped into six-person chorus lines out of which individual members keep breaking, fighting, rejoining, dancing, grabbing, quitting, whirling, until at the end everyone is spinning separately, a once-ordered cosmos in which every planet has turned selfish and mad.

This sort of thing is worth diamonds. Of itself it would justify seeing the opera, buying the videocassette. But it comes at a price. First, you are never going to persuade an Elizabeth Schwarzkopf or a Margaret Price to master and undergo these contortions. The Sellars/Smith company of singers is more than adequate vocally. Some are at times quite good. But none is able to achieve the expressive vocal power of at least a dozen other Mozart singers I have heard in these roles. And much of their own singing, however good or bad it might be, obviously has to be less clear and effective because of all this bending and twirling.

Peter Sellars could never have achieved such complex patterns of integrated movement except by means of a coherent and disciplined troupe of "resident" performers, willing and able to rehearse for long periods of time. To obtain the semi-gymnastic spectacle he desired (expression through gesture), some degree of vocal quality and projection (expression through words and music) had to be sacrificed.

Critics have made precisely the same observation about certain operas produced by Giorgio Strehler and Walter Felsenstein. You may not always get the greatest vocal performances in their productions. You may sacrifice something of musical expression. But the total integrated spectacle gives you so much more good theatre, they declare, that the sacrifice is worth it. The work of all three producers can be traced back to the theatricalist ideals of Vsevolod Meyerhold, Peter Sellars's distant Russian master. Neither *prima la musica* nor *prima le parole;* but in the beginning was the gesture. "What the audience sees is more important, I would venture to say, than what it hears, because we think in images" (Peter Sellars, 1980).

Peter Sellars has looked deeply into the Mozart–Da Ponte scores and librettos (and, I presume, deeply into himself and the world he inhabits) and found dark and ugly things. He has found men who beat and brutalize women, women possessed by lust for men who are not "theirs," couples involved in selfish, poisonous, mutually destructive relationships. These he has realized by onstage scenes of sex and violence so explicit that the reconciliation scenes that inevitably follow in Mozart (scenes that are virtually dictated by the "recapitulation" sequences of late-eighteenth-century sonata-form progressions) become virtually impossible to credit—which may be part of Sellars's plan.

When sex is "serious," it is presented in near-pornographic images: the Count shoving his hand under Susanna's short skirt, his head under her apron, as she stands backed up against a wall; Leporello's slide show of Giovanni's conquests, sleazy *Hustler* magazine–type shots of naked women whose eyes are blacked over; the nymphet who leads Giovanni, stripped and groveling, to his doom; Despina forcing Don Alfonso to crawl, while she rides him like a horse. Fiordiligi, Don Giovanni, and Cherubino all perform whole scenes in their underwear. When sex is "comic" in Sellars's operas, it is little more than a series of sophomoric crotch jokes.

Almaviva throws his wife to the floor and kicks her, holds a gun to her head. Ottavio hurls, drags, slams, and shoves Donna Anna about. Masetto *does* beat Zerlina. Ferrando and Guglielmo, when they pretend to discover their fiancées' false marriage contract, shove them to the floor and start choking them.

In each opera, someone reaches a point of such manic frustration that he or she simply has to toss things around, smashing eggs or cans or bottles all over the set. Silent characters in black lurk menacingly about. All of these qualities are incarnated in the set and background action of *Don Giovanni:* a street cracked apart by a deep hole in which cocaine addicts snort and bodies are dumped; bloody hands held up in the shadows; undressed people twitching and crawling, as a garbage can bursts into flame.

Peter Sellars claims, correctly, that most of the dangerous emotions he depicts can be traced to the original texts. All three operas are far more about real sex than most people pretend. In the two more serious works sexual politics and class warfare are combined. Parts of *Don Giovanni* are harsh, cruel, and full of hate. Almaviva is a wildly jealous, proud, lust-driven, vengeful man. No *dramma giocoso* based in large part on a strong man's supposed right to have sex with any woman under his power—as both *Figaro* and *Giovanni* are—can be taken simply as a sunny good joke. *The Marriage of Figaro* is the opera of the double standard par excellence: the Count can seduce every woman in reach, and continue to expect his wife to forgive him; if she so much as compromises herself by appearances, she could be dismissed or even worse. Each opera is studded with antimale and antifemale arias, attacks on the cruelty of the one and the infidelity of the other.

All of this is there in the texts. Peter Sellars has simply taken it more seriously than anyone before him. He has also taken seriously each threat in the librettos to kill someone else or oneself. When Don Ottavio sings again and again, "Morte mi da," he shoves a pistol in his mouth. (The use of diner cutlery as a weapon attenuates the seriousness of these threats in *Così*.)

One could counter by insisting that most of this "dangerous" content is simply part of a convention in classical comedy—lustful men, fickle women, illicit amorous intrigues, and deceived spouses are as much a part of ancient stage tradition as empty rhetorical threats to kill or commit suicide—and that Peter Sellars is wrong to take all these things so modernly/seriously, as if they were aspects of some sordid contemporary "case" involving adultery, wife beating, and rape. A great deal of recent scholarship on Mozart has devoted itself to demonstrating the degree to which he and Da Ponte were simply trying to follow contemporary and popular Viennese conventions in their intrigues. Da Ponte wrote, then Mozart wrote music for, plots that they both hoped would sell.

Something of the inherited tradition, like the long-lost-parents discovery scene, is irreducibly present in these operas, and can never be dissolved in any modern directorial acid solution. (Of course, the damnation-to-hell of Don Giovanni is an inherited convention as well, which Mozart "believed" in no more than did Molière.) But Mozart did raise the moral and emotional intensity of these situations far beyond that of his time or, for that matter, of a generation later (cf. Rossini). His (and Da Ponte's) more bitter antifemale and antimale outbursts go well beyond the requirements of "tradition." For all the semifarcical, half-inherited nature of their plots, Mozart and Da Ponte were in fact breaking away from the tradition. Mozart, at least, took a great number of these human passions quite seriously indeed.

Even if such things were "mere conventions" in the eighteenth century, is Peter Sellars wrong to insist that we cannot accept them so comfortably today? If he can in fact "make them play" as dire and dangerous for a contemporary audience, is he not justified in doing so?

The problem, as I see it, is that he can do that only by ignoring many of the clear and explicit meanings of the score. Almost all of Sellars's justifications for his new readings are drawn from Da Ponte's librettos, or from speculations on Mozart's ideas—*not* from Mozart's music. What Mozart's role was in proposing, crafting, or editing these librettos we shall never know. But he did write all the music. And the music says things very different from what Sellars is reading in the text, and depicting on the stage.

These are, in the end, three very different operas, with very differing degrees of "darkness." But taken all in all, most of their music is positive, even joyful; most of their scenes are either comic or humane. There is in the music of all three—even *Don Giovanni*—an all-integrating balance (or at least a willing embrace of disparates), a cohering power that Sellars lacks. Mozart's scores say much more than do Da Ponte's texts—or Peter Sellars's antimusical redactions of them. As many attentive students of these operas have pointed out, it is Mozart's music, far more than the words of his librettist, that makes clear the implicit "values, social situations, and general ideas," to quote Sandra Corse, that provide the intellectual content and examine the moral meanings. In the end, I can only conclude that the producer didn't understand, and hence didn't trust, the power of Mozart's music.

My most common response as a spectator to the Mozart–Da Ponte productions at Purchase was that I was listening (or trying to listen) to music that drove in one direction, wphile watching a stage spectacle that drove in the other. All too often, I felt the music was *denying* the sense of what was happening on stage.

The scores, whether read on the printed page or heard carried through the air, along with two hundred years of production history, indicate that to strip away most of the comedy, politesse, and reconciliation from these operas, revealing almost everyone in them as ravaged or monstrous, as grossly "real," is in fact to resist or ignore not only Mozart's genuine historical context, but also his hard-won, sometimes barely achieved musical balance. He clearly delighted in broadly mixed, all-embracing genres; in breaking down altogether the walls between farce, laughing comedy, sentimental comedy, and tragedy. He relished the challenge of containing them all in resolved musical structures that demonstrate the moral and emotional complexity of human beings. Ignore or deny the positive, redemptive attitudes so tightly woven into the texts and scores of the Mozart–Da Ponte operas—as Peter Sellars has done—and you will end up by shrinking them painfully, turning them into something much smaller than they are.

(1990)

CHAPTER SEVEN

Norma: The Case for Bel Canto

One popular view of Vicenzo Bellini's *Norma* is that the title role is so outrageously difficult to sing—and the work itself so little worth doing if you haven't a soprano up to the mark—that the opera has only survived, in the years since its première in 1831, as a vehicle for a few particularly endowed *prime donne:* Giuditta Pasta, Maria Malibran, Giulia Grisi (all three of whom Bellini heard before he died at thirty-three), Lilli Lehmann, Rosa Ponselle, and Maria Callas.

Like many popular views, this one is grounded in truth, but also muddled with imprecision. There is written into the role of Norma, Druid priestess and woman scorned, as much potential for dramatic excitement as into the roles of any of the great tragedy queens of Racine. God knows it isn't an easy part to sing, with its demanding mixture of vocal and emotional textures, its C's above (some go for D's) and B-flats below the staff, its long-breathed lines and octave drops and showpiece trills. One must be able to sing a strong, natural-sounding contralto and some of the highest coloratura ever written. The role of Norma calls for an authentic bel canto soprano voice, one that can be both mercurial-birdlike and witchy-dramatic, which drastically reduces the field of available singers at any time.

Moreover, the dramatic challenge of this deep and complex part is at least as great as the musical. Alongside a good Norma, most Italian opera heroines—including other Bellini heroines—can seem poor butterflies indeed. It may well be that only the six sopranos I have just named have met both challenges at once, and have achieved something near to the full potential of this role.

It is impossible to describe accurately the voices or performances of singers who died before we were born, or before the invention of accurate recording devices. There is so much disagreement over the vocal qualities of living opera singers that I am even hesitant to cite "eyewitness" accounts. But in comparing critical descriptions made by their contemporaries of all six of these Normas, what I found striking was the constant use, over a century and a quarter, of the same terms. As Harold Rosenthal once wrote, "The great Normas of operatic history have to a greater or lesser extent all been great singing actresses: mistresses of dramatic declamation and outstanding personalities—Lilli Lehmann, Rosa Ponselle, Maria Callas." "The singer," remarked another critic, "must translate into musical phrase and cadence the emotions of a character under stress, as Pasta and Malibran did—and as Callas has done." Listening to Callas in Florence in 1952, a third critic wrote, "I realized what Stendhal and other chroniclers of the nineteenth century meant when they spoke of Malibran and Pasta." "We can well believe," comments John Ardoin in *The Callas Legacy*, "that her balance between drama and agility came the closest in modern terms to those qualities of Giuditta Pasta."

Of every one of the six (except perhaps Ponselle), it was acknowledged that the vocal instrument itself could be impure, even unbeautiful, but that the singer converted this sometimes steely edge into operatic gold by her range, control, and agility; by musical intelligence, accuracy, and style; and by theatrical presence and histrionic skill. Writing in 1856, Paul Scudo said, "Beautiful, intelligent, and passionate, Pasta made up for the imperfections of her vocal organ by means of incessant work, and a noble, tender, knowing style. An actress of the first rank, [she] submitted each breath to the control of an impeccable taste, and never left a single note to chance." Stendhal, a passionate admirer (and personal friend) of Giuditta Pasta, admitted that she (like Callas) had a voice made up of three distinct ranges—"not all molded from the same metal, as they say in Italy; but the fundamental variety of tone produced by a single voice affords one of the richest veins of musical expression which the artistry of a great soprano is able to exploit." "From the start," Sergio Segalini concludes his analysis of the singer for whom the role was created, "her limitations were obvious; but by dint of sheer effort, Giuditta Pasta forged an extremely accomplished technique that allowed her to become the ideal interpreter for Bellini and Donizetti. She was never able to erase her vocal asperities, nor give to her voice the exquisite beauty of a Maria Malibran. But thanks to those very asperities, she learned how to bring an infinite variety of vocal colors to her interpretations."

From the start to the finish of her relatively brief career, many critics and operagoers were offended by Maria Callas's metallic timbre, her sometimes forced or shrill high notes, the audible shifts among her three vocal ranges. But "these and others were precisely the accusations made at the time against Pasta and Malibran," says the Italian musicologist Eugenio Gara, "two geniuses of song (as they were then called), sublime yet vocally imperfect."

Most of the great Normas began as mezzos, or even Wagnerians, and then channeled that power into bel canto. Lilli Lehmann and Maria Callas were perhaps the only two sopranos in history who could sing well both Norma and Brünnhilde, sometimes two or three nights apart—a feat comparable, someone once wrote, to winning gold medals in both weightlifting and the hundred-yard dash. (Lehmann insisted that she would rather sing three Brünnhildes than a single Norma.) All six apparently worked at their craft with demon-driven intensity. Lehmann would sing each phrase through hundreds of times in practice, go through an act three or four times running. Callas did the whole "Casta diva" nine times in one rehearsal for her American première. Each of the six applied extraordinary intelligence to her analysis and creation of the role. "It should be sung and acted with fanatical consecration," declared Lehmann. Each was able to electrify audiences by her mere presence on a stage.

It is uncanny how the same tributes recur: each of these Normas is called "hypnotic," "riveting," "electrifying," "unforgettable"; each is described as having exact pitch and control; each is praised for recitatives and fioriture sung expressively, not for mere fill or show; each is called a genius of dramatic gesture and timing. Almost everything written of the earlier divas has also been said of Callas's interpretation. As *Time*'s critic put it after her 1954 Norma in Chicago: "She may not have the most beautiful voice in the world, but she certainly is the most exciting singer. . . . She can be likened to no singer in the immediate past." Andrew Porter wrote, "There is a real sense in which Callas, appalling though her vocalization often is, recalls the 'old' singers." The chain was unbroken—here was a heroic coloratura, a "prototype of the legendary singers of old." How such a tradition, such a "chain," is maintained is impossible to determine: Maria Callas's voice teacher, Elvira Di Hidalgo, was a Rossini singer of what she regarded as the Malibran mode, a musician fiercely committed to the old bel canto style. Another of Callas's mentors, Tullio Serafin, had conducted Rosa Ponselle in the role thirty years before. "I am enthralled," wrote Harold Rosenthal of Callas's 1957 London Norma, "when she is onstage as with no other artist today. When all is said and done, opera is more than singing; it is music drama; and Callas' Norma is a dramatic creation of the highest order. . . . We will tell our children and grandchildren about it."

One needn't wait for once-in-a-generation near-perfection to hear a performance of bel canto opera. The extraordinary success of Maria Callas may have inspired other singers and impresarios to resurrect many works by Bellini, Donizetti, and Rossini, after decades of apparent neglect. But these roles had never died out in Italy. There, the provincial and major houses have kept *Norma* and her challenging sisters in the repertory since their early nineteenth-century premières: one Italian critic has listed twenty-three Normas worthy of note between Pasta and Callas. He also reminds us that the opera experienced long periods of absence from major houses—three twenty-year lapses at La Scala, two thirty-year gaps at the Met.

More than ten years ago, Andrew Porter unearthed forty-seven different recordings of "Casta diva," Norma's famous first-act prayer: two verses of heartbreakingly beautiful melody over simple string arpeggios and a solo flute, which soar weightlessly in long curves around the key of F, then spill over into wild, repeated trills. The cavatina climaxes in two series of fortissimo high A's, leaping up to B-flat and then trickling rapidly down. It is gorgeous, it is touching, it is fiendishly demanding. It can be made to correspond precisely to the secret inner pain and confusion of the traitor/priestess, poignantly pleading with the moon-goddess to temper the audacious zeal and ardent hearts of her people. And it seems that every soprano in sight, from Adelina Patti to Helen Traubel, wanted to prove that she could sing it. Giuditta Pasta, who sang the first Norma at her La Scala debut, insisted at first that the aria be cut: she found it "ill adapted to her abilities." But Bellini talked her into it before opening night. Rosa Ponselle used it as her audition aria for Gatti-Casazza at the Metropolitan in 1918, and fainted halfway through.

Since Callas revived *Norma* for the non-Italian world in 1948 (she sang her last in Paris in 1965), any number of singers have had a go at the role, often in explicit imitation of her style. The most noteworthy of the present generation have been three divas gifted at coloratura, if not at compelling dramatic recreations. Joan Sutherland (who played Callas's maid in 1952) sang Norma first in Vancouver in 1963. Beverly Sills began her series in Boston in 1971. Montserrat Caballé, the most nearly satisfactory of the three, started singing the role in Barcelona in 1970. Unfortunately, because of the renewed popularity of the opera (and perhaps the challenge inherent of the role), many sopranos whose abilities come nowhere near the demands of the role have attempted to sing Norma in recent years.

There is no one left alive to recall Lilli Lehmann's Normas of the 1890s, there can be very few who remember Rosa Ponselle's of the 1920s. (One can still hear their "Casta diva" and "Mira, o Norma" on old recordings.)

Most of today's critics were brought up with the Callas version. Her 1952 *Norma* was one of the first classical LPs I ever bought. I saw her sing the role two and a half times. (The half was in Rome in January 1958; she sang Act I, then refused to sing any more, because of a throat problem. A major scandal ensued, and she was banned from the theatre for life. "Vietato a Callas di Cantare a Roma!" screamed page one Roman headlines the next day.)

Like most Callas-trained observers, I have been to some degree discontented with every other Norma I have heard since. What I feel we are missing in other Normas of the last twenty years is the dramatic dimension that only a few great singing actresses have been able to give to the part.

The other half-truth in the popular view of *Norma* is that the opera itself—the noise and motion surrounding the central role—is pretty commonplace stuff. Liszt writes of "the weak, effeminate, poor-spirited Bellini." Berlioz compares him to "a grinning puppet." My old 1930s *Victor Book of the Opera* seems to damn the opera with faint praise: "Those who weary of declamatory modern opera, in which the

BELLINI, *Norma*, Maria Callas, Paris Opera, 1964. Photograph by
Roger Pic.

music is constantly changing in agreement with the most swift and subtle moods that emotion throws upon the stage . . . will have no quarrel with the simplicity of *Norma*."

More than one commentator has dismissed most of the score as hurdy-gurdy stuff: thin, catchy, repetitive, predictable. "Serious" Italian orchestration, after all, is supposed to have come in with Verdi (who, while defending Bellini's melodies, found him weak in harmony and poor in instrumentation). And though the central triangle may afford lean and passionate drama, the Druid business around it has befuddled more than one producer—a lot of chorus members forever trooping in and out in long robes to sing bouncy songs about how much they hate the Romans. "What on earth is one to *do* with *Norma?*" is the critic's rhetorical excuse for static productions.

Frankly, I'm not sure. Apparently it worked—as a production—for twelve thousand people in the ancient Greek amphitheatre at Epidaurus in 1960, where Callas had real hills and trees as a backdrop. A La Scala effort at modern abstract design in 1973 pleased almost nobody. Any producer who tries to get rid of the long robes and thick tree trunks is slapped for being insufficiently Druid.

The Egypt business, the politics of *Aida*, works because it is so essentially integrated into the human story. The politics of *Norma* is not. Two Gallic priestesses falling in love with a Roman proconsul complicate the intrigue, of course. Adalgisa is especially ashamed to *abbandonar la patria*. The sacred gong Norma bashes three times is at once the Druid war cry and a wild gesture of personal revenge. The fire in which she burns is punishment for treason as well as for breaking her vows of chastity. ("Casta diva," indeed.)

But Oroveso and the chorus really serve no essential dramatic function. They think they're finally going to get a chance to fight when the gong rings in Act III, and they break into the wild "Guerra, guerra" chorus, *allegro feroce*, under Norma's frenzied urging. But their subjugated, static role is exactly the same at the end as it was at the beginning. Felice Romani gives them some wonderful lyrics full of *sangue* and *vendetta*: the Tiber will run with blood when our Druid battle axes beat down their eagles. But it's all hopeless wishful thinking. These forest-dwelling religious cranks obviously haven't a chance against Rome. And the music Bellini gives them (with that one exception) is about as warlike and barbaric as a holiday march. Bars and bars of it are spent just getting them on and off stage.

As for the orchestration generally, I think Bellini was more knowing and dramatically skillful than Verdi gave him credit for. Things most operagoers feel rather than recognize, such as tonal shifts (Herbert Weinstock, Domenico de Paoli, and Pierre Brunel have all analyzed the music well), silences, and suspensions, were worked out as carefully as the more obviously expressive gestures—violins *allegro agitato* or creepy-crawly low strings to hint of danger; repeated notes to signify inner agitation; tender love lyrics easing out of crashing chords; a full palette of woodwind colors. The chorus-moving music may get to be a drag, and that overly jaunty E-flat march keeps coming back. But some of the orchestral interludes (listen to the poignant, three-theme D-minor prelude to Act II) are seductive and appropriate, and the singers' line is usually deftly underscored by the musicians'.

In any case, the vocal line itself, recitatives included, is almost always dramatically apt as well as beautiful, which is not an easy thing to achieve. Herbert Weinstock argues that every trill, every chromatic run, and every ornamentation of Norma's arias make perfect dramatic sense. Some historians of eighteenth- and early nineteenth-century opera have argued that its vocal embellishments (except as individually vulgarized by celebrity singers) were never mere vehicles for technical virtuosity, as later singers sometimes made them appear. Most often, they assert, these runs and shakes and scales and trills were intended to be dramatically expressive—of fury, madness, ecstasy, or rapture. In the case of many bel canto operas, I am not persuaded. But I agree that every one of Norma's "ornaments" can be made to serve as an expression of inner feeling.

Even "Casta diva," best remembered for its long-breathed, floating, rising-and-falling legato, would lose half its meaning without the coloratura outburst with which it concludes. Of Norma's violent attack on Pollione ("Ah, non tremare"), Brunel comments, "Norma's extreme vehemence, transformed into sheer fury, expresses itself by means of her *fioriture*." The three diabolically difficult low trills—E-flat, G-flat, B-flat—that Norma has to sing in Act II (*con furore*) on the accented dotted quarter notes of "*A*-dal-*gi*-sa *fia* punita" (Adalgisa will be punished) are the physical manifestation of her unbearable internal rage. The unaccented syllables here are sung to doubled sixteenth notes; after a fourth trill on the tonic B-flat, she leaps to a rapid run (up to A) above and down the staff to complete the dire and vengeful sentence: "*Nel*-le fiamme perirà," "She will perish in the flames."

Even Wagner (an unlikely defender) recognized this quality in Bellini. "They think me an ogre in all that concerns the musical school of Italy," he wrote in 1837, "and they set me up in especial opposition to Bellini. No, no, a thousand times no! Bellini is one of my favorites, because his music is all heart, deeply felt, closely and *intimately bound up with the words*" (my italics).

Wagner's evaluation of Bellini's music underwent a number of revolutions. His successive, perhaps overlapping views are worth considering in any assessment of Bellini's skills that is to go beyond the "swan of Catania" legend—that of a mellifluous craftsman who wrote bel canto arias for world-famous canaries to sing, and then suffered the fate of dying romantically young.

In 1837, Wagner was recommending the study of Bellini as "a cure for the intellectual abstruseness of German composers." He had conducted *Norma* at

Magdeburg in 1835, and at Riga in 1837, making additions to and changes in the orchestration. At Paris in 1839, he wrote a new aria (never used) for Oroveso to sing. Later, in an essay on Spontini and Rossini, he mocked the "consumptive variations" on Rossini's already thin themes that Bellini and Donizetti had fed to the public. Wagner seems to have mellowed after a visit in 1860 to the sixty-eight-year-old Rossini, when some of his early enthusiasm for Bellini appeared to return. By 1871, however, he was calling *Norma* "insipid and threadbare." In 1880, the conductor Anton Seidl wrote to Francesco Florimo, who was collecting letters and memoirs for a book on Bellini, that after playing him some melodies from *Norma* on the piano, Wagner had remarked, "Despite a certain poverty, there is real passion and feeling here. It only needs to be sung by the right singer to make a deeply moving effect."

It would be unwise, I think, to base a case for bel canto opera on either the chorus or the orchestration of *Norma*. "What enchanted us in Bellini [the younger Wagner again] was the pure melody, the simple nobility and beauty of song. Surely it can be no sin to assert this." In the end, the case rests on the words and music Romani and Bellini wrote for Pollione, Adalgisa, and Norma—words and music rendered, not by nightingales and star tenors belting out concert arias and ensembles, but by three proud, suffering, and complicated people.

Pollione was first sung by Domenico Donzelli, who wrote Bellini to brag of his range, "from the bass D up to the high C." "When he gave out his high notes," according to a contemporary observer, "there was some misgiving as to the peril of his blood vessels." Giovanni Martinelli and Giacomo Lauri-Volpi played the role early in this century. In my younger years, the biggest name tenor to take the role was Mario Del Monaco; the best looking, Franco Corelli—neither to universal satisfaction. But it cannot be pretended that the role is particularly heroic: *Norma* is a woman's opera, in which both tenor and bass serve as foils.

The first Adalgisa, Giulia Grisi, was soon to sing Norma, which makes clear that Bellini intended the role for a soprano rather than a mezzo. In my time, Ebe Stignani sang the part of the timid virgin *giovanetta* until she was old enough to be Callas's mother. The role offers less dramatic range than Norma's, but almost as much opportunity for vocal display. (The vocal scale, as written, is identical.) This is, in fact, one of the great supporting roles, and some of the finest sopranos (and mezzos) have been happy to undertake it: Barbieri, Cossotto, Horne, Simionato, Swarthout, Thebom, Troyanos. The proper blending of different timbres between the two women is crucial, and the casting of two sopranos of similar vocal quality (as is sometimes done) is inevitably a mistake.

The Norma–Adalgisa duets in fact demonstrate the difficulty of casting the central role. It has been convincingly argued that the "ideal" voice for a Norma is what the French call a *falcon*, which is to say a powerful mezzo-soprano with an extended upper range. To differentiate the roles, then, and distinguish the blending vocal vibrations within their duets, the younger woman should be sung by a pure, high lyric soprano. But although a modern "extended mezzo" (Grace Bumbry, who has sung both Adalgisa and Norma, is one example) may be able to do justice to many of the expressive demands of the role, and achieve the strength and vocal color necessary for certain aspects of the character, it is unlikely that she will be able to soar freely into the uppermost notes of the part, or master the high coloratura. For this reason, we usually hear Norma sung by a soprano, Adalgisa by a mezzo—with portions of the latter role either cut or (in the duets) transferred to Norma.

Giuditta Pasta did in fact have the unique combination of resources the role demands, and it was specifically for her voice that Bellini crafted this very nearly unsingable role. (Maria Malibran has been considered a "stretched contralto"— someone who has to work even harder to make the role her own. Of both early divas, as of Maria Callas, it has been claimed that repeated performances of the role did harmful and painful things to their vocal cords.)

In addition to being the most vocally demanding and physically strenuous female role in Italian opera ("the Isolde of La Scala"), the character of Norma encompasses a psychological encyclopedia of emotions. When she enters late in the first act, she immediately berates the chorus in imperious recitative: "Who *presumes* to dictate a reply to the all-seeing Norma?" Seconds later, she is breathing out her heavenly prayer for peace, establishing at once her priesthood, her dominion, her tenderness (and her vocal powers). Prayer and rites over, she moves into a rich, yearning aria (which no one on stage hears) of her guilty love for Pollione. Three scenes later she herself sings (in witchy recitative, down to B-flat below staff) of the *diversi affetti* in her breast, her mingled love and hatred for her and Pollione's sons. Then, almost at once, she opens up into a voluptuous free duet encouraging Adalgisa in her new love, half in recollection ("O, rimembranza!") of her own—an outburst of pure beauty.

She ends with a leap to high C and a chromatic run by exact semitones down to A, which Adalgisa gets to repeat twenty-one bars later. Then the two match voices for one of Bellini's more spectacular a capella cadenzas, to express what they think is a happily shared feeling. Pause for breath.

"Where's he from, your new lover?" "From Rome." "Ro-ma!" (E-flat, drop to F-sharp). In comes Pollione. "E-i! Pol-lion!!" (an octave drop down, an octave leap up. As one critic pointed out, Callas always sang both exclamation points.) Horns, woodwinds; staccato violins suddenly race up two octaves: *L'ira di Norma*.

She rounds on Pollione in one of the most spine-chilling lines of all opera: "Tremi tu? e per chi?" (You are trembling? And for whom?); and then answers her own question by leaping into an aria, *con tutta forza* ("Tremble for yourself, evil one, for your children—*Trema per me!*"), of violent, shuddering scorn. Raging inside the glorious lyric line, she shifts halfway to Adalgisa, and introduces the second great ensemble of warring emotions, B-flat major, 9/8 time: Norma is madly cursing Pollione, Adalgisa is in agony, Pollione is defying her gods and yet pleading for Adalgisa, all at the same time. Pierre Brunel has analyzed this magnificent trio in persuasive detail:

> The rhythm is always vigorous, the vocal ornaments allow each separate accent to emerge clearly: accents of pity in Norma, accents of heartbroken lucidity in Adalgisa, accents of impotent effort in Pollione. The characters are not tearing one another apart: their griefs superimpose in a lyrical ascent that achieves a sort of gravity by means of the trinity of treason, deceit, and sin. After a few measures in which the orchestra makes use of a discreet chromaticism, an *allegro risoluto* in E-flat major starts the movement again, which is soon to pick up speed: Norma runs after Pollione, who tries to drag off Adalgisa. The girl refuses, despite Norma's orders—"Follow him!" Bellini multiplies the scenic indications in this dramatic intermezzo.
>   The final part of the trio (*allegro agitato assai* in G minor) once again opens with Norma's invective against Pollione—"*Vanne, sì*": she turns on him and covers him with curses. Over a shivering accompaniment of strings her voice rises, implacable, up to the solemn and ultimate threat, "*Te sul onde,*" at which point the melody—with a vigor now equal to that of her voice—reaches its ultimate expansion. Norma's vocal line is reprised by Pollione and Adalgisa in duet, the one trying desperately to defend his love, the other renouncing the man she loves in order not to hurt Norma; but soon the great curse rises again to dominate their voices. And this frantic trio goes on, to the point of exhaustion, even though the sacred bronze has already sounded in the temple, and the chorus of Druids is heard calling on Norma to accomplish her holy rites.

And so on it goes, a virtually unbroken gamut of violent emotional changes our singer-actress must make credible, until the moment when she beats the sacred shield, announces her own guilt, and, shrouded in black, marches into her own funeral pyre. Surely she is, as Pollione at last comes to realize, a *sublime donna*.

Wagner, I think, made two crucial points about *Norma*. Of course the opera is "thin" ("consumptive," "threadbare") when compared with the orchestral density and vocal variety of *Tristan* or the *Ring*. But (a) the music of the three leads, and Norma's in particular, is "intimately bound up with the words" to a degree that even Verdi, a supremely astute man of the theatre, rarely achieved, and that Bellini himself accomplished in no other opera; and (b) the music "only needs to be sung by the right singer to make a deeply moving effect." Wagner's third point, regarding Bellini's sublime gift for touching melody ("His music is all heart. . . . There is real passion and feeling here"), I will simply take as a given. It is one of the points on which even Bellini's detractors seem to agree, and one that I am unable to analyze or explain.[1]

I have mentioned a number of qualities that have been singled out in the praise of one great Norma after another: size and range of voice, control, agility, accuracy, musical intelligence, theatrical "presence," "intensity," professional dedication, and an expressive—rather than a routinely musical, let alone an exhibitionist—treatment of every note in the score. Many of these qualities, I believe (some of them virtually demanded by text and score), feed into and in the end blend with the character of Norma herself. Certainly range, control, dedication, a conscious theatricalism of effect, and an instantaneous, mercurial shifting between emotions are characteristics of the role as well (ideally) of the singer who dares to enact it. (There are parallels with Floria Tosca, at least in Callas's interpretation of the part: a passionate opera singer playing a passionate opera singer. But both role and character in Puccini are less powerful, wide-ranging, and "true," I believe, than their counterparts in Bellini.)

The astonishing breath control critics cite again and again in describing the great Normas—the viola- or cellolike legato line sustained with micro-minute dynamic control ("a perfectly pitched high and soft E-flat at the end of a difficult aria"), as if the singer had no more need to breathe in than a stringed instrument has—seems to me to represent Norma's own superhuman efforts at self-control. The mad outbursts of "impossible" coloratura singing up and down, above and below the treble staff render audible what happens when this control breaks down.

Callas's notorious "three voices," or three distinct vocal registers (what one critic calls her "chameleon voice")—the fierce, growling, dark contralto; the warm, floating, flutelike *mezza voce;* the steely and uncertain highs—might even, in this particular role, be identified with the outrageously variable aspects of Norma's character: proud priestess, tender mother-lover, vengeful woman scorned. Other observers have remarked how Callas was able to give Norma's frequent and difficult descending chromatic glissandi a strangely melancholic tone, as if the down-

---

1. Friedrich Lippmann, in an article in *Analecta musicologica,* does a fairly persuasive job of analysis on Bellini's long, "developed" melodies in *Norma*—the great arcs of melody built out of simple, two-measure elements; the "diathematic" climb, then the descending line retarded, kept from falling to its close again and again; immediately a new ascent, in a new key, using similar short elements, with the same poignant intensification by means of retards and repetitions.

Similarly, Lippmann analyzes the uniquely tension-filled, internalized *crescendi* of Bellini's arias and scenes; his famous descending chromatic lines, his instant (and demanding) shifts from fortes and fortissimos to *piano subito* and vice versa; and his harmonic skill. By these and other means, Lippmann argues, Bellini was able to make of the Neoclassical "bravura" aria something intensely personal and internal: a highly sensual, even ecstatic form of soprano expression, almost never reaching a point of repose, which at once defined the "Romantic" sensibility and created a vocal form that is still very difficult to resist.

scale fall revealed some secret inner pain. "Her secret," Eugenio Gara writes, "is her ability to transfer to the musical plane the suffering of the character she plays."

I do not know what makes one soprano's voice seem to convey more of "passionate womanhood" than another's. Despite all of the reams of "intimate" analysis that have been written about the lives of both Maria Malibran and Maria Callas (both of whom, like Bellini, died early enough for legend—Malibran at twenty-eight, Callas at fifty-four), I have no sure reason to believe that this expressiveness is bound up with a singer's private, offstage experience. Great acting is great acting; great singing is great singing. Neither need be a reflection or translation of the kind of person an actor or singer is, the kind of joys or pains she (or he) has experienced.

Callas's vocal quality and control, her dramatic expressiveness, and her onstage demeanor in the role of Norma (and I presume that this is at least partly true for the five other great interpreters as well) went, of course, far beyond bel canto, in the simplistic sense of "beautiful singing." (To singers and voice teachers of the pure style, the phrase *bel canto* has always meant a great deal more than that.) One could argue, in fact, that the sum of her characteristics often fell short of "beautiful singing." It also achieved something more intense and more compelling than the vivid theatrical recreation, the "illumination" of a fictional character—something for which actors from Garrick to Olivier, from Mary Garden to Fyodor Chaliapin have been praised.

Since the disappearance of castrati, the female dramatic soprano has been the single most impressive and compelling vocal range in opera: the highest, the most potentially moving, the most astonishing; the farthest, in effect, from the way we talk. Opera, as several commentators (among them Hélène Seydoux) have remarked, depends absolutely for its historic, enduring, and immediate power on the female soprano range, which is at once ethereally high (like E-string notes above the fingerboard on a violin) and, by the standards of most human beings, "superhumanly" powerful. An all-male opera—Britten's *Billy Budd* for example—can, like an all-male chorus, be tremendously powerful; but it will always be the odd, one-in-a-hundred exception. When you add to the potential range and power of a dramatic soprano the (literally) breathtaking agility of a coloratura—as any acceptable Norma must do—you have the makings of the sublime operatic, perhaps even musical experience, in purely auditory terms.

In *Opera, or the Undoing of Women*, Catherine Clément argues that this spellbinding vocal phenomenon—the human voice at its most beautiful, its potentially most expressive—has too often been "wasted" on weak, pliable, long-suffering heroines. Most of the female characters in opera are seen as either the creatures (Clément's view) of crude and cruel male librettists and composers who were simply converting their or their cultures' male-chauvinist fantasies into operas; or

(Hélène Seydoux's view) of male artists secretly frustrated by their cultural obligation to "act like men," when what they really wanted to do was cry. (They express their female inner selves, according to Seydoux—who regards opera as an innately bisexual art—through their suffering heroines.)

But can one honestly say that of Norma? Catherine Clément's analysis of Norma, like her analyses of other "undone women" in opera, is rapturous and opaque. But she does seem to grant the Druid priestess a large measure of independence, of pre-Christian, pre-Roman female strength: the strength of a witch or sorceress, even more than that of a lover and mother.

> These furies, these goddesses, these women with fearsome arms and inspired eyes [a not inaccurate image of Callas on stage], these Turandots and Normas collected the witch's inheritance in the nineteenth century. . . .
>
> Man gave them the law that makes them women and mothers; then comes the day when the husband and father betrays the woman, who has become undesirable. That is where Norma's story begins. . . . Norma and Adalgisa are the past and the present of a single colonizer-lover; the conqueror takes forcibly, seduces, and carries off; that is his pleasure, that is what moves him. . . .
>
> [The sorceresses, the weird women, the goddesses] have not disappeared. . . . They revive in every woman burdened with a heart too full of misfortune. . . . If I find something really to love in all these torn women, it is because, under the opera lights, they bear the attenuated but recognizable features of a redeeming paganism. . . . Oh, it is not that paganism triumphs; these women always lose, but that's what they are singing—their resistance to the one God . . . the one clung to by man.

In Norma's face-to-face confrontation with Pollione, writes Clément, "she, the priestess, she, the possessor of divine power, can kill him or save him." Only when faced with the possible exposure and death of his new love, Adalgisa, does the Roman man melt, beg, implore. Now, according to Clément, Norma has what she wants: the man on his knees. Now she can willingly denounce not Adalgisa but herself, and escape the world by means of "the flight of a sorceress, who finds a way to constrain her faithless lover by fire."[2]

2. This was not, by the way, Maria Callas's interpretation of the finale. The part of Norma, she once told an interviewer, appealed to her more than all the other roles she had played because "when she finds herself in a terrible crisis of love, she chooses death rather than hurt the man she loves, even though he has betrayed her." To biographical critics such as Sergio Segalini, Callas "destroyed herself" precisely by playing roles like Norma—a role with which, he insists, she "identified fiercely"—with such self-destructive intensity. Clément's reading (in her 1979 book) also ignores Norma's final, maternal plea to Oroveso to spare her children. If anything, one could argue, she becomes most vulnerable, most unlike a goddess, at the moment of her self-sacrifice. In an essay on the character of Norma published in September 1980, Clément appears to acknowledge this:

> Between Medea, all charged with manic laughter—in which laughter we recognize her divinity—and the human priestess who has in fact had children by the Roman officer, the gran-

Some of Clément's analysis is beyond my understanding. But I do hear in almost all of Norma's music, especially as rendered by Callas, the sound of "womanhood" at its most various, most powerful, most defiantly independent of men. For the character of Norma, Bellini created not simply vocal lines that evoke a woman's conjugal and maternal love, or the violent pain of a woman rejected by a man. (Italian opera is full of such women—including, of course, Callas's other signature role, Cherubini's Medea.)

I also hear, in the two great Norma-Adalgisa duets (especially "Mira, o Norma," but also in "O, rimembranza!"), the defiant power of a "sisterhood" that goes far beyond rivalry over a man. So, not surprisingly, does Catherine Clément in her 1980 essay:

> How does the music [of the Act I duet], latent in Adalgisa, awaken in Norma the source of tenderness? Here it is that is born in her the memory, and with it the sweet melody accompanied by plaintive flutes. Here is love, sung in doubled unison.
>
> An astonishing duet; an astonishing rapport. One sings—and the other sings too. A cello accompanies the deeper voice, another cello accompanies the younger. And Norma replies; Norma admits; Norma remembers. Nothing can stop Adalgisa now: she is transported by the cries of love at its most irrational. And Norma? Norma relives it all as if in an echo. Hallucinated, she discovers herself once more in the "other woman": an essential substructure for the "hysterical," womb-to-womb identification by which every female relationship takes place. We swim with them in a fluid love that pours itself out in all directions: a love in which Pollione (the still-unmentioned object of the same love that these two women bear for him) serves as the conduit between one and the other. Adalgisa is captivated by the marvelous way in which love begins, and Norma is captivated by Adalgisa in love. The two women are in love with the same love: "he," the man who, in the pre-dawn light, whispers to one the same tender words he once whispered to the other, "he" is never named. "He" does not exist, beyond the united beating of two women's hearts. . . .
>
> Norma does not find tenderness in the chaste, cold moon. She does not find it in the faithless Roman Pollione. She finds it only in Adalgisa. True love duets take place only between two women: pure accounts of sublimated passion meet each other there—and nowhere else. Tender Adalgisa, a private shelter of sweet unawareness, inhabited (not that she knows it) by the past of another woman . . . and tender Norma, who would rather die than condemn

---

diose power of myth has declined. Romanticism cares more for tenderness. . . . It cannot cope with the epic style. Its heroines are no longer goddesses, but divided women, in which the divine spark shines only in sudden flashes. The greatness of Medea is terrifying, inhuman. That of Norma is human, sweet, even in her rages—each of which is aborted: at the moment she wants to kill her children: at the moment she wants to denounce Adalgisa. Norma's full strength is expressed in these moments when her rage is aborted, and transformed into abnegation.

her younger rival. In their interreflecting mirrors, Norma and Adalgisa are one for the other the ideal Narcissus—which is what we call love; which is also what we call motherhood. When it directs itself to an absent man, we call it death.

A male critic, Pierre Brunel, hears something of this same "unison of hearts" in the female duet:

> The duet, properly called (*assai moderato* in F major), "O, rimembranza," admirably displays Norma's essential psychological motivation: a sympathy based on identification, as the Adalgisa of today merges with the Norma of yesterday. To an accompaniment of arpeggios, a solo flute introduces the melody to which Adalgisa is about to confide her evocation of the beginnings of her love:
>
> Sola, furtiva, al tempio
> Io l'aspettai sovente;
> Ed ogni di più fervida
> Crebbe la fiamma ardente.
>
> Alone, in secret, at the temple
> I often waited for him;
> And each day more and more fervent
> Grew the burning flame.
>
> But already Norma has begun to confide to the identical melody the emotion that she had once felt at the sight of Pollione. So that this duet of confession is at the same time a duet of recognition: ecstatic recognition, at first . . . then more and more troubled, up to the cadenza ("Ah! si!") which leads into the second movement (*più animato*, in C major): "Ah si, fa core, abbracciami"— "Ah yes, be brave, embrace me." Norma, overcome by emotion, takes upon herself the responsibility of releasing Adalgisa from her vows. Adalgisa, in ecstasy, sings the same *allegro* theme, and asks the older woman to repeat her unexpected encouragement. The duet concludes on a long cadenza for two voices in unison, which gives the impression of a perfect accord.

Similarly, Norma's mysterious dominion over *i druidi*—and, ultimately, over the Roman as well—goes beyond mere political power, the occasional and anomalous power of a Semiramis or a Cleopatra or an Elizabeth I. Norma rules them, as she rules us, by her voice. It is far and away the strongest thing in the world this particular opera creates. In fact, there seems to me almost no innately, profoundly female emotion (if a man may risk such speculation) that Norma's music does not contain. If Callas's "reedy," "resinous," "steely," "metallic," "hard-edged," "swordlike" instrument and her "tigerish" demeanor (typify them as you will) dismayed certain critics enamored of the birdlike purity they preferred in their sopranos, these precise qualities may have allowed her to embody, in this most powerful of female operatic roles (Isolde is all love; Brünnhilde goes out of her mind), all that the soprano voice is capable of expressing of the supreme and independent difference of the gender it represents.

(1975, revised 1991)

CHAPTER EIGHT

Hugo Sung and Unsung:
Or Why We Put Up with Dumb Opera Plots

Whenever Verdi's *Ernani* comes around, music critics who pretend to know it well try to find nice things to say about it. It's pretty good "for early Verdi." It has some exciting arias, duets, and ensembles. It has its "occasional elegances."

But there's no getting away from the fact that nowadays it's generally regarded as distinctly lesser Verdi—one of those dark, Spanishy love-death-and-honor operas full of bouncy pop tunes sung by romantic caricatures in elaborate sixteenth-century costumes who have somehow to work their way through a nearly incomprehensible plot.

Over the last ten years, the opera has usually been performed in two or three places in the world every season, which puts it about twelfth in the list of Verdi's most frequently heard operas. But if Verdi's *Ernani* has declined in favor since the nineteenth century (when it was one of the repertory staples), it is still at least regularly performed, and by some of the most famous singers in the world. The once-notorious play on which it is based—Victor Hugo's *Hernani, ou l'honneur Castillan*—has virtually disappeared from the living stage, despite the determined "historic preservation" efforts of the Comédie-Française. "No modern play-going audience," writes William Weaver, "would sit through a straight-faced production of *Hernani*."

This is not 100 percent true. A few modern versions of the play seem to have worked. I sat through a tolerable one in New York in 1974. But like many enduring nineteenth-century Italian operas, *Ernani* borrowed its characters and its plot from a once-popular play now far less well known than its lyric successor. Comparing the cases of Victor Hugo's plays and the music dramas they inspired may help us to understand what makes for longevity in opera, and why so many standards in today's opera repertory have been based on dramatic originals most of us would not tolerate on the spoken stage.

It is difficult today to conjure up the semilegendary reputation of Victor Hugo, who dominated so much of the imagination of his century. He can be compared only to other nineteenth-century demigods like Goethe or Tolstoy—men who combined extraordinary creative powers with profound cultural influence, and received the kind of mass adulation that turned them into near-mythical figures while they were still alive. By the end of his long life (1802–1885), Hugo was nearly adored by millions of his fellow citizens, whose respect for him almost equaled his own self-esteem.

His rise to glory was sudden, but well planned. "Je veux être Chateaubriand ou rien," he had written in his journal at fourteen. He would be either the equal of the great early Romantic master, or nothing. He set out by entering (and winning) prestigious poetry competitions, and attracting high-placed support, with pompous proroyalist odes. The popularity of Walter Scott, and the visit to Paris of a troupe of English Shakespearean actors in 1827, led Hugo to try his hand at passion-filled, anticlassical verse dramas set in earlier times and un-French places. The first, based on Scott, was a one-night fiasco. The second, a wildly unhistorical romance called *Cromwell*, turned out to be unperformably long. The third, *Marion Delorme*, was banned by the state censors. The fourth, *Hernani*, was a hit.

It was a hit partly because Victor Hugo and his circle of would-be literary revolutionaries packed the house on opening night, and for thirty-eight nights thereafter, by distributing hundreds of free tickets to their friends, and to long-haired students and artists who could be depended on to make noise on their behalf. The ensuing *bataille d'Hernani* has become part of the Hugo myth, a colorful episode now entrenched in French literary history.

At first, the outrageous spectacle of these exuberant young dandies drowning out the hisses of their disgusted elders convinced people that a revolution of sorts *had* taken place, and that Victor Hugo's new liberal Romanticism had displaced for all time the tired decorums of the Classical theatre. Locked in a dark theatre for five hours before the opening night curtain, the Hugolians also led radical cheers, sung revolutionary songs, left sausage skins in the foyers, and urinated in the corridors. The play drew record crowds (who kept on hissing and cheering), was disliked by most of the actors and critics, and was written about by a great many of the people who attended. Théophile Gautier described the scene in his *Histoire du romantisme*:

> It was enough to cast your eyes on the audience to realize that this was no ordinary performance. Two ways of life, two parties, two armies, even—I am not overstating—two civilizations were there, hating one another cordially (as one can only hate in literary quarrels), asking only for war, and ready to convert one into the other. The general attitude was hostile, elbows were getting sharp, the least contact would be enough to set off the battle; and it wasn't hard to see that this particular longhaired young man was soon going to find the well-barbered gentleman next to him an unspeakable cretin, and find himself unable to keep this opinion to himself.

Hugo went on to write three more, increasingly melodramatic plays for the Comédie-Française (he could turn out a play in three weeks; Verdi took at least three months for an opera) and three for the commercial, or "boulevard," theatres. In the same period (1830–1843), he fixed his reputation as the most popular French romantic author by publishing *Notre-Dame de Paris* and four new volumes of verse; befriended the Duchesse d'Orléans, wife of the heir-apparent; was elected (on his fifth try) to the Académie Française; established his lifelong liaison with Juliette Drouet, who had acted a small part in one of his plays; imagined himself somehow "saving" France; and grew immensely rich. By the end of this time, another young cultural/political revolutionary—Giuseppe Verdi, the composer of *Nabucco*—was being hailed in Italy as "the Victor Hugo of his party."

The dismal failure in 1843 of *Les Burgraves*, the last play Hugo wrote for the stage, marked the end of the short reign of high romantic drama as far as new Paris offerings were concerned. But for most of the next century, actors and actresses of the broad, grandiloquent style (like opera stars of today) insisted that these works be kept in the repertory as display pieces for their talents.

Mlle. Rachel, a stage goddess of the 1840s and 1850s, relished the juicy role of Tisbe in Victor Hugo's *Angelo*—the prototype of Ponchielli's opera *La Gioconda*. In 1867, *Hernani* was given a lavish revival for the Paris International Exposition, which nearly led to a second *bataille* because its author (like his hero) was then a political exile, sulking in the Channel Islands and hurling poetical insults at a government he despised. When the Second Empire collapsed in 1870, Hugo returned to Paris in triumph to witness the historic pairing of Sarah Bernhardt and Mounet-Sully in both *Ruy Blas* (1872) and *Hernani* (1877). The Divine Sarah used these two plays as sturdy vehicles for the rest of a long and fabulous career, helping to keep them alive in the United States as well as in Europe. She also undertook revivals of Hugo's even more melodramatic *Angelo*, *Lucrèce Borgia*, and *Marion Delorme* in 1905 and 1911, when she was in her sixties. Throughout her career, Bernhardt was praised as an "operatic" actress. She preferred works like Hugo's because of the opportunities they provided her for stage spectacles, passionate confrontations, great death scenes, and sublime solo "arias" for her silvery voice. "Avoiding any trace of interpretive nuance," remarked the critic Francisque Sarcey of one of her Hugo performances, "she presented a sustained caress of sound, the very monotony of which possessed indefinable delicacy and magnetism. All she needed to do was add the music of her voice to the music of the verse."

At Hugo's death in 1885, two million people watched his state funeral procession. His hearse was followed by eleven wagon loads of flowers to the Panthéon; streets were renamed in his honor. Beginning with the centennial of his birth in 1902, a spectacular revival of *Les Burgraves* was followed, night after night, by a worshipful ceremony of tribute on stage at which the two leading ladies recited his verses and crowned his bust with a laurel wreath.

By 1920, *Hernani* had been performed 734 times at the Comédie-Française—most frequently between 1877 and 1910, when it was given an average of fifteen times a year. (The total count for all of his plays at the French national theatre by 1920 was 1,694; by 1980, 2,748.) In 1927, the Comédie celebrated the centennial of the Romantic movement (which they dated from Hugo's 1827 "Preface to *Cromwell*") by offering, among other things, glamorous new productions of *Hernani* and *Ruy Blas*. The *Hernani* centennial in 1930 brought a new Paris production and a flood of newspaper and magazine articles on the 1830 *bataille*. Colette thought a 1938 centenary revival of *Ruy Blas* by Paul Dux, with its stylized and witty decors, the theatrical event of the year.

Since then, Hugo—especially via *Hernani* and *Ruy Blas*, both by 1984 around the 1,000 mark—has been one of the ten "staples" of the Comédie-Française repertoire. This may, of course, be attributed to the conservative nature of the house and its audiences. Shifting tastes over the past two decades have led to fewer performances each year there of noncomic nineteenth-century works. For more than a century, many serious critics have persisted in regarding Hugo's stage works as hopeless.

Even so, at a time when the 300-year-old "Maison de Molière" was venturing into Arrabal, Beckett, Ionesco, and Brecht, there were notable new productions of Hugo's *Ruy Blas* in 1960 and 1979, and of *Hernani* in 1952, 1972, and 1974. Both have been filmed, recorded, and shown on French television. Some of the new regional and experimental theatres and *maisons de culture* in France, though they tend to be identified with avant-garde playwrights and directors, have also had a go at reinterpreting Victor Hugo.

But these occasional exhumations do not add up to anything like a Hugo revival, or a return to the "Hugolatry" of the nineteenth century. At each new production, critics have usually shown grudging respect for the two "museum-piece" classics (*Hernani* and *Ruy Blas*), while dismissing the lesser plays as Manichean melodramas with comic-strip plots. On the whole, they save their praise for the daring of the producer and the skill of the actors, who have somehow managed to inflate these moribund works back into a semblance of life.

In non-French-speaking countries today, Hugo's reputation rests primarily on two novels, *Notre-Dame de Paris* (or, if you prefer, *The Hunchback of Notre Dame*) and *Les Misérables*, and even more on the films and the stage musical they have inspired. It could be argued that so rapturously poetic a playwright (Hugo's better plays were written in rhymed verse, and are full of intricate sonic effects) was bound to suffer from translation. But for a good part of the nineteenth century, bad translations and atrocious rewritings of Hugo's plays held the stage in England and the United States, despite the fulminations of puritan critics at their tasteless French freedoms. (The French Romantic theatre, wrote the American actress Fanny Kemble in 1836, was the result of reckless experimenting on the part of "M.

Hugo and his fellow radicals—a disgrace to any Christian and civilized people.")
In time, they gave way to even simpler crowd pleasers, like *The Count of Monte Cristo* and *Cyrano de Bergerac*—the only French nineteenth-century Romantic costume dramas still regularly performed in this country. Albert Takazaukas's off-off-Broadway production of *Hernani* in 1974 was the first revival of that play in New York in 103 years.

Since the Hugo boom ended, the point has been tiresomely often made that, however despised or ignored or forgotten he may have become as a playwright, his characters and plots *have* survived—thanks to the opera stage. "It is depressing to note," Eric Bentley wrote in 1948, "that French Romantic Drama is a portentous failure, that *Hernani* is a schoolmaster's classic far inferior to anything of Schiller's (not to compare it with Shakespeare, as Matthew Arnold did), and that the plays of the French Romantics succeeded best, when they succeeded at all, on the operatic stage for which God, if not always their authors, intended them." George Bernard Shaw put it even more succinctly, when reviewing a London production of *Ernani* in 1892: "The chief glory of Victor Hugo as a stage poet was to have provided libretti for Verdi."

That he did twice, for *Ernani* and *Rigoletto* (which is taken from his 1834 play *Le Roi s'amuse*). Verdi also considered operatizing *Cromwell* and *Ruy Blas*. This world's-most-famous author, who had nothing but scorn for Italian opera and who twice went to court to keep musical adaptations of his works off the Paris stage, became, against his will, one of the most fruitful sources of plots for nineteenth-century composers. Unfortunately, these composers never sent the author a penny in royalties—which was the main reason for Hugo's scorn, and his litigiousness. Although a friend of many men of music (Berlioz, Liszt, Saint-Saëns), Victor Hugo did generally regard contemporary composers (especially Italians, and more especially Rossini) as woefully inferior to the earlier masters. "Music has brutalized Italy," he once wrote to Meyerbeer, explaining his refusal of another opera proposal, "and at this moment it is on its way to brutalizing France. I do not wish to participate in this work of devastation."

But even if, as a French critic once said, Victor Hugo didn't love music, music certainly loved Victor Hugo. Hostile critics today tend to call his plays "operatic." Friendly nineteenth-century composers agreed. The *New Grove Dictionary of Music and Musicians* credits him as the source of sixty-eight completed operas (including nineteen based on his novel *Notre-Dame de Paris*, the first five to his own libretto) as well as sketches or projects for other operas by Bellini, Bizet, D'Indy, Honneger, Massenet, and Mussorgsky. Hugo's texts and plots have also served the composers of ballets, overtures, serenades, film scores, Broadway musicals, symphonic poems, and incidental music. His poems (there are twenty volumes of Victor Hugo poems) have provided lyrics for songs by Saint-Saëns, Berlioz, Fauré, Franck, Liszt, D'Indy, Lalo, Massenet, Rachmaninoff, Chabrier, Delibes, and

Gounod; even Wagner had a try. Hugo, naturally enough, preferred his own "verbal music" to theirs. He accepted incidental music in his play *Lucrèce Borgia* (he even helped to write it) on the condition that it not be so good that it would distract people's attention from his words.

Of these sixty-eight operas, only four survive in the world repertory today: Donizetti's *Lucrezia Borgia* (1833), Verdi's *Ernani* (1844) and *Rigoletto* (1851), and Ponchielli's *La gioconda* (1876). There are occasional performances of Saverio Mercadante's *Il giuramento* of 1837, which is based, like Ponchielli's opera, on Hugo's *Angelo, tyran de Padoue*. I'm not counting Boublil and Schoenberg's phenomenally popular musical *Les Misérables* of 1984, although both friendly and unfriendly critics—I tend toward the friendly—have called it an opera.

One explanation for Hugo's popularity with opera composers was offered by Francisque Sarcey, writing in *Le Temps* in the 1870s. He compared Hugo's methods, intentions, and effects to those of the librettist and composer of an opera, and concluded they were in many essential ways the same. Like a typical nineteenth-century opera composer, he wrote, Hugo stressed collisions of passions and spectacular tableaux, often at the expense of dramatic plausibility. He included pauses in the action where the "musician" in him could take over, with a poet's versions of arias, duets, trios, and choruses. He supported these scenes of verbal music with extreme and "operatic" gestures. (Doña Sol, the heroine of *Hernani*, is given eighty-seven acting directions in the script—falling to her knees, fainting, etc.) Sarcey's analysis of scenes from Hugo's plays shows them to be constructed precisely like operatic *scenas*, with cavatina-cabaletta arias preceded by recitatives, and love duets that are "pure verbal music." Doña Sol's wedding night "duet" with Hernani—

Pas un nuage au ciel; Tout, comme nous, repose.
Viens, respire avec moi l'air embaumé de rose!

—which only concludes with the lovers' death, was one of Sarah Bernhardt's triumphant moments. Her "vocal success with Victor Hugo's Spanish heroines," a biographer has written, "was that of a lyric soprano interpreting *jeunes premières rôles* in romantic verbal operas."

People at every level of sophistication enjoy making fun of Italian opera plots. The resident faculty of my Harvard house, pressed to come up with a silly skit for one Christmas entertainment, seriously considered doing a straight reading through (in English) of the libretto to *Il trovatore*. One popular television critic used to devote a whole column to retelling the plot of any opera being shown on TV, to amuse down-to-earth readers by his demonstrations of the stupidity of this upper-class art.

Ernani can seem, in the printed text, more than usually foolish, because of the extraordinary condensation of Hugo's story that Verdi's librettist, Francesco Maria Piave, had to perform. Singing words, except perhaps in Gilbert and Sullivan patter songs, takes a good deal longer than speaking them on stage. A play of 2,000 lines of French verse has to be reduced to an opera libretto of fewer than 1,000 lines of Italian. Carlo's famous soliloquy at the tomb of Charlemagne ("Costor sui sepolcrali marmi") contains 87 words. Hugo's original, one of the most celebrated spoken arias in all Romantic drama, contains 1,537.

Room also has to be left, in about the same overall viewing time, for orchestral overtures and interludes and the obligatory Italian opera choruses, which rarely do anything to further the action. The opening chorus of *Ernani* is a piece of totally gratuitous "local color." Critics have had harsh words for Victor Hugo's long speeches of transparent exposition ("Let me tell you all about your childhood, my daughter . . ."). But by pruning them all ruthlessly, Verdi and Piave leave us often totally bewildered as to why their characters are behaving so passionately and so strangely. It takes Hugo a full act to explain Elvira's (Hugo called her Doña Sol, but Elvira scans better in Italian) confusing personal relationships with her demon-lover Hernani and her protector Don Ruy Gomez de Silva. Piave gets it all over with in twelve lines and concludes, "Si rapisce"—"Let's abduct her." Ernani's colorful band of brigands immediately and jauntily agrees. Any audience following the script can be forgiven for finding the whole business highly unlikely.

A few lines later, Ernani makes a fleeting reference to "the sadness of his exile"— what exile? the viewer wonders; and exiled why?—a matter that Hugo had time to explain at exasperating length. Scene 2 has scarcely opened, with Elvira lamenting her enforced nuptials and her true love's absence, when the king, suitor number three, forces his way into her chamber, tries in a few lines to seduce her, fails, then tries to drag her off, when (surprise!) Ernani emerges from a secret door and stops him, and then Don Ruy Gomez enters through another door—shame, chaos, confusion, quartet with chorus, end of act.

One can relate similar confusions (or absurdities) resulting from condensation in the libretti of the other surviving "Victor Hugo" operas: *Rigoletto*, *Lucrezia Borgia*, and *La Gioconda*. In each case, whatever its own weaknesses, Hugo's original is both clearer and richer, with more complex and better-motivated characters; more interesting admixtures of the comic, the grotesque, and the political; more spectacular moments of theatre; and verbal outbursts and combats of far greater emotional intensity. Of course, these are precisely the elements that the composers tried to supply by music.

Changes in popular taste over time are no easier to explain than popular taste at any given time. Theatrical historians assert that the likes of Ibsen and Shaw displaced, and in time wiped out, the high-minded historical tragedies (and melodramas) of Schiller, Dumas, Hugo, and their successors—just as they were sup-

VERDI, *Rigoletto*, Cornell MacNeil, San Francisco Opera, 1961.
Photograph by Carolyn Mason Jones. Courtesy of the San
Francisco Opera.

posed, in their time, to have displaced the last tired wave of Neoclassicism. Exposure to more authentic forms of realism, to more persuasive and intelligently constructed plots, to characters, actions, and language closer to our own lives (so goes the argument) left a new generation of theatregoers embarrassed by the very plays their parents and grandparents had adored. The showy, poetic tirades, the pompous emotional pretenses, and the absurdly entangled intrigues of nineteenth-century "costume drama" came, in time, to be virtually banished from Western theatre stages—only to find themselves preserved in Western opera houses.

Why? Why are we still listening to *Ernani, Rigoletto, La Gioconda, Lucrezia Borgia?* Why should plots, characters, themes, speeches, and motivations we regard as intolerable on the spoken stage still be perfectly acceptable to us in opera—indeed, deserving of $50 and $100 tickets, bravos, and tossed bouquets?

Any "explanation" of a cultural phenomenon can be only speculation. You know why you go to such operas better than I do. But let me offer a few possible reasons for the survival of these dramatic dinosaurs.

1. Singers who can guarantee full houses (either because they sing well or because they're famous or both) still want to sing roles in these operas. So to fill up an opera house, the impresario lets them name the operas they want to perform. Why do they want to sing these roles? In part because of cultural lag (*their* idols and teachers sang them, they learned the parts long ago, they're part of the standard repertoire); and in part because, in the accepted manner of nineteenth-century Italian opera, these roles were written as display pieces designed to show off the beauty and skill of brilliant voices. The case is identical to Sarah Bernhardt's performing in Hugo's tragedies well into this century, because she (and her audiences) loved the opportunities they offered her to display her "operatic" talents.

2. In a similar way, opera impresarios (and to a lesser degree, conductors and musicologists), who know much more about music history than you and I do, have a personal stake in keeping alive these operas of the past. Like the singers, they have devoted much of their careers to studying them, and their taste to admiring them. (One may win points among one's professional peers for "rediscovering" forgotten old masterpieces.) Authentic audience taste, in the modern world of high-priced opera, has only a marginal effect on repertory choices in many cities. In the nineteenth century of Hugo and Verdi, plays and operas lived or died (like Broadway shows today) on the basis of popular appeal. Today, subsidies, season ticket sales, foreign language performances, and the somewhat sheepish behavior of opera audiences, trying hard to like what they're told they should like, greatly muffle the effect of popular appeal.

3. We, the audiences, actually do love the show-off arias and ensembles, however dramatically irrelevant or impossible they may be, and the jaunty (or luscious, or clever, or hummable) music of Donizetti or Verdi or Ponchielli. We love

it so much we don't care if it surrounds and supports a logically impossible, humanly incredible, or morally reprehensible drama. Let Lucrezia poison five enemies on a whim, and still insist that we admire her for her motherly love. Let a hunchbacked, foul-mouthed jester pay to have his lecherous boss murdered, and then find the body of his dying daughter (dressed as a boy) in the sack instead. Let La Gioconda keep forgiving her hated rival because the rival happens to be wearing a rosary (or a crucifix) that reminds La Gioconda of her own long-suffering mother. Let everybody keep pouring out poison and then antidotes for poison or make-believe Romeo-and-Juliet poison till we can't tell the dead and dying from the healthily napping. We don't care.

We don't care, as long as we get to hear Pavarotti singing "La donna è mobile," or Caballé singing "Ernani involami," or Domingo singing "Cielo e mar," or Sutherland singing "Com'è bello," or any one of a hundred other worthy singers rendering other memorable tunes from these operas, and a good orchestra sweeping us through the interludes and bouncing us through the dances. We can't usually understand what these people are saying when they sing in opera anyway (almost never, in Verdi's "crossed-purpose" ensembles). Bewildered as we may be when we read the libretto (or the supertitles), we still tend to yield to voice, music, and spectacle in the opera house. "The public still goes to the opera to achieve that wordless transport effected through song," writes Charles Affron, in a book on Hugo and Musset. "Absurdities of plot and character . . . are forgotten because a singer makes beautiful sounds. . . . Disbelief is suspended because it cannot for a moment be engaged."

4. This argument may seem anti-intellectual and unfashionable, but there is also the possibility that our great-grandparents were right: whatever we may pretend, we secretly do like melodrama. And perhaps we should. No one I know has put the case for the seriousness of melodrama more powerfully than Eric Bentley—the wisest drama critic of this century, the same man who dismissed Hugo's *Hernani* as "a schoolmaster's classic":

> Intensity of feeling justifies formal exaggeration in art, just as intensity of feeling creates the "exaggerated" forms of childhood fantasies and adult dreams. It is as children and dreamers—one might melodramatically add: as neurotics and savages too—that we enjoy melodrama. . . . Melodramatic acting, with its large gestures and grimaces and its declamatory style of speech, is not an exaggeration of our dreams but a duplication of them. In that respect, *melodrama is the Naturalism of the dream life.*
>
> The melodramatic vision is in one sense simply normal. It corresponds to an important aspect of reality. . . . Melodrama is not a special and marginal kind of drama, let alone an eccentric or decadent one; it is drama in its elemental form; it is the quintessence of drama.

5. One can argue that the music of a good Italian romantic opera tells a story of its own, apart from and as if parallel to the story told by the libretto. In the best cases, this independent musical plot can be something coherent, logical, organically unified, and legitimately moving, even when the libretto and onstage action are not. I feel this to an impressive degree with Donizetti's *Lucrezia Borgia;* not at all with Ponchielli's *La gioconda.*

6. And finally, there are cases where the music does illuminate, enhance, uplift, and ennoble these admittedly somewhat flimsy stories. By some peculiar alchemy, an inspired score seems able to render them almost mythical or sublime, and make their "unnatural" actions and emotions matter profoundly. As A. Richard Oliver writes in "Romanticism and Opera":

> Hugo's *drames* in particular competed, over the author's objections, with Shakespeare's plays and Scott's novels as the most popular source of opera plots. *Le Roi s'amuse* is much better known to the theater world through its transformation into *Rigoletto; Angelo* into *La Gioconda.* The simple fact was that the *drame romantique* hungered for musical adornment. The unbelievable characters and the contrived plots it shared with the *melodrame* were admirably suited to musical enhancement, whereas plays offering air-tight, credible incident and psychological insight were not. Hugo, tone-deaf and anti-operatic though he was (he was amazed that Verdi could make four people speak at the same time in *Rigoletto*), realized this too late, as his attempts to shore up his moribund *drames* with music amply testify. It is very likely that the greatest theatrical event of the 19th Century in Western Europe was the opera. It sucked the blood out of all the other forms of drama and left them lifeless.

I could argue such a case with no difficulty for *Rigoletto,* in which Verdi spun Hugo's poetic straw into musical gold. Hugo (who also came to admire *Rigoletto,* and was enraptured by the quartet) may have been correct, however, in regarding Verdi's version of *Hernani* as a crude and cheapened travesty of his play. It requires, at the very least, singers, a producer, a conductor—and an audience—who can somehow force themselves to take it all very seriously.

(1984)

CHAPTER NINE

Sex and Religion in French Opera

Most operas that continue to hold the stage deal with "romance" (men and women falling in and out of love with one another) and either heroic or comic adventures: warfare and duels, quests, confusions of identity, tragic misunderstandings.

The romantic content of opera is frequently rendered more interesting (and more musically productive) by coyness, jealousy, divided loyalties, insecurity, hopelessness, or loss on the part of the lovers. Occasionally (*Fidelio*, *The Magic Flute*, *I vespri siciliani*) the adventurous or idealistic portions of an opera plot may take on uncommon seriousness and depth.

But it was left for French librettists and composers, by and large, to convert operatic romance into physical lust; to take their characters and adventures not simply from legend, history, or "everyday life," but from the supposedly sacred mysteries of religion; and then to concoct for our delectation strange and steamy combinations of the two.

One mustn't be too assertive about national characteristics, in opera or anything else. As soon as I ventured to claim that French opera writers were more sex obsessed than others, someone would bring up the great humping themes of Strauss's *Der Rosenkavalier* and Shostakovitch's *Lady Macbeth of Mtsensk*, or the epic lusts of Monteverdi's Nero and Poppea. The minute I suggested that French librettists and composers waded more deeply than others into religious waters, I'd be asked about *Parsifal* and all of Verdi's heroines' heavenly prayers. No opera that premiered in Paris quite equaled Strauss's *Salome*, a spicy stew that combines the Bible and Krafft-Ebing in almost equal parts.

But the French, once they got seriously into popular opera (around 1830), demonstrated a unique fascination with religious texts, plots, emotions, and paraphernalia; and, for the time, a uniquely free (uniquely "French"?) display of sexual passion.

Religion came first. Eugène Scribe, the phenomenally popular playwright and librettist who virtually invented French grand opera (with some help from Parisian designers and composers), enjoyed using superdramatic episodes taken, very loosely, from European history. And because medieval and Renaissance spectacles were very much in vogue—the first Meyerbeer/Scribe grand opera came out the same year as Victor Hugo's *Notre-Dame de Paris*—he opted for fifteenth- and sixteenth-century plots, which inevitably involved religious controversies.

La Juive (Halévy and Scribe, 1835) involves a Jewish father and daughter who stand heroically firm against the malevolent anti-Semitism of the Christians of Constance (Germany) at the time of the Church council of 1414, and the defeat of the Czech reformer Jan Hus. *Les Huguenots* (Meyerbeer and Scribe, 1836) pits Catholics against Protestants in the Paris of 1572 and climaxes—Scribe enjoyed bloody climaxes—with the St. Bartholomew's Day massacre. *Le Prophète* (Meyerbeer and Scribe, 1849) tells of a weird sect of Anabaptist rebels who briefly took over the city of Münster in 1534 and crowned one of their duped followers as prophet-king and son of God. Betrayed to his enemies, the prophet blows up a whole palace on his head and theirs in the final scene (rather like Saint-Saëns's Samson), as a challenge to the Paris Opera's stage crew and a treat for the haut-bourgeois audience.

Given the Paris Opera's crowd-pleasing commitment to lavish stage spectacles, the religious settings and sentiments in these early French "grand" operas permitted not only onstage wars and the boilings-in-oil of heretics, but also an almost endless succession of gorgeous religious rituals and processions. These demanded recognizable and moving choral music and impressive church or cathedral sets.

The French were not the only opera makers to seize on this most familiar of all sources of scenic and musical extravaganza. *Boris Godunov*, *Cavalleria rusticana*, *Die Meistersinger*, *Tosca*, and *Peter Grimes* all include scenes set in or near Christian churches, with religious rituals in progress. (The protagonists are usually engaging in contrapuntal, secular goings-on in the foreground.) There are plenty of other operatic scenes, French and non-French, set in convents and monasteries, in which resident monks or nuns provide the background chorus. Jewish and pagan temple settings enlarge the list. All of these afford potentially spectacular, emotionally satisfying, and naturally choral surroundings.

But no nineteenth-century Italian, German, or English opera company came up with anything to equal the Münster Cathedral coronation scene in *Le Prophète*, or the parade of prelates in *La Juive*.

The cortège advances in the following order: the trumpeters of the Emperor, the flag-bearers and crossbow-men of the city of Constance, the masters of the different guilds and societies; the alderman, the archers of the Emperor; then the men at arms, the heralds, the trumpeters of the Cardinal, his crossbow-men, his banners and those of the Holy See; all the members of the church council, their pages and their clerks; the Cardinal, on horseback, with his pages and his gentlemen; the halberdiers, the heralds of arms of the Emperor, carrying the banners of the Empire; then finally, the Emperor Sigismund, on horseback, preceded by his pages, surrounded by his gentlemen, his equerries, and followed by the princes of the empire. . . . The trumpets sound, the organ is heard, the crowd of people lift cries of joy. . . . At the appearance of Sigismund and the officials of the Empire, the bells of the Cathedral and of the other churches in the city are rung, and the sound of cannon is heard.

As one French critic wrote in 1835, "If one is not careful, the Opera will become a power capable of throwing its armies into the balance of power in Europe."

Without trying to clarify the tangle of church-state relations in France after the revolution, I should point out that in all of these operas the leaders of the established church come off as villains—an image apparently acceptable to the ardent anticlericals of Paris in the 1830s and 1840s. Scribe was willing to attribute the most passionately "religious" convictions ("Kill the Jews! Slaughter the Protestants! C'est le voeu de Dieu, le Dieu Vengeur!") to the most morally corrupt of men. The hysterical, sadistic professions of the Anabaptists in *Le Prophète* are worthy of the Reverend Jim Jones.

So far, though, not much sex. In *French Grand Opera: An Art and a Business*, William L. Crosten writes, "Melodrama viewed with righteous horror any portrayal of physical passion. . . . Homely, middle-class virtue held the field. Indeed, it could scarcely be otherwise in a libretto written by Scribe. . . . In his plays he constantly sustained the sanctity of marriage and the solid virtues of domestic life."

The Catholic Valentine readily switches religions to marry her Huguenot lover, but the only things she ever embraces are his feet and his faith. Jean the Prophet loves his mother more than the dear orphan Berthe, and Rachel ("La Juive")—although she accuses her Christian lover Leopold of "having commerce" (oh, the shame!) with her—is clearly less devoted to him than to her father and her religion.

One of the safer ways to mix sex and religion, French opera writers found, was to push back further into history, to Biblical or Early Christian times. Then, according to lascivious legend, our puritanical, flesh-denying forefathers (whether Christian or Jewish) were confronted and tempted on all sides by the devotees of orgiastic pagan religions, who were forever trying to seduce them into wicked ways. This gave Paris opera producers the chance to stage great pagan orgies and barbaric rituals in suavely decorative early Third Republic style. Composers and librettists got to write splendid sex versus religion duels between jezebels and saints.

In all three major works of this genre—Saint-Saëns's *Samson et Dalila* (1877), and Massenet's *Hérodiade* (1881) and *Thaïs* (1894)—although antipagan virtue eventually triumphs, all three of the male puritan heroes (Samson, John the Baptist, and Athanaël) find the sexual lures of their temptresses impossible to resist, thereby proving themselves solid nineteenth-century Frenchmen as well as sorely tried saints. (Richard Strauss's John the Baptist, you may recall, never once flinches before all of Salome's lures, which of course drives her mad.)

Saint-Saëns's Samson sings:

> Despite myself, my steps have led me to this place;
> I want to flee, but alas! I cannot.
> I curse my love . . . and yet, I love still.
> Fly, fly this place that my weakness adores. . . .
> Your tears reawaken my grief. . . .
> Delilah! Delilah! I love you. . . .
> Let God's thunder strike me down,
> Let me perish in His flame;
> My love for you is so great
> That I dare to love despite God Himself.

Dalila then sings her big aria. God sends the requested thunderbolt. Samson prays for strength to resist her wiles. She runs into her house (or tent). More divine thunder and lightning. "Samson lifts his arms to heaven, as if pleading to God. Then he runs after Dalila; stops; and finally enters her house." Doomed.

Massenet's olden-time heroes hold out, or at least pretend to hold out, a little longer. Most of the sex in his *Hérodiade* (as in Strauss's *Salome*) is found in Herod's own sick daydreams and in the ambience of his pagan court. "As the curtain rises [Act II, Scene 1], Herod is nonchalantly reclining on the couch [white leather, covered with rich stuffs]. Nubian, Greek, and Babylonian slave girls lie around the back of the chamber, and around the king's couch, in lascivious and picturesque poses." ("Dans des poses lascives et pittoresques"—isn't that a lovely phrase?) They proceed to do naughty dances for him, and quench his thirst from an amphora full of aphrodisiac vin rosé.

At first, John tries very hard to convert Salomé's infatuation for him into a mystic or spiritual love for the one true God:

> Love me then if you must, but as one loves in dreams, where in contemplation
> of the ideal one is wrapped in a mystical flame which transfigures that love
> which our sinful flesh enslaves. Banish all these transports of unholy desire!
> Lift up your soul to heaven!

But Salomé will have none of it. And by Act IV, poor John is in a state, tormented by the image of her sinful flesh. He resolves his dilemma, *en vrai français*, by presuming that God gave him this "intoxicating flower" to press to his lips: "Thou has given me a voice to praise Thee, O Lord—and a soul to love!"

Pre-Christian prophet and pagan courtesan offer themselves together to die, "clasped in a supreme embrace," singing:

> Ah my dearest, it is good to die while loving,
> When our days burn out like a dying flame,
> Our love, in the shining radiant heavens,
> Will solve the mystery and find life everlasting.

Tristan and Isolde couldn't have put it better.

The case of Athanaël in *Thaïs* is more perverse and peculiar still. A saintly desert fanatic, he spends two acts singing of the joys of self-denial, all the while lusting for the sex queen of Alexandria he's pretending to try to convert. Thaïs, meanwhile, is yielding to his arguments, which ruins his whole game. She renounces her lovers and their splendid gifts, sets fire to her palace, and becomes a desert nun, starving herself to death as repentance for all of the gorgeous sins we saw her committing in Acts I and II. Well produced and performed, this opera can still dramatize with terrific intensity the classic French warfare (cf. André Gide) between the seductive appeal of puritan austerity and the impulse toward total sensual abandon.

In her salad days, Thaïs had warned Athanaël (as Carmen warns her admirers), "Be careful not to fall in love with me." Athanaël burns with feverish jealousy of all of the men who have enjoyed her body, and talks her into the most dreadful acts of mortification. He transforms Alexandria's highest-paid whore into Saint Thaïs of the Bleeding Feet. Only then does he acknowledge the beast within:

> In vain I flagellated my flesh, in vain I beat myself! A demon possesses me. . . .
> Ah! to see her again, to make her mine! I long for her! Yes, I was mad, mad not
> to have understood—that she alone was all I wanted, that one of her caresses
> was worth more than heaven! Oh, I would like to murder all those who have
> loved her.

Never has the natural intensity of French religious sentiment been so intimately fused with the natural intensity of French sensual passion. Athanaël is almost as demonic in his unholy lust as Claude Frollo, the evil priest of Hugo's *Notre-Dame*.

Devils and hell are as much legendary as they are specifically "religious"—Don Giovanni's fate is no more theologically "Christian" than Parsifal's. But when French composers invoke devils and hell, it is usually in a distinctly Catholic and

MASSENET, *Thaïs*, Beverly Sills and Sherrill Milnes, San Francisco
Opera, 1976. Photograph by Susan Ehmer.

sexual context. Their devils mock religious hymns, trample over pious believers, and are impotent in the face of crosses and holy water. And the three best-known devils in French opera—Meyerbeer's (in *Robert le diable*, 1831), Berlioz's (in *La Damnation de Faust*, 1846), and Gounod's (in *Faust*, 1859)—all display their diabolic natures most actively in conjuring up debauched female spirits and in trying to arrange for the sexual violation of virgins. The virgins (or ex-virgins), of course, end up in heaven, but not always before the devil has had his way with them— another instance of the unholy, uneasy means French opera writers found to satisfy warring Gallic urges.

The Meyerbeer-Scribe devil (named, of all things, Bertram) is a fairly soppy and ineffectual spirit. But he does, by means of a famous aria, summon up the "ghosts of faithless nuns" from the graveyard of a ruined convent, who abandon themselves to an orgiastic dance. His son Robert later turns up in the bedchamber of his chaste beloved, threatening to rape her. Her angelic tears and pleas not only deter, but also reform him.

It's hard to tell how much hanky-panky actually goes on in Berlioz's *La Damnation de Faust*. On their first encounter, Faust and Marguerite sing of (and presumably act out) a wish to clasp each other gently in their arms. Later, deserted, she recalls one perfect kiss. This Marguerite is imprisoned, not, like Gounod's heroine, for murdering her illegitimate child (which would indicate she did more than kiss), but for killing her mother accidentally with a sleeping potion Faust gave the girl to keep her mother out of the way during his "visits of love." So perhaps more did go on than gentle clasping and perfect kissing.

In general, however, Berlioz plays down sex in the lives of his protagonists— their passion seems, on the whole, rather blissful and pure—and plays up religion. An Easter hymn recalls Faust to the "holy calm of peace" he once knew. Méphistophélès leads a mocking parody of "Requiescat in pace" ("Religious music touches me," he admits, "for sentimental reasons"). He and Faust ride over praying peasants on their final mad gallop to Hell.

One of the hardest things to take in Gounod's version is his smarmy blend of winking prurience and *eau-bénite* religiosity. The composer was a pious Catholic believer who wrote twenty-three masses, seventy-seven religious canticles and motets, hymns, church organ music, and sacred oratorios, including a tedious "redemption" trilogy that Victorian England adored. The vigorous Christianity of Meyerbeer and Halévy is here reduced to the thin, sweet prayers of a spineless and angelized female, who rather too easily succumbs to the jewels and wiles of the devil-driven Faust—a man who craves her primarily *because* she is chaste and pure. Virgin ravishing is an essential ingredient in the religio-erotic ragout of French opera, whether the virgin be male or female.

After Marguerite is discreetly deflowered during the Act II interval, she tries to pray for forgiveness (in one of opera's better-known church-and-choir scenes, for which Gounod had to ask permission of the papal nuncio); is tormented by Méphistophélès and his hellish "voices"; and collapses from the strain. In the very next scene, Méphistophélès conjures up the "famous courtesans and queens" of antiquity in an attempt to melt whatever is left of Faust's virtue, by means of the usual lascivious operatic spectacle. Marguerite prays some more, dies, and goes to heaven, to another Easter hymn. This almost embarrassingly enduring opera—it *does* have some spirited and memorable music—may be the ultimate reduction of sick sexuality and denatured religion into a thin stream of lyrical sentimentality, a kind of music drama virtually unique to the French.

Other French composers, from Jules Massenet (*Marie-Madeleine, Le Jongleur de Notre-Dame*) to Arthur Honneger (*Jeanne d'Arc au bûcher, Le Miracle de Notre-Dame*), wrote specifically "pious" works for the opera and concert stage or incorporated bits of religious kitsch into their works. Anita ("la Navarraise," in Massenet's 1894 opera of that name) wears a little lead figurine of the Virgin Mary about her neck. A lovesick girl accused of whoring, she prays to her little idol for her lover's safety ("Protect him, most holy Virgin, *Vièrge purissime*"); passionately kisses it when he returns; and, when he denounces her, is only stopped from stabbing herself to death by finding the little lead Virgin in the way.

The two most enduring French operas (along with *Faust*)—Bizet's *Carmen* (1875) and Massenet's *Manon* (1884)—may seem to have plenty to do with sex, but not very much with religion. Both have as their heroines women we are meant to admire (or at least forgive) for their sexual promiscuity. They may in the end be "punished" for it, but it is obviously intended to be part of their charm—for us, as for all of their onstage admirers. Both operas were roundly attacked by contemporary moralists when they first appeared. Writing of *Carmen* in 1885, Félix Clément denounced "the shame of such a subject, the like of which has never, in two centuries, dishonored a stage dedicated to the delicate pleasures and divertissements of polite society."

Manon is only fifteen when she runs off to live in sin with Des Grieux, and sixteen when she runs off with someone older and richer. Verdi's Violetta Valéry may be "la traviata" (the wayward one, the courtesan), but Massenet's Manon is infinitely looser, and more treasured by her creator for her sins. In her most winning air ("Profitons bien de la jeunesse"), he captures a poignant, Ovidian sense that all should be forgiven to a young, beautiful creature trying to fight the passage of time:

> Let's make all we can of our youth,
> These days that Spring leads in:
> Let's love, and sing, and dance without stopping—
> We'll never be twenty again!

Carmen's opposite number—equally charming, amoral, and characterizing—is the Habañera: "L'amour est enfant de bohème."

> If you don't love me, I love you—
> And if I love you—look out!

Both women, we accept, sleep with the baritones as well as the tenors. Manon does retain, through it all, her love for Des Grieux, as Carmen does not for Don José. The dramatic difference is important (it helps make *Carmen* the tougher opera), but the moral difference is not. And in both cases, I think, something remains of the Thaïs/Dalila/Salomé syndrome, the French fascination for wicked women who manage to melt the virtuous resistance of holy men. Des Grieux is, after all, on the brink of Holy Orders when Manon rushes to his seminary to test her seductive powers. Her triumph lies in her *de*-converting the chevalier/abbé from the Church. It's one of the classic "sex and religion" scenes in French opera.

"O my God! Purify my soul with your sacred fire, and erase with its radiance the shadow that still rests at the bottom of my heart!" he prays before she arrives. Once before him again, in his priestly robes, Manon weeps, falls to her knees, begs his forgiveness and his love. He denounces her perfidy, insists his love is dead. *Look* at me, she pleads, listen to me, feel the touch of my hand!

"I love you!"

"Do not speak of love here; it is blasphemy!"

"I love you!"

"Ah, be still! Speak not of love!"

"I love you! . . . I will never leave you. . . . Come!"

"Ah, Manon! No longer can I struggle against myself."

Like Samson, he defies his God for a woman of dubious virtue. "Let the heavens collapse on my head; my life lies in your heart." And another one bites the dust.

Religion in *Carmen* is pretty well confined to Micaela's prayer, and to a general sense that life back home in Navarre was more God fearing and simple. In Prosper Merimée's short story, on which the libretto was based, José was originally destined for the Church, and made to study for the priesthood. If Bizet's librettists had picked up on this, it would have fit him nicely into my pattern of "seduced male saints" in French opera.

Even without this clue, *Carmen* retains, I believe, a great deal of the excruciating moral/sensual tension of the French opera tradition. José (this is, I grant, a very personal reading) is not only a mama's boy at heart (and a virgin—"jamais femme avant toi"), his nature and values shaped by a naïve country Catholicism; he is also, by Carmen's well-informed standards, a hopelessly inadequate sexual partner. He moons over a withered flower and a chaste kiss from his mother, while Escamillo stabs his bull right to the heart in a bloodstained arena, and Carmen lets out a shriek of joy and pride. Driven mad by a fundamental sense of male insufficiency, José—still more a "priest" (or an altar boy) than a free and adult man—finally penetrates Carmen the only way he can. Unfortunately, no self-respecting tenor is likely to accept my interpretation of the role of José—just as Jon Vickers violently rejected the concept of Peter Grimes as a tormented homosexual—so you probably won't see it enacted on stage.

It would be satisfying if I could put forward some logical and persuasive explanation for this persistent, almost obsessive use of sex and religion (and more specifically, sex versus religion) in French opera. But a dozen operas, by half a dozen composers, don't represent a culture. And of course I'm leaving out all those (*Lakmè*, *Pélleas*, *Louise*, etc.) that don't fit my case.

Still, there is something unusual here, a play of dangerous forces rarely indulged in by non-French composers. The strange, divided nature of French Catholicism is certainly part of the explanation: on the one hand, Rabelais and Voltaire, ravaged monasteries, Jules Ferry and Emile Combes, *Le Canard enchaîné*, priests as figures of fun; on the other, distinguished Catholic writers, elite Jesuit schools, convents full of holy nuns (cf. *Les Dialogues des Carmélites*), all those sweet female saints, the great cathedrals, abbeys, and pilgrimage churches. Four separate apparitions of the Virgin Mary were reported in France during what historians still describe as the faithless nineteenth century.

The unique place of sexual passion and prowess in French culture is even harder to document and define. It may be enough to recall that, for several centuries, France, and especially Paris, was the place where frustrated or curious men from other countries and cultures inevitably went in their search for greater sexual freedom and adventure, and found women eager to help; and to recall as well the astonishing sexual candor (unique in Europe) of French literature and painting. I'm not sure how to interpret or explain either of these forces, but they have had a lasting effect on French opera.

(1983)

CHAPTER TEN

Nuremberg Used and Abused

The imagination of the nineteenth and twentieth centuries has burdened the mastersingers' city of Nuremberg with an almost unbearable weight of symbolism. Like other of the world's dream cities (Alexandria, Istanbul, Paris, Venice), Nuremberg has been seized on by people living elsewhere to represent one thing or another, because of either real or imaginary qualities in its history and nature.

But few other cities have paid so heavy a price for the dream images of them that non-natives have created and maintained. The story of Nuremberg is unique and impressive—particularly its story in the late fifteenth and early sixteenth centuries, the period that most of its idealizers choose to idealize. But that story has been rewritten and misread, used and abused many times since then.

The first people to invest the old imperial city with their own fantasies were German Romantic writers and painters of the late eighteenth and early nineteenth centuries. They half-discovered, half-invented a stage-set image of quaint old Nuremberg, which continues to work well in opera. These men were followed by Baedeker-toting tourists, who followed their predecessors' directions in search of the authentic *altdeutsch* picturesque: crumbling riverside castles, steep dormered roofs, high half-timbered buildings projecting over narrow cobbled lanes. For better and worse, Nuremberg has also been chosen to serve private symbolic functions by Teutonic chauvinists from Richard Wagner to Adolf Hitler, men who were trying to rewrite European history in order to prove that Germania was and always had been number one.

Reconstructing the "real" Nuremberg of its own Golden Age (from the birth of Albrecht Dürer, say, to the death of Hans Sachs, 1471–1576) requires that one abandon all subsequent images of the city. Independent since 1219, Nuremberg grew in prosperity mainly because it was, for most of that one century, at the crossroads of a dozen trade routes. With a population of about 25,000 citizens behind its walls (and perhaps another 20,000 dependents outside), it was one of the largest and richest cities in the German-speaking empire. Since 1422, even the imperial castle on the hill, about which it had grown, had been the property of the all-powerful city council.

The forty-two members of the council had sole and absolute power over virtually every activity in the city. They kept Nuremberg as tightly self-contained and rulebound a little beehive as Europe has ever known. The councilmen, almost all wealthy patrician merchants from the top forty families—those stout fellows one sees in paintings and engravings, with their fur-trimmed robes and velvet berets—established an intricate set of laws and an extensive civic bureaucracy to govern wages and prices, weights and measures, foreign relations, dance steps, the length of jackets, the quality of herring, and the texts of poems.

Wagner to the contrary, they forbade the town craftsmen to form guilds, so as not to risk protest demonstrations or a dispersal of their own power. A street riot like that of *Die Meistersinger*, Act II they would have put down in no time. Not only had they no emperor, prince, viceroy, or bishop to tell them what to do; the council actually ran the town's thirteen Catholic churches, convents, and monasteries. It appointed their pastors, administered their finances, legislated their morals. When Luther came along in the 1520s, this puritanical and fiercely independent city slipped from Catholic to Protestant with scarcely a ripple. Both Sachs and Dürer publicly welcomed the new dispensation. The council happily took over the rich monastic properties in the name of the city. Unfortunately, the Lutheran distrust of sacred images marked the end of rich commissions for many of Nuremberg's celebrated artists.

"Celebrated" may be overstating the case. Nuremberg of 1470–1570 was almost as famous for its fine craftsmanship as it was for its stable government, its mercantile prosperity, and its thick double circuit of walls. But what we think of as "art" was rarely taken with any special seriousness, despite the modern aesthetic assertions of Wagner's Pogner and Sachs. In sixteenth-century Nuremberg, Dürer was certainly respected, but primarily for his magical-realist technique and his popular woodcuts. For all of his 3,848 songs, 133 comedies, and 530 poems (by his own count)—or perhaps because of them—Hans Sachs was regarded as a kind of droll civic father figure. But he was no more considered a serious "artist" than were the other versifying Rotarians who attended the weekly meetings of his Shopkeepers' Singing Club.

To mystical Germans looking at the city through the rose-stained glasses of a later generation, Nuremberg appeared as "the Florence of the North." But take away Dürer—who probably preferred Italy anyway—and one is left with a few highly skilled wood and stone carvers, glaziers, engravers, and goldsmiths, whose workshops were judged by the city fathers no more important than those that turned out Nuremberg's excellent (and profitable) bells, cannons, scissors, toys, clocks, trumpets, and locks.

After his Italian travels, Dürer became part of a small Nuremberg cenacle of humanists—one or two of them genuine scholars, the rest fascinated dilettantes. But their private readings, their translations from the Greek and Latin, and their heady *conversazioni* had no effect whatever on the hard-working, penny-counting habits of their townsfolk, who—like Wagner's mastersingers—resisted every effort at innovation. As Gerald Strauss writes in *Nuremberg in the Sixteenth Century:*

> From the mastersingers with their mass of punctilious rules guarded by official watchdogs, to the small band of humanists who dissected and criticized each other's books, from the physicians, so vain of their professional reputations, to the Protestant theologians who knew truth when they saw it, men spoke and acted by codes according to which they approved and censured.
>
> The new, the different was everywhere regarded with suspicion. Nuremberg was emphatically an unintellectual society. . . . Not a single thinker, poet, or scholar was able to impress his mind upon the city's civic personality. Nuremberg would have been exactly what she was had no one written a book there or, for that matter, read one.

For a short while—as long as prosperity maintained, as long as churches and rich merchants needed new buildings and decorations, as long as costly wars could be avoided and powerful nation-states had not rendered them obsolete—cities like Nuremberg could at least feel contented, secure, and self-righteous. With the shift of trade routes to Atlantic ports, the emergence of Protestantism and the trauma of the Thirty Years' War, and the consolidation of power in the united kingdoms of Spain, France, and England, snug and prosperous little cities like Nuremberg lost much of their energy, their spirit, their very reason to exist. This lack of continued prosperity helps to explain why Nuremberg remained frozen in its sixteenth-century form. It was like an ancient ship caught in the ice, waiting to be discovered.

After three decades of religious wars, the city slept in its economic and cultural decline for the better part of two centuries. Educated Germans of the Enlightenment saw nothing but dark, clumsy Gothic crudeness in the native art and traditions it embodied. Passing through en route to Frankfurt in September 1790, Mozart (who rarely noticed the scenic attractions of the cities in which he performed) only "breakfasted in Nuremberg, a hideous town," as he wrote to his wife. During the seventeenth and eighteenth centuries, more progressive German cities had adopted new and sophisticated French or Italian models, or had turned to ancient Greece and Rome for their inspiration.

It was Goethe himself, in an outburst of youthful enthusiasm for Strasbourg Cathedral in 1770, who gave the first notable German stamp of approval to the old native style. He went on to praise Hans Sachs, the almost forgotten cobbler-poet. Most historians attribute the cultural rediscovery of Nuremberg itself to two Berlin University students, Ludwig Tieck and Heinrich Wackenroder, who took a walking tour of the South during their spring break in 1796. They loved what they saw of Italy and the Rhine valley; but Nuremberg was a revelation. "Nuremberg, thou once world-famous city!" wrote Wackenroder. "How gladly did I wander through thy crooked alleys; with what childlike love I contemplated thy old-world houses and churches, which so firmly bear the stamp of our old native art! How deeply do I love the products of that age, which bear so racy, strong, and genuine a character!"

Wackenroder and Tieck helped persuade a whole generation to "honor the German masters" (as Wagner's Sachs commands). At an exhibition on "the Romantic discovery of Nuremberg," held at the city's German National Museum in 1967, misty, past-evoking paintings and drawings of the city by twenty-five Romantic artists were displayed, along with rapturous, loving descriptions of the city by many of Germany's most famous early nineteenth-century writers. The tricentennial of Dürer's death was celebrated in Nuremberg in 1828 with an embarrassing excess of fervor. Longfellow—a great admirer of Goethe, the German lyrists, and German culture generally—celebrated his visit to Nuremberg in 1836 with one of his drippier poems ("Through these streets so broad and stately, / These obscure and dismal lanes, / Walked of yore the Mastersingers, / Chanting rude poetic strains").

After the poets and painters came the tourists. From 1883 on, the indispensable Baedeker guides to southern Germany led the seeker-after-art dutifully past every even marginally noteworthy building, sculpture, and painting in the city. While declaring "there is probably no town in Germany so medieval in appearance," they also reminded their English-speaking readers that "great care should be taken to ensure that the sanitary arrangements are in proper order, including a strong flush of water and proper toilette paper."

"Year by year," began a guidebook of 1907, "many a traveller on his way to Bayreuth, many a seeker after health at German baths, many an artist and lover of the old world, finds his way to Nuremberg." It was "a city of the soul," with "a flavour indefinable, exquisite."

By the mid-nineteenth century, a proper grand tour would have been unthinkable without a wistful pause at Nuremberg. The only qualms expressed by the Victorian and Edwardian guidebook writers were over the recent, almost too exact imitation-old Gothic buildings in the city, which tourists had a hard time distinguishing from the genuine article; and over the increasing number of factory smokestacks that were beginning to surround the jewel-casket of Germania.

Die romantische Entdeckung Nürnbergs—the Romantic discovery of Nuremberg—was more than just a local version of a European cultural craze, a trendy taste for the picturesque past. Unlike comparable "Romantic discoveries" in England or France, it was also part of an aggressively antiforeign movement, part of a defensive, irrational, even monomaniac chauvinism.

Nuremberg satisfied the needs of romantic travelers, poets, and painters because it offered a virtually "unspoiled" image of a fourteenth-to-sixteenth-century town. But it also satisfied the needs of Germany-firsters, because they thought it the purest possible representation of just how wonderful German culture could be, with no alien admixture of anything French or Italian.

This is one of the most important reasons Richard Wagner chose Hans Sachs, the burgher-mastersingers, and the common *Volk* of sixteenth-century Nuremberg to serve as both background and (much of the time) foreground for his most accessible and most popular opera. Sachs, he declared, was "the last embodiment of the artistically productive national spirit . . . something different from the Latin type." Wagner carefully studied historical accounts for his text, then incorporated into it actual verses of Sachs's, folk songs, and a Lutheran congregational chorale. He consciously strove for a musical style more simple and old-fashioned than his own norm at the time.

In 1867, he had published a long essay entitled "German Art and German Politics," which has been called "his commentary on *Die Meistersinger.*" In it, he wrote, "Ever since the regeneration of European folk-blood, considered strictly, the German has been the creator and inventor, the Romantic the modeller and exploiter; the true fountain of continual revolution has remained the German nature. In this sense, the dissolution of the 'Holy Roman Empire of the German Nation' gave voice to nothing but a temporary preponderance of the practical-realistic tendency in European culture"—which had now, he insisted, reached a nadir of spiritless decadence. The Thirty Years' War, he declared, had utterly destroyed German civic culture. It left all German art, for two barren centuries, in the hands of the petty princes. They, unfortunately, had simply imported or imitated spineless Latin art: tinny Italian operas, insipid ballets from France ("a vain and light-minded nation").

Late in the eighteenth century, a few prescient Germans, led by Lessing and Winckelmann, recognized their "Ur-kinsmen in the divine Hellenes." (Wagner, like Hitler, regarded the ancient Greeks' as the only culture equal to the pure German.) Then the sublime Goethe symbolically wed Greek Helen to German

Faust. Next, Schiller inspired a generation of patriotic German youth to an ideal of *Volk und Vaterland*, around the time of the 1814 Wars of Liberation.

But since then, Wagner insisted, there had been nothing; or at least nothing better, in German theatre, than Rossini and Spontini, Dumas and Scribe, the penny-dreadful melodramas of Kotzebue ("the corrupter of German youth, the betrayer of the German folk"), fatuous actors and singers. Worst of all were the operatic travesties that Rossini had made out of Schiller's *William Tell* and Gounod out of Goethe's *Faust*—"a repellent, sugary-vulgar patchwork, with all the airs and graces of a lorette, wedded to the music of a second-rate talent." Somehow, Wagner declared, German art had to find its folk roots again; and particularly German theatre, the folk art par excellence.

And where were German writers and composers to find their ideal inspiration? Not, surely, in the decadent, Paris-aping court theatres. Certainly not in the soulless, Jew-dominated commercial theatre. No—look to "the Mastersingers of Nuremberg, [who] in the prime of classic humanism, preserved for the eye of genius the old-German mode of poetry."

Many observers have stressed the elements of historical authenticity in *Die Meistersinger*, from the correct architectural settings Wagner demanded for the 1868 première to David's recital of the mastersingers' rules and tones and modes. But more important than the opera's historicity, I believe, are the uses to which Wagner put it.

Most of what Wagner wants to say is communicated musically of course, and can never be reduced to a prose statement. He is "saying" things in this opera about true love and true art that have nothing specifically to do with German art or German culture. But in addition to his conscious choice of setting and subject, Wagner does from time to time repeat in the opera the ideas of his essay.

Viet Pogner (who has traveled far *in deutschen Landen*) is distressed that the courtiers of other provinces make so little of the solid burghers of Nuremberg—who, after all, alone in the wide German Reich still care for art. When he learns that Walther von Stolzing—a knight, after all—wants to gain entry into their guild, he feels that the "good old days" have returned. Hans Sachs argues with his fellow masters that, if they genuinely want to show the people how highly they honor art, they will let the people themselves judge their work; that way *Volk und Kunst* will bloom and thrive together. All of this comes close to Wagner's own prose prescription, published the year before the opera's première, for a popularly based revival of true German art.

But nowhere in the opera are Wagner's own cultural and political opinions more clearly voiced than in Hans Sachs's final exhortation ("Habt Acht!") to the people, who then take it up en masse as the opera's closing chorus.

WAGNER, *Die Meistersinger*, Karl Ridderbusch, Salzburg Easter Festival, 1974, rehearsal. Photograph by Siegfried Lauterwasser.

Beware! Evil tricks threaten us:—
If the *Deutsches Volk und Reich* should once decay
Under false foreign rulers
Soon no prince would understand his people any more,
And foreign mists, with foreign trifles,
They will plant in our German land;
No one would know any more what is German and true,
If it did not live in the honor of the German masters.
Therefore I say to you:
Honor your German masters! . . .
And if you favor their endeavors,
Even if the Holy Roman Empire should dissolve into dust
For us there would still remain—Holy German Art!

The link between Wagnerism and National Socialism, between the muddled social thinking of Richard Wagner and that of Adolf Hitler, has been written about too much already. Although the two men shared certain noxious racial and German-nationalist notions, Wagner *did* also create works of art that even the most scrupulous humanitarian can enjoy without guilt. Wagner cannot be blamed for the fact that Hitler enjoyed Wagner's works even more than some of us do—and no work more than *Die Meistersinger*, which the Führer is reported as having seen more than two hundred times.

Long before Hitler, *Die Meistersinger*'s vision of Nuremberg and Old Germany, and especially Hans Sachs's notorious "curtain speech," had made this work a special favorite of the newly unified German empire. It was adopted as a kind of propaganda piece by those who wanted to assert not only German national unity, but also German superiority over "false foreign rulers."

Under the guiding spirit of H. S. Chamberlain, the dogmatic English anti-Semite who had married Wagner's daughter Eva in 1908 (and who first met Adolf Hitler in 1923), the annual Wagner Festival at Bayreuth became more and more an Aryan-nationalist celebration. When, after a ten-year wartime hiatus, the festival reopened (with *Die Meistersinger*) in 1924, it was firmly committed to the new National Socialist cause. At the opening performance that year, the audience rose to its feet at Sachs's "Habt acht!" and remained standing to sing "Deutschland über Alles" at the close.

Nine months before, in September 1923, Adolf Hitler had personally chosen the city of Dürer, Sachs, and *Die Meistersinger* to be the site of his National Socialist German Day—the first of nine increasingly spectacular Nazi Party rallies to be held in Nuremberg. Flowers and flags were laid on, the imperial castle was illuminated, and the market square was roped off for speeches.

Hitler liked the visual image of the city, its symbolic fortress–castle, the islanded river that ran through it, its surrounding walls with their sturdy gates and round towers, the hill-forest of steep roofs and church spires within. It seemed to give ancient Germanic roots, and thereby a spurious authenticity, to his movement. After 1933, it also asserted a connection between the Third Reich and the First— that loose federation of more than three hundred German states and independent cities, called (for no good reason) the Holy Roman Empire, which had begun to offer some form of allegiance to a German "Kaiser" (i.e., Caesar) in the year 962.

For almost two hundred years (1355–1523), Nuremberg had been the city in which every new emperor held his first Reichstag, or parliament, of German leaders. For more than three hundred years (1424–1796), Nuremberg had the honor of serving as the civic safety-deposit box for the sacred imperial relics and regalia.

These two distinctions, in Hitler's view, made Nuremberg the symbolic holy city of the First Reich; so he determined to make it his as well. In a folio of photographs of old Nuremberg, published in Bremen in 1940 for American readers, the author made explicit the connection between the old city and the new: "From the Heidenturm of Kaiser Freidrich Barbarossa, in the Burg, float the colours of the new Reich, and over the Market Place which bears the Fuhrer's name Young Germany marches every year. The Old City gives the proud consciousness of a great imperial and civic tradition, the town of the Reichsparteitag faith in the future."

Today, thanks to old newsreels and Leni Riefenstahl's 1935 film *Triumph of the Will*, most people probably identify the Nuremberg rallies of 1927–1938 with the immense parade ground and arena southeast of the city. But the old city of Dürer and Sachs played its role as well, in these morale-building propaganda rituals.

Hitler was always officially received in Nuremberg at the 1618 Town Hall, with its great vaulted chamber dating from 1332. Each year the mayor of Nuremberg offered him some splendid and symbolic gift: one year an engraving of Dürer's "Knight, Death, and the Devil"; the next year, copies of Charlemagne's crown, orb, and scepter. Before Hitler's arrival, all of the church bells of the city were ordered to ring for half an hour. The roads were hung with Nazi banners; the window boxes were filled with flowers. Hitler received visiting foreign diplomats in the old imperial castle, where he expounded on the beauties of old Nuremberg. (He had tried, he explained, to clear the medieval sector of all "trashy imitations," and to restore its ancient charm.)

Day after day, the wide, winding streets of the city were filled with marchers (from 500,000 to 1,000,000 party members descended on Nuremberg in September for the 1930s rallies), parading twelve abreast: first the Hitler Youth with drums and banners; then a torchlight parade of up to 180,000 party leaders; and finally the "march-past" of the Führer in "Adolf-Hitler-Platz" by 100,000 SA and SS men, and a closing serenade under his hotel window.

A highlight of the 1935 and 1936 rallies was a gala performance for the party elite at the Nuremberg Opera House of *Die Meistersinger*. For these performances, Hitler himself commissioned new sets and costumes, which were reproduced for almost every subsequent production of the opera during the Third Reich. The Festival Meadow set for Act III was backed by a long row of banners in perspective, exactly like those at the *Parteitag* rallies.

One is tempted to believe that the next two nightmares in the life of this much put-upon city were visited on it as punishments for its symbolic role as what Allied reporters liked to call the "birthplace" or the "nursery" of Nazism; "the heart of the world's enemy," in Rebecca West's phrase. But this may not have been the case.

Nuremberg was bombed eleven times between September 1944 and April 1945, most devastatingly on January 2, when a thousand RAF planes all but obliterated the historic center in one twenty-minute raid. This was done not because it was Hitler's favorite city, not because of the Nuremberg laws or the Nuremberg rallies; but because it was an "important industrial and communications center" (something the romantic guidebooks rarely mentioned), manufacturing aircraft engines as well as pencils and toys. It was besieged and shelled for five straight days by the U.S. Seventh Army in the last days of the war, not because it was "quintessentially German," but because the two SS-Panzer divisions remaining within its walls put up such a ferocious resistance.

At the end, three-fourths of the buildings in the old town were destroyed. What was left for the Allied armies of occupation were piles of rubble stinking faintly of disinfectant, under which lay at least 2,000 dead Germans. Half the population had fled; the remaining half lived on as best they could, many without food, in cellars and bomb shelters. The city's total wartime toll was estimated at 8,000 dead, 12,000 missing, and 350,000 homeless. No German city except Dresden had been so totally wiped out.

On April 28, 1945, the London *Times* correspondent inventoried the incredible damage done to what he called "the finest medieval city in Germany." " 'The best thing would be for the citizens to go and find a vacant piece of ground and build a new town,' " he quoted one Allied officer as saying. "This cannot be rebuilt," declared a member of the U.S. prosecution team in the fall of 1945.

But it was rebuilt. The "old city" tourists visit today is in great part a reconstruction. The pale stonework in the facade of St. Sebaldus's Church is all new; the darker stones inserted here and there were recovered from the ruins. Again and again, guidebooks and placards note, "Destroyed in 1945." The more important buildings, beginning with the castle, the two great churches, and the Dürer house, were rebuilt to look more or less as they did in the sixteenth century; the ruins of others were simply cleared. A few—including St. Catherine's, the mastersingers' church—were left as ruins. A little Disneyland imitation of an Old Nuremberg street was built for quick-stop tourists behind the Frauentor gate.

In *On Trial at Nuremberg*, Airey Neave wrote in 1978, "There are many reasons why Nuremberg in that October after the war was a most hated city. It had given its name in 1935 to the laws by which Jews were deprived of their rights as citizens. . . . If the highest Nazis were to be tried what better place could there be than Nuremberg? . . . Was it not here that Hitler's oratory had turned Germans into savage hordes calling for blood?"

In fact, Nuremberg was chosen for the international trials of Nazi war criminals because—as General Lucius Clay told Justice Robert Jackson, who was to head the tribunal—it had the only law court building still standing in any German city: the 1877 Palace of Justice, which Rebecca West called "an extreme example of the German tendency to overbuild. . . . Its mass could not be excused, for much of it was a waste of masonry and an expense of shame, in obese walls and distended corridors."

Twenty-one Nazi leaders were lodged in the prison behind this building, while U.S., English, French, and Soviet judges heard testimony from them, their attorneys, and their adversaries six hours a day, five days a week in Courtroom B. After nine months of hearings, sentences were passed. On October 17, 1946, eleven of the Nazi leaders were hanged in the gymnasium of the prison.

The most famous of Hans Sachs's utterances in *Die Meistersinger* is his nationalistic exhortation, often misread and exploited during the Third Reich. But to my ears, his profoundly moving Act III soliloquy is Wagner's definition of the best possible symbolic role that this ancient city could have played in the heart of its tormented, sometimes dangerous, even barbarous land. Reflecting on both the history of humankind and the mindless riots of the night before, the old man begins to despair of his city, his land, his century.

> Wahn! Wahn!
> Uberall Wahn!

> Madness! Madness!
> Everywhere madness![1]

Everywhere he sees people tormenting and beating one another, even themselves—"the old madness without which nothing can happen."

Midway in his reflections, Sachs pauses. The satisfying, stately, steplike "Nuremberg" motif breaks like sunlight through the melancholy clouds:

> Wie friedsam treuer Sitten
> Getrost in Tat und Werk,
> Liegt nicht in Deutschlands Mitten
> Mein liebes Nürenberg!

> How peacefully with its faithful customs,
> Contented in deed and work,
> Lies in the middle of Germany
> My beloved Nuremberg.

More than any subsequent fantasy of *altdeutsch* charm, *volkisch* art, or Teutonic superiority, this winning quatrain of Sachs's does describe the actuality of sixteenth-century Nuremberg—a solid, stolid, unified, hardworking, and contentedly conservative community. Had it been allowed to retain this image, and not been forced to serve the imaginative needs of others for so many years, the history of a city, a country, perhaps even a world, might have shared more of the benevolent humanism of Wagner's Hans Sachs, and less of the *Wahn* of his confused compatriots.

(1986)

---

1. Or "folly," "fools," "illusion," "delusion": the word doesn't translate easily.

CHAPTER ELEVEN

Whatever Became of the Breastplates?

Faced with the astonishing array of visual and dramatic interpretations of Wagner's *Der Ring des Nibelungen* offered during the last twenty years, it's sometimes hard to realize that for three-quarters of a century—from the première performances at Bayreuth in 1876 to the first post–World War II performances there in 1951—most operagoers saw the *Ring* done by performers going through much the same motions, in much the same costumes, against sets that were altered only very gradually, all over the Western world.

One reason for the durability of the original, Victorian-Teutonic conception was that Richard Wagner created it himself. He commissioned and oversaw the creation of the first sets and costumes, and meticulously directed the première cycles himself. After his death in 1883, his widow, Cosima—who personally ran the Bayreuth Festival with an iron fist until 1906 (and who lived on until 1930 to be sure that her docile son Siegfried kept the rituals intact)—insisted that all subsequent performances be copies of what she declared she remembered of her husband's originals.

Wagner had written stage directions of minute and often unrealizable detail, which Cosima insisted (and many orthodox Wagnerites still insist) must be followed to the letter. ("A flash of lightning breaks through the cloud; in its light, a Valkyrie on horseback becomes visible; on her saddle hangs a slain warrior." "Fafner drags himself further up the knoll and spits from his nostrils at Siegfried. Siegfried avoids the venom, leaps nearer, and stands to one side. Fafner tries to reach him with his tail. When Fafner has nearly caught Siegfried, the latter leaps with one bound over the dragon, and wounds him in the tail." *Und so weiter.*)

The composer commissioned a friend and disciple to sit in on the 1876 rehearsals and "to note down everything I say, even the smallest details, about the interpretation and performance of our work, so that a tradition goes down in writing."

WAGNER, *Die Walküre*, Leipzig Opera, 1974. Photograph by
Helga Walmüller.

(These notes were published between 1880 and 1896.) In founding his own festival
theatre at Bayreuth to produce the *Ring*, Wagner also created a world headquarters
and began a family directorate, which were to exert a quasi-dictatorial, profoundly
conservative power over *Ring* productions there and elsewhere for decades to
come. According to David C. Large, "Wahnfried [the Wagner household at Bay-
reuth] sought conformity to a Bayreuth 'ideal,' and when this was not forthcom-
ing it tried to scuttle the offending production by withholding rights or personnel. . . . Cosima continued to view the production of her husband's work outside
Bayreuth as a kind of sacrilege, as a 'betrayal' of Richard's memory."

   There are few visual images of the original productions beyond the detailed,
highly romantic paintings of the artist Josef Hoffmann, from which the Brückner
brothers at Coburg created the actual painted sets. Hoffmann's sketches for the
Rhinemaidens' undersea rocks, Hunding's lofty wooden hut with the mighty ash

tree in its center, Alberich's and Mime's high rocky caves, the Gibichungs' elaborately carved hall, and the "Wild, Wooded, and Rocky Valley on the Rhine" where Siegfried meets the Rhinemaidens are all vivid, busy, melodramatic renderings of an exaggerated nature and a mythical past conceived by a conventional German landscape artist of the time. We do have photographs of the original Brünnhilde (with her horse) and the original Wotan, wearing or bearing the winged helmets, bumpy metal armor, white gowns and blue cloaks, crossgartered sandals, armlets, spears, long wigs, and beard that defined these characters visually (on stage and in caricatures) for many decades to come. One prize shot shows the original Rhinemaidens, including Lilli Lehman, "swimming" atop their precarious machines, while swathed head to toe, as Shaw complains, in "muslin *fichus* and tea-gowns," their hair arranged in fashionable 1876 coiffures—Rhinemaidens quite unlike the topless, Rubensian nixies who cavorted in Hoffmann's original designs.

We also have photographs of Angelo Neumann's Leipzig production of 1878, which he toured all over Europe during the next eleven years, and of the second Bayreuth production of 1896, both of which were based very closely on the original. We have photographic (and of course verbal) records of other nineteenth-century versions as well, most of which took their cue from the original.

It is impossible to recover to a present-day imagination the impact of these early productions. Wagner's whole grandiose idea, his voluptuous New Music, would still have to seem "modern" to us. The conventions of painted backcloths, two-dimensional rock-and-foliage wings, and clumsy pseudohistoricist costuming would have to be things we simply took for granted.

Professional critics and amateur observers of the time who made mention of the staging devoted most of their attention to the technical innovations. They wrote of steam machines that covered the stage with colored mists and clouds to mask the transformations, not always on cue; of how well the mechanical dragon or the magic fire scene worked (less than flawlessly, in 1876); of how well deceived they were by the undersea illusions. "Never before," wrote the Vienna critic Eduard Hanslick (who had mixed feelings about the music) "has such an accumulation of scenic wonders been offered at an opera." But he judged these devices, as he judged most of Wagner's music, to be mere nervous stimulants, so much sensual opium for the rational mind.

At Munich, one Brünnhilde actually did leap on her horse and charge into the final "fire"—as Wagner's stage directions required. But Cosima dismissed this as a mere circus trick. Many critics mocked the "children's pantomime" effects of the serpent and dragon, while admitting they might impress unmusical tourists. The original rainbow bridge to Valhalla was derided as an obvious, flower-garden prop. Hanslick complained about the tired, tethered horses and the ludicrous live rams. J. W. Davidson, of the London *Times*, thought the scenography at Bayreuth not nearly so good as that currently visible on stages at London, Paris, and Vienna.

From 1896 on (when Bayreuth finally mounted its second *Ring*), critics took issue with the fixed, semaphoric style of acting Cosima imposed there, which many thought more forced and unnatural than what her late husband's actors had done twenty years before. In 1889 Shaw wrote, "Bayreuth has chosen the law of death. Its boast is that it alone knows what was done last time, therefore it alone has the pure and complete tradition, or, as I prefer to put it, that it alone is in a position to strangle Wagner's lyric dramas note by note, bar by bar, *nuance* by *nuance*." In 1896, he judged the Bayreuth style of acting to be an amateurish display of tableau-vivant attitudes, the striking of stupid poses by singers who were often little more than "animated beer casks." (From earliest days, *Ring* tourists mocked the girth of "youthful" Siegfrieds and "enchanting" Brünnhildes. Romain Rolland, at Bayreuth in 1896, described "the vast padded bulk" of a Sieglinde: "From bust to backside she is as wide as a city wall.")

What is remarkable, in view of these criticisms, and of the epochal changes that were to take place both in the Western world and on Western stages during the half century that followed, is how durable these images and methods were to prove. Photographs and accounts of *Ring* productions and performers in Berlin, Paris, London, New York, and Vienna well into the 1930s and 1940s depict staging very little changed from the century before. Hans Kautsky designed new *Ring* productions for the Royal Opera at Berlin (1912–1913), the Metropolitan Opera in New York (1913–1914), and the Vienna State Opera (1930) that satisfied another generation with the same breastplates and helmets, the same stock crags and caves and Nordic carvings and dark, fussy trees. (He did risk "cinematographic" projections in Berlin for the entry of the gods into Valhalla, but the jerky silent-film movements went out of synch with the music and destroyed the illusion.)

World War I, a flurry of anti-Germanism, and the beginnings of Modernism in the arts came and went; large singers in horned helmets and bearskins and long blonde plaits went on standing still or making traditional gestures against romantic-naturalist mountain crags and picturesque trees. The "golden years" of Wagnerian singers (Flagstad, Melchior, Lorenz, Leider, Schorr et al.) were, for the most part, leaden, unchanging years for theatrical design, as far as *Ring* productions went. The reactionary cultural nationalism of the Nazi leaders (who, as we have seen, effectively turned the Wagner festival into an annual party celebration between 1933 and 1942) accounted for some of this paralysis in Germany. It is harder to explain on the stages of London, Paris, and New York.

The standard argument still made in favor of mounting a "traditional" *Ring* production (the Metropolitan Opera's version of 1989 was intentionally patterned after much earlier Bayreuth productions) is that "this is what Wagner wanted." To this, antitraditionalists counter with two objections.

First, "what the author wanted," even when it can be surely known, is in many cases irrelevant. The text (or score) exists; the author doesn't. It's ours now, not his, to make of what we will. ("It is in vain," wrote Shaw, "for Bayreuth to contend that by faithfully doing what was done last time it arrives at an exact copy of what was done the first time when Wagner was alive, present and approving. The difference consists just in this, that Wagner is dead, absent and indifferent.")

"Respect for the work," a sense of responsibility to the notes on the staves, does seem to me a worthwhile trait in a producer—respect, at least, for what the producer finds worthy of respect. But this need not imply a total and slavish respect for the author, with all of his quirks and crotchets; and Wagner had more than his share. In any case, the world has turned a few times since 1876, and what Wagner wanted more than 125 years ago isn't likely to be what he'd want today. It certainly isn't what his two grandsons (who have run the Bayreuth Festival since 1951) have wanted for the past 40 years.

Second, despite the strange cultural phenomenon called "Wagnerism"—a near-deification of Wagner (Wagner the thinker, as well as Wagner the musician) that spread through Europe and the United States between 1870 and 1900—and despite his claim to have created total and indivisible art works, no aspect of the composer's work has stood the test of time *except* his music: not his philosophy, not his historical and aesthetic theories, not his mythologies, not his plots and librettos, certainly not his racial theories, and not his ideas and ideals on operatic staging. Although he was (like Verdi) a very astute man of the theatre, responsible for a number of important theatrical innovations, Wagner's vision of the stage possibilities of even his own works was radically limited by European tastes and traditions of the second half of the nineteenth century.

There were innovative, antitraditional productions of Wagner's *Ring* before 1951, which went against the gospel according to Bayreuth. The holy city itself risked a few concessions to abstraction and stylization. Beginning in 1933 (with the Nazis breathing down his neck), the skillful designer Emil Preetorius gave Bayreuth—as he also gave Berlin, Milan, Rome, and (as late as 1958) Vienna—versions of Wagner's *Ring* cycle that, while they followed the Master's stage directions, reduced a great deal of the Victorian fussiness into symbolically simple and powerful forms. As early as 1905, Alfred Roller designed a *Ring* for Mahler at the Vienna Court Opera that dispensed with horses, rams, and Teutonic motifs altogether, reduced the ride of the Valkyries to a projection of clouds, and created looming, elemental mountain shapes that dismayed the Viennese old guard. In the 1920s, adventurous stage designs in many German cities—Munich, Freiburg, Baden-Baden, Hannover, Frankfurt (all by Ludwig Sievert), Dortmund, Düsseldorf, Duisberg, Berlin, and Dresden—began incorporating the experiments and discoveries of modern art, particularly German Expressionism, into productions of Wagner's *Ring*.

These drew on the unrealized stage ideas of Adolphe Appia and others (geometric abstractions, projections on cycloramas, the use of traps and revolves, stark use of lighting and symbolic colors), as well as on the strange "inner visions" of modern painters. Sievert's were perhaps the first consistently stylized productions: bare stepped acting platforms in front, an imagined Rhine valley beyond, crystalline mountain shapes, minimal projections in the distance. (Lee Simonson's new *Ring* for the Met in 1948, with its stylized, unromantic cliffs and sharp-angled acting platforms, was very similar to Sievert's.) The gods in his *Das Rheingold* stand on a stark, bare segment of curved earth—an impressive image later used by Wieland Wagner. In Sievert's productions, and Emil Pirchan's even more minimalist version at Berlin, Erda is simply a giant mask emerging from the earth.

The single most important scenographer ever to turn his attention to the *Ring*—the Swiss designer Adolphe Appia (1862–1928)—was turned away by Cosima as a presumptuous upstart. Appia had been working since 1892 on a series of timeless, stunningly simple, geometric designs for Wagner's music dramas, the drawings for which are now regarded as one of the landmark creations in the art of the stage. But when he showed them to the Widow of Bayreuth in 1896, she dismissed him and wrote to a friend, "Appia seems not to know that the *Ring* was performed here in '76 and that as a result there is nothing more to be discovered in terms of sets and productions." In the end, he had to settle for a sadly cheapened version of his magnificent designs (and then, for only half a *Ring*) at Basel in 1924–1925. The Wagner brothers' productions of 1951–1975—and the many stripped-down, light-created, atmospheric/abstract versions that followed—owe more to Appia than to anyone else: the first modern theatre designer to dispense with all inessentials in order to carve stage places out of changing washes of color and light.

Partly because of its identification with the Nazi cause, partly because of Germany's postwar poverty, the Bayreuth Festival was not resumed until 1951. When Wieland Wagner, the composer's grandson, offered the first postwar cycle at Bayreuth that summer, the effect was shocking, profound, and internationally felt. During the next twenty-five years, he and his brother Wolfgang (Wieland died in 1966) created four complete new productions of the *Ring* (1951–1958, 1960–1964, 1965–1969, 1970–1975), all in the radical New Bayreuth style.

The New Bayreuth style (which, abandoned by the Bayreuth Festival in 1976, is of course "new" no longer; producers since 1970 have been trying to find ways to rebel against it) has been explained in three ways. One, because Germany was strapped for cash in 1951, this was the least expensive way to mount a new *Ring* cycle that could still be impressive. Two, the legacy of 1933–1945 had left the traditional Teutonic style of production—which Hitler saw as a tangible demonstration of his vision of a heroic "master race"—in hopeless political disfavor. The only way to start the festival anew was to dump the old style altogether, strip the stage bare of its nationalist associations, and begin with a "less is more" Modernist style. Three, despite the howls of traditionalist Wagnerites, such a style was in fact quite defensible in and congenial to the 1950s and 1960s, of a piece with related movements in architecture, painting, sculpture, and film.

Interpreted most economically, the *Ring* tetralogy calls for a minimum of eleven different scenes. It would be tiresome to try to describe the forty-four different ways in which the Wagner grandsons chose to evoke these scenes between 1951 and 1976. Anyone familiar with the San Francisco *Ring* productions of 1967–1972 (Paul Hager/Wolfram Skalicki), or with any of the seven different *Rings* designed by Günther Schneider-Siemssen between 1964 and 1989, will have some idea of the New Bayreuth style—although these designers never settled for stages quite as abstract and unfurnished as those of the brothers Wagner.

In general, the New Bayreuth style focused on a central, circular acting area— although the stage disk (or ring) was sometimes tilted, rendered concave or convex, even cracked and broken into pieces. This area was subtly and diffusely lighted; a world of darkness lay beyond its edges. Lead singers, usually in simple robes or tunics, posed about the disk. They had spears when called for, but no helmets or armor. Groups (of Nibelungs, Valkyries, or Gibichung soldiers—120 of the latter, in three fixed choral rows, for Wieland's first *Götterdämmerung*) cluster or move in carefully fixed patterns. There are no walls, no ceilings, no mountains, no trees. On the flat disk are placed the fewest possible objects—rocky lumps, for example, to serve as seats or an anvil.

Variations over the twenty-five years occurred mainly in the lighting of the stage and the gigantic cyclorama behind it. A complex console was created to control hundreds of lights and projectors, which could create violent, moving thunder-clouds; washes of subtly shifting color; the mottled shadows of a forest. Light and color changes could be precisely timed to the movement of the score. Abstract background sculptures were created to indicate a wall of gold, a wooden palisade, totemic deities, a tangled organic forest. Stark, dramatic projections on the cyclorama could evoke a golden vertical pile for Valhalla, horizontal waves for the Rhine.

Wieland was generally regarded as the more ingenious and creative of the pair. The original conceptions, refined over the years, were his. Few stage images of Wagner's *Ring* have ever matched the potency of his Siegfried and Brünnhilde standing alone on a bare curve of earth, surrounded by an infinity of blue; or the sudden emergence out of sheer blackness of the neck and flame-breathing head of a giant dragon, dead center behind Siegfried, alone on his flat circular disk. For his second series, in 1965 (which he had originally hoped to persuade the sculptor Henry Moore to design), Wieland Wagner devised great archetypal images and primeval idols. When the Nibelung's gold was piled up in front of Freia, it assumed the shape of a female fertility goddess.

For several years, Wieland Wagner had to defend his stagings each summer against the outrage and boos of traditionalists, frustrated by all that was missing, and by his defiance of his grandfather's explicit instructions. But gradually variations of his style spread to other of the world's opera houses. By the 1960s, these "eternal," light-created, un-Germanic settings began to seem more appropriate for Wagner's philosophy-drenched legends than detailed, pseudoarchaeological reconstructions of Old German places and times. For one thing, they enabled viewers to read into the action almost any meaning they wanted. For another, they seemed, in their global, evocative, ever-changing play of light and space and color at one with, as if created by, the music. The minimalist staging and absence of spotlights, as Ernest Newman pointed out, at once reduced the negative effect of mediocre acting, and enhanced the fundamental narrative role of the orchestra.

Like Shaw—who had confessed in 1922 that his favorite way of attending the *Ring* was to sit in the back of a box with his feet up and "listen without looking"— Wieland Wagner had come to feel, long before 1951, that the romantic settings and exaggerated acting styles of his father's and grandfather's generations ("those papier-maché castles, those pseudo-naturalistic forests, those fat ladies in helmets, with all their lusty shouts") worked against the music they were supposed to incarnate and complete.

The cracked disk, the lowering dark skies, and the more menacing, overalled, and helmeted Gibichung army of Wolfgang Wagner's 1970–1975 series heralded the end of this powerful, long-dominant mode. At the same time, they pointed to more bitter and specifically political interpretations to come. This, the last of the Wagner brothers' productions of the *Ring*, was stark, abstract, hieratic, timeless (like all their stagings); and, by 1970, just a bit dull. After the *journées de Mai* in Paris in 1968, and similar intergenerational protest movements elsewhere, Western culture was felt to have made another sharp turn. It was time for *Ring* productions to catch up.

Outside of Bayreuth, between 1950 and 1975, production styles ranged from the antique-traditional (Paris, 1955), through handsome but not abstract stylizations (Milan, 1950; Hamburg, 1956; Vienna, 1957–1958), to productions like those designed by Paul Hager (San Francisco, 1967–1972), Jörg Zimmermann (Milan, 1968), and Günther Schneider-Siemssen (London, 1964; Vienna/Salzburg/New York, 1967–1975), which seemed closely related to what the Wagner brothers were doing. The latter all made use of "timeless" costuming, huge curving symbolic sets, a minimum of stage furniture, dazzling atmospheric projections, and fabulous (if often dim) lighting effects. In these cities, too, however, some critics and audience members began to wonder if there were not other, more "relevant," more immediately exciting alternatives to the New Bayreuth style.

When the new revolution came, it came with a vengeance: first at Kassel, in West Germany, in 1970–1974; then at Leipzig, in East Germany, in 1973–1976; finally, and most notoriously, at the centennial *Ring* at Bayreuth in 1976.

The 1974 Kassel production was defiantly eclectic and disunified. In it, Siegfried was a bearded hippie; Wotan a Texas millionaire; Nibelheim a concrete bunker; and the Gibichungs, Nazis. The gods decayed into hate-filled, senile creeps in wheelchairs; the Norns' broken future-telling rope became a computer that suddenly went down. Wotan and Alberich embraced at the end, apparently the sole survivors of a nuclear war.

At Leipzig, director Joachim Herz (one of the several protégés of the late, great Walter Felsenstein of East Berlin, who continues to exert considerable influence in European opera production) told a consistently ugly, anticapitalist tale, the roots for which can be traced back to interpretations of the *Ring* written by left-polemicists like Shaw and Theodor Adorno. Wotan is again a power-hungry capitalist; the dragon becomes an armor-plated tank, with Fafner's head emerging from the turret. The dwelling place of the gods (like that of San Francisco's 1985 *Ring*) is a Neoclassical temple in decay. A gang of factory workers—the ones who really built Valhalla—gathers at the end of *Das Rheingold* to watch as the gods move on to their own destruction. Siegfried and Brünnhilde make love on a battle-field. Wotan marches in Siegfried's funeral procession surrounded by drooping imperial eagles. *Götterdämmerung*, in fact, begins long after *Siegfried*, in a sleek chrome-and-glass world. The wedding takes place on a turbine-factory floor, surrounded by fascist eagles on columns, banners, saluting leagues of uniformed thugs.

The Patrice Chéreau/Richard Peduzzi Bayreuth production of 1976 is perhaps well enough known by now not to need description, thanks to international television broadcasts, videodisks and cassettes, the forests of newsprint and rivers of ink that have been devoted to it. In this extremely controversial staging, the producers pushed the interpretation of Wagner's *Ring* as an allegory of the evils of the Industrial Revolution even farther than their brothers at Leipzig or Kassel. The Rhinemaidens become whores at a hydroelectric plant, in an opening scene that led to screams of fury from the first-day audience at the Master's temple on Green Hill. Costumes and sets depict not the medieval Rhineland or some abstract mountaintop out of time but (for the most part) Western Europe in 1876.

The production (conducted by Pierre Boulez) was, for all that, vivid and compelling, with acting of an intensity never before seen at Bayreuth (and rarely elsewhere in Wagner), and a few potent, unforgettable symbols—Foucault's world pendulum, Wotan's mirror, the great industrial wheels, the Valkyries' beautiful ruined castle or cathedral wall. Nibelheim is an underground factory full of slave laborers; Hunding arrives surrounded by a sinister mob of goons; Gunther and Gudrune wear fashionable evening dress; the tanklike dragon turns back into a giant—four production ideas that have since become near-clichés. Alberich was no dwarf, but the giants were truly gigantic: singers sitting on the shoulders of athletes, draped by huge costumes, swinging great apelike arms. Mime's forge was a mammoth steam-operated press. Brechtian "alienation effects" were provided by Loge drawing the curtain himself at the end of *Das Rheingold*, smirking knowingly at the audience; and by the mob/chorus turning, as the closing flames subside (there is no flood) to stare at the audience, as if defying us to come up with a better world.

Since 1976, the castle has indeed collapsed, the river overflowed, the house of the gods gone up in flames. Productions of every imaginable sort, from the most safe and picturesque to the most grotesque and nonsensical, have poured out at a rate never known before. At least thirty important new *Ring* cycles have been completed in the last twenty-five years, in Seattle and Dallas, Bologna, Florence, and Turin, Aarhus and Brussels, Buenos Aires and Cardiff, Zurich and Geneva, Nice, Strasbourg, and Marseilles, Warsaw and Barcelona—as well as the traditional world opera capitals, and of course all over Germany and Austria. Bayreuth has come up with two more new *Ring*s, in 1983 (Solti/Hall/Dudley) and 1988 (Barenboim/Kupfer/Schavernoch), each more unusual and disturbing than the last.

The bizarre and sometimes very specific updatings among these—the productions that have attracted the most publicity—wrench the music dramas out of their legendary or mythical settings and shove them into other, real-looking (or futuristic) worlds. Their producers have cast off the New Bayreuth "essentialist" style as something fraudulent and safe, and used Wagner's *Ring* instead to make specific comments about the contemporary (or nineteenth-century, or Western bourgeois) world. In Germany, in particular, they have made explicit reference to the Third Reich/Wagner connection (the Gibichungs often become Nazis pure and simple). They have treated the gods as decadent and criminal, Nibelheim as an oppressive capitalist slave-factory, and the whole epic as a tale of modern bourgeois greed and abuse of power, whether they choose to set it in 1876, 1945, or in some utterly bleak era after an imagined nuclear war.

A serious critical analysis and response to the new interpretations and productions of Wagner's *Ring* of the past twenty years would take another essay at least as long as this one. More "liberties" have been taken, more extravagant conceits have been displayed, more novel readings of lines, scenes, and characters have been offered in these last two decades than in the near-century of productions before.

I cannot comfortably justify a return to 1876; but neither can I champion interpretations of Wagner's *Ring* that profoundly diminish the stature and significance of such characters as Wotan, Siegfried, and Brünnhilde (as many of these do) to levels far below the import of their music. If "What Wagner wanted" is no sure guide to production, most critics will still insist that producers can and should be guided by "what the music tells us." A producer may ignore (they concede) the stage directions, even skim over some sung German words that contradict his stage action or scenes; as long as he agrees that what matters most is the music, and the drama implicit in it.

But who is to say precisely what drama *is* implicit in so fluid, so complex a score? Leitmotivs "mean," for the most part, only because Wagner or his commentators say they do. Except for a few almost obvious ones—the Magic Fire music, for example—would we "know" that certain chords and sequences "mean," say, Revenge, or Fate, or Renunciation, or God's Stress, if we didn't have program notes or a guidebook to tell us? Aestheticians and musicologists have argued for centuries over what and how music "means." Until they all agree, and we agree with them, we cannot hold producers to a fixed and single interpretation of a line, scene, or character, because "the music says so."

Chaos, as Wagner himself sometimes suggested, is likely to be the rule, rather than the exception, in our world (and in productions of *Der Ring des Nibelungen* that try to reflect or comment on that world) until another cruel divine order emerges to force things back into unity. *Ring*s devoted to the evils and collapse of Eastern European communism are surely on the drafting boards already, now that *Ring*s devoted to the evils and collapse of capitalism and fascism are becoming routine. Be grateful if you have the opportunity to see a contemporary *Ring* that is as compelling to look at as it is to listen to; thoughtfully (not narrowly or spitefully) of our time; on the whole generous to Wagner, rather than mean-minded and reductive; one that makes provocative sense, and still seems to grow out of the music, which is (fortunately) larger than all of these postmodern *Konzept*s put together.

(1990)

CHAPTER TWELVE

What Makes *Otello* Work?

The composition of *Otello* was a much less Shakespearean feat; for the truth is that, instead of *Otello* being an Italian opera written in the style of Shakespeare, *Othello* is a play written by Shakespeare in the style of Italian opera. It is quite peculiar among his works in this aspect. Its characters are monsters: Desdemona is a prima donna, with handkerchief, confidante, and vocal solo, all complete; and Iago, though slightly more anthropomorphic than the Count di Luna, is only so when he slips out of his stage villain's part. Othello's transports are conveyed by a magnificent but senseless music which rages from the Propontick to the Hellespont in an orgy of thundering sound and bounding rhythm; and the plot is a pure farce plot: that is to say, it is supported on an artificially manufactured and desperately precarious trick which a chance word might upset at any moment. With such a libretto, Verdi was quite at home: his success with it proves, not that he could occupy Shakespeare's plane, but that Shakespeare could on occasion occupy his, which is a very different matter.

Shaw on Verdi (1901), even at such length, is irresistible. He is also at least partly irresponsible. He was promoting Wagner by putting down Verdi, and G. B. Shaw by putting down Shakespeare. A substantial portion of his reputation is based on such clever and outrageous half-truths.

Of course, Verdi's opera is not Shakespeare's play, any more than Shakespeare's play is Giraldi Cinthio's story. In fact (although I am about to do it myself), I find it tiresome that people keep writing more and more words about the enigmatic Englishman's play when they pretend to be writing about Verdi's opera.

My guess is that several thousand words have been written about *Othello*-with-an-H for every one devoted to *Otello*. Shakespeare's 283-year head start has a lot to do with this—and the fact that words seem to be better suited to the analysis of structures made out of other words than to those made out of musical notes. Verse drama, moreover, has a longer pedigree and a loftier academic prestige than mere opera.

But beyond that, apart from musical analysis, Boito/Verdi seem to have left the critic who wants to comment on something more than particular singers, conductors, and sets relatively little to talk about. They so strip-mined and refined their original that most of the endlessly fascinating questions Shakespeare's 25,000-plus words give rise to simply don't exist for the reader or analyst of the 6,500-word libretto (not counting repeats) that Boito writes and Verdi sets to music.

When Othello lost his H, Iago became Jago, and Desdemona began accenting the second syllable of her name, all three changed utterly. They awoke, in fact, in a totally different world: different because it was made out of music; because it was operatic; because it was Italian; because it was, in imaginative terms, Boitan and Verdian; and because it was a world conceived and brought to life in the 1880s rather than the early 1600s.

One gross example of the difference between their two worlds: *Othello* is one of the most savagely and explicitly *sexual* good plays ever written. I am referring not to coy bawdy jests or to traditionally safe literary euphemisms (hot blood, wanton sports, the rites of love). I mean compellingly vivid references to, and images of, sexual intercourse:

an old black ram
Is tupping your white ewe . . .

Your daughter cover'd with a Barbary horse . . .

making the beast with two backs . . .

The gross clasps of a lascivious Moor . . .

the general camp,
Pioners, and all, had tasted her sweet body . . .

Would you, the supervisor, grossly gape on,
Behold her topp'd? . . .

Were they as prime as goats, as hot as monkeys,
as salt as wolves, in pride . . .

and then kiss me hard,
As if he pluck'd up kisses by the roots,
That grew upon my lips, then laid his leg
Over my thigh . . .

to be naked with her friend abed,
An hour, or more . . .

Lie with her, lie on her . . .

All of this, and so much more like it, has proven fertile ground for literary and psychological analysts of the play. But there is not one word of it in the opera. The word *whore* (repeated ten times in the play) is softened to *vile courtesan*—and even that *parola orrenda* appalls Des DE mona down to an E-flat shudder. The homoerotic leg-over-thigh image from Cassio's supposed dream is neutered into "as if kissing the internal image with tender anguish."

George Marek has attributed this bowdlerization to Verdi's own "Italo-Victorian" tastes. Marvin Rosenberg has written of (and defended) similarly emasculated versions of the play that were being edited for young English female ears during the same century. My point is simply that a good deal of the ripest, juiciest source of interest . . . is gone.

Italo-Victorian or no, Arrigo Boito is regarded as a poet of some distinction. Scanning his libretto for repeated, musically accented words in search of some sort of poetic pattern that might explain the opera's power, I discovered about twenty words that recur again and again. Listening to the opera sung (even if one knows no Italian), one may find these repetitions weaving a kind of visionary emotional world.

Evviva! and *Vittoria!* are hard to miss. But then they're likely to crop up in the chorus of any Italian opera even vaguely related to war. Otello the hero is characterized by full-voiced war words such as *tremendo* and *trionfale*. His color (*nero, fosco, tenebre, oscure*) is contrasted to Desdemona's ivory hand and white brow (*eburnea mano, candido giglio della tua fronte*). Jago is partly conjured up by diabolic diction (*demonio, Satana, inferno*) and the evil adjectives he evokes (*crudel, atroce*). Set against him, the two nineteenth-century Italians posit a Catholic *paradiso* of *Dio, angeli, Madonna*.

Ciel here means "heaven," and more. It is Otello's stock angry oath, as well as the starry sky that once signified his love. *Notte* means "night," but also his and its blackness, and their lost night of love.

The words one hears over and over begin to tell a story of their own. These Mediterranean nights, and the citizens who dwell under them, are forever shot through with sparks, fire, lightning (*fulgor, fulgido, fulmini, ardente, fuoco*). Horror and its derivatives (*orror, orrido, orribili*) are on everyone's lips. And lips—*labbra*—form the most constant physical image. *Bacio* (kiss) three times triggers the opera's most poignant motif, but it is also used in many uglier contexts. *Credo, prego, giuro, temo* (believe, pray, swear, fear): the four oft-asserted verbs tell half the plot. *Onesta* (honest) and *cieco* (blind) are perhaps unavoidable, given Shakespeare. But all of the mud, blood, and tears (*fango, sangue, lagrime*) seem to be Boito's. The opera begins with *una vela* (a sail) and moves through Jago's *velen* (venom, poison) to *vel, velo, veli, velami* (veils and mists, handkerchiefs and fogs).

This analysis is still skeletal, unfinished; it is not yet enough to elicit much response. I have said that Otello's new world is operatic as well as Italo-Victorian and Boitan. By this I mean not simply that it is drama set to music, but that, for all its austere innovations, it respects certain operatic conventions that may or may not contribute to a successful total effect.

I am overwhelmed with admiration for Verdi's ingenuity in forcing some of these conventions to make great dramatic sense. Suffering females' prayers are a stock-in-trade of sentimental operatics. And an Ave Maria isn't even an original prayer. But never has that prayer ("at the hour of our death"), or any other prayer in an opera been tuned to a higher intensity of precise dramatic meaning. Scene-setting music is often obvious and cheap—but not when it hurls us so bodily into the action as the opening of *Otello*. Everyone in opera repeats lines at the end of an act. But when has a repeat been more horrifyingly right than Jago's seizing up of Otello's oath at the end of Act II?

Among Shakespearean scholars, there is a theory that Iago represents (among other things) Othello's inner self, that what he is doing is only speaking aloud, or bringing to clear consciousness, his master's unconscious fantasies, fears, and demands. As I watch Verdi's pair at the end of Act II—Jago forcing Otello back down onto his knees so they may swear vengeance as one—the stunning harmony of these two voices, often singing an exact octave apart, seems to justify this idea, which in turn feeds all the more power into the musical moment.

Other operatic conventions don't come off so well. One can make a case for them (Boito does) as necessary light interludes, and the opera is sewn together well enough around and through them. But I could live without the bouncy Act I fire-lighting chorus, and those simpering maidens and mandolins in Act II. I almost wish Verdi had been courageous enough to scrap the very idea of artificial ensembles, as he scrapped so much other dead wood in *Otello*. I want to *hear* Jago arguing with his wife in Act II, not have their lines swamped by Otello's and Desdemona's. And the louder-and-louder Act III closing septet (quintet, really, with voice-unders; Otello mutters only ten words) has always struck me, for all Verdi's efforts, as more operatic convention than music-as-drama.

And yet a good *Otello* (which one is actually more likely to find than a good *Othello*)—its poetry stripped bare, its eroticism censored, inflated by operatics—can still move us in profound, complex, and serious ways. Why?

Reviewers, like operagoers, tend to concentrate on stars first, producers second, and (if we're lucky) conductors and orchestras third. But in looking over a lot of old reviews, I discovered a few that began to hint at one reason for *Otello*'s enduring power.

One is Horst Koegler's astonishing review, in *Opera* magazine, of Walter Felsenstein's 1959 production at the Komische Oper of East Berlin. This critic thought it the most powerful Othello, opera *or* play, he had ever seen—*even though* it was inadequately sung. The director had "liquidated" asides and other conventions.

Hanns Nocker, according to Koegler, outplayed Laughton, Welles, Robeson, and Bondarchuk—even though "one could scarcely hear" his singing.

Then there was a French reviewer, at the Orange Festival in 1975, who insisted that Jon Vickers would be a great Otello "even if he lost his voice." This reminded me of a Friday evening in San Francisco, November 1970, when James McCracken did precisely that. Kurt Herbert Adler, the company's general director, came on stage before Act IV to inform us that the celebrated tenor had lost his upper voice, but that he had agreed to sing out the opera even so. We all applauded gratefully. But in fact, dummy that I was, I had been quite moved by the thin falsetto of McCracken's high notes at the end of Act III. It had seemed to me a creepy, convincing, dramatic innovation, a means of communicating uncontrol to the brink of madness.

Verdi himself says (and I almost believe him) that the whole of Jago's role can be sung successfully mezza voce. Some of the most powerful "arias" in the opera (Otello's harrowing Act III monologue is one example) are really better acted—gasped and choked, whispered and sputtered—than traditionally and beautifully "sung."[1]

What all of this adds up to is a hint of one possible source of the opera's persistent, non-Shakespearean power. Of course, there's still the whole Joseph Kerman, drama-in-the-music aspect to consider. But the emerging point is that this opera, like no other in the classic Italian repertory, is an opera for actors. What potency it has inheres in those three characters—what Otello, Jago, and Desdemona can be made to mean for us, do to us, evoke in us in terms of a vision, a statement, a complex of emotions.

This has something, but not very much, to do with logic. Much of what these three characters do and say, like their nonsinging 1604 counterparts, doesn't make real-world sense. By cutting Shakespeare's Act I, Boito and Verdi actually gain a small increment of credibility, if that matters. At least we aren't obliged to believe that Otello and Desdemona go to bed together for the first time ever during the opening act, and that he murders her about thirty hours later. Although some critics and producers interpret the love duet as a "wedding night" symbol, the

---

1. In *The Dyer's Hand*, W. H. Auden writes:

Since the ultimate goal of Iago is nothingness, he must not only destroy others, but himself as well. . . .

To convey this to an audience demands of the actor who plays the role the most violent contrasts in the way he acts when Iago is with others and the way he acts when he is left alone. With others, he must display every virtuoso trick of dramatic technique for which great actors are praised, perfect control of movement, gesture, expression, diction, melody and timing, and the ability to play every kind of role. . . . When he is alone, on the other hand, the actor must display every technical fault for which bad actors are criticized. He must deprive himself of all stage presence, and must deliver the lines of his soliloquies in such a way that he makes nonsense of them. His voice must lack expression, his delivery must be atrocious, he must pause where the verse calls for no pauses, accentuate unimportant words, etc.

libretto allows and even encourages one to imagine any number of weeks or months of similar bliss back home in Venice.

Even so, if you test the action against mere reason it *will* seem absurd. Roderigo is persuaded to pick a fight with, and later try to kill Cassio for less than no cause. Jago teases Otello down from blissful loving faith to *Miseria mia!* in just seventy-nine bars. If a conductor were to follow Verdi's tempo markings exactly, the Moor's whole moral collapse would take exactly three minutes and eight seconds. And I don't think you can learn as much about Jago as some people think just by reading the words of his *Credo*. By that standard, he may well appear a mere stock nineteenth-century Mephistopheles of no particular human interest.

For me, the potential excitement in Verdi's Jago lies in the quality of the baritone voice each singing actor brings to the role. In a way, Verdi was never more humble, more the selfless servant of his librettist and of imagined future productions than when he scored the words for this extraordinary part. Jago's melodic line does not order the singer how to sing or even (considered by itself) evoke much in the way of a performance. Instead, it invites a great baritone to do what he can; then gently, deftly, but with exquisite self-assurance underscores and punctuates the part. (Sandra Corse has suggested that Jago's vocal line as written—the recitativelike declamatory bursts, the unpredictable musical emphases, the rapid changes in dynamics and irregular pauses—does "suggest obsession." But that still leaves a great deal for the performer to add.)

The role of Desdemona, too, "works" only if its interpreter can make it work. She has all of the lilting lyrical opportunities any prima donna, or easily pleased audience, could wish for. But she is also asked to be, indeed must be strong, made of ductile steel. Brabantio's daughter is much more mature, much more her own woman, than Rigoletto's.

And Otello's jealousy, rapid, illogically induced, and operatic as it may seem, can also be made real enough to hurt very deeply. Much of the reason for this, I believe, lies in the fact that the surface of it is appallingly authentic.

The kind of morbid sexual jealousy that leads to murder has been frequently studied by criminologists and psychiatrists. According to R. R. Mowat in *Morbid Jealousy and Murder*, delusions of a lover's infidelity were the major factor in at least 12 percent—in some tests, as high as 23 percent—of British murder cases available for study—and that leaves out the one-third of murderers who also killed themselves, and hence weren't available for study.

It doesn't "explain" either Shakespeare's Moor or Verdi's to say that he "fits the pattern" of real-world jealous murderers. But I think much of the potential power of this role is related to the precision with which his behavior conforms not only to actual cases, but also to what Freud saw as a near-universal impulse in normal people—in Othello's case, an impulse yielded to so spectacularly that our own healthily repressed instincts may well be touched.

VERDI, *Otello*, Victoria de Los Angeles and James McCracken, San
Francisco Opera, 1962. Photograph by Carolyn Mason Jones.
Courtesy of the San Francisco Opera.

Your average insanely jealous murderer is a man in his late forties ("declined into
the vale of years"), considerably older than those who murder for other causes or
who are judged sane. ("Age itself predisposes to a paranoid development and
jealousy seems only a too natural reaction for the unhappily married husband.")
Eighty-five per cent of the time, he kills, not the supposed rival ("Cassio lives?"),
but his wife or mistress. ("The rival is in a way a delusional presence who has little
real existence and is therefore difficult to attack.") Sixteen percent have prior
assault convictions (note the blow in Act III). Ultimately, 66 percent confess ("I
killed her"), and almost 50 percent attempt suicide ("He stabs himself").

Why do they kill? Psychiatrists generally agree with Karl Jaspers that there is
almost inevitably some "primary" delusional experience, some antecedent cause,
since the actual evidence of infidelity is usually pathetically slight, even self-created.
"Almost anything will serve as evidence of the presence of another, and it is usually
concluded that sexual intercourse has taken place. The jealous man sees a handkerchief on the floor"—*un fazzoletto!*—"a hair on the bed, a wet cloth in the bathroom,
newspapers in a ditch, and attaches to all the same import, and is again convinced."
The morbidly jealous man needs to believe his wife is unfaithful. "The vast major-

ity of cases cannot be corrected by new experience or instruction," writes E. P. Bleuler, "as long as the condition which gave birth to them continues."

In many of the cases studied, an intervening, if not primary, condition is sexual impotence. For whatever reason (age—"the young affects / In me defunct"— alcoholism, disability, nervous block), the man cannot perform. Unable to bear the shame of blaming himself, he blames his wife ("How *could* I touch anything so foul?") and begins to imagine good reasons for not touching her. If not that, the root cause is often seen to be some other form of injured pride or self-esteem in an overly possessive, hypersensitive, secretly insecure male. *She* is to blame for all that happens to *him*. (Otello is recalled to Venice, and slaps Desdemona.)

The French psychiatrist Daniel Lagache, in *La Jalousie amoureuse*, thinks a paranoid jealous man likely to be one who, perhaps because he has known no women before (had Otello?) and is slightly afraid of sex, has formed an impossible feminine ideal to which he expects his spouse to conform (*la gloria, e paradiso, e gli astri*). When she betrays the first sign of even civil interest in another man, he leaps to the worst conclusions. If she is not perfect (this is a Freudian, mother-related formulation), then she must be unspeakably foul. "The rival commonly suspected is a friend," according to Lagache, "someone regularly associated with the household . . . a dominant person with superior social and economic standing." Elaborate, paranoiac spying rites then alternate with vile accusations, slaps, threats, and attempts to force out foul confessions. Out of private need, the man imagines erotic promiscuity, and projects his imaginings onto the woman.

Otello's behavior, in other words, is exactly that of hundreds of modern murderers studied in England, France, Sweden, Germany, and the United States. The murder, when it finally comes (more likely by bludgeoning or beating than by strangling or smothering), is commonly regarded by the man as an act of justice ("Confess! . . . Beware of perjury!") as well as a means of ridding his world of an intolerable presence.

Well, enough of this. Otello is a role in an 1887 Italian opera, not the hypothetical creation of a modern French psychiatrist, let alone some whimpering 1960 paranoiac in the Broadmoor Asylum for Criminal Lunatics. Intriguing as such parallels may momentarily be, they have a dangerously reductive tendency. Otello is obviously a conception much grander and more open than any real-life, morbidly jealous murderer. Otherwise the role could never go on, year after year, affecting so many people so deeply. But I do believe that the first catch, the first painful hook or hold he gets on us, may derive from the superficial authenticity of his awesome emotions.

Let me offer one last, private suggestion as to a possible source of this opera's power. Verdi's score is not all *orrore*, *notte*, *tremendo*, not all drenching sea storm, sinister evil, and strangled declamation. There are also a few brief moments of heart-catching beauty—moments usually triggered by a rising vocal or violin phrase that leaps to one single lovely note and then descends.

Like most operagoers, I suspect, I love these rare bits, and I tried to track them all down. Almost every one, I found, made musical-emotional reference, not to joy now, but either to hope of joy to come (the Act I duet), or to an agonized, Proust-like remembrance of joys past:

O: Now and forever, farewell, sacred memories. . . .

D: But it was with this hand that I gave my heart.

O: But oh grief, oh suffering! They have robbed me of the vision that kept my soul content. . . .

D: And one day on my smile
Hope and kisses bloomed. . . .

—and, of course, the final "un bacio . . . un bacio ancora."

At first, reading or playing these splendid, silvery moments again and again, I thought the impact was wholly musical; I was yielding to some trick of tonality and orchestration. But the effect seemed too sure and too lasting for that.

Then I thought it might be only "Verdian." Perhaps *he* could not face up, as Wagner could, to full-out Love Present. Because of some inner weakness akin to Otello's, Verdi had to hide behind a fiction of love remembered or yet to come.

And then I remembered fourteen of the strongest and truest lines Shakespeare ever wrote. And I wondered whether both of these great men in the end might not have been onto the same awful secret:

The expense of spirit in a waste of shame
Is lust in action, and till action, lust
Is perjured, murderous, bloody, full of blame,
Savage, extreme, rude, cruel, not to trust,
Enjoyed no sooner but despised straight,
Past reason hunted, and no sooner had,
Past reason hated, as a swallowed bait,
On purpose laid to make the taker mad.
Mad in pursuit, and in possession so,
Had, having, and in quest to have, extreme,
A bliss in proof, and proved, a very woe.
Before, a joy proposed, behind, a dream.
All this the world well knows, yet none knows well
To shun the Heaven that leads men to this Hell.

(1978)

CHAPTER THIRTEEN

The Odd Couple: Offenbach and Hoffmann

There are a number of worthy and still-popular operas by composers who wrote only one (the best known is perhaps Beethoven's *Fidelio*), or at least only one that survives in the repertory. What makes Offenbach's *The Tales of Hoffmann* unique is that it's the one enduring serious opera composed by a man who earned his reputation, and his lasting place in social and musical history, by writing 105 decidedly *non*serious works, usually identified by diminuitive labels like "operetta," "opéra comique," or "opéra bouffe." Arthur Sullivan, who learned a great deal from Offenbach, tried to make a similar leap into the ranks of serious composers with his romantic opera *Ivanhoe*, which he wrote after eleven successful comic-opera collaborations with W. S. Gilbert.

But *Ivanhoe* has disappeared, whereas Offenbach's serious, symbolist, death-and-devil-haunted work is still regularly revived, with all-star casts and lavish new productions, at major opera houses in Europe and the United States. It's as if the world's most popular comedian had a try at playing Hamlet just before he died, and pulled it off successfully.

Or almost successfully. Even favorable critics still tend to describe *The Tales of Hoffmann* as Offenbach's "problematic," "potential," or "unresolved" masterpiece. Scholars, conductors, and producers keep rewriting its text and score, rearranging its scenes, and making new cuts and additions, which doesn't always make the opera more clear. (Offenbach died before he finished it, so the game is fair.) No two commentators can even agree on what the opera means, which is rarely the case with Offenbach's lighter-hearted hits.

The three bass/baritone villains, plus Lindorf, are usually sung by the same actor, to make a dramatic and metaphysical point, and to save on singers' fees. The parts of Hoffmann's three loves (four, if you count Stella, who usually has two words to say) are written for radically different vocal types, and are traditionally assigned to three sopranos. But occasionally one singer—Joan Sutherland and Beverly Sills have both done it—will accept the challenge of playing all of these roles. This may either clarify or muddy the plot. Sometimes a dancer is hired to mime the part of the *automate* Olympia—as Moira Shearer did on film—while an unseen soprano trills her lines offstage. The four character-tenor servants may be thriftily combined in one singer as well.

Hoffmann's friend and protector Niklausse may or may not also be his muse. Her (or his) role may be minimal or substantial, depending on whose version of the text you use. The character of Hoffmann may be played as if staggering drunk or sober, in his twenties or his forties, or as if visibly aging through the three tales. Placido Domingo (who began singing the role at the age of twenty-four, and was still singing it twenty-five years later) has said that he sees the poet as about twenty with Olympia, thirty-four with Antonia, forty-five with Giulietta, and nearing fifty with Stella.

But then sometimes Giulietta's scene is played before Antonia's, which complicates that approach. Because the recitatives were not composed by Offenbach, some producers scrap them altogether and substitute spoken dialogue borrowed from the original play. The prologue and epilogue may be expanded to explain and unify the opera, or they may be dropped altogether. Two of the most popular musical numbers in the opera—Dapertutto's "Scintille, diamant," which he sings to the diamond he is about to offer Giulietta, and the "septet" (for six solo voices, plus chorus) that climaxes this scene—although set to music by Offenbach, were inserted after his death. In recent years, some scrupulous conductors have elected to remove them, and to turn Coppélius's evil "eye-selling" aria back into a trio.

For many years, producers were content to take the libretto and stage directions literally. They recreated the three central scenes as exotic, twisted love stories "evoked" by the poet Hoffmann out of his own past. He appeared on stage introducing these tales to his companions in Luther's tavern in Berlin, while Mozart's *Don Giovanni* (starring his current lady-love) was in progress at the opera house next door. Some producers even left the tavern and its inhabitants visible as a "frame set" throughout, to make this tale-telling concept more explicit.

Lately, the three love stories have been depicted in more psychodramatic ways, as the bad dreams of a drunkard, or the distorted and fantastic products of Hoffmann's sick imagination. In such versions, Hoffmann's double may lie asleep at his desk, or on his bed, all through the opera. The characters in his dreams or fantasies may wear masks, dress in black, or move like hellish puppets about a barren, claustrophobic space. Walter Felsenstein and Patrice Chéreau (among other producers) have endeavored to render their versions of the opera more "Hoffmannesque" and less "Offenbachian." In his austere Paris Opera production of 1974–1978, Chéreau

OFFENBACH, *The Tales of Hoffmann*, Placido Domingo (right) and
Michael Rees Davis, San Francisco Opera, 1987. Photograph by
Marty Sohl.

claimed he had tried to suppress all "the wretched 19th Century theatrical naivete," and "to eliminate anything that smacked of Paris 1880."

The confused and problematic nature of *The Tales of Hoffmann* is partly the result of Jacques Offenbach's untimely death, which left producers with a text that cries out for reconstructive surgery. But it is even more the result of his uncharacteristic choice of a source.

In 1851, Jules Barbier and Michel Carré (who also reduced Goethe's *Faust* and Shakespeare's *Romeo and Juliet* to texts for Gounod) wrote a play entitled *Les Contes d'Hoffmann*, which opened at the Théâtre de l'Odéon in Paris on March 21. For this play, the two authors very loosely combined bits of three fantastic stories by the German writer E. T. A. Hoffmann (1776–1822), plus references to four or five others. They then concocted the ingenious stage conceit that these stories were episodes from Hoffmann's own past, which he was relating to his tavern companions on a single evening shortly before his death.

Hoffmann did hang out at Lutter and Wegner's wine cellar in Berlin after 1814, where he traded stories with his friends, and probably drank too much. But his own life—at least his documented life—was far less exotic and adventurous than were his weird Romantic tales. As far as we know, the real Hoffmann was never in love (a) with a mechanical doll who went all to pieces, (b) with a great singer doomed to die if she sang, or (c) with a Venetian prostitute who stole his reflection—although he did write stories about unfortunate lovers in each of these situations. He dreamed all of his life of traveling to Italy, but never escaped the King of Prussia's domains. He developed a passionate infatuation for a fifteen-year-old singing pupil when he was thirty-five, the memory of which seems to have haunted him for years. But he appears to have remained faithful to the Polish woman who had married him in 1812, and who supported him through a life of considerable poverty and pain.

Ernst Theodor Amadeus Hoffmann (he changed his third name from Wilhelm in honor of Mozart) is still taken quite seriously by scholars of German literature, and by cultural historians examining that phase of European art and thought we call Romanticism. Almost all studies of Hoffmann's writing are in German, and a great part of his literary work—which includes forty-nine tales, two novels, several semifictional essays on music, and a great deal of music criticism—has never been translated into English. Most of his life was divided between music (which he adored) and the law (which paid the bills). Only in the last years of his life did he begin to write the strange, supernatural stories that won him a brief but extraordinary international vogue. His tales were widely translated during the 1830s and 1840s (especially in France) and had a marked influence on authors like Gogol and Dostoevsky; Gautier, Nerval, and Baudelaire; Thomas Carlyle and

Hans Christian Andersen; and two American authors of "tales of mystery and imagination" very like his, Nathaniel Hawthorne and Edgar Allan Poe.

Although Hoffmann's own musical compositions (including eight operas) have been judged tame and uninspired, his music criticism was prescient and occasionally profound. He wrote passionate defenses of Bach, Gluck, Mozart, and especially Beethoven, whom he worshipped, and of the spiritual nature of music in general. Robert Schumann named two of his piano cycles (*Fantasiestücke* and *Kreisleriana*) after Hoffmann's creations. Tchaikovsky's *Nutcracker* ballet is based on a few of the healthier episodes in one of Hoffmann's bizarre children's stories. Delibes's ballet *Coppélia* makes use of the same story as Act I of Offenbach's opera. Wagner and Weber both acknowledged the influence of his musical ideas. Busoni and Hindemith used his plots for operas.

But virtually no one (except scholars) reads Hoffmann any more. For reasons of cultural change, he comes as near as any significant nineteenth-century author can come to being "unreadable" today, unless one is dutifully studying his puzzling time. The force that has almost singlehandedly kept his name alive outside of Germany (and German departments) is an odd opera written by a fabulously popular German Jewish Parisian best known for his satiric and sexy operettas. Professional Hoffmannites profess to be dismayed that the public reputation of their idol has been sustained almost solely by *The Tales of Hoffmann*, this confusing musical mélange of his life and work put together by a composer they regard as hopelessly frivolous and (even worse) French.

Jacques (originally Jakob) Offenbach was born near Cologne in 1819. His father, an itinerant cantor and music teacher named Isaac Eberst, had adopted the name of his native town, Offenbach-am-Main. He brought Jacques to Paris at the age of fourteen. There he was first a music student, then an orchestra cellist, then, successively, a salon performer, a conductor, a composer, a theatre manager, an entrepreneur, and ultimately an international celebrity and bon vivant. In the process, he became (despite a German accent and a Jewish nose his detractors loved to mock) more Parisian than the Parisians—and decidedly more so than the second emperor himself, Napoleon III, son of a Corsican, married to a Spaniard. Naturalized a French citizen in 1860, Offenbach was awarded the Légion d'Honneur in 1861.

The French Second Empire (1852–1870) is a period that gossipy amateur historians adore and serious moralizing historians deplore. In all of their accounts of Paris during these hectic, high-colored eighteen years, Jacques Offenbach—Orpheus in Paris, the king of the Second Empire, the Mozart of the Champs-Elysées—looms so large that he has become (along with Charles Garnier's extravagant new opera house) an overly facile symbol for all of Second Empire Paris.

His career as the favorite entertainer of Le Tout Paris (i.e., the fifty-six hundred well-to-do Parisians who "mattered," out of almost two million) began at the International Exhibition of 1855, when he leased a fifty-seat theatre on the Champs-Elysées and began grinding out one-act, three-character musical farces that were livelier and funnier than anything on stage at the Opéra-Comique. Visitors to the fair, pleasure-seeking Parisians, and a young soprano he discovered named Hortense Schneider helped fill the little *bonbonnière* every night. When the fair ended, he moved to slightly larger and more comfortable quarters in the Passage Choiseul (the theatre is still there), for which he wrote a silly *Mikado*-like chinoiserie called *Ba-ta-Clan*. In the process, Offenbach invented what we now think of as the comic light opera. Gilbert and Sullivan, Franz Lehár, and Johann Strauss, Jr. all followed in his path.

In the next fourteen years, Offenbach wrote 64 more operas bouffes or comiques, which divides out to an average of 4.6 a year. He also ventured his first serious opera, *Rheinnixen*, for Vienna in 1863. It ran for eight performances, and survives today only as a footnote to *The Tales of Hoffmann*, because Offenbach had the wit to transfer its hypnotic, waving barcarole from the Rhine to the Grand Canal.

Among Offenbach's full-length, full-cast effusions during these years (he wrote music like a man possessed, scribbling scores on a lapboard in jolting carriages, or while carrying on animated conversations at his Friday night soirees) were *Orphée aux enfers* (*Orpheus in the Underworld*), of 1858; *La belle Hélène*, of 1864; *La Vie parisienne*, of 1866; *La Grande Duchesse de Gérolstein*, of 1867; and *La Périchole*, of 1868.

Today, all five of these witty, establishment mocking, melodically captivating shows are still regularly performed, either as light relief by the world's grand opera companies, or as regular fare at today's equivalent of the Boulevard musical theatres of the Second Empire.

In point of fact, they often seem slightly ill at ease in modern-day performance. The Met's pompous, kitschy *La Périchole* of 1956 was a case study in how to submerge a great operetta in overproduction. Régine Crespin is great fun to watch, and a joy to hear, as Offenbach's grand duchess. But she could never (and would never) ape the raw raunchiness of Hortense Schneider, "La Passage des Princes," a fleshy sexpot offstage and on who was meanly caricatured as "Nana" by Émile Zola—a liberal reformist who despised Jacques Offenbach and all of his works and pomps:

> The big wench slapped her thighs and clucked like a hen, shed round her an odor of life, a sovereign feminine charm, with which the public grew intoxicated.
>
> From the second act onwards everything was permitted her. She might hold herself awkwardly, she might fail to sing some note in tune, she might forget her words—it mattered not: she had only to turn and laugh to raise shouts of

applause. When she gave her famous kick from the hip, the stalls were fired, and a glow of passion rose upward, upward, from gallery to gallery, till it reached the gods. . . . Hand on hip, she enthroned Venus in the gutter alongside the pavement. And the music seemed made for her vulgar voice—shrill piping music, music that recalled the Saint-Cloud Fair, with wheezings of clarinets, and playful trills on the little flutes.

Most current producers insist on rewriting Offenbach's operetta texts to incorporate twentieth-century gags, and on importing Top 40 Offenbach hits from his other operas, to satisfy the mobs they hope to attract. But originally these works emerged from and criticized the air, the life, and the style of a city whose intense, false, fleeting image they helped to fix in the world's imagination. Between their thumping, intoxicating carousel *galops* and their mock-lyric outbursts, these sharp, satirical comedies inevitably included asinine aristocrats (or deities) not unlike Napoleon III, the Empress Eugénie, and their comic-opera courtiers; outrageously "French" sexual license; and sharp jabs at grand opera. We can catch alluring glimpses and faint sounds of Offenbach's Paris from the music and lyrics of these scintillating works. But we can never recapture the genuine thrill of recognition, the journalistic precision of the effect they must have had on Parisian theatregoers of the years between 1858 and 1868.

Nathanael rushed in, impelled by some nameless dread. The Professor was grasping a female figure by the shoulders, the Italian Coppola held her by the feet; and they were pulling and dragging each other backwards and forwards, fighting furiously to get possession of her. Nathanael recoiled with horror on recognizing that the figure was Olimpia. Boiling with rage, he was about to tear his beloved from the grasp of the madmen, when Coppola by an extraordinary exertion of strength twisted the figure out of the Professor's hands and gave him such a terrible blow with her, that Spalanzani reeled backwards and fell over the table among the phials and retorts, the bottles and glass cylinders, which covered it: all these things were smashed into a thousand pieces. But Coppola threw the figure across his shoulder, and, laughing shrilly and horribly, ran hastily down the stairs, the figure's ugly feet hanging down and banging and rattling like wood against the steps. Nathanael was stupefied—he had seen only too distinctly that in Olimpia's pallid waxed face there were no eyes, merely black holes in their stead; she was an inanimate puppet. . . . And now Nathanael saw a pair of bloody eyes lying on the floor staring at him; Spalanzani seized them with his uninjured hand and threw them at him, so that they hit his breast.
    Then madness dug her burning talons into Nathanael and swept down into his heart, rending his mind and thoughts to shreds. . . . His cries passed into a brutish bellow that was awful to hear; and thus raging with the harrowing violence of madness, he was taken away to the madhouse.

This passage from "The Sandman," the tale on which Offenbach's Olympia episode is based, is not untypical of the breathless, antirational, willfully Romantic and supernatural works of E. T. A. Hoffmann. The original "tales of Hoffmann" are populated by monstrous dwarfs, magic potions, bizarre transformations, cabalistic lore, various succubi, and diabolic powers, as well as good ordinary European gentlemen (usually artists) driven mad by insensitive bourgeois, by all manner of obsessions, and by fiery, though never consummated, sexual passions. In their time, these stories were treasured, like early Romantic music, as a liberating escape from the strict rationalism of the eighteenth-century Enlightenment. Today, they are analyzed microscopically by Freudian psychologists and literary critics.

The real source, I believe, of the nagging puzzlement many people still feel at Offenbach's *The Tales of Hoffmann*, for all its musical and vocal felicity, derives not from its incompleteness or its internal inconsistencies, but from the uncomfortable union of composer and subject.

Why did Jacques Offenbach, the original gay boulevardier, choose for his ultimate text, the one most dedicated effort of his life, a play based on the life and works of so alien an artist? Or to put it more simply, what has Offenbach in common with Hoffmann? It is as if a Parisian prince of light collaborated with a Prussian prince of darkness, resulting in the opera we know.

Hoffmann's biographers and critics tend to be offended by Offenbach's shallow, tuneful redaction and reduction of their dark hero and his works. Offenbach's biographers and critics acknowledge that he achieved a greater musical sophistication and range of vocal expressiveness in *Hoffmann;* but on the whole they prefer his earlier operettas to this strange Teutonic swan song. Siegfried Kracauer has written, "All the same, this [*The Tales of Hoffmann*] was not the most significant of his works. Others, like him, had wrestled with demons, but no one but he could have written the *Offenbachiades*." According to James Harding, "*Les Contes d'Hoffmann* will always be an interesting but unequal achievement. . . . His most truly rounded genius should be discovered in *Orphée*, *La belle Hélène*, *La Vie Parisienne*, *La Grande-Duchesse*, *La Périchole*."

Trying to fit the opera to the man, biographers strain to find or force connections between *Hoffmann* and Hoffmann. Offenbach was, after all, Légion d'Honneur or no, German born, too. After the ignominious French defeat by Prussia in 1870, a number of popular papers dragged out his German origins as a sign of subversion (he had fled his adopted country during the war), and denounced him as "Herr Offenbach," a "tool of Bismarck," *le grand responsable*. They pointed at the cynical "decadence" of his popular works as one of the reasons for France's defeat. "The brilliant theatrical era that opened with *La belle Hélène*," argued one critic in 1871, "contributed, by its spirit of satire and disrespect, to the woeful work done by unbounded skepticism, triumphant materialism, and social decadence." "Our unfortunate country will plunge into ruin if she does not quickly recover her good sense and good taste by throwing out once and for all these impudent corroders of the theatre," wrote another in 1873. The mockery of German militarism in *La Grande Duchesse de Gérolstein* no longer amused the authorities. Productions of the work in France were banned in 1875.

After the Franco-Prussian War and the Commune, the tide of Parisian taste turned (at least temporarily) against the larking, mocking "Offenbachiades." The composer had not had a genuine hit since *La Périchole* in 1868, and even that represented an effort on his part to write something more lyrical and sweet than his norm, something in tune with a public that was growing tired of the cynical amoralism of *La Vie parisienne*. His health had been in painful decay since the early 1860s. By 1875, he was nearly paralyzed with rheumatism and gout, and sometimes had to be carried from chair to carriage, from carriage to chair. He was reduced to putting on pumped-up Las Vegas–revue (or English pantomime) versions of his old hits just to pay his bills. In 1875, one of his more grandiose ventures as a theatre manager went bankrupt. He had to rent out his beloved seaside villa (the Villa Orphée, named for the operetta that financed it) and agree to a money-making tour of the U.S. centennial celebrations in 1876. On his way back across the Atlantic, he was overheard making fun of the new French Republic by a French republican senator, who passed on an exaggerated version of his remarks to the sensitive, left-leaning Paris press. A minor scandal ensued.

All of this, his biographers claim, plus a sense that his end was near, disposed Jacques Offenbach to see in the darkly visionary, deeply German, death-obsessed Hoffmann a kindred spirit during his own declining years. According to James Harding:

> The libretto had poignant undertones for him. In 1878, when he finally began work on it, he sensed that death could not be far off. Like Antonia, he also knew that making music would hasten his end, but an impulse that could not be denied forced him on. *Les Contes d'Hoffmann* was his own story and symbolised his own career. . . . Prematurely aged and ill with the stabbing pain that scarcely ever left him, he thought of an old ambition, one he had nurtured since the earliest days. . . . He wanted to be the composer of a real opera, of a work of art. . . . *Les Contes d'Hoffmann* was to be his testament. It so possessed his whole being that, unconsciously, he reached back into his past, towards his roots and the music of his native country. . . . The main flavour of *Les Contes d'Hoffmann* is German.

Siegfried Kracauer claims:

> The reason he coveted it so ardently [the Barbier and Carré libretto] was that he was now actually living in Hoffmann's ghost world. . . . As an old man

doomed to die he resembled Hoffmann himself; like the latter, he, too, was now wrestling with evil spirits. . . .

He discovered that he shared the fate of Hoffmann, the hero of the drama— nay, more, that he was Hoffmann's double. Like Hoffmann, who had never achieved any of his three loves, Olympia, Antonia, or Giulietta, he had never attained the object of his love, grand opera. Like Hoffmann, he had been fooled by an evil spirit, who had estranged him from his true vocation. . . .

This opera was the judgment that Offenbach passed on himself; and the music, which is full of the panic of a child lost in the dark, betrays how many demons stormed in upon him during the process, in which his whole artistic existence was at stake.

I've tried hard, but I just can't buy this romantic notion of an identification in extremis. It reminds me of a past generation of Mozarteans who were certain they heard some "metaphorical shudder," some "fatalistic plunge," some "tragic despairing gloom" every time Mozart composed a work in a minor key, and then presumed there must be some deep, biographical impulse behind it. The very score of Offenbach's last opera seems to puncture such speculations.

The music of *The Tales of Hoffmann* is richer, more varied and expressive than that of his operettas. But it's still Offenbach: still full of joy and esprit, still far more French than German, still wholly at odds with the fundamental spirit of its source. Everything Offenbach ever wrote, it seems to me, leads up to it—given, for once, that he had real time to write and a serious artistic purpose. The party scenes of the Prologue, at Spalanzani's, and in Venice; the mechanical doll's coloratura, the comic-character turns are all precisely the sort of things he had been dealing with for years. Comparing modulations, rhythms, melodic structures, and orchestration song for song and scene for scene (which would take another essay), one could, I believe, demonstrate that the best of Offenbach's operettas are very close musical cousins of *The Tales of Hoffmann*.

This runs counter to the kind of "autobiographical" explanations of works of art many people enjoy. But I honestly believe that Jacques Offenbach had virtually nothing in common with Ernst Theodor Amadeus Hoffmann—or no more, let us say, than Charles Gounod had in common with Goethe or Shakespeare. Given all one can honestly learn about the composer from his letters, memoirs, and music, the romantic fantasy that in his dying years he felt compulsively drawn to his native German roots just doesn't hold up—let alone the idea that he felt some occult kinship with E. T. A. Hoffmann, this concocter of infernal, neurotically overimagined fairy tales out of another world.

I think that Jacques Offenbach simply wanted a good story for his legacy-opera: one that would allow him to indulge all of his known compositional skills; still be popular enough to be taken on by the Opéra-Comique (as it was); ensure his own artistic immortality; and, as he promised his wife just before he died that it would do, make their grandchildren rich.

From the time it was first produced in 1851, people had talked of Barbier and Carré's play, *Les Contes d'Hoffmann*, as a natural for musical setting. Olympia, after all, has to waltz wildly and sing brilliantly. (Originally, her voice was an offstage English horn.) Antonia is a star soprano by definition—and a dying consumptive soprano at that, in the manner of Violetta or Mimì, who hears her dead mother singing Schubert's "Marguerite." In her scene in the play, Hoffmann is a composer as well as a poet, and Dr. Miracle accompanies her dying air on his magic violin. Stella, too, is an opera star, based on a character in Hoffmann's essay-story about Mozart's *Don Giovanni*. Barbier and Carré wrote drinking songs for the two outer frame scenes and for Giulietta's Venetian orgy. Much of the play was written in verse; the text lent itself to musical setting with remarkably little revision.

Offenbach had been tempted by the play in 1851. By the time he declared his interest to Barbier a second time, in 1878 (Carré was by then dead), the author had already completed an opera-libretto version for another composer, who generously gave up his prior claim when he learned that Offenbach was interested. Barbier then rewrote his libretto to fit Offenbach's musical ideas—but not, from the evidence, all that much.

All of this leads me to believe that Offenbach felt no special attraction to Hoffmann; rather, that he liked Barbier and Carré's cleverly condensed, largely demystified theatrical-exotic Parisian stage version; and felt that, given his own musical skills, he could do something very special with it. Taking great pains for once in his life—he spent the better part of two years on his unfinished score—he managed, before he died, to do precisely that.

(1987)

CHAPTER FOURTEEN

The Janáček Boom

"I compose and compose as though something were urging me on. I no longer saw any worth in my work, and scarcely believed what I said. I had become convinced that no one would ever notice anything of mine."

In 1916, when he wrote these lines, Leoš Janáček had good reason to feel neglected. He was already sixty-two. He had been composing assiduously, in his own quirky way, since he was eighteen. And he was unknown outside of the provincial capital of Brno (population about 200,000) where he had spent almost his entire life. There, in the capital of Moravia (now central Czechoslovakia) he taught school, conducted choirs, wrote operas and textbooks, collected more than two thousand local folk songs, and minutely recorded the noises made by people, dogs, chickens, and insects, which he developed into an elaborate theory of "natural" composition.

In 1904 he finished his third opera, *Její pastorkyna*, which we now know as *Jenůfa*. When it was rejected by Karel Kovarovič, director of the Prague National Theatre, Janáček offered it to the Brno Theatre, where all but one of his nine operas were to have their premières. They played it a few times in 1904, 1905, and 1906; a few more times in 1910. And that was it.

Eventually, the determined intercession of friends won over the difficult Kovarovič. (In 1877, Janáček had panned one of Kovarovič's own operas, and biographers attribute the director's long resistance to *Jenůfa* to a twenty-nine-year grudge.) But Janáček's friends managed to get the two men to embrace during an opera intermission, persuaded Janáček to accept all of the revisions Kovarovič demanded in the score, and personally guaranteed the first six performances against financial loss. With its title changed from *Her Foster-Daughter* to *Jenůfa*, his opera got its first big-city performance on May 26, 1916.

Sixty-four years later, this same opera is scheduled for performance in a dozen cities around the world. The other four Janáček operas that appear regularly in the repertory, all written after his sixty-sixth year—*Kátya Kabanová* (1921), *The Cunning Little Vixen* (1923), *The Makropoulos Case* (1923), and *From the House of the Dead* (1928, first performed posthumously in 1930)—were seen in at least eleven cities outside of Czechoslovakia in 1980.

Berg and Stravinsky may get more attention from the musicologists, and Benjamin Britten's operas may be more accessible to English-speaking fans. Occasionally a new production (of Schoenberg's *Moses und Aron*, say, or Aribert Reimann's *Lear*) will focus public attention momentarily to another twentieth-century composer. But the operas of Leoš Janáček have been performed more frequently and more regularly around the world than those of any other modern composer during the last thirty years.

In addition to keeping most of his operas in the regular repertory somewhere all of the time, the Czechs have staged a Janáček Festival at Brno or Prague every ten years since 1948, to celebrate the decades since his death. In 1948, they did all five of the operas just mentioned, plus *The Excursions of Mr. Brouček* (1920), a surrealistic satire in two disconnected parts. "I doubt if *Mr. Brouček* will ever penetrate outside Czechoslovakia," wrote Desmond Shawe-Taylor after seeing it at the 1958 festival. Since he wrote that, the opera has been done at Munich, Münster, Florence, West Berlin, the Holland and Edinburgh Festivals, Vienna, Düsseldorf, and London.

For the 1958 festival, the Brnovians also unearthed three of Janáček's early flops, *Sárka* (1888), *The Beginning of a Novel* (1894), and *Osud* (1906), all of which then lapsed back into obscurity. In 1965, they opened a new, modern, 1,400-seat opera house in Brno, and called it the Janáček Theatre. The 1968 festival was held there, a few weeks before the Soviet invasion of Czechoslovakia. (A fall conference on the composer had to be called off.) In 1978, seven of his operas were performed in the new theatre and two in other halls in one long eleven-day Janáček glut. Making amends for their decades of neglect, the Czechs now export productions to other countries, and have dutifully been putting Janáček's collected works onto records.

Because much of the power of Janáček's music drama depends on Moravian folk song and speech rhythms, it is natural that a great deal of the sales campaign on his behalf has been carried on by compatriots. Max Brod and Maria Jeritza (and the young pianist Rudolf Firkusny) were among those Czechs who helped him during his lifetime. Today, Czech conductors like Rafael Kubelik and Bohumil Gregor, Czech singers like Nadezda Kniplová and Sona Cervena, and Czech producers and designers like Bohumil Herlischka and Josef Svoboda carry on the fight. But international-class producers from other countries—Günther Rennert, Jonathan Miller, Volker Schlöndorff, Walter Felsenstein (and Felsenstein's protégés, Götz Friedrich and Joachim Herz)—have contributed to the Janáček boom. Incomparable singing/acting roles like that of Emilia Marty in *The Makropoulos Case* and the two domineering matriarchs in *Jenůfa* and *Kátya Kabanová* have attracted some of the world's finest sopranos.

Between 1951 and 1978, the English National Opera (known until 1968 as the Sadler's Wells Opera) mounted six Janáček operas, persuaded of his importance by conductor Charles Mackerras. (Mackerras has reedited the scores of both *Kátya* and *Makropoulos*, and conducted complete recordings of these and other Janáček operas.) The Deutsche Oper am Rhein repeated this feat between 1971 and 1977, and capped it by staging the first non-Czech cycle of the six operas in Düsseldorf between November 26 and December 4, 1977. In 1980, the combined forces of the Scottish and Welsh National Operas set out on the same project, introducing one Janáček opera a year in Cardiff, then moving it to Glasgow and on tour the year after. Elisabeth Söderström (who sings these operas in four different languages) has helped make Janáček a popular hit in Sweden. Argentina saw its first *Jenůfa* in 1950; Australia, in 1976.

The French and Italians, who prefer to hear operas in their own languages, have discovered that Janáček's spiky phrases translate badly into Romance tongues. So he has not conquered the same place in the repertoire there he holds today in Germany and Great Britain. But after a few exchange visits from the Czechs, even the French and Italians began to grant him a hearing. Rome saw a native *Jenůfa* in 1952 and 1976; La Scala has done its own *The Cunning Little Vixen* (1957), *From the House of the Dead* (1966), and *Jenůfa* (1974). Paris got *Kátya Kabanová* in 1968, and its first *Jenůfa* in 1980.

The United States follows rather than leads in matters operatic, for a variety of good reasons, mostly financial. Although Maria Jeritza of Brno (who had sung the lead in the Vienna première in 1918) brought *Jenůfa* to the Met in 1924, it was quickly dropped after a few performances. "'What a crew!' we may say of the people of *Jenůfa*," wrote Ernest Newman in a review of that production. "A more complete collection of undesirables and incredibles has never previously appeared in an opera. To the crude story Janacek has written music that is obviously the work of a man who, however many works he may have to his credit, is only a cut above the amateur."

Thanks to the patriotic fervor of Jan Popper, I was able to see a complete *Jenůfa* in May 1957, staged by his Opera Workshop at UCLA, where I was briefly a student. (His graduate teaching assistant at the time was a young Iranian named Lotfallah Mansouri, later to become general director of the opera companies in Toronto and San Francisco.) In his more violent moments, Popper, who was born in Liberec, Czechoslovakia, even looked a bit like his idol.

But no professional American production of a Janáček opera was given again until 1959, when the Lyric Opera of Chicago borrowed a Covent Garden production of *Jenůfa*. San Francisco introduced *The Makropoulos Case* in 1966, also with lead singers imported from London. The Metropolitan only got back on the bandwagon in 1974, reviving *Jenůfa* after a fifty-year sleep. *Kátya Kabanová*—to my mind, the best of Janáček's operas—received its first regular season U.S. performance in San Francisco (with Kubelik conducting and Söderström as Kátya) in 1977, following a few small school and festival productions. *From the House of the Dead* was given a powerful NET television production in December 1969, and Colin Graham staged the Santa Fe Opera's *The Cunning Little Vixen* in the summer of 1975.

I cite all of this to establish that the operas of Leoš Janáček have, in rather recent years, established themselves in the world repertory at least as strongly as those of any other modern composer. ("Modern," as I'm using it, is not a matter of dates. *Der Rosenkavalier* and *Turandot*, which I would not call modern, were written after *Jenůfa*.) The story of how this happened reveals something about the accidents whereby our "taste" is constructed—even after genius has done its part.

Far away in Brno, chattering in Czech, quarreling with half the people in town (including his wife), and composing according to his private theory of the "musical curves of speech," Leoš Janáček had an uphill climb to establish an international reputation. But he died at least moderately famous in 1928, having made up in his last twelve years for the obscurity of his first sixty-two. His seventieth birthday celebrations in 1924, an invitation to visit England in 1926 (a year that saw many new stagings of *Jenůfa*, particularly in Germany), and the composer's death two years later helped to release a minor flood of honors, testimonial articles, and productions of his operas and other works all over the German- (and Czech-) speaking world. At his death, his Viennese publisher printed a black-bordered advertisement listing the ninety opera houses, from Aachen to Zlen, that had already put on *Jenůfa*.

It is difficult to explain what happened next. A British music critic was astonished a couple of years ago at the prospect of having to review eight new recordings of Richard Strauss operas. He remarked on the typical "period of post-mortem disapproval" all composers are supposed to go through, and thought that the thirty years between Strauss's death and transfiguration seemed unnaturally short. Another, more cynical commentator once remarked that "it takes approximately twenty years to make an artistic curiosity out of a modernistic monstrosity; and another twenty to elevate it to a masterpiece."

If they are right, then the abrupt decline in Janáček's reputation after 1928 may not require any complex explanation. Critical articles continued to be written about his operas throughout the 1930s and 1940s, but the performance record shrank to almost nothing. England and America heard none of the operas at all. The Vienna tally for *Jenůfa* before 1964 was: 1918, ten performances (with Jeritza); 1926, two; 1948, five. The Czechs gave up on all of his operas except *Jenůfa* (which they liked for the "local color"), and finally dropped that from the repertory as

JANÁČEK, *Jenůfa*, Anja Silja, Glyndebourne Festival Opera, 1989.
Photograph by Guy Gravett.

well; Dvořák and Smetana were so much easier to love. *The Makropoulos Case* was given only six performances in Prague between 1928 and 1956.

In histories of opera written before 1970, Janáček is inevitably shoved onto a side track labeled "folk" or "national" opera, along with Albéniz and Vaughan Williams, and there dismissed in a paragraph or less. Very few of the many books published on modern music in the 1930s, 1940s, and 1950s had anything at all to say about the man who now so dominates the modern opera scene. As Ray Ellsworth wrote in 1965:

> The truth is that after Janáček's death the world's small interest in his work rapidly declined, and he was regarded as little more than a provincial master for two decades (1928–48). It was not until after the Holland Festival's performance of *Jenůfa* in 1951 that Janáček's fortunes picked up beyond Central Europe.

The start of the Janáček revival, I think, can be traced to 1948. That was the year of the first six-opera cycle in Prague, the year the BBC first broadcast *Jenůfa*, and the year Charles Mackerras came back a convert to London after a year's study in Prague. Mackerras has eloquently described his experience:

> In 1947 I sat with my young student wife [Mackerras himself was then twenty-one] in the gallery of the National Theatre in Prague, listening for the first time to a Janáček opera. It was *Kátya Kabanová*, conducted by that greatest of Czech conductors, Vaclav Talich,[1] with whom I was studying at the time. . . .
>
> What a revelation that performance was to me! Here was a composer whose name I hardly knew, who had been dead twenty years, writing an opera in an entirely different idiom from anything I had ever known, who used the human voice and the inflections of his strange sounding language in an absolutely original way, and whose instrumentation and harmony produced colors and sounds unlike anything I had heard before. . . .
>
> I took vocal scores of several operas of this virtually unknown composer back to London in 1948, and was fortunate in being able to interest Norman Tucker of Sadler's Wells in Janáček's work. Of course, these piano scores gave very little idea of what Janáček's orchestration sounded like. . . . I managed to secure a tape of *Kátya* through the B.B.C., and during a playback gave a sort of running commentary to Norman Tucker and Desmond Shawe-Taylor, who had heard a lot *about* Janáček, but very little of his actual music! They were as enthusiastic as I had always been, and the first English performance of a Janáček opera was given on April 10, 1951, at Sadler's Wells.

1. In fact, Talich had reorchestrated *Kátya*, as he had other Janáček operas, "to beautify and normalize it." Mackerras later made heroic efforts to recreate the scores of both *Kátya Kabanová* and *The Makropoulos Case* as Janáček had originally written them.

I have no doubt that much of the rise in Janáček's popularity can be attributed to the selling powers of Charles Mackerras, backed by the faith of Norman Tucker and the support of a few critics like Desmond Shawe-Taylor. In 1954, the Janáček centennial, Rafael Kubelik (then a better-known conductor than Mackerras) took over the Sadler's Wells *Kátya*, with a considerable rise in its critical and popular success. This led to an invitation for him to conduct a Covent Garden *Jenůfa* in 1956—a production that went on to Chicago. Eventually, these two fervent Janáčekians were to serve as musical directors at London's two opera houses, positions of considerable power and influence in the opera world.

Gré Brouwenstijn's *Jenůfa* at the 1951 Holland Festival also attracted important attention. "Festival productions" tend to be visited by foreign opera lovers and critics and written about at length, more than regular season productions; and the Holland Festival is more adventurous than most. The Dutch continued to demonstrate their dedication by introducing two later and more difficult operas, *From the House of the Dead* (in 1954) and *The Makropoulos Case* (in 1958). Walter Felsenstein, a legendary man of the theatre, offered *The Cunning Little Vixen* at the Komische Oper of East Berlin in May 1956, and critics from all over Europe came to see it. (It eventually ran for more than two hundred performances. Thanks to a fellow student from Berkeley who was writing a dissertation on the director, I got to see Felsenstein's *Vixen* during my first trip to Europe in 1957, just six months after my first *Jenůfa* at UCLA.)

After that it took only the Prague Music Festival and the International Janáček Congress of 1958 (with the world première of *Osud* and resultant world publicity) and then Chicago's *Jenůfa* in 1959 to settle the case: in ten years, Leoš Janáček had somehow become a "classic of modern music."

I count an average of ten different professional productions of his operas outside Czechoslovakia each year between 1955 and 1960. The Prague National Theatre sent a 299-person contingent to the Edinburgh Festival in 1964, which performed two Janáček operas in productions considerably more impressive than those Britain had seen heretofore. They returned in 1970 with three more. They went to the Holland Festival with more exports in 1976 and 1977. Munich, Wexford, Glyndebourne, Prague, the Paris Théâtre des Nations: the publicity value of these summer festivals was enormous. Opera house administrators all over the world were getting the word.

At the start of the Janáček revival, critics were more divided on his merits than they are today. The first British production, in 1951, received so hostile a reception from most of the newspaper critics that some observers expected it to be the last.[2]

---

2. Adrienne Simpson cites a number of these unfavorable reviews in the Cambridge Opera handbook to *Kátya Kabanová*. Here are some examples:

Five years later, the Covent Garden *Jenůfa* gained reviews that were "respectable, no more." Claudia Cassidy, then the terror of the *Chicago Tribune*, called *Jenůfa* "one of the dullest operas I have had the misfortune to see" in 1959.

By the 1960s, a more tolerant (or more open-eared) generation of critics, who were able to see and compare more good productions of his work, began to write of Leoš Janáček as a more-or-less settled master, and of his operas as among the century's most important. One reviewer of Joachim Herz's highly stylized 1962 *Kátya* in Leipzig wondered if it might be the most "beautiful and perfect" thing written since *Tristan* and *Otello*. In the 1970s, production after production drew superlatives—"unforgettable," "all but unbearable," "one of the most emotionally shattering evenings I have ever experienced in an opera house." The pinnacle seems to have been reached in Götz Friedrich's 1972–1974 productions of *Jenůfa*, starring (who else?) Elisabeth Söderström.

There are still dissidents. Daily newspaper reviewers in several cities feel free to admit they do not find Janáček's music interesting to listen to, and they complain—as his detractors have done all along—of his unsystematic and fragmentary construction. Many professional critics are able to muster more enthusiasm than I can do for *The Cunning Little Vixen* and the first two acts of *The Makropoulos Case*. Many musicologists and composers have a hard time taking seriously the work of so freakish and instinctive a musician, one so ignorant (or so defiant) of the Bach-Beethoven-Wagner-Berg tradition of thematic development and symmetrical composition. ("He approaches composition as if music had not been invented before!" complained one scholar.)

If your approach to music is predominantly analytic, this schoolteacher from Brno may drive you berserk. Charles Mackerras once identified forty variant "themes" for Emilia Marty alone; the composer recommended that people not bother looking for "themes" at all. One tendency of scholars of this sort is to lump Janáček along with Charles Ives as a cranky, irregular regionalist who ignored all serious mainstream developments and pasted together "found sounds" in a way that, for some occult reason, still excites the uneducated listener.

Uneducated listeners—even those who may love opera—sometimes feel that these great waves of taste wash over their heads without anyone ever asking them

---

[Janáček is] a rather simple-minded fanatically industrious old man chained to his theories of peasant speech-melody, and impotent as a writer of large-scale works. (*Musical Times*)

[Janáček is] rather a scrap-by-scrap composer, finding it difficult to think consecutively for more than two or three numbers at a time. (*Sunday Times*)

The music is so short-winded and the phrasing so abrupt and broken up that one is never conscious of a continuous flow. It is a kind of perpetual recitative, and one waits in vain for a release into the clear waters of pure song. (*The Stage*)

The spirit of enterprise that animates Sadler's Wells is, of course, to be fostered by all possible means. It is doubtful, however, whether their latest operatic venture has been worth all the time, energy, and youthful talent expended on it. (*Glasgow Herald*)

what they think. The impresarios decide what to produce. The critics tell us what to admire. All we can do is buy it, or not.

Or not. Therein lies, perhaps, one of the most interesting aspects of the "Janáček boom" of the last thirty years. "There is some sort of credibility gap here," wrote the editor of *Opera*, after raving about Elisabeth Söderström in *Jenůfa*. "Every writer and commentator confirms that Janáček is one of the greatest opera composers of this or any other century—and yet the public is slow to respond."

Through thirty years of reports on the Janáček revival, one keeps reading of unsold tickets and half-empty houses, of crowds that bleed out between acts. From everywhere comes the same story: empty seats at Glyndebourne, "pitifully small" audiences in London, entr'acte quitters at San Francisco. The 1956 *Jenůfa* was the worst financial failure at Covent Garden since the war. Twenty-three years after its London première, Mackerras's version of *Kátya Kabanová* was still drawing only 43 percent capacity houses. Reviewers the world over keep remarking on the composer's lack of public appeal. "Texas, when all is said and done, is still *Carmen* country." "The Dutch people who are fond of opera clearly love only the most popular pieces." "The Vienna public, like its London counterpart, does not exactly turn out in droves to see this kind of production." "Unless more people attended the second performance than the first [of *From the House of the Dead* at Sadler's Wells] this is likely to be more in the nature of an obituary notice than a review."

Not until the Düsseldorf cycle of 1977 and the London *Mr. Brouček* of 1978 was there any mention of a near-sellout for a Janáček opera. All along, there have been bravos and multiple curtain calls from the fervent few. But only in the 1980s, perhaps, and only in those few cities where Janáček operas were well and frequently performed, did the general operagoing public begin to agree with the critics. "*The Makropoulos Case*," wrote a London critic in 1971, "doesn't pack the house, but neither did *Elektra* at Covent Garden twelve years ago. Education of the public taste is a slow process."

Many forces have contributed to the resurrection and reestablishment of Leoš Janáček's operas in the last 30 years: the power of creative individuals, the strategic guesses of company managers, the divided opinions of critics, the relative inertia of public opinion. What looks like value in the arts is always open to manipulation and revision, is never carved by God in the bedrock of earth. The extreme, I might almost say decadent, argument that artistic preference is nothing more than vogue was put by the editor of *Opera News* when the Metropolitan Opera decided the time had come round for Janáček again in 1974:

Fashions in music are an intriguing phenomenon, no less so in the realm of opera, where Leoš Janáček has now taken his rightful place after a long, fitful existence. Suddenly *Jenůfa* has become a staple in many opera houses, and the Met has done proudly in bringing it back into the fold. *Kátya Kabanová* crops up in Berlin, Vienna, London; *The Makropoulos Case* in New York, San Francisco, London. And so it goes.

He went on to cite similar "vogues" for Cavalli, Monteverdi, Handel, and Berlioz and "the 1950s craze for the Baroque." Now that the Callas-inspired bel canto revival "seems to have peaked," he wrote, "singers, conductors, and directors are scouring other obscure corners for novelty"—Korngold, Massenet, the lesser-known Mozart. What next? he wondered: Spontini? the Russians? a Weber revival? In any case, he concluded, "Now it's Janáček's day."

Aware as I am of the forces of fashion, whim, and the marketplace in establishing what passes for taste, I can't be quite as cynical as that. I believe that one could demonstrate why, among Janáček's operas, at least *Jenůfa* and *Kátya Kabanová* are likely to hold the places they have won as long as opera companies and audiences continue to exist in something like their present state. Except for Britten's *Peter Grimes*, in fact, I know of no other modern operas that can satisfy at once the critic's demand for original and viable contemporary music, inextricably wedded to a credible and moving text, and the opera audience's desire for real people they can care about, caught up in serious human plots; and all of this expressed in waves and cries of music that cut deep into the heart.

(1980)

CHAPTER FIFTEEN

Herr von Words and Doctor Music

The very salutations of their letters are a clue. For almost thirty years, through more than five hundred surviving letters, they most commonly address each other as "My dear Dr. Strauss" or "Dear Herr von Hofmannsthal." (Actually, the poet had a better right to the title than the composer. Hofmannsthal had an earned Ph.D., University of Vienna, class of 1898. Strauss's doctorates—Heidelberg '03 and Oxford '14—were both *honoris causa*.)

Ten years into their correspondence, Strauss begins using "My dear friend"—an intimacy the poet permits himself only ten times in his 304 letters. Only once in the entire published correspondence does one of their first names appear. Birthday letters, letters of congratulations for honors and successes, even letters on illnesses or bereavements have a chill, carved in marble effect. For two men who worked so productively together for so long, their celebrated correspondence is astonishingly cool, formal, distant—and, very often, frankly hostile.

One could argue that the words-and-music collaboration of Da Ponte and Mozart (three operas), like that of Boito and Verdi (two operas), produced a considerably more substantial body of work than the six operas created by Team Hofmannsthal-Strauss between 1909 and 1929. (The first, *Elektra*, had already been produced as a play in 1906, when Strauss saw it and decided he wanted to set it to music. The libretto of the last, *Arabella*, was essentially finished when Hofmannsthal died in 1929. Completing the score and arranging for production took Strauss another four years.)

Whatever the qualitative sum, the numbers are impressive. No other composer/librettist pair in the history of opera managed to write so many works that have remained in the international standard repertory and—for all of the dispraise of their detractors—seem likely to remain there. In addition to the first and the last, they collaborated on three other enduring works—*Der Rosenkavalier* (1911),

Ariadne auf Naxos (1912, revised 1916), and *Die Frau ohne Schatten* (1919)—and one flop, *Die ägyptische Helena* (1928), which is occasionally revived by Strauss die-hards in places like Munich and Santa Fe.

But despite their frequent, formal professions of admiration, if not for each other, at least for each other's talent; and despite the poet's everlasting agonizing over the fragility of their "relationship," like some anxious modern lover arguing with a partner—"*I beg of you, do not inflict on me this injury;* do not injure us both, do not injure our relationship!"—they were never, as far as one can tell, friends; scarcely even friendly.

Their motor trip together through northern Italy in March 1913 comes to the reader of the correspondence as something of a shock. It was one of their rare face-to-face encounters. Strauss, typically, was the one to offer the invitation. Hof-mannsthal, typically, raised objections. "Your kind, attractive proposal that I might accompany you on a car journey from Ala was altogether unexpected, and not easy to fit in with everything I had planned. But . . . this personal contact (which we have never before had over anything we have done before) might greatly benefit our chief joint work"—by which he meant *Die Frau ohne Schatten*, the opera they were working on at the time.

During most of their acquaintance, Strauss lived at Garmisch, near Munich; Hofmannsthal, in a village near Vienna. But even when cars and chauffeurs (let alone trains) were available, they almost never made the effort to meet. When Strauss accepted the post of co-director of the Vienna State Opera in 1919 (an appointment his "dear friend" had bitterly opposed), which obliged him to spend a few months of each year in the city, Hofmannsthal still found excuses not to visit or receive him. "It is most kind of you to offer to come out here, but please don't think of it under any circumstances; the tram journey of one and three-quarter hours each way is torture, and I do not enjoy visitors."

Although he occasionally traveled about Europe on literary and theatrical busi-ness, Hugo von Hofmannsthal—the classic neurotic artist—preferred either to stay home at Rodaun, tending his fragile nerves and coddling his fragile genius; move to Salzburg for the international theatre festival that he and Max Reinhardt had essentially created; or venture from time to time out to Alpine spas or sunny Italy in a quest for calm and for mental health. The more robust Richard Strauss, meanwhile (ten years older than the poet, he outlived him by twenty years), toured all of Europe, including Russia, virtually nonstop, conducting and promoting his (and their) works, spreading his (and their) reputation, enjoying the rewards of an international celebrity. He also traveled twice to the United States and twice to South America. It is he who oversaw the premières and new productions of their joint works, and reported dutifully on them back to Hofmannsthal: "I have just concluded a magnificent triumphal progress with your works: first *Rosenkavalier* at the Hague and in Amsterdam . . . full houses at unheard-of prices; a Strauss

Week in Mannheim, with *Salome*, *Rosenkavalier*, and *Ariadne*, staged very prettily and wittily by Dr. Hagemann . . . finally *Ariadne* and *Elektra* in Switzerland, with a downright triumphal success." "On Monday the one hundredth *Rosenkavalier* came off gloriously in Dresden, with a full house and an impeccable performance. Afterwards, in cheerful company, we thought of you gratefully with much admiration." "I believe that *Ariadne* has inaugurated a new theatrical era in Italy. A pity you weren't there!"

One result of this willed separation is the fact that they had to do much, perhaps most, of their collaboration by mail. This is a godsend for us, because a byproduct was one of the most revealing and provocative correspondences in the history of art. The two writers, in fact, grew aware of just how good their letters were, and had a censored selection of them published in 1925.

To musicians and musicologists, what is most fascinating about the Strauss-Hofmannsthal letters is the detailed image they provide of the collaborative creative process, of the conception and slow growth of important works of art. Through the letters (and the many surviving draft texts and scores), we can trace in close detail the means and steps by which their six operas came into being. Articles, theses, and books have been written on the "genesis" of each of the Strauss-Hofmannsthal operas, because the two men left scholars so much wonderful material to play with.

Reading the earliest letters in a sequence can be quite exciting; the reader feels privy to the very conception of a new work. Strauss asks Hofmannsthal for a particular kind of plot or libretto. Hofmannsthal replies that he can't possibly provide *that*, but he sends instead a sketch of some of his own new-forming notions. Strauss, ever desperate for material, usually accepts the poet's ideas and sets to work.

In May 1916 (to follow the case of *Arabella*), Strauss writes that he'd like to do another "love opera." Six years later, when *Die Frau ohne Schatten* (an idea of Hofmannsthal's) is finally finished, Strauss returns to the theme: "I feel like doing another *Rosenkavalier* just now." Trying to be helpful, his collaborator writes that he is steeping himself in Stendhal, Scribe, and Musset, looking for ideas for something "light and conversational." Strauss continues to insist that he wants "a second *Rosenkavalier* [by far their biggest 'hit'], without its mistakes and longueurs." By September 1923, the poet has decided to set the new work in Vienna of 1840. A year later, turning back to the project from a heavy, symbolic Salzburg Festival drama, he decides to shift the action forward to the seedier 1880s, and digs out of his drawer the scenario of "a bourgeois comedy of the Scribe sort" he had sketched two years before. By November 1927, he has reworked it into the notes and character sketches for a "lighter *Der Rosenkavalier*," which he happily sends to Strauss.

Then the arguments, the rewrites, and the refinements begin. In the case of each opera, the evolving work keeps changing its shape and direction under pressure first from one man, then the other. In the process, each "invades" the other's field. Strauss tells Hofmannsthal how to create his characters and plots. Hofmannsthal tells Strauss how to write music.

Much of this is simply two craftsmen exchanging requests or suggestions, the way an architect and a builder might leave notes for each other. Here I need eight more words, says Strauss. Please write me a short scene for Orestes; what I want here is something more passionate; I must have a great musical conclusion in the form of a trio. Hofmannsthal takes issue with Strauss's musical characterization of one of his literary creations: "[Ochs] must whisper, not bawl, for God's sake! It cut me to the quick to hear him shout the word 'Hay' at *fortissimo*."

It is Hofmannsthal who first proposes that "an old-fashioned Viennese waltz, sweet and yet saucy," pervade the last act of *Der Rosenkavalier*. He warns Strauss away from "a Wagnerian kind of erotic screaming" in the love duets. The complex, elusive, creatively frustrating conception of *Ariadne auf Naxos* (rewritten Molière comedy-plus-musical divertissement) is from the start 100 percent Hofmannsthal's idea. To his first proposals, Strauss sends back a list of the vocal ranges, set numbers, and orchestration he desires, for the poet to keep in mind as he drafts his text.

"That was a brilliant idea you had in the moonlight between San Michele and Bozen," Hofmannsthal writes of their *Die Frau ohne Schatten* discussions on the 1913 Italian tour—"of accompanying the upper world with the *Ariadne* orchestra, and the denser, more colorful world with the full orchestra." He alters his poetic diction to suit. Sometimes the poet—who could not read music—indicates the sort of music he hears in his mind's ear by evocative descriptions or vivid metaphors. For Helena, he wants something "diabolic and the same time amusing." "When I mention 'gurgling' I have in mind the noise of water 'speaking' in a pipe."

"This is the only way to collaborate," writes Hofmannsthal of their early work on *Ariadne I*. "There will be other occasions when I shall ask you to comply with requests of mine; where, in certain episodes, a given text requires a more subordinate attitude from the music, as was the case in the Marschallin's scene. Here, on the contrary, the whole thing is to be simply a framework on which to hang the music, well and prettily. We must not merely work together, but actually *into each other's hands*."

And yet how often, and how radically, did these two men work at cross-purposes, rather than together. Each developed formal epistolary conventions to defer or blunt the edge of his attacks. But the attacks came all the same, and when they came, they could be devastating.

Their letters are sprinkled with assertions of admiration by each man for the other's work. "How great and pure a joy it is to me to work for you." "You're

STRAUSS, *Der Rosenkavalier*, Manfred Jungwirth, San Francisco
Opera, 1971. Photograph by Ken Howard.

Da Ponte and Scribe rolled into one." But often these are only a kind of stroking before a slap. Their letters are also full of pretenses of humility or self-effacement. These, too, however, are usually rhetorical preludes to a critical blast. "Of course, I know nothing of music." "Of course, we musicians have no taste."

The formulas of civility and the veneer of false friendship are kept in place right up to the brink. "I know you will take what I am about to say in the right spirit." "Don't get angry if I venture to come forward as a critic of your music." "Forgive me if I use very harsh and unduly strong language." And then it breaks, it erupts, explodes, pours out in a brutal, bitter, or venom-filled stream.

On receiving a libretto into which Hofmannsthal insists he has poured his whole soul, which is the best thing he has ever done, Strauss replies with a blunt, unfeeling list of all of its radical flaws. Of the first *Ariadne* idea, he writes, "Personally, I am not particularly interested by the whole thing." Of a proposed text for the second *Ariadne*, he says, "To be quite frank, I have so far not found it to my liking at all. Indeed, it contains certain things that are downright distasteful to me."

He doesn't basically like the libretto for *Die Frau ohne Schatten* either, he tells the poet. It has no real people in it, he can't get inspired, the musical result is cold, and all of his friends find it too obscure. "The characters [of *Arabella*] are not interesting . . . and so far I've been unable to warm to any of them. . . . The thing doesn't even begin to come to music."

If Strauss can be abrupt and unfeeling, Hofmannsthal's outbursts can be petulant, aggrieved, extravagant, and vicious. He will label Strauss's most innocent actions as treason, his least compromise (on a singer, or stage production) as a diabolical betrayal, or as evidence of the composer's crude crowd-pleasing instincts. In many of the letters, Hofmannsthal comes very close to calling Strauss a vulgar, tasteless, Bavarian clod.

He regards the composer's idea of a *female* composer for *Ariadne II* as "a travesty" that "smacks of operetta." (To Hofmannsthal, the word *operetta* implied something beneath contempt.) "This strikes me, forgive my plain speaking, as odious." Some of the composer's more radical ideas for revising the plot of *Ariadne* he calls "rubbish . . . nonsense . . . a stylistic absurdity . . . truly horrid!" "I feel quite faint." "Your proposals I consider, if you will forgive me, beneath discussion. They demonstrate to me that your taste and mine are miles apart." He icily dismisses *Intermezzo*, for which Strauss had written his own libretto.

In June 1916, piqued over another matter, Hofmannsthal writes an unusually nasty letter in which he declares that he has never liked much of the music for *Der Rosenkavalier* either—but then he decides not to mail the letter. Two months before he died, in 1929, he returned to scratch that sore open again. His friend, the playwright Arthur Schnitzler, he wrote Strauss, had never liked the "lapse into farce" of Act III. "As a matter of fact it is you alone who must take the blame for that 'lapse into farce.' You wrote me incessantly, letter after letter, saying that there was nothing in it to make one laugh, that in a comic opera one ought to laugh, and so on, and yet I believe to this day that the third act without this trend would have become far more beautiful still."

In some ways, Hofmannsthal's letter of August 1, 1918, opposing Strauss's candidacy as co-director of the postwar Vienna State Opera (a letter that Hofmannsthal wanted to include in their 1925 collection and that Strauss did not), shows most clearly the breadth of the chasm that lay between them. In it, the poet comes flat out and says that he regards Strauss as too much of a manipulative egotist, too neglectful of higher standards to be the right man for the job; as a man whose music, for some reason, was more valuable and civilized than Strauss was himself.

Strauss's response was a masterpiece of tact and restraint, and Hofmannsthal eventually came round. Later, he wrote, "What touched me profoundly on this occasion was the infinite kindness and forbearance with which you reacted to my opposition against your coming to Vienna."

In general, Strauss can rise above the poet's temperamental outbursts. He either ignores them, coolly refutes them, or, occasionally, concedes a point to keep the peace. "Why do you always turn so poisonous [he wrote in 1927] the moment artistic questions have to be discussed in a businesslike manner and you don't share my opinion?"

Hofmannsthal's typical reaction to criticism, even to what he regards as insufficient praise, is a fit of old-fashioned pique. He is hurt, wounded, cut to the quick, sensitive to slights real or imagined, so easily offended, so ready to offend: "I have sacrificed everything for you!" More than once he proposes breaking off all contact forever. Yet in these "fits," he sometimes reaches a plateau of lucidity from which he sees clearly what irreconcilably and absolutely different men they are.

> There is something wrong between the two of us (you and me) which in the end *will have to be* brought out in the open. . . .

> Although we have known each other for so long and mean so well by each other . . . I do not think there is anyone who knows me so little.

> I am a much more bizarre kind of person than you can suspect; what you know is only a small part of me, the surface; the factors which govern me you cannot see.

The poet seems to be right: the union of these two talents and temperaments does look like a mésalliance. But it would be pointless to ask whether either man could have created "better" operas with another collaborator, since no one acceptable appeared. Hans Pfitzner, a popular German composer of the 1920s, kept hinting to Hofmannsthal that *he* would like a libretto. ("I told him," Hofmannsthal wrote Strauss, "that, if I did have an idea for an opera, I would write it for you.") Famous writers like Gerhart Hauptmann and Gabriele D'Annunzio let it be known that they would like to work with Strauss. For better or worse—as long as both were alive—neither man could comfortably conceive of collaborating on an opera with anyone else. (After his first partner's death, Strauss wrote operas together with three other men—operas less popular and respected than his better-known earlier works.) "If you now estrange me from yourself," Hofmannsthal wrote after the first *Ariadne* fiasco, "you can find in Germany and abroad men of talent and rank who will write opera libretti for you, but it won't be the same."

Hofmannsthal's defense of their embattled partnership (which he compares to a tired old marriage) was, in effect, that he drove Strauss to do his best work *in spite of* the composer's own "baser," crowd-pleasing tastes and instincts. The poet was especially certain that this had taken place with *Die Frau ohne Schatten*—a play that Strauss never fully understood, made up of characters and ideas with which he was often unsympathetic. At the very time Strauss was begging the poet to help him become "the Offenbach of the twentieth century," Hofmannsthal was writing, "You have every reason to be grateful to me for bringing you . . . that element which is sure to bewilder people and to provoke a certain amount of antagonism. . . . This 'incomprehensibility,' it is a mortgage to be redeemed by the next generation."

Which, in effect, turned out to be true. Ignored or resisted during Strauss's lifetime, *Die Frau ohne Schatten* only began to attain universal acceptance ten years after his death, with the U.S. première (at San Francisco) in 1959, followed by impressive first or new productions at Munich, New York, Vienna, Salzburg, London, and Paris.

These ill-matched collaborators were separated by fundamental differences of temperament, background, intellect, and taste. But what set them most strenuously at odds are two other issues. Strauss believed that music is more important than words, and Hofmannsthal believed the reverse; and each man regarded himself as an artist in no way inferior to the other.

Long after his first partner had died, Strauss wrote (with Clemens Krauss) an opera called *Capriccio*, in which he stages a debate—which is never resolved—on the question "Which comes first—words or music?" (*Wort oder Ton?*) "Prima le parole, dopo la musica" (first the words, then the music) may express a good working rule for the collaborative process; but does de Casti's phrase, around which *Capriccio* is built, also express a hierarchy of artistic values?

Hofmannsthal thought it did. For all of his profound frustration with the ultimate inadequacy of words to say all that people need to express, he was a

European man of letters to the core. He hated having his sublime (or clever) texts swamped out of recognition by Strauss's often voluptuous music, his profound symbols and ideas "canceled out" by an unsympathetic score. And for all Strauss's conscientious concern to make clear and audible the lyrics of his operas, the composer obviously believed in the superior expressiveness of music.

Don't all composers care more for music, all librettists more for words? Perhaps. But either they are somehow able to collaborate as a sort of pair of Siamese twins, composing *together*, four hands to the task, each anticipating the other's instincts and style (Brecht and Weill, Rodgers and Hart, Gilbert and Sullivan), or—and this is certainly the case with all enduring operas of the first rank—the *composer* is, without question, acknowledged by both as the leader of the team: Prima la musica, dopo le parole.

Hofmannsthal would have none of that. Alone among the composers of operas regularly and consistently performed, Strauss worked most often with a librettist who regarded himself as the composer's artistic equal or better. Norman Del Mar has written, "History knows of no other instance of an author of the highest rank acting unaided as the librettist to a great composer."

Actually, history knows of a few one-shot instances—Maeterlinck and Debussy, Auden and Stravinsky. A number of serious and respected twentieth-century writers (Apollinaire, Claudel, Cocteau, Colette, E. M. Forster) have written performable opera libretti. But I cannot imagine any of them (or Da Ponte, Scribe, or Boito) writing to his composer-partner, as Hofmannsthal did to Strauss, "I know the worth of my work; I know that for many generations past no distinguished poet of the rank with which I may credit myself amongst the living, has dedicated himself willingly and devotedly to the task of writing for a musician."

Hofmannsthal insisted that for a producer to alter one syllable of his final text would be as vandalistic as to alter a note of Strauss's score. He saw to it that his dramas were published as he wrote them, not as revised for performance. He kept trying to push Strauss toward forms of composition in which the *word* would take command, toward a conscious decision "to entrust the *decisive role* to the voices."

"Once a melody seeks to dominate the scene . . . that is invariably the beginning of the end." "If only it were possible to . . . reach a 'less-of-music,' to reach a point where the lead, the melody would be given rather more to the voice, where the orchestra . . . would be subordinated to the singers." In the case of *Ariadne auf Naxos*, in particular—the occasion of their most bitter conflicts—he insists that Strauss regard his role as nothing more than a "decorator" of his lines, as the author "not of the substance, but of the trimmings."

Hugo von Hofmannsthal is an important poet and playwright, if not perhaps the reborn Goethe he sometimes seemed to think himself—important, at least, in the context of German literature. He is a more important writer than most of the "men of letters" who have collaborated on operas. But his artistic arrogance, his adamantine refusal (or inability) to understand the nature of his co-creator, or of opera as most of us experience it—which is to say, through the music and singing first— probably did as much to set limits to Strauss's achievements as an opera composer as the latter's own uncertain taste and antimodern instincts.

(1989)

CHAPTER SIXTEEN

The Twentieth Century Takes on Shakespeare

Why even bother trying?

Verdi pulled it off, more or less, three times. But the annals of opera are littered with the corpses of failed musical versions of Shakespeare's plays, from forgotten seventeenth- and eighteenth-century masques, through Italian bel canto tragedies and French romantic mush, to Samuel Barber's *Antony and Cleopatra*.[1]

Shakespeare's thirty-six-plus plays have held the spoken stage with unparalleled strength and endurance primarily because of their author's uniquely conjoined skills. He could make the English language perform magical tricks through new born diction and lavish imagery, through outrageous insult or tearful understatement, through silence or surfeit, through his ability to manipulate and interweave the language of many different classes and types of people. He was a master plotcrafter who could create characters more subtle and complex (or, when called for, more winningly simple) than those of any other playwright. And his theatrical imagination—his ability to make and dissolve whole worlds within a "wooden O"—was no less wondrous than that he gave to Prospero in *The Tempest*.

None of these qualities is readily recapturable or reproducible on the operatic stage. Verdi's two tragic versions (*Macbeth* and *Otello*), for all their grand music,

---

1. Those interested in exhuming some of the remains might look into Winton Dean's thorough and thoughtful review of "Shakespeare and Opera" in Phyllis Hartnoll, ed., *Shakespeare in Music*, and to the 187 Shakespearean operas Dean has traced for his appendix. Versions of *The Tempest*, more than half of them German, lead the pack, with 31 operas. *Romeo and Juliet* is next, with 14. In addition to the composers mentioned in this essay, the roster includes Balfe, Berlioz, Bloch, Halévy, Holst, Orff, Salieri, Smetana, Thomas, Vaughan Williams, von Suppé, Wagner, and Zandonai. Writing more than twenty years ago, Dean had high praise for Britten's *A Midsummer Night's Dream* ("the most successful Shakespearean opera since Verdi"). But in general he doubted "whether the present condition of music is favourable to Shakespearean opera. . . . Certainly the advanced techniques have contributed almost nothing so far."

are, as drama, Italo-Victorian reductions of their originals, with truncated plots and characters simplified to nineteenth-century opera dimensions. The ingenious musical-dramatic synthesis and concision of *Otello* make it one of the most moving and powerful operas ever written. But only in *Falstaff*, I believe, was Verdi able to equal, even occasionally exceed, the rich human comedy of the plays from which he drew.

To fit a Shakespeare play into an opera timetable, you must first cut from one-half to two-thirds of the lines. This, and the fact that Shakespeare's stage permitted him numerous and instant scene changes impossible in opera, will force you to reduce and probably rearrange the plot, to omit characters, scenes, and subjects. Your actors, then, will be obliged to *sing* their scraps of these intricate lines—over an orchestra, yet. It is enough of a challenge for most stage directors of Shakespeare to get their actors to enunciate intelligibly the spoken lines.

Music, of course, can do magical things of its own, as Shakespeare was the first to acknowledge. (Prospero confesses that he requires "some heavenly music . . . to work mine end upon their senses.") But all of the odds would seem to be against any composer of a Shakespearean opera being able to preserve more than a handful of the very things that make his source sublime.

Composers of this century (or at least of what music historians call the "post-Puccini" era) are faced with an additional challenge in trying to turn Shakespeare into opera. For all of his exuberant innovations, Shakespeare worked with and within strictly conventional forms: five-act structures, iambic pentameter rhythms (or prose for low comics), rhetorical set pieces, inset songs, line-for-line exchanges, and so on. So did most opera composers, up to about 1920. The trick, which Verdi accomplished fairly well, Bellini, Rossini, and Gounod less well, is to translate Shakespeare's conventions into your conventions.

But now there are no accepted, agreed-on musical conventions. Try to compose in the successful idioms of earlier times, and you doom yourself to emotional falsity and transparent contrivance. But the supposedly more "honest" musical styles of our time—atonal rows and note clusters, fragments of disconnected rhythm, bizarre orchestration, notes played or sung at random—have in general proven ill-suited to the deep and sustained human/dramatic wholes one looks for in opera, and especially in Shakespeare.

One could cite many contemporary attempts to make operas out of Shakespeare, by composers and librettists rash enough to have rushed in where their betters feared to tread. I'd like to consider just three: Benjamin Britten's *A Midsummer Night's Dream* (1960), Samuel Barber's *Antony and Cleopatra* (1966), and Aribert Reimann's *Lear* (1978)—which is, in my opinion, the most artistically successful of the three.

Britten's *A Midsummer Night's Dream* is the best accepted, most often performed modern operatic version of a Shakespeare play. Premiered at Britten's own Aldeburgh Festival in June 1960—in a hall seating 316—his *Dream* was taken over by the Royal Opera at Covent Garden (2,250 seats) in 1961, with a larger orchestra, a starrier cast, and a Gielgud/Solti production. It received its U.S. première in San Francisco that same year and has since been performed hundreds of times in dozens of cities. Particularly memorable productions since the first have included Walter Felsenstein's in East Berlin (1961–1964), conducted by Kurt Masur—like almost all of Felsenstein's operas, it was meticulously rehearsed for several months and stage-imagined with incomparable intensity; John Copley's Covent Garden revival of the 1970s; a 1978 Jonathan Miller version for the Welsh National Opera; an abstract/modern, Peter Brook–influenced Aldeburgh revival (1980); and what may have been the best recreation so far ("What a pity Ben never saw such a production in his lifetime," wrote the editor of *Opera*), a Peter Hall–produced, Bernard Haitink–conducted dream of a *Dream* mounted for Glyndebourne in the summer of 1981.

Britten wrote the part of Oberon, king of the fairies, for a countertenor, which puts many people off (including me: that cold, eerie timbre simply cannot convey changes of emotion). But all of the best countertenors around have had a go at the role, including Alfred Deller, Russell Oberlin, and James Bowman. Walter Felsenstein persuaded the composer to let him use a baritone instead, singing the part an octave down, as other producers have done with Handel and Gluck. Oberon's consort, Tytania, is a sort of queen-of-the-night coloratura who gets the opera's most ravishing vocal music. San Francisco first heard Mary Costa, then Jennifer Vyvyan, who created the role. Gielgud and Solti used Joan Carlyle; Hall and Haitink, Ileana Cotrubas. The other key solo role, the low-comic Bottom the Weaver, has been most memorably performed by Owen Brannigan (Aldeburgh, 1960; San Francisco, 1971) and Geraint Evans (Covent Garden and San Francisco, 1961). (San Francisco's first Hermia—a relatively minor role—was Marilyn Horne.)

Britten was fascinated with the possibilities for musical rendering of sleep, dreams, and supernatural beings, and he clearly loved the play. He enjoyed casting young boys in his operas (here, Puck and the four fairies) for the pure, "church choir" timbre of their unbroken voices. Oberon's countertenor and the unique orchestral forces and chords Britten assigned to each of Shakespeare's three character groups (the courtly lovers, the fairies, and the "rude mechanicals") further enriched his musical palette.

Britten and Peter Pears, his life companion and tenor of preference, skillfully and felicitously cut and rearranged Shakespeare's text themselves; nothing that matters seems to be absent. They added only a single line of their own, to explain the omitted first act. Unfortunately, this doesn't mean that one *hears* all those magical words. Tytania's and the boy fairies' enchanting songs, in particular, and some of the rustics' rapid exchanges are often impossible to understand.

One great problem post-tonal composers have in creating long narrative works is that of finding credible sources of coherence and unity, barred as they believe themselves to be from the old games of set-piece arias and ensembles, expected repeats, and harmonic progression. Britten, the most popular modern opera composer, leapt happily into this challenge with an ingenious arsenal of the most various, eclectic, and nondoctrinaire devices. Some of these suit Shakespeare's own imaginings wonderfully well. Others blunt, thwart, or bury them. All of them together yield a work of considerable musical appeal.

For the enchanted wood by moonlight in Act II, Britten created a haunting, mounting series of pianissimo chords (the first for muted strings, the second for muted brass, the third for woodwinds, the fourth for harp and percussion) that keep returning in varying fashion to ensnare the whole cast in a magic web of sleep. Each character or group of characters is provided with a "motivic" set of instruments all its own. I especially like Puck's tooting trumpet and ratatat drum, and the silver-bell celesta that accompanies his and Oberon's spells. The quarrel among the four courtly lovers grows into a rousing, "operatic" quartet. All of the otherworldly scenes are kept chromatic, although tonal (i.e., in shimmering semi-tone progressions, à la Wagner). For the finale in Duke Theseus's court, we return to old-fashioned diatonic keys and chords. In fact, for the rustics' inset "Pyramus and Thisbe" skit in this scene, Britten wrote a full fourteen-number mock bel canto Italianate opera in miniature. Flute/Thisbe's "mad song" on discovering her dead lover ("Asleep, my Love? What, dead, my dove?") is an *allegro grazioso* takeoff on *Lucia*, which Peter Pears sang to a fare-thee-well at the première (and for the recording). Some critics take offense at this as a knowing sophisticate's in-joke. I find it a perfect counterpart to Shakespeare's own mockery of the ranting Senecan tragedy he helped to displace.

Shakespeare's early fairy comedy is full of musical cues ("Music, ho! Music such as charmeth sleep") that Britten, like Purcell and Mendelssohn, enjoyed picking up on. His *Dream* is a clever, occasionally a beautiful little opera, which, to be appreciated fully, should probably be studied closely, then seen more than once in a smallish opera house—preferably with rustics who can act as well as Geraint Evans, a baritone Oberon (heresy!), a world-class Tytania, and a stage director with the imagination of Walter Felsenstein or Peter Hall. The orchestra is wonder-fully expressive, and the fairy choruses (and all of Tytania's music) are as enchant-ing as they are unintelligible. But both the lovers and the rustics can seem dull, unromantic, or unfunny for most of the opera—until the lovers are allowed to soar into one of Britten's overlapping-line ensembles, and the rustics get their chance to "act," opera buffa style, instead of jerkily declaiming lines that are meant to be comic.

Britten's short-breathed, discontinuous musical idiom, for all its sweetness and ingenuity, cannot reach the pearl-like purity and magic of the original. It's a prize of an opera, but the delicacy and finesse of the fairy poetry, the wit and humor of the rustics' rehearsals and the lovers' quarrels, and the mind-spinning evocations of otherworldly realms all still beg to be read, and heard, as Shakespeare wrote them.

The story of Samuel Barber's opera, *Antony and Cleopatra*, is almost a tragedy in itself. First suggested by conductor Thomas Schippers, it was commissioned by Rudolf Bing to open the new $60 million Metropolitan Opera House at Lincoln Center; then hyped as only the Met knows how to hype, and outglittered at its own première (in September 1966) by the diamond-studded celebrity crowd and Franco Zeffirelli's ostentatious production. Totally sacked by the opening night critics, it has resurfaced only three times since, thanks primarily to the efforts of Gian Carlo Menotti, the composer's close friend and sometime collaborator. The first was a production Menotti helped rewrite for the Julliard School in 1975; the second, a Paris concert version in 1980; and the third, a stripped-down staging at Menotti's own two carbon-copy summer festivals, at Spoleto in Italy and Charleston, South Carolina, in 1983. Barber never attempted another opera—in fact, very little work at all—in the fourteen years of life that remained to him after the Metropolitan fiasco. Devastated by his failure (according to Richard Dyer, music critic of the *Boston Globe*), he kept trying to rescore this opera into the success he thought it deserved.

The opening night critics and reporters picked first on the new opera house, then on the distracted audience, then on Zeffirelli's C. B. deMille production ("like five *Aida*s rolled into one"), and only last on Barber's poor opera. "Paste amid the Diamonds," *Music and Musicians* called it. Almost everyone was kind to the all-American cast and conductor (Leontyne Price, Justino Díaz, Jess Thomas, Ezio Flagello, Rosalind Elias, Belan Amparan, Thomas Schippers). But "the end impression," wrote Roland Gelatt in *High Fidelity*, was "of a passionless, uncommitted, Meyerbeerian spectacle—a piece of manufacture more than a creation."

Zeffirelli, who not only directed the production but also designed its sets and costumes and wrote its original libretto, does appear to have something to answer for. To display all of the new Met's stage machinery, he designed golden-cage pyramids that opened and closed, an assemblage of metal rods or slats ("Venetian blinds," everyone called them) that kept rising and descending, a mammoth sphinx that moved "around the stage like a lost locomotive" (on opening night, it crashed into the metal slats), and a full-size floating barge for Cleopatra. He staged the whole sea battle of Actium on motorized toy boats. He so overcharged the Met's new revolve with his legions of soldiers, Roman senators, and Egyptian attendants (and a camel) that it stopped revolving. His costumes were no less grandiose. Winthrop Sergeant, in *The New Yorker*, called Zeffirelli's production "appallingly pretentious, appallingly arty, and, in most cases, destructive."

But even after the later productions, and the 1983 Spoleto recording, with all Zeffirelli's kitschy pyramids and casts of thousands cleared away, after all of Barber's and Menotti's tinkering with score and text, few critics have found it easy to say many favorable things about this ill-fated work. The best Andrew Porter could venture, on the occasion of the Julliard School revival, was that the opera deserved "a third chance," preferably not in English, with a carefully reedited score—"perhaps a century or so hence."

Britten's *Dream* is an excellent small opera that is simply not the equal of Shakespeare's play. Barber's *Antony* (well, two-thirds of it) is a terrible opera that bears no resemblance whatever, artistic or imaginative, to Shakespeare's original. Granted, Zeffirelli snipped the *lines* out of Shakespeare. But half of them you can't understand, even on the recording. And almost everything important is gone. The music that replaces it is, with a very few exceptions, lifeless and uninspired.

Barber was not troubled by the Modernist agony of fitting a traditional text to a nontraditional musical language because, in terms of musical style, he never quite made the post-Puccini leap. He could do a few lyrical things very well—elegiac farewells, tenderly aspiring death scenes, solo airs (and one gorgeous trio) that resemble the best of his songs. But all of his arrivals in Rome sound like something off the sound track of MGM's *Quo Vadis*. When we zap back to Egypt, harps arpegg, woodwinds wail, a bell tree tinkles, antique cymbals clash. In general, his orchestral scoring is thick, plodding, old-fashioned, and obvious. His vocal scoring—a slight gesture to this century—tends to be declamatory rather than lyrical, the notes jabbed out with little audible reference to the words or emotions they are supposedly carrying. Powerful Shakespearean lines are shot out abruptly in off-accent notes; moments of high passion are italicized by swooning strings. Barber's Cleopatra, in the end (despite Leontyne Price's heroic efforts), is almost as flat as his Antony, his Caesar, or his Enobarbus.

That said, I must admit to being moved by the stately, hieratic, musically sustained final act (real vocal lines soar over a weeping continuum of strings and funereal drums), which contains the deaths of the two protagonists. My only suggestion for a revival would be to perform this (with two superb leads) as a one-act opera on its own—perhaps in a triple bill between Puccini's *Il tabarro* and Schoenberg's *Erwartung*—to demonstrate Barber's place in musical history.

What could, or should, an opera composer have done with Shakespeare's *Antony and Cleopatra?*

Left it bloody well alone.

Most of Shakespeare's overreaching global poetry in this play is out of the reach of any composer. So are the wild, inconstant passions and triple-edged emotions of Cleopatra's most famous lines. The characters of *Othello* are simple and clear. The world of *King Lear* is unnatural and stark. *Antony*, by contrast, is altogether this-worldly, as subtle and various as its heroes and locales.

How to portray in music time and space so condensed, passions so mercurial, all of the lies of love? Lose the psychopoetic context, the sense that in these two mixed-up, middle-aged lovers' lives lies the whole world, and you lose all. Composers may conjure up movie-music melodies and follow-the-dots orchestration to stand for Egyptian lust and Roman power. But as I read this magnificent play, I hear, at most, a few trumpet fanfares, slow background chords, minor string ostinatos, occasional underlinings—in a phrase, "incidental music." The words are far too grand to be taken over by mere music. "The very richness of the poetry," writes Roland Gelatt, "poses an almost insuperable hurdle for a composer to clear. Shakespeare is already operatic without the addition of music. . . . Before we begin laying into Samuel Barber too heavily for his failings, we should pity a composer whose task is to find a musical setting for lines as freighted with their own music as these."

King Lear, by contrast, may be viable as music drama for the very reasons that many drama critics have thought it unperformable on the spoken stage. It overreaches spoken stage realism and seems "too much" in every way. There is too much madness, too much evil, too much cruelty, pathos, insult, suffering, folly. Even the play's strongest defenders have regarded key scenes as "unactable." It *can* be done on stage (though it rarely is). But it probably works best in an old-fashioned, high-grandiloquent style, like Donald Wolfit's; or in an austere, existential, hyperstylized fashion, like Peter Brook's. In a nonrealistic setting of genuinely inspired and deeply felt music, it is just possible that some of these "unperformable" or "unbearable" effects could be achieved as well as or better than in a spoken, Shakespearean production.

The words are crucial, of course. But in this case one could conceivably lose most of them, "score the subtext" (World in Chaos, Evil in Control), and suffer much less than in cutting a more poetic whole, such as *Antony and Cleopatra*. There are a few indispensable lines that probably should be heard, particularly in the scenes of "heartbreaking" pathos of Acts IV and V. But Aribert Reimann and his librettist have saved most of these, and stilled the thunderous orchestral cacophony long enough for us to hear them.

Moreover, this seems to me one case wherein the problem of adapting a conventional play to an anticonventional musical language can be, and largely has been, got round. To begin with, *King Lear* is the most unconventional, the most nearly hysterical, the most outré and outrageous play Shakespeare ever wrote. Its poetic imagery can be so elaborate and so concentrated as to be almost opaque. Whole speeches are uttered in mad, meaningless, repetitive syllables. It is so much a play of the mind, of the timeless, universal, tormented human mind, and so little a play dependent on medieval or Renaissance conventions, that Reimann's shrieking, snarling, crashing, no-holds-barred score probably suits its essence better than any more conventional musical idiom could do.

Although Reimann's *Lear* is more cacophonous (and certainly louder) than any of the Modernist works (Berg's, Schoenberg's) from which it descends, and is composed around even more intricately thought-out musical structures than theirs, I find myself—most of the time—able to yield to it completely, as I cannot yield to most of the operas of his atonal or serialist predecessors.

Why? Partly, I suspect, because Aribert Reimann's music is broader, more free, and less doctrinaire—although no less intense and unlovely—than theirs. This allowed him the freedom to shift, in some of his interludes and in his final scenes, for example, to soft, clear, almost lyrically expressive music. Here, he will use nonmetrical melismas; there, notes locked into metronome-paced bars. Here, 48 strings are ordered to play 48 separate lines, creating a brain-disorienting cloud of noise; there, a single cello or brass flute will sing a heartrending solo. The double-range music he gives to Edgar/Mad Tom may well enlarge this role beyond anything a speaking actor could achieve. Reimann's *Lear* orchestra has been augmented by five extra percussionists to keep the din going on seven gongs, six drums, five bongos, five tom toms, five temple blocks, five wood blocks, four tam tams, cymbals, a hanging bronze plate, metal foil and blocks, and wood chips. Be prepared.

The more I listen to this fractured, free, apparently undisciplined music, the more I ponder this mad-looking score (which someone once described as a looking like an army of trained ants marching across the page), the more "right" it all seems, line after clangorous, oppressive, fortissimo line. The manic declamations, the violent coloratura, and the insisted *Sprechgesang* in the vocal line counterweigh precisely the orchestral frenzy of the world. In the midst of a storm that is clearly as symbolic as it is real, Shakespeare's Lear cries, "Blow, winds, and crack your cheeks"—and Reimann's winds do.

Dubious or hostile critics (including me, on first hearing) faulted Reimann's *Lear* for scanting the positive, redemptive, good-guys' half of the drama: the half represented by the later Lear, Cordelia, Edgar, Kent, the Fool, Gloucester, France, and the good servants. One's overwhelming impression, as the curtain fell, was of a universe totally dominated by, indeed made out of, chaos and evil.

But now I realize that this is also my overwhelming final impression on reading or seeing the play. Decades of Shakespearean scholars have tried to convince us that *King Lear* is really about Christian virtue triumphing over pagan vice. But it isn't. It's about an ugly, evil, unfair, godless world, which both William Shakespeare and Aribert Reimann knew to exist.

What remains for a contemporary composer who might still want to make use of this richest and most fertile of literary sources?

In July 1985, a new opera based on *The Tempest* by John Eaton (libretto by Andrew Porter) opened at the Santa Fe Opera. Two other operatic versions of this play were in progress that year, by Lee Hoiby and Peter Westergaard. In defensive advance explanations of his version, John Eaton (a Princeton-trained, Indiana-based composer, whose *The Cry of Clytaemnestra* was performed in San Francisco in 1981) tried to make his strange mixture of tones and tempi, his overlaying of electronic music and microtone vocalizing with jazz and Renaissance ensembles all

REIMANN, *Lear*, Thomas Stewart, San Francisco Opera, 1985.
Photograph by David Powers.

seem reasonable, apt, and "relevant to our post-Hiroshima experience." John Rockwell of the *New York Times* found the result (as I found *Clytaemnestra;* I haven't heard *The Tempest*) "relentlessly ugly." "The pervasive impression," he wrote, "is of dissonant sludge, the many styles and colors mixed into aural mud."

Other composers, closer perhaps to Aribert Reimann's temperament, may find fit matter for contemporary visions of horror and evil in Shakespeare's more bitter plays, such as *Troilus and Cressida* (William Walton's opera made use of Chaucer's poem, not Shakespeare's play) or *Timon of Athens. Macbeth, Coriolanus,* and some of the history plays might be reimagined for our time musically, as many directors have reimagined them for the legitimate stage.

But despite the successes of Britten and Reimann, my last advice is the same as my first. It's probably wisest for a composer to leave Shakespeare alone, and to search for stories and texts among lesser writers, whose genius will not so embarrassingly overshadow one's own.

(1985)

CHAPTER SEVENTEEN

Artists on the Opera Stage

The idealistic fantasy of a "total art work" is one that regularly visits the imaginations of opera producers, probably because they see themselves as already halfway there. With a good score matched to a good libretto, the union of at least two arts—music and literature—appears to be taken care of, presuming a producer has available musicians and singing actors who can do them justice. The producer, stage director, and cast will try to assure that the result is good theatre. All that remains is to incorporate good dancing, good architecture, and good art. Then the total art work is achieved, and the muses are pleased.

Richard Wagner wrote and dreamed of such a *Gesamtkunstwerk*. But he never really got beyond his private vision of words and music united. Productions of Wagner's music dramas during his lifetime were limited by the abilities of available singers and musicians, by traditional nineteenth-century theatre practice, and by set and costume designs—the "art and architecture" of opera—of the most conventional romantic-realistic style, which lagged far behind the Wagnerian visions they were supposed to help audiences see.

The most thoroughgoing attempt to realize a union of all of the arts on the musical stage came about in ballet, rather than opera. It was the work of Serge Diaghilev and his Russian Ballet, first in St. Petersburg, then (from 1909 to 1929) in Paris. For a single production, *Le Train bleu* in 1924, Diaghilev assembled the combined talents of Pablo Picasso, Darius Milhaud, Jean Cocteau, Coco Chanel, Henri Laurens, and the choreographer Bronislava Nijinska. In 1911, Diaghilev got Gabriele D'Annunzio, Claude Debussy, and Leon Bakst to collaborate with Michel Fokine on another of his ballets. He persuaded André Derain to work with two composers—Satie and Milhaud—as well as George Balanchine, on a Ballets Russes creation of 1926.

At no period before or since have so many major visual artists been involved in theatrical production. Perhaps the nearest comparable phenomena are the collaborations of Martha Graham with sculptor Isamu Noguchi between 1935 and 1950, and those of choreographers Merce Cunningham and Paul Taylor with a number of important American artists during the last thirty years.

The world of modern dance, by virtue of its relative plotlessness and abstraction, may lend itself more readily than opera to interpretations by modern artists. And yet the list of twentieth-century painters and sculptors who have designed sets and costumes for the opera stage is an impressive one. From the early-modern generations, André Derain, Maurice Utrillo, Oskar Kokoschka, Marc Chagall, Giorgio De Chirico, László Moholy-Nagy, André Masson, Pavel Tchelitchev, and Henry Moore have all designed opera productions. Among artists come to fame more recently, Louise Nevelson, Eugene Berman, John Piper, Salvador Dalí, Victor Vasarély, Maurice Sendak, Bernard Buffet, Robert Indiana, and David Hockney have all had the chance to impose their visions on the opera stage.

The earliest known artists of the stage were in fact architects: sixteenth- and seventeenth-century Renaissance and Baroque architects whose impressive designs, more often for pageants, masques, and processions than what we would call "operas," have come down to us in the form of pen sketches (like Inigo Jones's), illustrations for books (like Sebastiano Serlio's), or, in the case of Vincenzo Scamozzi's great all-purpose set for Palladio's Teatro Olimpico in Vicenza (1585), as permanent pieces of theatre architecture. (The Teatro Olimpico is still occasionally used for operas.) Four generations of the prodigiously talented Galli da Bibiena family of Bologna designed opera settings (as well as buildings) all over Europe. Their sketches for stage scenery are now collectors' treasures. Perhaps the best way to appreciate the Bibienas' unique and brilliant style is to visit the little court theatre at Bayreuth designed by Giuseppe and his son Carlo in 1748. It remains to this day the perfect rococo opera setting.

A number of serious artists worked for the opera stage in the nineteenth century. The great Berlin architect Karl Friedrich Schinkel designed a memorable *Magic Flute* in 1816, among other theatrical commissions. But in general the century witnessed a serious division between stage design, which tended toward more and more extravagant, "period-style" illustration, and what we now think of as important nineteenth-century art. By midcentury, the artists we now regard as major tended to see themselves as independent, self-expressive rebels, at war with the ultraconservatives who managed and supported the government, the church, the museums, and the major opera houses—a condition that was to maintain well into this century.

Beginning with Adolphe Appia's radically purified designs for Wagnerian operas, conceived in the 1890s (for the most part theoretical and unproduced; the widow Wagner would have nothing to do with such blasphemy), a vigorous and exhilarating new movement in stage design swept through the twentieth century. Russian Constructivists, Parisian Cubists, Bauhaus theorists, and a number of other French, Italian, and (in particular) German "total art work" movements fed into this bubbling stream.

The leading figures in innovative opera design, however, were now primarily theatre professionals, not moonlighting painters and architects: people like Alexandre Benois and his son Nicola from Russia, master stage artists who designed scores of operas all over Europe throughout most of the century; Alfred Roller, president of the Vienna *Sezession*, presenting fresh versions of Wagner and exciting Strauss premières; Edward Dulberg, working with Otto Klemperer at the Krolloper in Berlin (which also commissioned opera designs from Oskar Kokoschka and László Moholy-Nagy); archmodernists of the *Neue Sachlichkeit* school, creating radical designs for new and traditional operas in several German cities before, during, and after World War II; Caspar Neher, Bertolt Brecht's chief designer, who began a tradition of astonishingly imaginative opera design at the Komische Oper in East Berlin; Josef Svoboda, Czech wizard of light. The most notorious were Richard Wagner's own grandsons Wieland and Wolfgang, who gave Bayreuth and opera production generally a new lease on life after 1951, mounting austere symbolist productions washed in light and pure color. Brilliant designers from the legitimate stage (Oliver Smith, Ralph Koltai, Rene Allio) and major filmmakers like Visconti, Zeffirelli, and Bergman added their talents to the opera stage. A reaction against abstract "Appian" (or neo-Bayreuth) austerity led to a new cycle of imaginative, evocative, semirealistic design.

Now all styles coexist in most of the world's major opera seasons. The most adventurous (and sometimes the most ludicrous) new work continues to be done by designers for the state-subsidized German houses, and by traveling French and Italians. Since the 1950s, American opera companies have been able to share in the international excitement, with productions designed not only by historic masters such as the Benois *père et fils* but also by many of their celebrated successors, like Alfred Siercke, John Conklin, Jean-Pierre Ponnelle, Günther Schneider-Siemssen, and Pier Luigi Pizzi.

With so many distinguished professional stage designers to choose from—men and women with years of training in theatre design, close relations with stage mechanics and opera artists, familiarity with the demands of production, and a mastery of lighting and scenic composition—why would the producer of an opera call on a painter or sculptor who is probably unfamiliar with all of these things? And why would a famous artist agree to spend weeks, perhaps months, designing sets and costumes to serve someone else's work—sets and costumes that will, in the end, probably be made by other people, regarded by critics as "mere illustration," and stored in a warehouse (or even destroyed) once the production is over?

Sometimes the answers to these questions are simple: (a) for the publicity; (b) for the money. There is reason to suspect less-than-idealistic motives whenever press and public begin to identify the production of an opera not with its composer, its conductor, or even its producer, but with its celebrity designer—a person who has in most cases never designed an opera before. Four interesting examples are "Dalí's *Salome*," "Bernard Buffet's *Carmen*," "Chagall's *Magic Flute*," and "Vasarély's *Tannhäuser*."

Peter Brook, at the time chief of production at Covent Garden, was reportedly so chagrined by the hostile press reaction to his and Salvador Dalí's 1950 *Salome* that he quit the company and stopped producing operas, at least for thirty years. ("Would that critics still had such power," one of them recently lamented.) On that occasion, Dalí avoided his more celebrated excesses, but his surrealist costumes and freakish pomegranate-and-peacock feather sets apparently reduced Straussian decadence to farce. Thirteen years later, Dalí made a second foray into opera, with a comic rewrite of a seventeenth-century Alessandro Scarlatti opera seria for Venice, which included a man on stage watching TV, the artist himself splashing paint, perfumed soap bubbles, one giant weeping eye, and paintings of elephants on legs a hundred feet high.

Bernard Buffet's designs for *Carmen* (Marseilles, 1962), with their black, spiky, knife-cut lines, cartoon-cubist outlines, and ink-scribbled costumes, look like any other example of this once phenomenally popular artist's work. They say "Buffet" far more than Bizet. Alongside the wonderfully imaginative opera designs of professional French scenographers working in the 1950s and 1960s, this contribution by a "real" artist looks unadventurous and tame.

Marc Chagall designed sets and costumes of considerable originality for several adventurous theatres in Russia before and after the revolution. But his designs for the Met's *Magic Flute* of 1967 simply imposed on the opera the artist's established and well-known style. Chagall designed 13 large painted curtains, 26 smaller curtains, and the costumes for a cast of 121, all in his personally symbolic, dazzlingly colorful signature style. It was a tour de force of sorts, not unlike his new ceiling for the Paris Opera of 1963. But (although the opera is certainly open to numerous interpretations) Chagall's designs seemed to have very little to do with Mozart or Schikaneder, in fact to war against their classic creation. As art critic John Canaday wrote after the New York opening, Chagall's decors for *The Magic Flute* represented "the biggest one man show in town. . . . The finesse, the delicacy, the wit, the tenderness of the music were not backed up. They were smothered."

Victor Vasarély's oeuvre involves precise geometrical arrays of lines and shapes, often ranked in stripes or grids or interlocking patterns to create vibrating "op art" effects. When he was invited to design a 1984 *Tannhäuser* for the Paris Opera, he turned Wagner's world into a series of giant distorted squares that shrank as they receded downstage, and changed color to suit the seasons. His backdrop for the Venusberg bacchanal was simply a huge mirror—which makes a certain psycho-erotic sense. The front curtain, one critic wrote, was in Vasarély's "own inimitable style that has nothing to do with the work but which will no doubt find a final resting place in some art gallery."

One odd commission was the engagement of the English sculptor Henry Moore to design a *Don Giovanni* in 1967 for Gian Carlo Menotti's Festival of Two Worlds at Spoleto. Moore took no fee, but in return demanded that there be no advance public mention of his participation. He also insisted, according to Menotti, on total control of the staging, which involved Mozart's dons and donnas posing about stark walls and courts dominated by typically Moore-ish reclining nudes and other giant abstract shapes made out of foam rubber. Generous critics insisted that Moore's strange, indefinable things gave the opera a "timeless" quality.

Menotti's engagement of Henry Moore is in one way typical of many artist-opera collaborations of the past forty years, in that it took place in a "festival" setting. Since the war, many European (and some American) opera festivals have been more willing to take risks—including risks on artist-designers—than have city-center companies in their regular seasons. Most of the famous postwar visual experiments at Bayreuth have been the creations of the Wagner grandsons themselves. The painter John Piper has designed for the Glyndebourne and Aldeburgh festivals in England. David Hockney's first two full-length opera designs and one of Maurice Sendak's were commissioned by Glyndebourne.

In its opening season (1933), the director of the Florence May Festival invited Giorgio De Chirico to design the sets and costumes for Bellini's *I Puritani;* between 1949 and 1952 De Chirico contributed three additional opera designs to the Maggio Musicale Fiorentino. His brother, another surrealist painter of note who went by the name of Alberto Savinio, designed the sets for Rossini's *Armida* (which starred Maria Callas) at Florence in the latter year. Wilhelm Fürtwangler invited the German Expressionist painter Oskar Kokoschka to design a *Magic Flute* for the Salzburg Festival in 1955; he also did a *Ballo in maschera* for Florence in 1963. The founder of the summer festival at Aix-en-Provence, who had the appealing idea of putting on opera productions each summer in the courtyard of the archbishop's palace, was committed from the outset to a policy of persuading leading French artists to design the painted drops and flats that separated the performers from the palace walls. Balthus painted a charming *Così fan tutte* for Aix in 1950. André Derain designed a candy-box *Abduction from the Seraglio* for 1951, and *The Barber of Seville* for 1953. André Masson contributed designs for Gluck's *Iphigénie en Tauride* in 1952—the same year that Lucien Coutaud designed a dramatic, fantasyland *Médée.*

Some artists seem to have been designing "stage sets" all of their lives. A great many of the best-known early paintings by Giorgio De Chirico, for example, look like ominous, empty stage settings waiting for something to happen. But although De Chirico was frequently asked to design for the stage, and in eight cases for opera, his theatre sets bear little resemblance to his "stage set" paintings. The former look disappointingly old-fashioned—stylistically clumsy painted drops that lack either the disquieting power of his best early painting, or the useful and novel vigor of good professional stage design. This is probably due to the fact that his opera commissions came well after his important, "metaphysical" early work. By the 1920s, in fact (when he was not simply copying earlier motifs), De Chirico was turning out—on canvas as on stage—casually imprecise visions of a classical world, painted in a sort of garish, primitive "Renaissance" style.

Since 1958, the American sculptor Louise Nevelson has been creating magnificent, otherworldly walls made up of shallow, precisely crafted wooden boxes stacked in grids, each box carefully inlaid with bits and pieces of machined and unfinished wood. The whole wall, which may be ten feet high and twenty feet long, is then spray-painted black, white, or gold, depending on the mood Nevelson wishes to create. These "environments" achieve a hieratic, sacred quality, like altars or altar screens for some primeval religion, and I can well imagine one serving as the background for an opera or a ballet.

In 1984, Nevelson designed a simple, flat version of one of those walls as the setting for Gluck's *Orfeo ed Euridice* at the Opera Theatre of St. Louis: a giant painted grid of gold-edged black rectangles variously filled with gold circular and triangular shapes. The chorus carried standards that repeated these motifs. The spectacular costumes and jewelry Nevelson designed for the opera's hellish, earthly, and heavenly creatures were not unlike the costumes and jewelry she designs for herself.

Certain artists specialize in dreamlike (or nightmarelike) visions, which seem appropriate to dream- or nightmarelike operas: *The Magic Flute*, *Le Coq d'or*, *L'Enfant et les sortilèges*, *The Cunning Little Vixen*, *A Midsummer Night's Dream;* or (among the nightmares) *Elektra*, *Erwartung*, and *Lulu*. This is probably the kind of "appropriate" collaboration the Metropolitan Opera had hoped for with Chagall's *The Magic Flute;* or that Jean-Louis Barrault intended when he engaged the aging surrealist André Masson to design the Paris Opera's first *Wozzeck* in 1963.

Neither venture was 100 percent successful—any more than the operatic collaborations of other "dream" artists, such as Pavel Tchelitchev and Giorgio De Chirico. Perhaps the incarnated dreams of genuinely visionary artists are too personal, too uniquely expressive of their own needs and impulses to represent or even comment usefully on the special visions of composers.

A few artist-opera collaborations seem to have worked either because the artist had thought long and deeply about a work he cared for very much; or because there was a particular affinity between his style and that of the composer. Despite the fact that he was sixty-seven years old and very ill, and had been doing little more than copying his own early works for many years, Maurice Utrillo was an obvious choice for the Opéra-Comique's fiftieth anniversary revival of Charpentier's *Louise* in 1950. Both composer and artist were in love with a fantasy image of *la vie de bohème* and Paris as it used to be. The sets Utrillo drew could have been (and perhaps were) borrowed directly from any one of the hundreds of loving views of Montmartre he had painted in the preceding forty-five years.

David Hockney's designs for Stravinsky's *The Rake's Progress* (first used at Glyndebourne in 1975) represent another apt meeting of minds. This time the meeting was not so much one between artist and composer, or artist and authors, as between the artist and what had been the composer's and authors' own original inspiration: a narrative series of paintings by the eighteenth-century English painter and engraver William Hogarth. Stravinsky's librettists, W. H. Auden and Chester Kallman, contrived the opera's plot from the story implicit in Hogarth's series. Hockney then took as his cue what one might call "Hogarth's world": its costumes and architecture; its taste for artifice, generality, and overt moralizing; the very lettering style; the cartoonlike drawings; the fussily filled panels and cross-hatching technique of Hogarth's popular engravings. Hockney found in these engravings a certain congruence to his own experiments in the early 1970s with eclectic, technically precise drafting. In the end, he believed (and most critics agreed) that his personal absorption and recreation of Hogarth's style not only suited a work drawn from Hogarth; but also echoed, or perhaps "shadowed," Stravinsky's own musical technique, which made obvious use of eighteenth-century borrowings. "Stravinsky's music," Hockney has said, "was a pastiche of Mozart's, and my design was a pastiche of Hogarth."

Robert Indiana, the artist of American pop images (the tilted-O "LOVE" logo, American Dream dart boards, road-sign letters, Marilyn Monroe, Model-T Fords), confesses to having been captivated by Gertrude Stein, and the Stein-Thomson operas, since he first heard of her and them in the 1950s. His second one-man show in 1964 began with a concert of Virgil Thomson's music, including excerpts from *The Mother of Us All*, composed in 1947 to Stein's text on Susan B. Anthony. After their meeting at that concert, the composer wrote a "musical portrait" of the artist. Later still, Indiana designed posters for an exhibition of the Stein family's art collections and for the opening of another Thomson opera.

In 1965, Virgil Thomson invited Indiana to design the sets for a UCLA production of *Mother*. Although they weren't used at UCLA, Indiana's sketches formed the basis for the Center Opera Company's production of *The Mother of Us All* at Minneapolis in 1967—the text rewritten by the artist to incorporate a Model-T Ford, a Mississippi River showboat, and various new characters identified by Miss America banners across their chests—and then for a definitive bicentennial production at the Santa Fe Opera in 1976.

The Stein-Thomson-Indiana interaction is one example, I believe, of an artist-designed opera at least as successful as the Diaghilev dance/art collaborations of the 1920s, or those arranged by the Merce Cunningham Dance Foundation since

STRAVINSKY, *The Rake's Progress*, Susan Patterson and Jerry
Hadley, San Francisco Opera, 1988. Photograph by Marty Sohl.

1956. Not only did the artist care profoundly for the opera he trying to make
visible; he was also able to work closely with the composer (as Alfred Roller had
worked with Strauss and John Piper with Britten). Indiana had evolved a flat,
sharp-edged, pop-iconic, circus colored personal style that drew from sources not
all that different from Stein's and Thomson's, and that helped to realize the full
potential of their opera. Alfred Frankenstein described Indiana's sets at Santa Fe as
combining "the best features of three great American entertainments: political
convention, a traveling circus and a beauty queen pageant."

In a relatively few cases, independent modern artists have grown so fascinated by
the challenge of designing for the opera stage that they have tried to master the
intricacies of production and the politics of collaboration. Through opera after
opera, year after year, they have made themselves into full-fledged and successful
artists of the stage. Some, like Natalya Goncharova (whose dazzling 1914 sets for
Rimsky-Korsakov's *Le Coq d'or* have never been surpassed), Alexandre Benois
(who remains my favorite opera designer of this century), and a few of their
Russian contemporaries are now better known for their stage designs than for their
gallery art. A number of Neoromantic French artists who first emerged in the

1920s and 1930s, like a few German and Austrian *Neue Sachlichkeit* painters, are also best remembered today for their theatre work.

In recent years, artists who have established notable reputations as designers for opera include Eugene Berman (1899–1972), John Piper (1903–), Maurice Sendak (1928–), and David Hockney (1937–). Eugene Berman, born in St. Petersburg, was identified by the 1920s as one of a group of "New Romantic" artists in Paris, along with his friends Christian Bérard and Pavel Tchelitchev—artists who rejected nonfigurative abstraction for variously stylized forms of pictorial realism highly charged with emotional appeal. Berman's own penchant was for a melancholy, lyrical kind of historical nostalgia, vestiges of dream castles and ruins, tattered draperies, haunting shadows, all exquisitely sketched in ink or painted in bright glowing colors.

After designing a number of ballets, both in Paris and in New York (where he moved in 1935), Berman designed five operas for the Metropolitan between 1951 and 1963: *Rigoletto*, *La forza del destino*, *The Barber of Seville*, *Don Giovanni*, and *Otello*, plus a *Così* for the Piccola Scala in Milan in 1956. (He moved to Rome to paint in the 1950s.) Berman's designs represented the most interesting and original work to appear on the Metropolitan stage during those years, and helped break its long tradition of stultifying historicist sets. A conservative among twentieth-century painters who was deeply attached to Italian Renaissance art and architecture, his work was highly successful on the opera stage, perhaps for those reasons. Berman knew well the operas he designed and respected the demands of the stage. A highly sophisticated colorist, stage architect, and manipulator of shadows, he knew how and when to twist realism into surrealism, and provided audiences with sets and costumes that were at once original, beautiful, and historically evocative, if not always clearly related to the opera in question.

John Piper is best known to followers of opera for his many collaborations with Benjamin Britten. Piper designed the first staged productions of *The Rape of Lucretia* (1946), *Albert Herring* (1947), *Billy Budd* (1951), *Gloriana* (1953), *The Turn of the Screw* (1954), *A Midsummer Night's Dream* (1960), *Owen Wingrave* (1973), and *Death in Venice* (1973). The two men were close friends of long standing—Piper's wife Myfanwy wrote some of Britten's librettos—and could work together in intimate and productive fashion. But Piper also designed sets for other plays, ballets, and operas (notably a *Don Giovanni* for Glyndebourne in 1951).

He was an extraordinarily versatile and popular artist. He illustrated books, designed stained glass windows (including a memorial window to Britten at Aldeburgh and the great baptistry windows for Coventry Cathedral), posters, ceramics, and fabrics. His ghostly, Impressionist paintings are saturated with a deep sense of place, time, and longing; of realism vanishing into ruin or dream; of a present haunted by the past. His style was at once accurate and evocative, highly personal and recognizable, yet always respectful of his subject. It served as well for travel guide illustrations, a wartime series of paintings of bomb-damaged churches, and a suite of twenty-six watercolors of Windsor Castle commissioned by the Queen Mother, as for the ghostly projections of *The Turn of the Screw*, and the flickering gold and blue images of Venice's palaces and canals that form part of Aschenbach's waking dreams in Britten's last opera.

Maurice Sendak is best known as an ingenious author and illustrator of books for children—at least thirty written by other authors (including both Grimms' and Andersen's tales) and twelve he has written himself. In November 1980 he began his series of opera designs (in collaboration with director Frank Corsaro) with a *Magic Flute*—the all-time favorite artist's opera—for the Houston Grand Opera. In this production, characters in eighteenth-century costume performed against a charming Sendak dream world of temples and grottoes, tropical foliage, and imaginary animals painted on a succession of drops, which drew more applause than the singing.

That same month, Oliver Knussen's operatic version of Sendak's book *Where the Wild Things Are* opened in Brussels. It was repeated at Glyndebourne, along with another of Knussen's children's operas, in 1983. In these, Sendak's sets and costumes essentially reproduced the artist's fancifully grotesque book illustrations. Meanwhile, the New York City Opera had produced his and Corsaro's version of Janáček's *The Cunning Little Vixen* in 1981. Glyndebourne introduced their production of Prokofiev's *The Love for Three Oranges* in 1982. In the summer of 1987, a double bill of Ravel's *L'Enfant et les sortilèges*—which has a story very like that of *Wild Things*—and *L'Heure espagnole*, two more fantasy operas with Sendak designs, were produced at the Glyndebourne Festival. An *Idomeneo* was produced at Los Angeles in 1990, in which I found Sendak's cartoonish decors ill-attuned to Mozart's opera seria.

After his remarkable success with *The Rake's Progress*, which has now been produced in several cities, David Hockney—one of the most successful and popular painters of his time—was next invited to design a *Magic Flute* for Glyndebourne in 1978. Drawing on manifold sources (Giotto, Paolo Uccello, Karl Friedrich Schinkel, eighteenth-century images of Egypt, etc.), Hockney created another series of obviously artificial drops and flats painted in unmodulated areas of glowing earth-and-sky tones, plus two marvelous images for the fire and water ordeals, and the finest realization I have ever seen of Schikaneder's impossible final-scene demand: turn the stage into a sun. These share the witty cartoon- or posterlike directness of Hockney's *Rake*, and add to it a greater eclecticism, exoticism, range of color, and outlandish perspective. The decors for both these operas have been used in several cities.

For 1981, John Cox asked David Hockney to design two three-part productions for the Metropolitan Opera. The first began with the Milhaud and Cocteau circus ballet *Parade*, originally designed by Picasso in 1917. It continued with two one-act

French operas, Poulenc's gaga *Les Mamelles de Tirésias* (1945) and Ravel's *L'Enfant et les sortilèges* (1925)—both based on scripts (by Apollinaire and Colette, respectively) written in Paris in 1917. The combination allowed Hockney to pay tribute to the early modern School of Paris artists the three works evoke (*Parade* included direct borrowings from Picasso; *L'Enfant* recalled Matisse), while playing some splashy colorist and Cubist games of his own. The second trio—an all-Stravinsky evening—included *Le Sacre du printemps*, danced on and in front of two great circles of changing color; an all-blue "Chinese porcelain" *Le Rossignol*, with dancers on stage and singers off; and *Oedipus Rex*, sung by formally dressed and arranged soloists and chorus, wearing huge white masks, on a great circle of blood-red light.

In December 1987, Hockney displayed the results of his greatest challenge so far—a new *Tristan und Isolde* for the Los Angeles Music Center Opera—a leap into musical drama deeper and more tragic than anything he had dealt with before. Despite some intentionally dazzling color combinations, a few provocative cartoonlike shapes (the sails of Isolde's ship, the steeply raked and regular "forest" outside her castle), and a transcendentally moving "light show" for the final scene, some observers—including me—felt that with *Tristan*, Hockney had ventured out of his depth.

Producers of opera, for the reasons I've been suggesting, keep inviting famous artists to design their productions, and famous artists keep accepting these invitations. If these idealistic, "total art work" collaborations often end in failure, this may reflect the fact that serious artists are *not*, by and large, entirely happy in the role of craftsworker-collaborator.

From Pablo Picasso to Robert Indiana, artists have insisted on the right to alter a libretto to suit their visual impulses. Whatever the libretto, the score, or the director may propose, the artist may insist on expressing his own private visions. He may dislike having these visions interpreted by mere follow-the-dots craftsworkers, whose job it is to enlarge the artist's inspired sketches into stage-sized drops and make-believe places. He may dislike the idea of his valuable efforts being regarded as anything less than permanent, although he can still exhibit, sell, and publish his sketches, as many contemporary artist-designers do.

Famous artists who have worked for the opera stage, unable to yield to the imagination of a rival artist, have often overwhelmed the works they were invited to illustrate and evoke. The result then is likely to be not a collaboration, but Chagall versus Mozart, De Chirico versus Bellini, Masson versus Berg. This seems to me true of some of the most celebrated Diaghilev *Gesamtkunstwerk* creations. Not only did Picasso force Cocteau to rewrite his scenario for *Parade;* he also obliged Massine's dancers to parade about in what were nothing more or less than his own 1914–1916 paintings come to life. The dancers were no longer human beings, but *Über-marionetten*, giant puppets encased in thirteen-foot-high body masks, walking cubic sculptures.

"The use of famous painters as set designers," Walter Felsenstein once remarked, "which is particularly popular with the French, is not only wrong but even grotesque. . . . The set designer . . . must give himself utterly to the stage if he is to explore and master the laws of the stage, which are so radically different from those of painting."

In a few classic cases, like the Indiana–Thomson collaboration (Fernand Leger's ventures with Darius Milhaud seem to have worked with comparable success), a fortuitous coincidence of artist's style and composer's style has yielded an onstage incarnation of the musical idea. If one can find an independent, visionary artist who is willing to collaborate, willing to participate, willing to learn the requirements of actors, singers, and musicians, willing to take his or her own private needs and submerge them into, or at least merge them with, those of other artists, there is a chance that our conception of an opera may be illuminated and enlarged—which in the end is the soundest justification for such rare and risky joint ventures.

(1987)

All but two of the essays in this collection were originally written for a magazine for operagoers that almost never makes use of footnotes. While writing them, I did not always keep precise records of the sources of my quotations, and in a few cases I've been unable to trace them. The notes that follow are intended to indicate a small fraction of the works I consulted, and to offer ideas for further reading.

In recent years, several interesting books have appeared that treat of opera (as I have tried to do) in aesthetic, literary, social, economic, or (in the largest sense) cultural terms. In this, they differ from most earlier books about opera. The latter were made up, on the one hand, of a vast and popular library of plot outlines, biographies of singers and composers, potted "histories of opera," gossip and anecdotage, and self-celebrating company histories; and, on the other hand, of a small number of works of serious music history and analysis that concentrated on opera.

The seminal work of the new sort, with which every subsequent author on opera must somehow come to terms, is Joseph Kerman's *Opera as Drama* (New York, 1956; rev. Berkeley, 1988). Kerman demonstrated that it was possible to write about the phenomenon of opera in a serious, scrupulous, and critical fashion, while remaining accessible to a wide, nonscholarly audience of readers interested in the form.

The "next generation" of such works—books from which I have learned a good deal—includes Peter Kivy's *Osmin's Rage: Philosophical Reflections on Opera, Drama, and Text* (Princeton, 1988); Herbert Lindenberger, *Opera: The Extravagant Art* (Ithaca, N.Y., 1984); Paul Robinson, *Opera and Ideas: From Mozart to Strauss* (New York, 1985); Gary Schmidgall, *Literature as Opera* (New York, 1977), followed by his somewhat more rambling *Shakespeare and Opera* (New York, 1990); and (with limitations) Patrick J. Smith, *The Tenth Muse: A Historical Study of the Opera Libretto*

(New York, 1970). I found Peter Conrad's *Romantic Opera and Literary Form* (Berkeley, 1977), and his *A Song of Love and Death: The Meaning of Opera* (New York, 1987) to be overwrought and overwritten, a melting of hundreds of ideas about opera into a magma of private sensibility; but both books bear witness to the emotional intensity of at least certain operas and certain opera fans.

Two recent collections of essays, *Reading Opera* (edited by Arthur Groos and Roger Parker, Princeton, 1988) and *Analyzing Opera: Verdi and Wagner* (edited by Carolyn Abbate and Roger Parker, Berkeley, 1989), both of which grew out of Cornell University conferences—Cornell has become something of a center of "new opera studies"—exemplify some of these serious, broadly based new approaches to writing about opera. The former strikes me as slightly perverse in attending to opera librettos as autonomous works (though to a lesser degree than does Patrick Smith's study), and then subjecting them to the heavy artillery of New Critical theory; the latter—readable, for the most part, only by sophisticated musicologists—frequently demonstrates (once again) how little musical analysis can demonstrate. Philippe Berthier and Kurt Ringger, eds., *Littérature et opéra* (Grenoble, 1987), another "conference proceedings" collection of mixed value, helps to bring these two disciplines together. I admire Lorenzo Bianconi, ed., *La drammaturgia musicale* (Bologna, 1986) for the editor's own valuable introduction and detailed bibliography. Bianconi and several of his contributors adapt something of my own attitude toward successful opera as the result of a combination of music, libretto, and specific theatrical realization, and retain a full sense of its *theatrical* force and potential. The book takes its theme and definition from Carl Dahlhaus's essay, "Drammaturgia dell'opera italiana," in Bianconi and Pestelli, ed., *Storia dell'opera italiana*, vol. 2 (Turin, 1987).

Among many shorter books and essays, I was impressed by Guy Verriest, "Esthétique et défense de l'art lyrique," *La Revue musicale* (Paris, 1977). It is one of very few works I have read—Peter Kivy's is another; Lorenzo Bianconi's introduction to *La drammaturgia musicale* is a third—that tries to define an "aesthetics of opera," as I have also done. Another is Jean-Jacques Nattiez, *Tétralogies: Wagner, Boulez, Chéreau* (Paris, 1983). In this book, Nattiez uses the 1976 centennial *Ring* at Bayreuth to demonstrate some provocative and original ideas about the many possible relationships among the creative process, the text, and the aesthetic reception of an opera.

William L. Crosten, *French Grand Opera: An Art and a Business* (New York, 1948); Gloria Flaherty, *Opera in the Development of German Critical Thought* (Princeton, 1978); Philippe-Joseph Salazar, *Idéologies de l'opéra* (Paris, 1980); John Rosselli, *The Opera Industry in Italy from Cimarosa to Verdi: The Role of the Impresario* (Cambridge, 1984); and Jane Fulcher, *The Nation's Image: French Grand Opera as Politics and Politicized Art* (Cambridge, 1987) are specialized studies that attempt to position the phenomenon of opera within nonmusical cultural contexts. Theodor

Adorno, so wise in other domains, is disappointingly superficial on "the sociology of opera" ("Opera," in *The Sociology of Music* [New York, 1976]; originally *Einleitung in die Muziksoziologie* [Frankfurt, 1962]; also "Bürgerliche Oper," in *Klangfiguren* [Frankfurt, 1962]). This strikes me as little more than an illogical and ill-informed "bash-the-bourgeois" tract. To Adorno, the very survival of opera is proof that Western culture is sick. Unfortunately, Rosanne Martorella, *Sociology of Opera* (New York, 1982), does not begin to do justice to this tantalizing subject either.

An edited transcript of a conference on the future of opera held at Venice in 1985 was published in *Daedalus* (Fall 1986). The distinguished participants rehashed all the usual laments about art versus box office, out-of-touch composers, ill-trained singers and audiences, inadequate subsidies, superstar egos, the impact of television, and the like. Although ultimate questions were quietly raised—is opera heading for extinction? are the grand old houses dying?—most of the *conferenciers* were professionally committed to the status quo, which may have disabled them from looking into the future with any special clairvoyance.

Most of my facts and figures regarding opera productions, companies, houses, and the like are derived from a few periodicals that try to "cover" the global international scene. *Opera* magazine, published in London since 1950, remains the most thorough and dependable of these, and I recommend it to any serious fan or student of opera. Some of its reviews and essays are superficial and ill-written, which may be inevitable given its remarkable breadth of coverage. But its monthly world surveys and season calendars are as valuable as its annual indexes. *Opera News* (New York, since 1939), *Opéra International* (Paris, since 1966), and *Opernwelt* (Zurich, since 1960)—all of which I find more provincial or nationalistic than the London-based magazine—I tend to consult as supplements to *Opera*. *Opera* does tend to give special prominence to what is happening in Britain. But the other three are even more interested in their own language or country of publication than they are in the opera world in general. *Opera News*, published by the Metropolitan Opera Association, serves in part to publicize Metropolitan Opera productions. Even so, its current editor, Patrick J. Smith, maintains a laudable independence.

L'Avant-Scène Opéra (Paris) is a richly illustrated bimonthly publication, each number of which is devoted to a single opera. Each forms a small monograph, including a full libretto in French and (for non-French operas) the original language; an accompanying scene-by-scene musical commentary; a series of essays on the opera (its composer and composition, sources, cultural context, important productions and interpreters, etc.); and—a feature I have found especially valuable—a record of important productions throughout the world since the opera's première, listing conductors, producers, and casts, as well as a critical "discography" and a bibliography of earlier publications about the composer and opera. Photographs from past productions are liberally reproduced. Between 1975 and

1991, 125 operas were treated in separate issues. Along with a complete set of back issues of *Opera* magazine, a complete set of *L'Avant-Scène Opéra* seems to me a good start for a working library on opera in our time.

Near-equivalents to *L'Avant-Scène Opéra* in English are the opera guidebooks published under the aegis of the English National Opera/Royal Opera (ed. Nicholas John) by John Calder in London and Riverrun Press in New York (forty-one had appeared as of 1991), and the Cambridge University Press opera handbooks, of which there are now about twenty-five. The slender ENO/Royal Opera guides typically include one or two complete librettos (in English and the original language), about thirty production photographs, and three or four short accompanying essays per opera. Each volume in the more substantial Cambridge series is edited by an expert on the composer in question, and offers several original critical essays (on sources, genesis and composition, stage and critical history, musical structure and analysis, and related issues), some of considerable importance.

Other periodicals dealing with opera (*Opera Journal, The Opera Quarterly,* and *Cambridge Opera Quarterly*) fall more into the typical scholarly/background essay pattern of academically subsidized journals, although they frequently publish more popular articles dealing with artists and issues of current concern. At the opposite end of the scale is the erratically published *Opera Fanatic,* a one-man show by Stefan Zucker in New York, which has to be seen to be believed.

Any book on the opera world today, including this one, runs the risk of becoming outdated by tomorrow. One possible exception—a book that deals intelligently, if lightly, with almost every aspect of the creation and production of big-time opera (primarily by means of interviews with many of those actively involved, especially in Britain), and may serve as a valuable basic resource for several years—is Meirion and Susie Harries, *Opera Today* (London, 1986), well-illustrated with photographs by Zoë Dominic and Catherine Ashmore. I have also found useful information in the background or interpretive essays published in individual opera company programs or members' magazines. Covent Garden's *About the House,* a member's magazine, frequently includes articles of substance. Like most critics, I inevitably learn useful things from the reviews of my colleagues. I try to read on at least an occasional basis the opera reviews published in several newspapers and magazines from the United States and Europe. I wish that a few other music critics (such as Martin Bernheimer of the *Los Angeles Times*) could be persuaded to follow Andrew Porter's lead, and collect their reviews in book form. *Musical America*'s annual *International Directory of the Performing Arts,* which serves primarily as a clearinghouse for classical music performers and those who represent or engage them, offers compendious and generally accurate listings of seasons, house statistics, and the like for opera companies and festivals in the United States and abroad.

An indispensable bibliographic source—in fact, the first place I tend to look when researching almost anything musical—is the *New Grove Dictionary of Music and Musicians* (London, 1980). Musicologists and music critics inevitably take issue with certain judgments and emphases of the *New Grove*, which was written by an international team of experts under the general editorship of Stanley Sadie. But there is still nothing even remotely like it in print in any language. Opera fans may wish to consult or buy, in place of the full $2000, twenty-volume set, individual volumes in the inexpensive series of New Grove paperbacks, which are composed of the frequently long and generally well-written articles originally included in the *New Grove* on such topics as Wagner, Mozart, or "Masters of Italian Opera" (a single volume containing the entries on Bellini, Donizetti, Rossini, Verdi, and Puccini), "Modern Masters," the Second Vienna School, etc. Each of these essays, in the *New Grove* and in the paperback series, is followed by a complete catalogue of compositions and a detailed bibliography of primary and secondary sources. Other basic reference tools I make use of include Alfred Loewenberg, *Annals of Opera 1597–1940* (Cambridge, 1943; 3rd ed., revised by Howard Rosenthal, London, 1982, with supplement for 1940–1980); and Riccardo Mezzanotte, ed., *The Simon and Schuster Book of the Opera* (New York, 1979; originally published in Milan as *Opera: Repertorio della lirica dal 1597*, 1978). There exist also a number of dictionaries, encyclopedias, and handbooks of opera, which I've never had occasion to use. Of the many one-volume histories of opera, the most comprehensive and useful in English seems to be Donald Jay Grout, *A Short History of Opera* (New York, 1947; 3rd ed., 1988). Ulrich Weisstein, ed., *The Essence of Opera* (New York, 1964), is a collection of more than fifty short statements about opera, from the Florentine camerata to W. H. Auden.

Of the critics of opera I discuss at some length in the Introduction, one can read further in Benedetto Marcello's parody, "Il teatro alla modo" (Venice, 1735), published in a lively English translation by Reinhard G. Pauly in *The Musical Quarterly* (July 1948 and January 1949). For further reading of Shaw, see George Bernard Shaw, *Shaw's Music*, ed. Dan Laurence (3 vols., London, 1981). Although the 2,500-plus pages of this collection include much that is magnificent—anyone who loves good music and good writing (and especially good writing about music) ought to read Shaw—many of the reviews are devoted to Shaw's unhappy encounters with second-rate British and French composers of the late nineteenth century, or represent one of the greatest cranks of all time at his crankiest. Good one-volume paperback "samplers" of Shaw's music criticism have been edited by Eric Bentley (*Shaw on Music* [Garden City, N.Y., 1955]) and by Louis Crompton (*Bernard Shaw: The Great Composers: Reviews and Bombardments* [Berkeley, 1978]).

Eric Bentley's critique of the 1962 Metropolitan Opera season can be found in *What Is Theatre? Incorporating "The Dramatic Event" and Other Reviews, 1944–1967* (New York, 1968). His defense of melodrama is included in *The Life of the Drama* (New York, 1964).

Andrew Porter has collected his reviews in *A Musical Season* [covering 1972–1973] (New York, 1974); *Music of Three Seasons, 1974–1977* (New York, 1978);

Music of Three More Seasons, 1977–1980 (New York, 1981); *Musical Events: A Chronicle, 1980–1983* (New York, 1987); and *Musical Events: A Chronicle, 1983–1986* (New York, 1989). Mr. Porter's reviews of operas published after 1986 can be found in *The New Yorker*.

In addition to *Opera as Drama*, the writings on opera by Joseph Kerman—in particular, his reviews of opera seasons in San Francisco and New York—are listed (along with his other writing on music up to the time) in a special issue of *19th-Century Music* dedicated to Kerman (Spring 1984). The specific reviews I cite were published in *Opera News*, *Hudson Review*, and the *San Francisco Chronicle*. Since this bibliography appeared, Kerman has written important essays in *Critical Inquiry* ("How We Got into Analysis, and How to Get Out" [Fall 1980], and "A Few Canonic Variations" [September 1983]), and in *The New York Review of Books*. His comments on the discomfort of musical analysts in dealing with opera comes from his review of Andrew Porter's essay on Verdi in the *New Grove Dictionary of Music and Musicians* in *19th-Century Music* (1982).

Although I have found no adequate book on the subject of opera production, which has become so important in recent years, readers interested in this subject may wish to consult—in addition to the polemics by A. M. Nagler, Henry Pleasants, and Guy Verriest cited in the text—Oswald Georg Bauer, *Richard Wagner, The Stage Designs and Productions from the Premières to the Present* (New York, 1983); Rudolf Hartmann, *Richard Strauss: The Staging of His Operas and Ballets* (New York, 1981), and *Opera* (New York, 1977)—all originally published in German. Readers can also consult monographs on, memoirs by, or interviews with individual producers of note from the last fifty years, most of them published only in the producer's original language: Joachim Herz, Jean-Pierre Ponnelle, Gunther Rennert, Walter Felsenstein, Wieland Wagner, Götz Friedrich, Joseph Svoboda, Herbert von Karajan et al. A few surveys have been published in France and Germany (e.g., Kurt Honolka, *Die Oper ist tot, Die Oper lebt: Kritische Bilanz des deutschen Musiktheaters* [Stuttgart, 1986]) on postwar opera productions in those countries, in particular those at the Bayreuth Wagner Festival.

One can learn a great deal about public reaction to innovative opera production by reading the letters to the editor in *Opera* magazine and the *Musical Times* (both published in London) since about 1970, and in the German periodical press generally. The 1989 Bayreuth Festival souvenir book bravely included a rich sampling of international press responses, both hostile and favorable, to the new Kupfer/ Schavernoch *Ring* production, which had opened the year before.

Although I have some doubt as to the usefulness of esoteric musical analysis (which is infrequently applied to opera scores, in any case), attentive and scrupulous musicologists can still suggest new and important meanings in operas to the musically literate reader and can call attention to new dimensions of creative ingenuity. Julian Budden, *The Operas of Verdi* (3 vols., New York, 1973/1978–

1981), and George Perle, *The Operas of Alban Berg* (2 vols., Berkeley, 1980–1985), are good examples of this kind of analysis, as are a few of the contributions to Groos and Parker's *Analyzing Opera*. The same is true of the essays that Anthony Newcomb has written on Wagner, which I presume will one day become a book: one of these can be found in the Groos and Parker collection; others are "The Birth of Music Out of the Spirit of Drama: An Essay in Wagnerian Formal Analysis," *19th-Century Music* (1981); and "Those Images That Yet Fresh Images Beget," *The Journal of Musicology* (1983). The estimable and well-edited quarterly *19th-Century Music* (Berkeley, 1977+) offered in its earlier years a number of astute analyses (and other scholarly commentary) on opera scores and texts.

For reasons of space and economy, detailed and critical bibliographic notes on the individual essays in this collection have had to be omitted. Readers interested in consulting these notes are welcome to write to the author for information.

Page numbers in italics refer to illustrations. Generally, opera composers' names are indexed only when they are specifically referred to in the text, and the names of characters and settings are not cited apart from the operas in which they occur. Institutions (but not periodicals) are indexed under the cities in which they are located.

Designer: Nola Burger
Compositor: Keystone Typesetting, Inc.
Printer: Malloy Lithographing, Inc.
Binder: John H. Dekker & Sons
Text: 10/13 Bembo
Display: Bembo